Bleisure Tourism and the Impact of Technology

Swati Sharma
Amity University, India

Narendra Kumar
Amity University, Ranchi, India

Vasco Ribeiro dos Santos
Polytechnic Institute of Leiria, Portugal

Karen Miranda-Fernandez
Asia Pacific Institute for Events Management, UK & Lyceum of the Philippines University, Laguna, Philippines

A volume in the Advances in Hospitality, Tourism, and the Services Industry (AHTSI) Book Series

IGI Global
Publishing Tomorrow's Research Today

Published in the United States of America by
IGI Global
Business Science Reference (an imprint of IGI Global)
701 E. Chocolate Avenue
Hershey PA, USA 17033
Tel: 717-533-8845
Fax: 717-533-8661
E-mail: cust@igi-global.com
Web site: http://www.igi-global.com

Library of Congress Cataloging-in-Publication Data

CIP DATA PENDING

ISBN: 9798369343548
isbn: 9798369348888
eISBN: 9798369343555

British Cataloguing in Publication Data
A Cataloguing in Publication record for this book is available from the British Library.

Table of Contents

Detailed Table of Contents

Bleisure, a term given to a combination of business and leisure into one trip, has become popular in recent years. This trend reflects a paradigm shift in the traditional dichotomy between work and leisure. Due to the novel nature of the concept many researchers have studied the bleisure travel experience and marketing practices to ensure maximum return for the travel industry. However, a gap in the literature was noticed that relates to the historical evolution of travel trends, tracing the roots of modern tourism and business travel. This chapter aims to provide insights into the cultural, economic, and technological catalysts that have fostered the rise of bleisure travel. The study aims to explore how societal changes, technological advancements, and economic shifts have shaped the way people travel for both business and leisure. The study uses secondary data for analysing the concept from published research papers, journal articles, published articles in the magazines and newspapers.

In the context of Zillennials—those born in the late 1990s and early 2010s—this study investigates the phenomena of bleisure tourism, which combines leisure travel with business travel. The study explores the socio-economic aspects influencing the travel activities of Zillennials and looks into the causes and origins of this trend. Since technological improvements have made remote employment and flexible scheduling possible, Zillennials are trying to balance work and play. The appeal of bleisure travel among this group is driven by the need for work-life balance, cultural immersion, and experience travel. By illuminating the preferences, attitudes, and decision-making processes of Zillennial bleisure travelers, this study seeks to throw light on their motives and actions. Businesses in the travel sector must comprehend how business and leisure intersect in the context of bleisure tourism in order to customize services that meet the specific requirements and preferences of this growing market.

This study explores the synergy between technology and bleisure tourism in Malaysia, investigating their combined impact on enriching travel experiences. The chapter aims to uncover insights and implications for the future of bleisure tourism in Malaysia by examining technological advancements, sustainability initiatives, and emerging trends. Findings reveal that technology has democratised travel, making it more accessible and personalised, while sustainability initiatives have promoted responsible tourism practices and environmental conservation. Moreover, emerging technologies such as virtual reality and artificial intelligence offer innovative ways for tourists to engage with destinations and cultural attractions. The study highlights the importance of continued research and collaboration in driving innovation and sustainability in the bleisure tourism industry, positioning Malaysia as a destination for tourists seeking memorable, responsible, and technologically enhanced experiences.

The rise of digital nomadism and bleisure tourism is reshaping work and travel paradigms, particularly in Southeast Asian countries like the Philippines. However, there is a dearth of studies that delve into the interplay between co-working spaces, digital nomadism, bleisure tourism, and cultural diffusion in the Southeast Asian context. This chapter employed a qualitative approach, conducting semi-structured interviews with co-working space visitors and owners in the Philippines to understand the dynamics of cultural exchange within these spaces. The findings reveal that co-working spaces foster cultural immersion, knowledge transfer, and professional networking among digital nomads and locals. These spaces serve as conduits for cultural diffusion, where both visitors and locals exchange cultural practices, language, and knowledge. The implications of this chapter underscore the need for co-working spaces to prioritize cultural sensitivity and implement safeguarding measures to ensure responsible and sustainable cultural exchange in the context of bleisure tourism.

Mobile applications play a pivotal role in enabling and enhancing bleisure travel experiences. These apps offer solutions for communication, itinerary planning, transportation booking, and leisure discovery, reflecting the evolving expectations of modern travelers for efficiency, flexibility, and customized experiences. Despite their benefits, challenges such as data privacy concerns and information overload persist. Looking ahead, the future of bleisure travel is poised for further transformation through advances in mobile technology, including augmented reality and artificial intelligence. However, a research gap exists in understanding the full spectrum of mobile apps catering to bleisure tourists' needs. This chapter aims to address this gap by classifying mobile apps for bleisure tourism, exploring their advantages, and identifying challenges and opportunities for innovation. By doing so, it seeks to contribute to a deeper understanding of the role of mobile technology in shaping the landscape of bleisure tourism in the digital age.

Preface

In recent years, a new trend has emerged in the world of travel, reshaping the traditional concept of business trips. Bleisure tourism, a portmanteau of "business" and "leisure," is gaining popularity as professionals increasingly seek ways to balance their work commitments with the desire for relaxation and exploration. Bleisure tourism represents a departure from the conventional notion of business travel, where professionals would visit a destination solely for work-related purposes. Instead, individuals now seize the opportunity to extend their stay, transforming business trips into a dual-purpose experience that combines work and leisure seamlessly.

One of the defining features of bleisure tourism is the intentional extension of a business trip to include leisure activities. This extension allows travelers to strike a balance between their professional responsibilities and personal well-being. In a world where the lines between work and life are increasingly blurred, bleisure travel provides a refreshing approach to achieving a healthier equilibrium. As the boundaries between work and personal life continue to evolve, bleisure tourism emerges as a transformative trend in the world of travel. By integrating work and leisure seamlessly, professionals can enjoy a more fulfilling and balanced travel experience. As this trend gains momentum, businesses and the travel industry as a whole are adapting to meet the changing expectations of modern travelers who seek a harmonious blend of business and leisure in their journeys.

The intended book aims to be a support tool for all readers who work directly or indirectly on the phenomenon of bleisure tourism, with special emphasis on how technology is shaping the MICE (Meetings, Incentives, Conferences, and Exhibitions) industry. Tourism is important for the economy, for marketing, and for regional and local development, and so is bleisure tourism. This book is an important contribution to the tourism literature, with a focus on the role of different stakeholders in bleisure tourism.

We envision this book serving a diverse audience, including:

- **Academics and Researchers**: Scholars and researchers in the fields of tourism, hospitality, business, and related disciplines can use the book to deepen their understanding of bleisure tourism, explore research opportunities, and stay updated on the latest developments in the field.
- **Educators**: The book can serve as a resource for educators teaching courses in tourism management, hospitality, business travel, and related subjects. It can be used as a textbook or supplemental reading material to provide students with insights into the complexities of bleisure travel.
- **Students**: Undergraduate and graduate students studying tourism, hospitality, and business can benefit from the book as part of their coursework or as a reference for research projects. It provides them with a comprehensive overview of the bleisure tourism phenomenon.
- **Industry Professionals**: Professionals working in the tourism and hospitality industry, especially those involved in business travel, destination management, and event planning, can gain practical insights from the book. It may help them understand the changing dynamics of traveler behavior and make informed decisions.
- **Tourism Boards and Destination Marketing Organizations**: Organizations promoting tourist destinations can benefit from insights in the book to tailor their marketing strategies to appeal to bleisure travelers. Understanding the factors influencing destination choices for combined business and leisure purposes can enhance destination branding efforts.
- **Consultants and Analysts**: Professionals providing consulting services or market analysis in the travel and tourism industry may use the book to stay informed about trends, potential market segments, and factors influencing the demand for bleisure travel.

We hope this book serves as a comprehensive guide and valuable resource for anyone interested in understanding and leveraging the potential of bleisure tourism in the modern world. As editors, we are thrilled to present this work and contribute to the ongoing discourse in the dynamic field of travel and tourism.

CHAPTER 1: AMALGAMATION OF TWO WORLDS: BLEISURE TRAVEL: A CONTEMPORARY CONCEPT IN THE TRAVEL AND TOURISM INDUSTRY

This chapter delves into the evolution and current state of bleisure travel, an emerging trend in the travel and tourism industry where business trips are extended to include leisure activities. By reviewing relevant literature, the chapter highlights the growing desire for a better work-life balance and the recognition that travel can be both productive and enjoyable. The authors explore the expansion of bleisure tourism from a business perspective and discuss its future implications, providing a comprehensive overview of this innovative travel concept.

CHAPTER 2: BLEISURE TRAVEL: THE RISE OF FLEXIBLE WORK AND ITS IMPACT ON TOURISM

This chapter examines the rise of bleisure travel in the context of flexible work arrangements. It traces the historical evolution of travel trends, focusing on the cultural, economic, and technological factors that have driven the popularity of combining business with leisure. Using secondary data from various sources, the authors analyze how societal changes and technological advancements have influenced the way people travel, providing valuable insights into the modern tourism landscape.

CHAPTER 3: CONFLUENCE OF BUSINESS AND LEISURE: A STUDY TOWARDS THE ORIGIN AND EMERGENCE OF BLEISURE TOURISM IN ZILLENNIAL CONTEXT

Focusing on Zillennials—those born in the late 1990s to early 2010s—this chapter investigates the socio-economic factors influencing their travel behaviors, particularly the blend of business and leisure. The study explores how technological improvements have enabled remote work and flexible schedules, driving the appeal of bleisure travel among Zillennials. By examining their preferences, attitudes, and decision-making processes, the chapter sheds light on the motivations and actions of this emerging demographic, highlighting the need for businesses to tailor services to their unique requirements.

CHAPTER 4: NAVIGATING THE BLEISURE FRONTIER: BEHAVIORAL EXPEDITION THROUGH TRANSTHEORETICAL LENS: A THEMATIC STUDY

This chapter investigates the behavior of bleisure travelers through the Transtheoretical Framework, identifying themes such as preparation, contemplation, action, and maintenance. By analyzing the experiences of 16 professionals, the authors provide insights into the motivations, challenges, and outcomes of bleisure travel. The study suggests intervention strategies and applies the AIDA model to bleisure tourism, offering practical guidance for future research and strategic planning in this evolving field.

CHAPTER 5: BEHAVIORAL RELIABILITY ON SOCIAL MEDIA FOR DESTINATION CHOICES IN BLEISURE TRAVEL

This chapter explores the impact of social media on bleisure travel, focusing on how travelers use these platforms to make destination choices. The authors analyze the role of social media in shaping travel behaviors, particularly in the context of Chandigarh, India. By examining the reliability of social media content, the chapter provides insights into how these platforms influence the travel industry and the decisions of modern travelers.

CHAPTER 6: EXPLORING THE FUTURE TRENDS OF BLEISURE TOURISM IN NEPAL

This chapter investigates the growing trend of bleisure tourism in Nepal, analyzing current trends and future projections. By examining the factors driving the increase in bleisure travel, the authors provide insights into how Nepal can harness this trend for economic and tourism growth. The chapter draws on existing literature and statistical data to offer a comprehensive overview of the potential impact of bleisure tourism in the region.

CHAPTER 7: DESTINATION MARKETING WITHIN THE SCOPE OF BLEISURE TOURISM

Focusing on Turkey, this chapter examines destination marketing strategies to attract bleisure tourists. The authors discuss the importance of promoting tourist attractions and developing activities that appeal to bleisure travelers. By evaluating Turkey's competitive advantages and future growth potential in bleisure tourism, the chapter provides practical guidance for researchers, businesses, and tourism professionals aiming to capitalize on this trend.

CHAPTER 8: HOW TECHNOLOGY IS REVOLUTIONIZING BLEISURE EXPERIENCES OF TOURISTS IN MALAYSIA

This chapter explores the synergy between technology and bleisure tourism in Malaysia, highlighting how technological advancements enhance travel experiences. The authors discuss the impact of digital tools, sustainability initiatives, and emerging trends on bleisure travel. By examining case studies and technological innovations, the chapter provides insights into how Malaysia can position itself as a leading destination for bleisure travelers.

CHAPTER 9: CO-WORKING SPACES AND DIGITAL NOMADISM IN THE PHILIPPINES: UNDERSTANDING BLEISURE TOURISM'S ROLE IN DIFFUSION OF CULTURE

This chapter investigates the interplay between co-working spaces, digital nomadism, and bleisure tourism in the Philippines. Through semi-structured interviews, the authors explore how these spaces facilitate cultural exchange, professional networking, and knowledge transfer among digital nomads and locals. The chapter highlights the importance of cultural sensitivity and responsible practices in promoting sustainable cultural diffusion in the context of bleisure tourism.

CHAPTER 10: ADDRESSING THE CHALLENGES AND PROPOSING SOLUTIONS TO BLEISURE TRAVELERS: INSIGHTS FROM IT PROFESSIONALS

This chapter addresses the challenges faced by bleisure travelers, particularly IT professionals, and offers practical solutions to enhance their experiences. By reviewing existing literature, conducting surveys, and interviews, the authors identify key obstacles such as time constraints, expense management, and navigating unfamiliar destinations. The chapter provides strategies for optimizing bleisure travel, including careful planning, leveraging technology, and stress relief methods.

CHAPTER 11: EXPLORING THE SYNERGY BETWEEN BLEISURE TRAVEL AND INFORMATION TECHNOLOGY IN INDIA: CURRENT STATUS AND CHALLENGES

This chapter examines the rise of bleisure tourism in India, driven by the country's growing business infrastructure and diverse leisure offerings. The authors discuss the benefits and challenges of blending business with leisure, focusing on major Indian cities. By analyzing advancements in transportation, digital connectivity, and accommodation, the chapter provides insights into how India can overcome hurdles and capitalize on the potential of bleisure tourism.

CHAPTER 12: MOBILE APPS FOR ENHANCED BLEISURE TOURISM EXPERIENCE: EXPLORING THE PROSPECTS AND CHALLENGES

This chapter explores the role of mobile applications in enhancing bleisure travel experiences. The authors classify various apps, highlighting their benefits and addressing challenges such as data privacy and information overload. By examining the future prospects of mobile technology in bleisure tourism, the chapter provides valuable insights into how these tools can shape the travel industry and meet the evolving needs of modern travelers.

CHAPTER 13: INFLUENCE OF SOCIAL MEDIA INFLUENCERS ON BLEISURE TRAVEL IN JAMMU AND KASHMIR

This chapter investigates the role of social media influencers in promoting bleisure travel in Jammu and Kashmir. The author analyzes how digital platforms like Instagram have reshaped travel narratives and contributed to sustainable tourism growth. By leveraging the visual appeal and wide reach of social media, influencers and travel agencies have successfully highlighted the region's potential for combining business and leisure, providing valuable insights into the transformative power of digital marketing in the travel industry.

As editors of this comprehensive reference book on bleisure tourism, we are delighted to present a collection of chapters that delve into the multifaceted dimensions of this burgeoning trend. Our contributors have meticulously examined the intersection of business and leisure travel, providing invaluable insights and practical implications for a diverse audience, including academics, industry professionals, and policymakers.

Throughout this book, we have seen how bleisure tourism represents a significant shift in the way professionals approach travel. This trend underscores a growing desire for a healthier work-life balance, as well as the recognition that travel can be both productive and enjoyable. Our chapters highlight how this dual-purpose travel experience can enhance personal well-being while meeting professional commitments.

We began with an exploration of the conceptual foundations and current trends in bleisure travel, setting the stage for a deeper understanding of its evolution and implications. Subsequent chapters examined cultural, economic, and technological factors, providing a historical context and shedding light on the driving forces behind this phenomenon.

Our contributors have also explored the role of technology in shaping bleisure experiences, the impact of social media, and the specific needs of different demographic groups, such as Zillennials and digital nomads. These chapters offer valuable insights into the behaviors, preferences, and decision-making processes of modern travelers.

Furthermore, this book addresses the challenges faced by bleisure travelers and proposes practical solutions to enhance their experiences. By examining the synergy between business infrastructure and leisure offerings in various regions, our authors provide a roadmap for destinations aiming to attract and cater to bleisure tourists.

As we conclude this preface, we hope this book serves as a comprehensive guide and valuable resource for anyone interested in understanding and leveraging the potential of bleisure tourism in the modern world. The insights presented here not only contribute to the ongoing discourse in the travel and tourism industry but also pave the way for future research and strategic planning.

We are thrilled to contribute to this dynamic field and look forward to seeing how the insights and strategies discussed in this book will shape the future of travel. May this work inspire new ideas, foster innovation, and encourage a harmonious blend of business and leisure in the journeys of professionals around the globe.

Swati Sharma
Amity University, Noida, India

Narendra Kumar
Amity University, Noida, India

Vasco Ribeiro dos Santos
Polytechnic Institute of Leiria, Portugal

Karen Miranda-Fernandez
Asia Pacific Institute for Events Management, UK & Lyceum of the Philippines University, Laguna, Philippines

Chapter 1

Amalgamation of Two Worlds:
Bleisure Travel - A Contemporary Concept in the Travel and Tourism Industry

Shilpi Gupta
https://orcid.org/0000-0003-0697-9945
Amity University Noida, India & Chandigarh University, India

Swati Sharma
https://orcid.org/0000-0003-2949-2363
Amity University, Noida, India

Prashant K. Gautam
https://orcid.org/0000-0002-1423-1358
Panjab University, Chandigarh, India

ABSTRACT

The travel and tourism industry has a significant impact on influencing the worldwide economy and fostering cross-border relationships. This diversified industry includes transportation, hospitality, leisure activities, and tourism-related services, which involve the movement of people for a variety of purposes, such as business, leisure, education, cultural exchange, and so on. Bleisure tourism is a new buzzword that reflects that business trips usually include opportunities for leisure. Bleisure travel is thus an amalgamation of the two worlds—"business" and "leisure"—and is an emerging concept in which travellers combine business visits with leisure activities. This chapter attempts to provide an overview of the relevant literature available in the topic of bleisure tourism, bleisure travellers, and emphasizing on the trends that

DOI: 10.4018/979-8-3693-4354-8.ch001

indicates a desire for a better work-life balance, as well as a recognition that travel can be both productive and enjoyable. This chapter also looks at the expansion of the bleisure tourism from business perspective, as well as its future consequences.

INTRODUCTION

A recent development that is steadily but gradually gaining hold is making it harder to distinguish between travel for work and vacation. This mix, called "Bleisure travel," represents a major shift in how business travellers arrange their trips. According to Economist, 2019 & Expedia, 2018 report, bleisure tourism, or travelling for business and pleasure at the same time, has become increasingly popular currently. Professionals who combine business travel with leisure time to avoid the all-work, no-fun nature of business travels are referred to as "bleisure travellers" according to the World Economic Forum, 2016 reports. The phrase "bleisure" describes a relatively recent and well-liked idea in travel and bleisure travellers' make the most of their experiences while traveling by extending business trips to include time for relaxation, exploration, and immersion into different cultures. This trend indicates that the Bleisure travellers' evolving their attitudes and purpose, as they strive to maximize their vacations by combining work and recreation. Travellers are no longer confined to the stuffy walls of hotel suites and conference rooms; instead, they are searching more and more for ways to mix leisure with business travel to make routine journeys extraordinary.

Professionals all over the world are starting to value the idea of relaxing getaways as a way to maintain a healthy work-life balance in the modern era. Combining travel for work with leisure time is known as "bleisure," a phrase derived from the terms "business" and "leisure." some studies which provides a brief overview of the development and future directions of business travel research, is based on a selection of academic as well as business resources. Implications for practice highlights a broad overview of the prospects while differentiating between various kinds of business travel (Lubbe 2020).

While the word "bleisure" has recently gained popularity, people have been known to mix leisure travel with work travel in the past (Mercan and Sandikci 2024). Ultimately, the business travellers aim for a state of well-being that places a priority on relaxation, attention to detail, safety, and security during the journey (Puerta, M., Pindado, J., González 2023). An expanding group of professionals known as "bleisure travellers" mix business travel with leisure time in an effort to strike a balance between their professional obligations and time for personal growth and relaxation. These tourists frequently prolong their business travels by a few days in order to see new places, experience the local way of life, and relax from work-related stress.

Professionals in the millennials and Generation Z, who value adventures and a healthy balance between work and life, are especially enamoured of this trend. For millions of people globally, travelling abroad for business is now a regular part of their job. Regardless of the organisational rationale, it is now likely that a large number of people work irregular hours outside of the official office, which has practically become a standard part of their working lives (Beaverstock et al. 2009). Study outlines how businesses use international business travel to connect their geographically dispersed divisions, exploring the venues and forms of business travel and lastly outlined how business travel affects the environment as well as the traveller (Beaverstock et al. 2009). However, the expansion of the travel and tourism industry is not disguised, and the sector has been innovative in introducing new segments frequently, one of which is Bleisure Tourism.

Travel for business that includes leisure is definitely not a new phenomenon; rather, it is a novel idea in tourist marketing tactics. The word “bleisure travel” is typically used to describe travel that combines elements of business as well as enjoyment. It typically manifests as business travellers extending their journey to enjoy recreational pursuits at the location they visit. The study looked at how the pandemic affected leisure travellers and how it would affect their future travel plans. The findings showed that vacationers are extremely demotivated, afraid, and frightened as a result of this worldwide pandemic. The results also showed that the foreseeable future of leisure travel appears unpredictable and hazy, which will have a significant impact on activities pertaining solely to business travel in addition to tourism and travel patterns.

By embracing the 'bleisure' theory, tourism destination management companies strive to expand into new areas and continuously produce inventive and imaginative products in order to remain competitive in the global market. By analysing the bleisure offerings using the data from DMOs' websites, this chapter adds to the body of literature. Additionally, the present investigation shows compelling reasons to target leisure travellers and provides DMCs with a number of useful implications (Ozdemir and Celebi 2023). Few studies have been done from an understanding of bleisure travel, and none from an analysis of bleisure travel. Many research have been done from the aspect of business tourism-related events and impacts. The phenomenon of employees engaging in leisure activities during their full-time working trips—especially managers and business travelers—has brought attention to the bleisure trend (Pinho and Marques 2021). From this chapter the authors’ are aiming on finding the overview of bleisure travel/tourism by highlighting the following:

a) Key Characteristics of bleisure travellers.
b) Possibilities in bleisure tourism around the globle.
c) Challenges faced by bleisure travellers and bleisure tourism.

This chapter looks at the reasons for the increasing popularity of bleisure travel, as well as its challenges and possible repercussions on the tourism sector. This chapter delves into the particulars, benefits as well, challenges, and possible future advancements of bleisure travel, offering an understanding of the manner in which it has altered business travel.

CHARACTERIZING BLEISURE TRAVEL AND TRAVELLERS

Essentially, bleisure travel is the ability to seamlessly integrate personal pursuits and professional obligations into a single journey. Travellers look forward to maximise the most of their trip, by prolonging a work trip by a few days or including leisure activities in the schedule. Interestingly, other from brief mentions of the administrative need for personal proximity, not much has been published about the representation aspect of international business travel. This study highlights five different sections pertaining to the bleisure travel, what more scholarly research on business travel needs to accomplish in order to advance our knowledge and comprehension of the development and application of travel in the modern era (Beaverstock et al. 2009).

When travelling for leisure, one isn't restricted by routines or job obligations and instead does it for the purpose of exploration, enjoyment, and relaxation. It makes it possible for people to go to new places, engage in leisure activities, experience other cultures, and make lifelong memories. Exploring, outdoor activities, induling in food walks, and vacations at the beach are prominent leisure travel diversions. Providing an extensive selection of services like customised holidays, guided excursions, and luxurious lodging, the tourism sector serves leisure travellers.

The business community and technology for travel are becoming more and more intertwined in today's business world. Technological developments have completely changed the way corporate travel is done, increasing productivity, efficiency, and satisfaction for business travellers. This thorough examination examines the numerous ways that technology affects corporate travel, focusing on important topics including communication, travel management, security, and sustainability. Through supporting local companies and promoting intercultural understanding, this kind of travel not only offers a much-needed respite and regeneration but also makes a big contribution to the global economy. Whilst, individuals that travel for business purposes visit different locations for conferences, seminars, client interactions, and training programmes. It is essential for promoting in-person contacts, developing and maintaining business connections, and spurring company development and innovation.

Leisure travel is characterised by its flexibility, with itineraries that permit last-minute alterations and longer stays. Leisure travellers frequently spend extra on excursions, entertainment, and distinctive lodging options including vacation destinations, unique stays or holiday homes. These expenses all contribute to their increased enjoyment of their trip.

On the other hand, business travellers mainly take trips for work-related events including client visits, seminars, workshops, and consultations. Their travels are primarily focused on professional growth, networking, and business engagements; they often take little time for relaxation. Business travel is typically scheduled or authorised by the employees' employers, sometimes with little notice and a focus on convenience and efficiency. These tourists usually have strict itineraries and set schedules, leaving little room for extended stays or deviations from the itinerary. Spending is mostly focused on commercial facilities, express services, meeting spaces, high-speed internet, and other services that boost productivity. Corporate hotels and serviced residences are among the preferred lodging options for business travellers because they provide necessary business amenities, easy access to business locations, and dependable connectivity.

Even with the popularity of online communication platforms, face-to-face interactions frequently lead to stronger partnerships, more successful negotiations, and a better comprehension of market dynamics. In order to ensure productivity and effectiveness, business travellers need to carefully plan and coordinate their travel, looking for suitable airline schedules, cosy lodging, and dependable transit alternatives. This chapter concludes with a list of North America's main attractions to illustrate how a variety of travel places may appeal to different types of travellers for a variety of reasons (Camilleri 2018).

Businesses spend a lot of money on business travel to support worldwide operations, grow their competitive advantage, and take advantage of new opportunities in a variety of countries. Working professionals from a range of backgrounds are embracing this phenomenon: from independent contractors wanting to maintain a nomadic technological existence to corporate executives addressing meetings. Due to the linked economies that support business travellers' daily needs as well as the necessity of business travel for the upkeep of corporate networks, corporate travel has become essential to the global economy (Beaverstock et al. 2016).

It's common to characterise business tourism as having a high economic significance (Lubbe, 2019). Demand for goods and supply variables, such as growing economies, population growth, globalisation, transportation system development, enhanced growth of specialised middlemen in addition to convention and exhibition centres and new business-related products, are key drivers of its expansion (Swarbrooke & Horner, 2001). Travelling for business-related objectives and with the primary goal of advancing the company's goals is referred to as business or business travel (Belén, 2013). It entails a worker travelling to and from another location of employment in order to attend an event, activity, or meeting. Additionally, on a single trip, business travel is mixed with other forms of travel(Puerta, M., Pindado, J., González 2023).

In the post-pandemic period, flexible work arrangements that deviate from the traditional within-office, nine-to-five schedule has become standard practice. The tourism and travel sectors are significantly impacted by the inherent place-and time-flexibility. The lines between job duties and travel are further blurred by this flexibility, which leads to flexible travel/tourism arrangements (Miao et al. 2024). Flexibility in administrative tasks, communication with co-workers and family members while travelling, and areas set aside for work are crucial. They also require additional services like room service, laundry, and transfers. Like any other traveller, the business traveller develops expectations and needs little more than accommodations to ensure a positive trip. Visitors wanting an equilibrium of business and pleasure frequently look for destinations with excellent business amenities (like conferencing facilities and trustworthy Wi-Fi) and enticing leisure alternatives (like attractive dining, outdoor pursuits, and that cultural highlights). In terms of funds and trip arrangements, the individual corporate traveller has a stronger financial reputation than the leisure traveller. They also don't carry personal items, therefore packing only what they need is a distinguishing characteristic (Puerta, M., Pindado, J., González 2023).

The modifications are driven by worries about how rising air travel will affect the environment, which will probably lead to new difficulties for business travel in the future. The following review of the function, characteristics, and outcomes of contemporary business travel is provided by a group of global specialists. The links between air travel and corporate travellers, the significance of movement in business, and the potential and difficulties presented by workforces that travel are among the issues discussed (Beaverstock et al. 2016). This project is an attempt to gather professional perspectives for the first time regarding Porto's possible growth in the leisure travel market. The purpose of this study is to advance knowledge about how locations may capitalise on this particular niche market for tourism, as well as what kinds of tourism-related assets are worth valuing and what particular features should be taken into account (Pinho and Marques 2021).

(Petrenko, Ekinil, and Provotorina 2023) outlines that, the study highlights the key characteristics of a bleisure vacation and lists the products and amenities that bleisure travellers most frequently request from lodging establishments. The rapid growth of bleisure travel makes it necessary to provide technology enabling bleisure guests to be catered to in business hotels. The majority of the theories currently in use about tourism motivations were created with leisure in mind, so they fall short of adequately explaining the intricate relationship between both business and leisure verticals. Therefore, in order to offer current viewpoints on the connection between travel for business and pleasure, the authors draw on social capital theory, belief theory, borderless career theory, and experiential education (Lichy and Mc-Leay 2018). Additionally, bleisure travellers are typically proficient in technology and prefer flexible work schedules. They easily organise their itineraries, reserve lodging, and find nearby attractions by using online resources and smartphone apps. Organisations are seeing more and more the advantages of encouraging bleisure travel, including higher efficiency, happier workplace, and higher employee retention rates. To promote this practice, employers might provide flexible travel guidelines and travel reimbursement policies. By spending money on food, accommodation, and recreational activities, bleisure travellers also boost the local economic benefits, which makes them an important market for the tourism and hospitality sectors.

The trend of bleisure travel is expected to increase as the boundaries between work and personal time become increasingly hazy. Their travels are mostly focused on sightseeing, adventure sports, visiting different cultures, eating, and shopping. In order to maximise their memories while taking advantage of travel discounts, these travellers frequently plan their trips far in advance. The companies providing corporate tourism services have their business with the employee's organisation. Nonetheless, the staff member who travels is the one who uses the corporate tourism service. As a result, it's important to evaluate and determine their expectations, needs, and profile(Puerta, M., Pindado, J., González 2023). (Aguilera 2008) outlined the analysis of transport activities produced by corporations has mostly focused on cargo movements and commuter trips. While the literature, especially in the field of industrial economics, has attempted to demonstrate the importance of in-person interactions in economic contact and the declining necessity of proximity as a precondition for initiating such contact, the topic of employee business travels has received little attention. (SOFRONOV 2018) highlights that, after food travel, corporate travel is the second- most preferred travel profile among Millennials. In addition, survey data showed that Millennials travel for leisure purposes in order to reduce the expense of their holidays.

The entire tourism and travel industry is evolving as a result of the distinct buying habits of millennials. Authenticity, fulfilment, and sustainability pique their curiosity. Experiences are more important to them than material goods. For instance, since these corporate travellers wish to network and get together hotel lobbies are crucial places for them to meet new people. In addition, they enjoy trying out real food and eating meals made using regional ingredients that are purchased straight from nearby companies. Instead than feeling like obnoxious tourists, they wish to feel like locals.

Presently, millennials are significant players in the travel industry, with a focus on business and leisure travel segments. They make up over 2 billion, or roughly 27 percent of the world's population (SOFRONOV 2018). There are notable differences between the travel habits, priorities, and motives of leisure and business travellers.

Leisure travellers travel mostly for their own pleasure, leisure, and exploration. In order to determine possibilities in the field of assisting bleisure travellers, the study glances at the characteristics and patterns in the growth of bleisure tourism, evaluates the overall amount of business-related lodging accommodations in Rostovon-Don, and lists the range of extra services that the hotel offers. The success of the fresh design can be attributed to the growing number of individuals in the labour market who fit into this new demographic and seek to balance their personal and professional lives in addition to their interest in travelling (Petrenko et al. 2023).

The emergence of employment trends predicated on the fusion of work and leisure is one of the most striking examples of the steady increase in velocities and social transformation that characterises accelerated civilizations. They continue to have an intricate link with high degrees of self-intensification when projected onto a positive concept of flexibility and self-control. To describe a more focused acceleration of this tendency that author call "job touristification," this paper reconstructs the fundamental elements of structured conduct like "bleisure" or "workcation"(López-González 2023).

According to Cohen's 1947 definition, business travellers are individuals who travel for work-related purposes (such as conferences, business meetings, etc.) and may also engage in leisure activities after work. Generally characterised as highly trained (the top) middle-income professionals, they like to view their travel as a benefit of their line of work, which entails comparable tasks in all of the destinations they visit. Migrant tourism workers are defined as (semi-)skilled workers in the tourism industry (such as bartenders, club supporters, disc jockeys, etc.) who migrate in pursuit of better employment prospects in their industry. They differ from the previously described group in that they exhibit a greater orientation towards tourist motives (Bassyiouny and Wilkesmann 2023).

Figure 1. Model of Bleisure Travellers

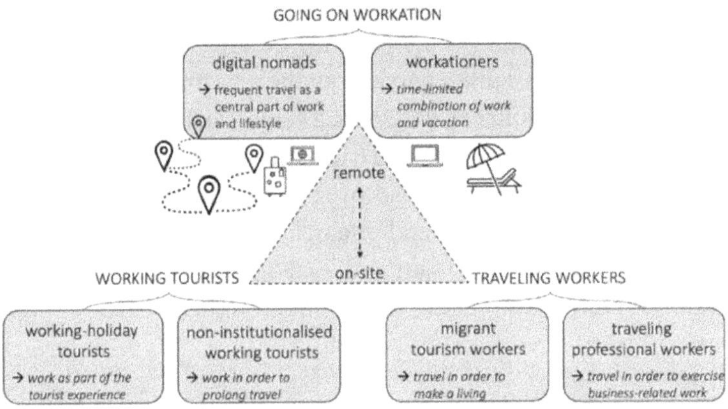

Source: Bassyiouny and Wilkesmann (2023)

According to the Department for Transport (2011), business travel accounted for 3% of excursion and 10% of the domestic mileage travelled in the UK in 2010. Even though it accounts for a greater proportion of trips in large cities with congested transport networks, this is an understudied sector. The results of the research about evolving business travel rules and procedures that impact travellers with luggage are discussed in this article. The goal of the study was to comprehend the mindsets and motives around the reduction of business travel, as well as the trade-offs that had to be made between cutting costs and carbon emissions and maintaining or increasing productivity in order to satisfy the demands of the company. The primary conclusions include the strategies and their effects on cutting expenses and carbon emissions, boosting productivity, and maximising the use of ICT.

The article continues by outlining how some elements can serve as both obstacles to and drivers of change. For example, clients who insist on in-person meetings with suppliers can also serve as catalysts for change by demanding details about emissions of carbon as a component of the Project for Carbon Disclosure (Roby 2014). Many new airlines operating short-haul point-to-point routes have emerged as a result of the EU's relaxation of air transport laws. Even though some of these routes—like those to Palma, Ibiza, Venice, and Nice—are obviously meant for pleasure travellers, anecdotal information indicates that a sizable portion of users utilise these services for business-related travel (Mason 2017). Both business and leisure tourists are able to indulge in leisure activities and visit attractions. As a result, the tourist spots need to have the necessary facilities and amenities. In this context, this study explains how locations might provide a variety of products to cater to a broad range of travellers. Products related to tourism can include, but are not limited to, travel to cities, the seaside, rural areas, ecotourism, wineries, cuisines, health, medical, religious, sports, cultural, or heritage tourism, educational, business (including meetings, incentives, conferences, and events), and more.

The majority of investigations on leisure travel have used a qualitative research methodology. In light of this, author carried out the research to create, using a meticulous procedure, a bleisure journey experience scale that has reliability and validity for evaluating business travellers' bleisure trip experiences. It was demonstrated that the scale, which has 28 elements spread over 6 dimensions, is valid and reliable. This study describes the theoretical and practical ramifications of the findings and suggests future research options (Tsaur and Tsai 2023).

The current study took advantage of these conditions to revisit three pre-pandemic literature topics:

(a) the advantages and disadvantages of a flexible lifestyle;
(b) the case for corporate travel in light of the availability of virtual conferences; and
(c) the influence of tourism on the corporate trip experience.

Nowadays, organisations frequently rely on connection and communication amongst employees who are spread out geographically. As a result, throughout the last couple of decades, corporate travel has grown significantly. To establish effective travel procedures, large corporations and government agencies frequently hire travel managers. This study examines the field of professional travel management (Gustafson 2012).

Comprehensive conversations with grounded business travellers conducted during the peak of the pandemic were analysed interpretatively, and the results showed that while less frequent travel enhanced work-life balance, it also elicited a need for experiences associated with tourism, such as novelty, change, and pleasure. Additionally, grounded business travellers reported that they had trouble fostering creativity at work and forming new business relationships as a result of not being able to be physically close to their colleagues due to the travel suspension. The study reinforced the idea that excessive flexibility is an exciting but stressful lifestyle by presenting the advantages and disadvantages of immobility in reverse. It demonstrated that virtual meetings cannot completely replace in-person interactions with coworkers, bolstering the argument for the need of business travel.

The study verified that tourism-related activities are significant elements of business visits by indicating that they function as anchor points for the rebuilding of thoughts and desires in the thoughts of grounded business travellers (Unger and Uriely, 2023). Bleisure travel has grown in popularity recently since the lines between work and leisure travel are becoming increasingly blurred.

This study looks at how bleisure marketing strategies are developed to entice business travellers to spend more money and have better experiences outside of business events. It also builds a chain of experiences for Bleisure tourism. In order to do this, a case study in the capital area of Japan was carried out. The findings demonstrated that local conference bureaus and exposition centres create a range of marketing initiatives with the aim of encouraging business travellers to spend more money, but these initiatives are still implemented haphazardly. Consequently, a Bleisure marketing plan was proposed (Chung et al. 2020).

POSSIBILITIES AND BARRIERS

While there are numerous benefits to travelling for work, there are also disadvantages. Finding the right balance between an individual's interests at home and their job commitments can be challenging for some people. Because of the employee's increased motivation to perform their job, the combination of business and leisure improves the productivity and profitability of the organisation. It also strengthens the worker's sense of kinship with the business. Business travel encourages dedication on the side of both the employer and the employee (Puerta, M., Pindado, J., González 2023). Thorough planning and efficient time management are required to guarantee that all obligations, both personal and professional, are appropriately attended to. Moreover, handling the complexities of trip planning, such as booking accommodation, transportation, and flights, may add another level of complexity to the vacation. As a result, it generates an ideal situation in which work and play are harmoniously combined.

To capture the chronology, dimension, and instability of this flex-work and flex-travel state, a theoretical framework is established. This approach has consequences for new travel trends as well as the possible alteration of both tourist environments and activities associated with travel. It is a reaction to the increasingly hazy boundaries between time and place dimensions and work-travel realms (Miao et al. 2024). When it comes to business, there are policy concerns and organisational logistics to consider when permitting leisure travel. Employers must have clear policies and procedures in place to guarantee that team member travelling adheres with company rules and regulations. Studies also highlighted that Overindulging in leisure or shopping can cause distractions, which can result in late arrivals at work and overspending on business trips. For Business travellers, travel agencies, lodging facilities, dining establishments, and other tourism-related enterprises will all profit from leisure travel. Because of this, research on bleisure travel, a relatively new kind of tourism, must be prioritised (Mercan and Sandikci 2024).

While the word "bleisure" has recently gained popularity, people have been known to mix leisure travel with work travel in the past. It is believed that bleisure travel can aid in raising employee productivity in light of the studies on the topic. People who travel for work frequently are separated from friends and family, which might lead to social distortion (Mercan and Sandikci 2024). The modern workplace's flexibility and the desire for a work-life balance have led to an increase in the popularity of bleisure travel. Despite this, it is hard to presume that merging these two realms has always been easy because of the differences between work and leisure, as well as the limited resources that travellers have, including time and energy. This study analyses travel features that cause tensions among employment and pleasure during leisure travel and affect travellers' subjective well-being through the use of a focus group conversation and a web-based questionnaire (Park, Lehto, and Kang 2024).

Culture and practical issues make bleisure travel much more challenging. Organising a vacation that meets the demands of both work and play requires careful planning, especially when it comes to scheduling travel companions. Legal and insurance concerns provide serious challenges as well; personal activities may not be covered by conventional work travel insurance, requiring supplemental coverage. In addition, regional variations in social norms and laws may erect further obstacles. Health and safety issues can complicate matters, particularly in the wake of international health emergencies. The inability to work distantly during free time can be attributed to technological constraints like inconsistent internet access and worries about data security. The regional and local economies are significantly impacted by business tourism, which also has significant growth potential. Some of the main factors that make corporate travel so appealing for destinations are minimal cyclical nature, regulated ecological impact, higher revenue for lodging and meeting spaces, enormous demand for meals and drinks as well as an increase in leisure activities (Pinho and Marques 2021).

Supporting sustainable bleisure behaviours also requires addressing ethical and environmental issues, such as the increasing environmental impact from more frequent travel. Numerous organisations have expressed interest in investing in online reservation platforms because to the potential for significant savings on reservation and ticket costs. Making a distinction between money spent on work and recreation could be necessary for this. Study illustrates how to use a broad comparative approach to determine the possibility that an enterprise travel division can cut corporate travel expenses while maintaining the same level of demand for travel and operational conditions (Bell and Morey 1995). This can mean setting limits on how much money is spent on work and play, defining what constitutes appropriate leisure activities, and managing insurance and responsibility concerns. Giving employees the resources and support they require can help organisations encourage productive bleisure experiences while lowering risks and responsibilities.

Hotel managers should concentrate on drawing in and providing for bleisure travellers as they represent a fast expanding and lucrative market for the hospitality industry. In addition to making profits from the purchase of business services, hotels that are able to draw bleisure travellers may also profit from the offer of additional amenities related to wellness, entertainment, and catering, along with from the sale of their primary accommodation service when the tour's duration is extended. Because of this, a lot of hoteliers are trying to connect with this expanding business and leisure market.

This study goals to examine how bleisure tourism services are organised in lodging establishments and to determine how important this industry is to the operations of commercial hotels in the Rostov area and the towns of Rostov-on-Don (Petrenko et al. 2023). The Porto case study highlights the requirement for cities to develop bleisure by considering the value of particular amenities such as locations, lodging, and assistance services; regional tourism resources such as environmental resources, cultural backgrounds, and traditions; accessibility and worldwide connectivity, particularly through air connections; hospitality, encompassing both qualified technical personnel and the hospitality sector and the advertising and promotional tactics of the destination(Pinho and Marques 2021).

The study examines the social effects of the mobile society using survey data from Sweden. The effects of overnight business travel on the capacity of passengers to establish distant communication and regional connections as well as the possibility of travelling can lead to the making of new acquaintances are among the important issues discussed (Bergström 2010). The number elderly American people who use a wide range of travelling and leisure-related services is rising. Despite the recent pandemic outbreak the tourism and hospitality industry has promising long-term prospects, particularly when it comes to the senior customer segment. There will be a greater variety of travel and leisure needs from older travellers due to conflicting reasons including longer life expectancies, greater capacity to take trips owing to greater earnings, yet greater well-being and social restraints. To meet the wide range of travel needs and capitalise on this expanding industry, it is expected that enterprises would need to provide travel possibilities and services for all budgets (Moschis 2022).

This study provides the idea emphasing on the precise assignment of appealing aspects from tourism activities to serve useful functions. To acknowledge the negative and alienating implications of this phenomena on the pursuit of a happy life, a critical model is proposed as a counterbalance to the optimistic narratives surrounding mobility and tourism (López-González 2023). The social sciences' current study on corporate travel and transportation has mostly concentrated on measuring and finding trends in this phenomenon. But an increasing amount of studies has also revealed the complexity and underlying causes associated with company adaptability. It is evident that business travel serves a wide range of purposes, and the motivations for it fluctuate significantly depending on the sector, nature of the work, and organisational setting. This leads to a lack of precision in the concept's definition and an overlapping with non-economic modes of movement. In this regard, business mobility theories offer little help to practitioners of transportation management (Jones 2013).

According to a poll of the top 100 corporate travellers, 32% of them have already implemented online booking systems, while the remaining respondents are evaluating them or plan to do so. Users take some time to get used to online booking systems, just like with other technologies. In the context of emerging technology, people need the correct incentives, the proper challenge, and an appropriate framework in place to compel them to modify their behaviour. When establishing adoption targets throughout the valuation process, managers, however, tend to forget this too quickly. It is not advisable to utilise polls from users about plans to use or embrace other IT services as a stand-in for consumption predictions (Alina M. Chircu 2001). This article evaluates how video-conferencing affects commercial aviation travel. With replacement rates between 2.5 and 3.5%, the results imply that video-conferencing has little impact on corporate air travel. Video conferencing is therefore not seen as posing a significant threat to the aviation business in the Norwegian market(Denstadli 2004).

(Arnfalk and Kogg 2003) outlined, how ICT and its advancements makes a shift from business travel to Virtual meetings. The author studied the environmental & economic impacts in this study and outlines that the effects include a greater understanding of how travel affects the environment and a greater interest in the alternatives that are accessible. This is most evident among those who have worked on the projects directly, but it is also evident among other staff members who have interacted with the project through surveys, interviews, and seminars. It is impossible to predict how much this would influence a shift in meeting behaviour (digital meeting or in-person), but author have observed that project management has made a deliberate choice to maximise project-related meetings (Gustafson 2012).

Only the most regular travellers felt that their trip was a hindrance to their ability to maintain local social connections, but even those participants who travelled only infrequently found significance in this experience. Even if there is no doubting the positive aspects of travel, it might not be feasible to outright reject the widely held belief that leading a life of mobility weakens cohesiveness in society and fosters isolation and solitude (Bergström 2010).

Travel for Business and pleasure encounters multiple challenges, usually arising from organisational directives and practical difficulties. Many businesses have stringent travel restrictions that make it difficult to combine work and play, making spending management more difficult and necessitating extra permissions. Reimbursement concerns emerge because employees frequently find it difficult to distinguish between work and personal expenses. Furthermore, the rigorous schedules associated with business travel can allow limited time for leisure pursuits, and any last-minute alterations to business plans may cause disruptions to leisure plans. Concerns about work-life balance also surface because combining work and relaxation can obfuscate boundaries, increase stress or burnout, and give the impression that one's level of devotion to one's career has reduced.

CONCLUSION AND FUTURE IMPLICATIONS

With the above review, author would like to conclude that the shift in perspective opened the door for bleisure travel, which allows travellers to make the most of their journeys by combining leisure interests with work-related objectives. Findings from both methods show that corporate travel management divisions are not exceptionally effective. It is anticipated that more businesses will start utilising internal travel management departments in a competitive market to assist in limiting the escalating costs associated with travel(Anderson, Lewis, and Parker 1999).

To curb down the implications and minimize the negative impacts on environment and practice the sustainability in travel, corporates are now switching into various other modes to accomplish business tasks like, webinars, hybrid conferences, meetings to protect the destination capacity as well as to facilitate the regenerative trends in tourism sector. This study claims to be outlining the results by adding relevant information to the body of knowledge on trip and life at work by highlighting the challenges in striking a balance between work and play in modern travel practices and providing travel managers with advice on how to reduce conflicts and maximise travel advantages (Park et al. 2024).

Experts were capable of to work remotely as technology developed and pandemic approached, which caused the distinction between work and leisure to become more hazy. People may now take control of their time and include leisure activities into their business travels thanks to flexible working hours and remote work arrangements, which have replaced the traditional nine to five office culture. In order to adapt to the evolving tastes and patterns of business travellers, numerous hotels globally have started introducing suitable loyalty schemes (Petrenko et al. 2023).

The findings indicate that, given a sufficiently extensive pool of firms, suitable benchmarking collaborators may be found that both fit the amount and degree of complexity of the business's diverse travel requirements and its operational setting (Bell and Morey 1995).

Furthermore, bleisure travel offers practical benefits to individuals as well as organisations. From a personal standpoint, it allows travellers to maximise their time away from their residence and the return on their travel expenses. Organisations can gain through encouraging bleisure travel by seeing increases in employee retention, job satisfaction, and productivity. Employees will have more freedom to combine work and play travel as remote employment becomes more prevalent. Extended stays in destination locations will be encouraged by this modification, giving professionals the opportunity to actually get involved in new surroundings without sacrificing work.

The review of literature provides constructive characteristics of the bleisure travellers which are highlighted below in figure 2, which will help the future studies to consider them while researching on Bleisure Travellers –

Figure 2. Key Characteristics of Bleisure Travellers

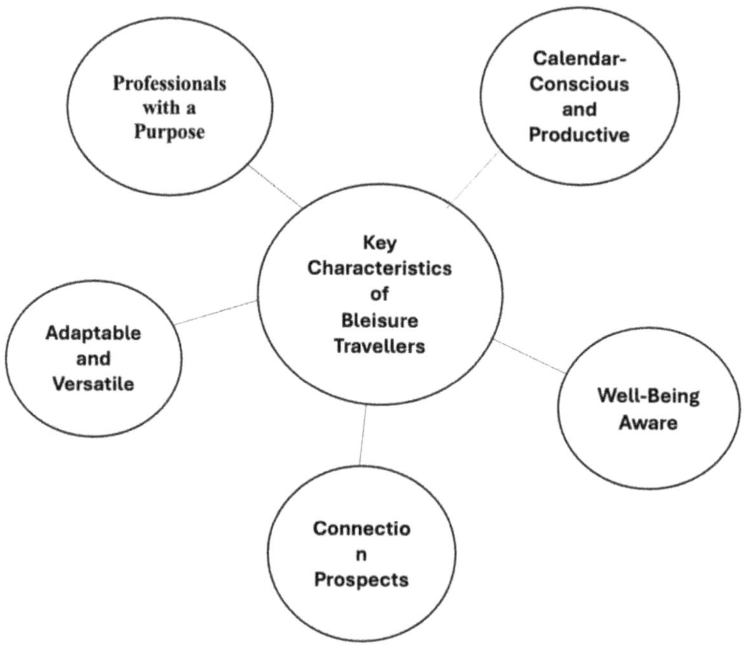

1. Professionals with a Purpose: Bleisure tourists are usually professionals on business trips. Prior to or following their professional commitments, they frequently prolong their stay to incorporate leisure activities. For these tourists, there's a chance to discover a place outside of the boardroom.

2. Calendar-Conscious and Productive: They have excellent time management skills, making the most of a business trip by fitting in extracurricular pursuits without sacrificing their commitments to their jobs. Their effectiveness enables them to combine work and play in a smooth manner.
3. Adaptable and Versatile: They can adjust to alterations in their working hours or surroundings and have a flexible mentality. They can take advantage of free time chances that present themselves while traveling thanks to this flexibility.
4. Well-Being Aware: When taking breaks, many bleisure travelers give careful consideration to their physical and mental well-being. When traveling, they might incorporate things like physical activity, spa services, or nutritious food options to keep their bodies and minds in check.
5. Connection Prospects: They understand that staying longer can lead to networking opportunities beyond just leisure. Informal networking can be just as beneficial at social gatherings and leisure activities as official business meetings.

From the review of literature possible challenges are highlighted as under which will help the future studies to consider them while researching on Bleisure Travellers –

1. Expense management: Travellers on a bleisure trip may have to pay more for lodging, meals, and recreational activities than what their employer pays for business-related expenses. This makes cost management challenging.
2. Travel Tiredness: Long stays and mixing work and play activities can make travelers feel exhausted. Going back and forth between work-related engagements and leisure pursuits without getting enough sleep can be mentally and physically taxing.
3. Organization Regulations: Certain companies may have stringent guidelines when it comes to extending business travels for personal use. These guidelines may include caps on the amount of money that may be reimbursed for out-of-town excursions or time limits on how long employees can stay.

Additionally, the role of technology is expected to be significant, since improvements in digital tools like smartphone apps and further addition to 6G connection will allow a different approach to work from almost anywhere. Improved mobile applications and platforms will make it easier to organise and manage leisure travel, seamlessly combining work and play schedules. Employers can alter rules to promote bleisure travel in light of the advantages it offers, such as increased employee satisfaction and retention.. In the future, bleisure travel will place more importance on environmentalism, regenerative tourism approach. There will be a greater need for eco-friendly accommodation, green transport alternatives, and accountable tourism practices as tourists grow more ecologically concerned. Businesses should also support carbon offset initiatives and encourage business travellers to select eco-friendly solutions when it comes to bleisure travel. Travel experiences that are tailored to each individual's preferences and improved by AI-powered recommendations will become more and more popular.

Travellers seeking out locations and lodgings with fitness centres, spa services, and wellness programmes will drive an increase in the incorporation of wellbeing and health-conscious activities into bleisure travel. This comprehensive method of travelling will improve general wellbeing and work-life balance, making leisure travel an appealing option.

There are certain restrictions with this study. The most significant flaw is the available of only secondary resources available in literature that raises doubts about the other aspects and results outcomes using the primary approach.

Authors would like to stress once again that the study's goal was to look into the features, related studies, understand the work-life balance and future trends in bleisure travel. Future developments in science and technology, shifting working cultures, and the growing popularity of remote work will probably have an impact on bleisure travel trends.

REFERENCES

Aguilera, A. (2008). Business Travel and Mobile Workers. *Transportation Research Part A, Policy and Practice*, 42(8), 1109–1116. 10.1016/j.tra.2008.03.005

Anderson, R. I., Lewis, D., & Parker, M. E. (1999). Another Look at the Efficiency of Corporate Travel Management Departments. *Journal of Travel Research*, 37(3), 267–272. 10.1177/004728759903700308

Arnfalk & Kogg. (2003). Service Transformation - Managing a Shift from Business Travel to Virtual Meetings. *Journal of Cleaner Production,* 11(8 SPEC.), 859–72. .10.1016/S0959-6526(02)00158-0

Bassyiouny, M., & Wilkesmann, M. (2023). Going on Workation – Is Tourism Research Ready to Take off? Exploring an Emerging Phenomenon of Hybrid Tourism. *Tourism Management Perspectives*, 46, 101096. Advance online publication. 10.1016/j.tmp.2023.101096

Beaverstock, Derudder, Faulconbridge, & Witlox. (2016). *International Business Travel in the Global Economy.*

Beaverstock, J. V., Derudder, B., Faulconbridge, J. R., & Witlox, F. (2009). International Business Travel: Some Explorations. *Geografiska Annaler. Series B, Human Geography*, 91(3), 193–202. 10.1111/j.1468-0467.2009.00314.x

Bell, R. A., & Morey, R. C. (1995). Increasing the Efficiency of Corporate Travel Management through Macro Benchmarking. *Journal of Travel Research*, 33(3), 11–20. 10.1177/004728759503300303

Bergström, G. (2010). Consequences of Overnight Work Travel for Personal Social Relations: Problems, Promises, and Further Repercussions. *Mobilities*, 5(3), 369–386. 10.1080/17450101.2010.494841

Bogdan, S. (2018). Millennials: A new trend for the tourism industry. *Annals of Spiru Haret University.Economic Series 18*, (3), 109–122. 10.26458/1838

Camilleri, M. A. (2018). *The Tourism Industry: An Overview.*

Chircu, Kauffman, & Keskey. (2001). Maximizing TheValue of Internet-Based Corporate Travel Reservation Systems. *Communications of the ACM,* 44(11).

Chung, J. Y., Choi, Y. K., Yoo, B. K., & Kim, S. H. (2020). Bleisure Tourism Experience Chain: Implications for Destination Marketing. *Asia Pacific Journal of Tourism Research*, 25(3), 300–310. 10.1080/10941665.2019.1708760

Denstadli, J. M. (2004). Impacts of Videoconferencing on Business Travel: The Norwegian Experience. *Journal of Air Transport Management*, 10(6), 371–376. 10.1016/j.jairtraman.2004.06.003

Gustafson, P. (2012). Managing Business Travel: Developments and Dilemmas in Corporate Travel Management. *Tourism Management*, 33(2), 276–284. 10.1016/j.tourman.2011.03.006

Jones, A. (2013). Conceptualising Business Mobilities: Towards an Analytical Framework. *Research in Transportation Business & Management*, 9, 58–66. 10.1016/j.rtbm.2013.08.003

Lichy, J., & McLeay, F. (2018). Bleisure: Motivations and Typologies. *Journal of Travel & Tourism Marketing*, 35(4), 517–530. 10.1080/10548408.2017.1364206

López-González, J. L. (2023). Job Touristification: Bases for the Critique of a Social Acceleration Phenomenon Manifested in Bleisure and Workation | La Turistificación Del Trabajo: Bases Para La Crítica de Un Fenómeno de La Aceleración Social Manifestado En El Bleisure y El Workation. *Cuadernos de Relaciones Laborales*, 41(2), 335–348. 10.5209/crla.87872

Lubbe, B. (2020). Business Travel: A Perspective Paper. *Tourism Review*, 75(1), 113–116. 10.1108/TR-05-2019-0178

Mason, K. J. (2017). *The Propensity of Business Travellers to Use Low Cost Airlines.*

Mercan & Sandikci. (2024). *Bleisure Tourism: Business and Leisure Together.*

Miao, L., Yang, F. X., Im, J., & Zhang, Q. (2024). Flexwork and Flextravel. *Annals of Tourism Research*, 106, 103763. Advance online publication. 10.1016/j.annals.2024.103763

Moschis, G. P. (2022). *Marketing Travel & Leisure Services.* Vol. Part F379.

Ozdemir & Celebi. (2023). *Bleisure Trends: Combining Business and Leisure Travel.*

Park, S., Lehto, X., & Kang, J. (2024). Balancing Work and Leisure: Unraveling Constraints on Work-Leisure Integration in Bleisure Travel. *International Journal of Hospitality & Tourism Administration*, 1–27. Advance online publication. 10.1080/15256480.2024.2344226

Petrenko, A., Ekinil, G., & Provotorina, V. (2023). Organization of Bleisure-Tourists Service as a Factor of Sustainable Development of the Tourism Sector of the Rostov Region. *E3S Web of Conferences*, 381. 10.1051/e3sconf/202338101084

Pinho, M., & Marques, J. (2021). The Bleisure Tourism Trend and the Potential for This Business-Leisure Symbiosis in Porto. *Journal of Convention & Event Tourism*, 22(4), 346–362. 10.1080/15470148.2021.1905575

Puerta, M., Pindado, J., & González, T. (2023). *The Resilience of Corporate Tourism : Bleisure*. Digitalization.

Roby, H. (2014). Understanding the Development of Business Travel Policies: Reducing Business Travel, Motivations and Barriers. *Transportation Research Part A, Policy and Practice*, 69, 20–35. 10.1016/j.tra.2014.08.022

Tsaur, S. H., & Tsai, C. H. (2023). Bleisure Travel Experience: Scale Development and Validation. *Journal of Travel & Tourism Marketing*, 40(1), 21–37. 10.1080/10548408.2023.2199773

Unger, O., & Uriely, N. (2023). Reflections on Hypermobility: A Study of Business Travelers during the COVID-19 Pandemic. *Tourism and Hospitality Research*. Advance online publication. 10.1177/14673584231184160

Chapter 2
Bleisure Travel:
The Rise of Flexible Work and Its Impact on Tourism

Devika Sood
https://orcid.org/0000-0001-7007-2905
Amity University, Noida, India

Monisha Juneja
https://orcid.org/0000-0003-3984-1598
State Institute of Hotel Management, India

ABSTRACT

Bleisure, a term given to a combination of business and leisure into one trip, has become popular in recent years. This trend reflects a paradigm shift in the traditional dichotomy between work and leisure. Due to the novel nature of the concept many researchers have studied the bleisure travel experience and marketing practices to ensure maximum return for the travel industry. However, a gap in the literature was noticed that relates to the historical evolution of travel trends, tracing the roots of modern tourism and business travel. This chapter aims to provide insights into the cultural, economic, and technological catalysts that have fostered the rise of bleisure travel. The study aims to explore how societal changes, technological advancements, and economic shifts have shaped the way people travel for both business and leisure. The study uses secondary data for analysing the concept from published research papers, journal articles, published articles in the magazines and newspapers.

DOI: 10.4018/979-8-3693-4354-8.ch002

1. INTRODUCTION

The combination of business and leisure (bleisure) is gaining popularity these days among various businesses around the world. Modern-day employees are willingly merging their jobs with leisure activities which have become part of modern work (Blackshaw, 2017). An important attribute of bleisure travel is using the free time during the business trip to engage in leisure activities (Lichy& McLeay, 2018). Business employees have interlaced their work lives with their personal lives to enjoy while on business trips (Caicedo-Barreth et al., 2020). A major break in the tourism economy was felt during the pandemic which was a 60% decline in international tourism in 2020 (OECD, 2020). However, in 2022 the amount of money spent by global businesses on travel increase to $1.3 trillion which was expected not till 2026 (Global Business Travel Association, 2023).Bleisure tourism arises out of the business motive but it mixes the leisure aspect of travel as well (Lichy& McLeay, 2018) while another study debates that travel motivation is difficult to point out (Pinho & Marques, 2021). The bleisure tourists can be divided into two groups: the first that travels as an individual as a part of a corporate event or conference guest who has limited leisure days on the business trip and the second is the business travellers who are accompanied by family or friends (Petrenko et al., 2023). Those bleisure tourists who travel alone enjoy their freedom and independence and are looking for establishing new social relations and gain a new viewpoint (Çulfacı et al., 2024).

The motivation for travel can be seen as an inclination a person has towards a particular tourism activity (Pizam et al., 1979) which is constantly changing with the changing times (Lee & Crompton, 1992; Phosikham, 2010). The existing literature lacks in identifying the emerging motives of bleisure travellers thus, making it important to study the cultural shifts and motives behind this travel. A survey by Global Business Travel Association (2023) reported 62% of bleisure tourists are saying they are travelling more than they did pre-COVID and 42% of them are saying they are adding vacation days to their existing business travel. Making bleisure tourism even more relevant in the new scenario. The existing literature is still in the infancy stages and this tourism concept has been overlooked by earlier studies (Pearce, 2015; Lichy, & McLeay, 2018). Understanding the concept of bleisure tourism will help the tourism service providers in keeping abreast with the changing times and enhance their services to meet the bleisure tourist needs.

Recognizing the growth of bleisure travel is important and explores the aspects that are driving its rise and expansion. This chapter outlines the brief history of the concept of bleisure tourism since its inception. The focus of the study is identifying the cultural shift, motivational factors, economic impact, and technological up gradation that it is bringing into the tourism sector. First the study explores the cultural shift that is reflected in the changing societal normand travel behaviour of the bleisure which would be important for the tourism service providers viewpoint (Lichy & McLeay, 2018). Then it study explores the motivational factor even though they are dynamic and ever-changing (Çulfacı et al., 2024). Further the study understands the economic impact by identifying the pattern and opportunities where the bleisure tourists can spend (Caicedo-Barreth et al., 2020). Fourth the chapter uncovers the latest technological advancement that will aid the bleisure tourists shaping their travel (Goecke, 2020). Lastly, the chapter summarizes the state and trends in bleisure post Covid.

2. HISTORY OF THE CONCEPT 'BLEISURE'

The term bleisure is relatively new that has been trending in the tourism industry in recent years. This term is a combination of both business and leisure. It can be summarised as an extended business trip that involves leisure activities undertaken at the destination. In 2000, researchers Pizam et al. concluded in their study that the line between work and leisure travel has faded. Davidson (2003) pointed out some of the unique characteristics of a traveller who is engaging in both work-related and leisure activities. Firstly, they would extend their trip to enjoy leisure activities and second, they would engage in tourism programmes during their work trip. While, Pinho and Marques (2021) stated in their research that the origin of the word bleisure can be dated back to 2009 when the younger workforce redefined their work travel routine. This point was further reinforced by Gale (2009) that the difference between travelling for work and leisure was becoming merged with a lesser distinction between the two.

Caicedo-Barreth et al. (2020) cited Martín (2011), who defined a business tourist as a person who travels outside their residence to complete a work assignment or be part of a meeting, conference or convention without getting any salary from the destination and the leisure activity came as a by-product of the work trip. Murchie (2014) further stated that the bleisure travellers were mostly those who had their own businesses and wanted to network over drinks. Around the same time, researchers Egencia & Expedia (2013) identified the bleisure age group as 18 to 34 years. García (2016) enforced that business tourism is in high demand and requires constant updating of tourism services and training of service providers to keep up with the demands.

Unger et al. (2016) referred to "hybrid travel" which a vast term was combining multiple aspects of tourism like work, medical visits, studies, and politics. Another term word that was used around the same time was 'bizcation' (Carlson Wagonlit Travel, 2016). But the term that finally got picked up was 'bleisure' (BridgeStreet, 2014; World Economic Forum, 2015, Lichy and McLeay, 2018). While other terms like "business event travellers" and "working tourist", have been used interchangeably to convey the same meaning that 'bleisure' does (Sohaili et al., 2022). Table 1. Summarizes the history of bleisure.

Table 1. Evolution and Significant Milestones in the History of Bleisure Travel

	Event/Study	**Description**
	Pizam, Uriely, & Reichel	Concluded that the line between work and leisure travel has faded.
	Davidson	Pointed out unique characteristics of a traveler engaging in both work-related and leisure activities.
	The Future Laboratories	Coined the term 'bleisure', identifying the fading line between business and leisure among professionals.
	Gale	Reinforced the merging distinction between traveling for work and leisure.
	Martín	Defined a business tourist and noted that leisure activity often comes as a by-product of work trips.
	Egencia & Expedia	Identified the bleisure age group as 18 to 34 years.
	Murchie	Stated that bleisuretravelers were often business owners who networked over drinks.
	BridgeStreet	Mentioned the term 'bleisure', helping it gain recognition.
	World Economic Forum	Further popularized the term 'bleisure'.
	Unger, Uriely, & Fuchs	Referred to "hybrid travel," combining aspects like work, medical visits, studies, and politics.
	Carlson Wagonlit Travel	Used the term 'bizcation' alongside 'bleisure'.
	García	Emphasized the high demand for business tourism and the need for constant updates in services.
	Lichy and McLeay	Their study helped popularize the term 'bleisure' in tourism research.
	Caicedo-Barreth, Pavón, & Santos	Cited Martín's definition of a business tourist.
	Sohaili, Aminudin, & Amir	Noted that terms like "business event travellers" and "working tourist" convey the same meaning as 'bleisure'.

3. CULTURAL SHIFT

Bleisure is a novel concept that is changing the tourism industry and shaping the different aspects of the tourism sector is worthwhile to understand (Chung et al., 2020). The term bleisure tourism has been derived from business and leisure tourism that cater to different aspects of the tourism experience (Yoo et al., 2016). Business tourism as the name suggests is related to the work aspect of the traveller. A business tourist travels to attend a meeting or complete a work-related commitment in order to advance in their career (Gustafson, 2014; Cohen & Gossling, 2015). While leisure tourist travels to immerse in the culture of a place and experience cultural sightseeing, dine at local restaurants or sunbathe on a beach (Leiper et al., 2008).

The corporate sector throughout the world is using the concept of bleisure like an incentive tour being offered to employees. The companies are encouraging the employee to combine their business trip with a mini-vacation, offering them to stay longer at the travel destination where they can take their family or friends (Petrenko et al., 2024). According to a recent study by Mercan and Sandıkcı (2024) it has been proven to increase employees' efficiency. As the employees can be accompanied by their family or spouse members in the bleisure trip which can't be done on a business trip. Researchers Pinho and Marques (2021) identified that millennials are changing the tourism industry based on their purchasing behaviour. They are attracted to experiences rather than tangible objects. This generation is on the lookout for authentic, genuine and sustainable experiences. The leisure activities enjoyed by bleisure tourists involve enjoying the local cuisine, and exploring the heritage and cultural sights followed by visiting art museums and galleries (Chung et al.,2020). Artistic and entertainment experiences are valued by the bleisure tourists that motivates them to extend their stay at the destination (Economist, 2019; Pinho& Marques, 2021). Researchers Tsaur & Tsai (2023) through their study created an experiences scale for the bleisure tourists. After thorough examining the validity and reliability tests the scale was developed having 28 factors spread over six dimensions that are "escapist experience", "job-related learning experience", "sociocultural experience", "prestige experience", "smart technology experience", and "entertainment experience.

It was the millennial generation that wanted to include business with leisure (Pinho & Marques, 2021) and the generation that preferred business travel came to second place in the order of preference after travelling for food (Sofronov, 2018). This concept has become popular with Generation Y or Millennials who spend a one fourth of the amount on leisure activities like guided tours, museums, concerts, galleries and sporting events (Pinho & Marques, 2021). This generation is conscience about spending on vacations as shown by statistical surveys which is why they tend to indulge in leisure activities on business trips or book a vacation next to the business travel (NCR, 2019). A study conducted by Expedia (2018) for over 2500 business tourists from all over the world that travellers who converted into bleisure tourists from business tourists were those who travelled at a place far away from their home for 2 or 3 nights rather than those who stayed for a shorter or longer than this time frame. This segments gets attracted by special or discounted rates for stay before or after their planned trip (Petrenko et al., 2023).

A recent study by Ezeuduji (2024) has cited Staines' (1980) compensation theory of work-life balance and conflict theory (Greenhaus & Beutell, 1985) to be in line with dealing with bleisure travellers' choices. Bleisure tourists use vacation time during business trips as a time to unwind and relax. Finding a balance between work and personal life is the underlying fact that the compensation theory is exactly what the bleisure traveller wants. Finding the equilibrium to battle the stress at work by practicing integrating work and leisure has been explained in the conflict theory. The companies are focusing on improving the mental health and general well-being of employees by promoting the bleisure culture among them. This would in turn make the companies profitable as they would be greeted with happier, relaxed (Batala & Slevitch, 2024), joyful and engaged employees (Ezeuduji, 2024).

4. MOTIVATIONAL FACTORS

Motivation is essential to understanding tourist behaviors and enhancing the tourism study literature (Uysal & Jurowski, 1994; Meng et al., 2008). For the traveller to be motivated, they must possess a psychological desire and work towards fulfilling this desire (Pearce & Lee, 2005). However, it is difficult to measure these multifaceted psychological desires as they are complex to observe and measure (Kluin & Letho, 2012). With the changing times the past travel motivation theories may not be relevant in the current scenario (Leong et al. 2015; Whang et al., 2016). As the literature on bleisure tourism is still in the infancy stage, the motivation theories that can comprehend this type of tourist are still being developed (Lichy & McLeay, 2018).

In tourism literature, the most commonly mentioned travel motivation theory is the push and pull framework developed by Crompton (1979). Push motivators are those that are related to internally driven desires that cover social interaction, leisure, and self-actualization (Kim et al., 2007). Over the years as further studies developed additions were made to the push factors like experiencing a new culture, (Ralston et al., 2004), escaping the daily routine, and self-exploration influence the volunteers working overseas (Pan, 2012) perception of the place, and challenge (Paraskevaidis & Andriotis, 2017). The pull factors are the outside attributes that the destination to be visited holds. This includes the weather, sites, attractions, and facilities (Correia et al. 2013). Some travellers are motivated by learning from new travel experiences as a way of discovery and like getting new opportunities to learn from (Stone & Petrick, 2013). These factors only cover the leisure motives of the travellers while the bleisure motives can be unfolded under the category of self-initiated expatriation (SiE) (Lichy & McLeay, 2018).

According to Frese & Fay (2001), the characteristics that make them fall in line with a bleisure tourist is that they are goal-oriented and ready to relocate to another country for work. Researchers Richardson (2006) and Thorn (2009) have provided a framework that can help in explaining the bleisure tourist motives. SiE are professionals that take up temporary work in another country (Howe-Walsh & Schyns, 2010; Doherty et al.,2013). They are driven by career development (Guo et al., 2013) and personal interests, family support, culture, and location (Dickman, 2012). Three theories that have been underlined by Baruch et al., (2016) help to understand their motives. First is the Boundary-less career theory explaining why the career paths are not bound in the same organization and explaining reasons why the individual seeks a career in a foreign country (Andresen et al., 2015). The second is the expectancy motivation theory that explains how SiEs get motivated to move abroad due to higher incomes, better lifestyles and enrich their skills. Third, the social capital theory describes the ways the organization creates social relationships among peers that can be used for career growth and success (Ramaswami et al., 2016).

Researchers Lichy and McLeay (2018) referring to previous studies and their study own have recognized bleisure travel interest based on motivations. First are the experiential learners who want to add to their previous knowledge (Kolb & Kolb, 2005), and the majority of bleisure travelers fall under this category (Lichy & Mcleay, 2018). Second, are the escapers who are looking for independence while travelling (Lo & Lee, 2011). The third category is holiday workers/ holidaymakers what to learn about the culture of the destination and are well-versed with the language (Lichy & Mcleay, 2018). Next is altruistic knowledge comprising senior academics who want to be engaged and have a willingness to learn (Paraskevaidis & Andriotis, 2017) and are motivated to travel abroad for research, publications, and career growth (Cunningham et al., 2016). Fifth are research-active trailblazers who are networking with like-minded people and increasing their reputation (Barros, 2006; Lichy & Mcleay, 2018) in their area of research.

Figure 1 illustrates the primary motivators driving leisure travel, business travel, and the integrated concept of bleisure travel.

Figure 1. Motivators for Leisure, Business and Bleisure (Prepared by Author)

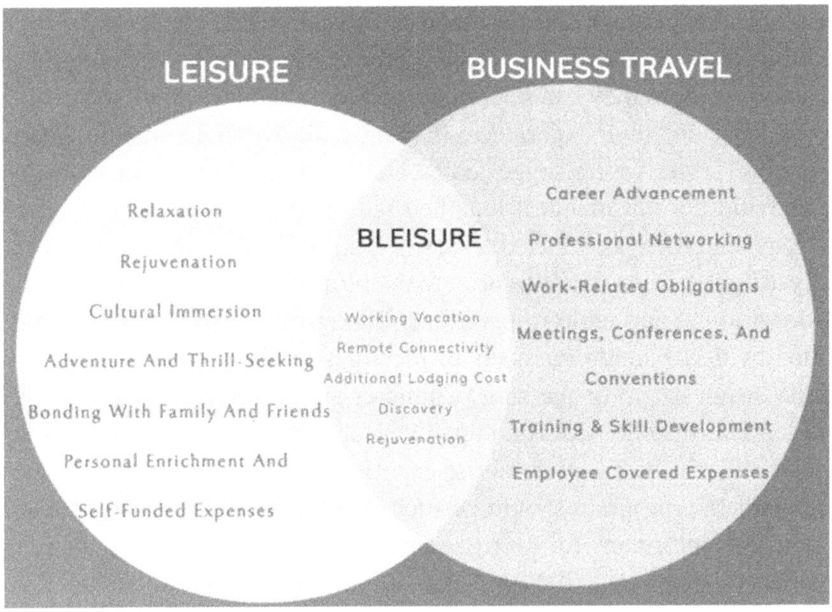

Leisure, bleisure, and business travel each offer unique motivations, yet they share common themes. Leisure travel is driven by relaxation and cultural exploration (Pinho & Marques, 2021) while bleisure combines work and leisure for a balanced experience. Business travel focuses on career advancement and networking. However, all three seek discovery, whether through new cultures, connections, or personal growth (Cook, 2023), reflecting a universal desire for exploration and memorable experiences. Figure1. depicts amalgamation of leisure and business travel to merge and form bleisure.

5. ECONOMIC IMPACT

Tourism providers need to look beyond the traditional leisure and business tourists. Both these categories of tourists have brought high economic returns separately (Lubbe, 2019). However, a new potential market has emerged called bleisure tourism that has yet to be explored and monetized (Caicedo-Barreth et al., 2020; Batala & Slevitch, 2024). Earlier literature supports that leisure tourists position value for money at the top while business travellers are concerned mostly with the value of service, as major travel expenses are covered by the company (Correia et al., 2013; Lichy & McLeay, 2018; Batala &Slevitch, 2024). This bleisure tourism market has an important economic impact on the local and regional businesses and has a high development potential as bleisure tourists wouldn't mind spending as long as the service quality isn't compromised (Pinho & Marques, 2021).

Bleisure tourists can be attracted to leisure activities after their business meetings or conventions where they can benefit by adding to the income of the destination along with enriching their experiences (Chung et al., 2020). Destination marketing organizations (DMOs) were suggested by UNWTO (2017) to make provisions for leisure activities for the attendees and their families while bidding for the business events. Expedia (2018) conducted a survey that highlighted that business tourists are likely to book leisure activities prior to their travel which includes entertainment events, local tours, and table reservations. This gives a good chance for revenue generation by DMOs and organizers of meetings to highlight such leisure events before the business trip or meeting (Chung et al., 2020). Collaboration between bleisure tourism stakeholders is a must to ensure a balance between the spending of the tourists and the positive tourist experience (Pinho, & Marques, 2021). A bleisure marketing program should be such that it promotes local businesses, develops ancillary programs for tourists, and fair distribution of profits among the shareholders (Chung et al., 2020).

The global bleisure tourism market is experiencing rapid growth and is expected to more than double in size over the next decade. According to Allied Market Research (2023), the global bleisure market was valued at $315.3 billion in 2022 and is projected to reach $731.4 billion by 2032, growing at a compound annual growth rate (CAGR) of 8.9%. This surge in the bleisure tourism market can be attributed to factors such as the rise in demand for work-life balance, digital transformation in the travel industry, and the increasing presence of millennials in the workforce. The top bleisure destinations are often business hubs that offer a variety of cultural, culinary, and entertainment opportunities. To address the challenges posed by the bleisure trend, such as increased travel costs and difficulty tracking expenses, businesses are adopting more flexible travel policies and encouraging employees to extend their trips for leisure purposes.

According to the study "Business Travel and Bleisure Tourism: A Study on The Travel Motivations of Academics" published in GSI Journals Serie A Advancements in Tourism Recreation and Sports Sciences in March 2024, the growth of the bleisure tourism market has significant economic implications. The study found that "the bleisure tourism market has an important economic impact on the local and regional businesses and has a high development potential as bleisure tourists wouldn't mind spending as long as the service quality isn't compromised" (Caicedo-Barreth et al., 2024) .

The economic potential of the bleisure tourism market is undeniable, with projected growth rates that outpace traditional tourism segments. By understanding the unique needs and preferences of bleisure travelers and collaborating with industry stakeholders, tourism providers can capitalize on this emerging and lucrative market opportunity (Lubbe, 2019).

6. TECHNOLOGICAL UPGRADATION

In the realm of bleisure travel, where business seamlessly intertwines with leisure, technological advancements have heralded a transformative journey, reshaping how professionals navigate their travel experiences. Previously, organizing bleisure trips necessitated extensive reliance on travel agents or corporate departments for booking flights, accommodations, and activities, leading to cumbersome coordination efforts. With the enhancement of information and communication technologies, tourism sector benefited and is called as an "information-intensive industry" by Starčević & Konjikušić, (2018). The advent of digital booking platforms like Expedia, Booking.com, and Airbnb has revolutionized this process. These platforms empower bleisure travellers with the ability to research, compare, and book various aspects of their trips within minutes, offering unparalleled convenience and personalization options (Goecke, 2020). Additionally, travel meta search engines aggregate prices from multiple suppliers, further streamlining the booking process and providing comprehensive options for travellers.

The evolution of online booking engines represents a significant milestone in the technological upgrade of bleisure travel. Platforms such as Expedia and Priceline, launched in the late 1990s, pioneered the concept of enabling customers to book their travel independently, without interference from airlines or traditional travel agencies (Goecke, 2020). This shift empowered travellers with greater autonomy and flexibility in planning their trips, laying the foundation for the seamless integration of business and leisure activities. Furthermore, the rise of remote collaboration tools like Slack, Zoom, and Google Workspace has empowered bleisure travellers to maintain productivity while away from their desks. These tools facilitate virtual meetings, cloud-based document sharing, and real-time communication, ensuring professionals can fulfil their work obligations without compromising their leisure time.

AI-driven platforms have further enhanced the bleisure travel experience by leveraging data analytics and machine learning algorithms to offer personalized recommendations tailored to individual preferences. From suggesting nearby attractions to optimizing travel itineraries based on past behavior, these advancements simplify the decision-making process for bleisure travellers (Agnihotri, 2024). Moreover, the concept of digital nomadism in bleisure travel has been complemented by the introduction of specific visa types tailored to remote workers and freelancers. These digital nomad visas allow individuals to reside and work in foreign countries for extended periods, aligning perfectly with the ethos of bleisure travel by providing flexibility to balance work commitments with leisure activities (Cook, 2023).

In addition to these advancements, the concept of digital nomadism has emerged as a prominent trend within the realm of bleisure travel. Digital nomads, individuals who leverage technology to work remotely while travelling, epitomize the fusion of work and leisure inherent in the bleisure ethos. These modern-day adventurers seek to break free from the confines of traditional office spaces, embracing a lifestyle that allows them to explore new destinations while maintaining their professional pursuits (Zimmerman, 2017). The rise of remote work and the increasing availability of high-speed internet access worldwide have facilitated the growth of the digital nomad community, enabling individuals to work from virtually anywhere (Agnihotri, 2024). From the hotels, the bleisure traveller expects necessary in-room facilities like uninterrupted Wi-Fi access, seamless long-distance calling services, more accessible electric sockets, and an ergonomically designed table and chair (Petrenko et al., 2023).

Furthermore, the introduction of specific visa types tailored to remote workers and freelancers, known as digital nomad visas or remote work visas, has further bolstered the appeal of bleisure travel for this demographic. By obtaining such visas, digital nomads can legally reside and work in foreign countries for extended periods, enabling them to fully immerse themselves in the local culture and lifestyle while balancing work commitments with leisure activities (Cook, 2023).

Figure 2. Evolution of Travel Technology and Bleisure (Prepared by Author)

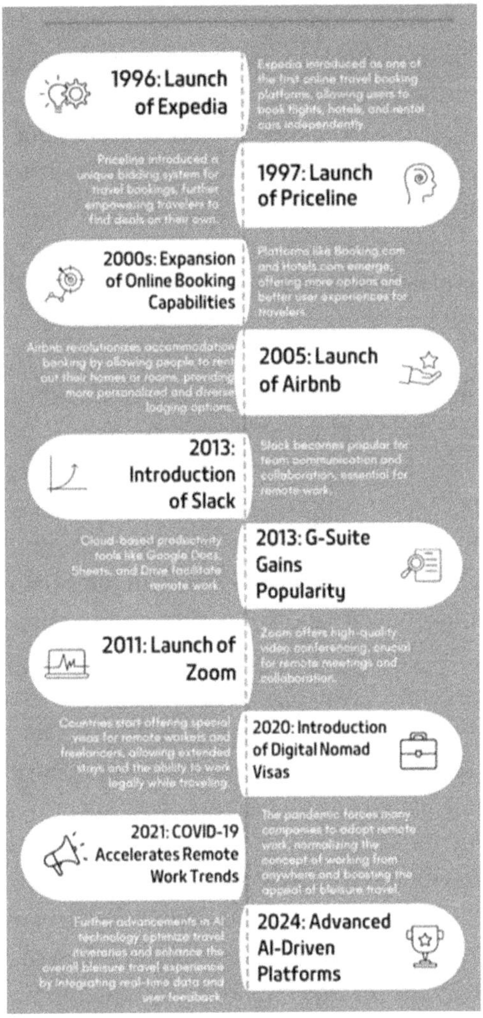

Figure 2 the figure demonstrates how each technological advancement has progressively contributed to the feasibility and appeal of bleisure travel, enabling travelers to efficiently combine business and leisure activities. The evolution of travel technology has provided the tools necessary for managing both work and leisure seamlessly, thus fostering the growth of bleisure as a significant travel segmentThis convergence of technology, remote work, and travel underscores the symbiotic relationship between bleisure travel and the digital nomad movement, shaping the future of work and leisure in the global landscape.

7. DISCUSSION AND IMPLICATION

Bleisure travel is a rapidly growing trend in the tourism sector that positively boosts the employee who is willingly travelling for work as it increases productivity and confidence. This study has prepared a timeline since the inception of the concept of bleisure by adding value to the existing literature available on bleisure tourism. Since early 2000's studies by Pizamet al. (2000) and Davidson (2003) showed the difference between business and leisure travel was slow fading. In 2008 the term 'bleisure' came into existence but not quite a well know term until 2014 and 2015 when it was mentioned by a BridgeStreet and World Economic Forum respectively. Even though the concept was being explored by various studies (Gale, 2009; Martín, 2011; Egencia & Expedia; 2013), but a noteworthy study by Lichy and McLeay (2018) on motivation and topology of bleisure tourist that the term becomes widely used in tourism research and in practice by stakeholders.

Variety of bleisure tourism stakeholders like business travellers, DMOs, hotels, dining outlets, and other local businesses are affected by the cultural, motivational, economical and technological factors. This chapter has summarised of the findings for each of these factors to enable it to fill the gap in the existing tourism literature. As the term bleisure is an amalgamation of business and leisure tourism it still has its unique features (Yoo et al., 2016). The categories developed by Lichy and McLeay (2018) for bleisure tourists on travel interest based on the motivations can assist the tourism facilitators in gaining a better understanding of this particular travel segment. The study concluded that such tourists have time constraints as they have to balance their work and leisure activities during the same trip. The second and third categories identified by the study as escapers and holiday workers have a greater chance to travel internationally for work which can be a potential target market for tourism service providers. While the last two categories altruistic knowledge seekers (senior academicians) and research-active trailblazers are a niche sector that should also not be overlooked by the service providers. Researcher Ezeuduji (2024) agrees that the academicians are the niche sector that should be catered to as they are commonly known to send papers to conferences at their favoured destination. Where they are bound to engage in leisure activities and share their experiences with their colleagues back home in the form of word of mouth publicity.

The generation Y or millennial's are the prime age group that is the bleisure tourist who values experiences over tangible items (Pinho & Marques, 2021). Researches Batala and Slevitch (2024) who have studied the pre, during and post trip experiences of bleisure tourists have concluded that such tourists would benefit from excellent and dedicated concierge consulting services that can alter the leisure activities to suit their free time, give good recommendations and help in making reservations for dining and booking tickets for entertainment activities. The tourism and hospitality service providers must adopt strategies to incorporate these distinct features of bleisure tourists. The business hotels are rethinking of launching apartments hotels to meet the growing demands of the bleisure tourists (Petrenko et al., 2023).

The economic impact of bleisure tourism is slightly different than pure leisure tourism as the former prefers service quality over value for money (Caicedo-Barreth et al., 2020). This segment of travellers can reduce the problem of seasonality (Çulfacı et al., 2024) Local and regional tourism can flourish by directing the bleisure tourists to these avenues. The bleisure tourists book leisure activities before the travel (Chung et al., 2020) and by giving discounted weekend stays it attracts more spending on leisure activities (Batala &Slevitch, 2024). According to Global Business Travel Association (2023) report bleisure travel spending is expected to be nearly $1.8 trillion by 2027.

The hospitality sector can benefit immensely from catering to the bleisure travellers. Researchers Petrenko et al. (2023) have suggested certain ways that can be sustainable for the hotels in the long run. They noted that the bleisure tourist will benefit from childcare facilities within the hotel premises, provide early check-in and late check-out at no additional cost, spa treatments, organised cultural programmes, offering discounts at food and beverage outlets, provide high-end meeting and conference equipments, and dedicated section of the website for bleisure facilities and amenities. Providing personalised service experience to such guests would be the ultimate game changer for the bleisure tourism (Ezeuduji. 2024).

Even though the widespread usage of digital technology enabled work from home during the pandemic it certainly gave rise to new applications and booking platforms for the bleisure tourist to use for their travel (Goecke, 2020). These platforms have enabled the bleisure tourist to have independence and flexibility for planning work and leisure activities. With constant upgradation of AI-driven platforms and remote collaboration tools, bleisure tourists are at an advantage to work and travel with ease (Agnihotri, 2024). This potential tourist can be attracted with personalized e-marketing strategies(Çulfacı et al., 2024). This chapter has uncovered the symbiotic relationship between bleisure travel and the digital nomad movement, shaping the future of work and leisure in the global landscape.

8. BLEISURE TRENDS POST-COVID-19

The COVID-19 pandemic has significantly impacted the travel and hospitality industry, leading to a shift in consumer behavior and the emergence of new trends. One such trend is the rise of "bleisure" travel, which combines business and leisure activities. As the world adapts to the post-pandemic landscape, bleisure travel is expected to transform the travel and hospitality sector (Yadav, 2023). The pandemic has accelerated the trend of remote work, with many employees proving their ability to be productive while working from home or other locations. This has led to an increased demand for flexible workspaces, particularly in hotels. Travelers are now seeking accommodations that offer comfortable and functional spaces to work, as well as amenities that cater to their leisure needs (Sommet Education, 2022).

Reversed Bleisure Model

Another trend emerging in the post-COVID era is the reversed bleisure model, where individuals perform work duties while on vacation, rather than taking leisure time during business trips. This shift is driven by the increased acceptance of remote work and the desire to make the most of travel opportunities. Governments, such as Dubai, have recognized this trend and are offering virtual working programs to attract overseas professionals (Thynk, n.d.). As bleisure travel becomes more prevalent, hotel guests are expected to have increasingly diverse requirements. They will want to use their time efficiently by balancing work and leisure activities, such as attending online meetings and exploring the destination. Guests may request specific amenities, such as soundproof rooms, movable partitions for privacy, and flexible childcare options. Hoteliers will need to adapt to these changing needs and provide comfortable and safe spaces for guests (Viacava et al., 2021). While the rise of bleisure travel presents challenges for the hospitality industry, it also offers opportunities for growth. Hoteliers must be prepared to cater to the needs of bleisure travelers by offering flexible workspaces, reliable technology, and a range of leisure activities. By adapting to these trends, hotels can attract a wider range of guests and increase their revenue (Zubair et al., 2022).

Figure 3 illustrates frequency of words that appear in the literature review. To summarize, the post-COVID-19 era has seen a significant rise in bleisure travel, with travelers seeking to combine work and leisure activities seamlessly. This trend has led to increased demand for flexible workspaces, a reversed bleisure model, and diverse guest requirements. Hoteliers must adapt to these changes to remain competitive and capitalize on the opportunities presented by the evolving travel landscape (Yadav, 2023).

Figure 3. Word Cloud Representing Trends in Bleisure (Prepared by Author)

CONCLUSION

Bleisure tourism comes with its own set of features and characteristics that make this new tourism trend different. The ever-changing consumer tastes and the pursuit of a work-life lifestyle are likely to impact the future of bleisure tourism. This type of traveller is looking for 'comfort, efficiency and flexibility' when they travel (Petrenko et al., 2023). This chapter outlines the brief history of the concept of bleisure tourism since its origin. Further, the study explores the cultural shift, motivational factors, economic impact, and technological upgradation that it brings into the tourism sector. The bleisure travellers are known for being skilled, well planned and organised while planning their trip (Ezeuduji, 2024). In essence, comprehending the development of bleisure travel and its underlying drivers is crucial for many stakeholders like travel service providers, DMOs, hotels, dining outlets, and other local businesses who have to adjust to these shifting trends. By staying in tune with the needs and wants of the bleisure travellers, service providers can stay competitive in a changing tourism environment. The recovery in the tourism sector after the pandemic has started which indicates that international travel is growing and increased competition among travel destinations is on the horizon. Bleisure tourism is vital to the growth of the tourism sector and understanding its features would benefit the tourism service providers. The COVID-19 pandemic has accelerated the rise of "bleisure" travel, where remote work allows combining business and leisure. This trend has increased demand for flexible workspaces in hotels and diverse guest requirements, presenting both challenges and growth opportunities for the hospitality industry. Hoteliers must adapt to these changes to stay competitive and capitalize on the evolving travel landscape

As the bleisure tourism market continues to grow exponentially, future research should focus on understanding the long-term implications of this trend on the tourism industry. This includes exploring the impact of bleisure travel on destination marketing strategies, the development of new tourism products and services, and the sustainability of the tourism industry as a whole.

In conclusion, embracing the bleisure tourism boom presents a significant opportunity for tourism service providers to stay competitive in a changing tourism environment. By understanding the unique features and characteristics of bleisure travelers, and adapting their offerings accordingly, service providers can capitalize on this growing market segment and drive the future growth of the tourism industry.

REFERENCES

Agnihotri, A. (2024, January 4). The Era of Bleisure Travel: Remote and Hybrid Work Trends Inspire a Fusion of Business and Leisure on Work Trips. *Hindustan Times*. https://www.hindustantimes.com/lifestyle/travel/the-era-of-bleisure-travel-remote-and-hybrid-work-trends-inspire-a-fusion-of-business-and-leisure-on-work-trips-101704342757445.html

Allied Market Research. (2023). Global Bleisure Tourism Market Outlook 2032. https://www.alliedmarketresearch.com/bleisure-tourism-market

Andresen, M., Biemann, T., & Pattie, M. W. (2015). What makes them move abroad? Reviewing and exploring differences between self-initiated and assigned expatriation. *International Journal of Human Resource Management*, 26(7), 932–947. 10.1080/09585192.2012.669780

Barros, C. P. (2006). Earnings, schooling and social capital of cooperative managers. *Annals of Public and Cooperative Economics*, 77(1), 1–20. 10.1111/j.1370-4788.2006.00295.x

Barten, M. (2024). 7 Tips for Hotels to Attract More Bleisure Travelers. Retrieved from https://www.revfine.com/bleisure/

Baruch, Y., Yochanan, A., & Tung, R. (2016). Career Mobility in a Global Era: Advances in Managing Expatriation and Repatriation. *The Academy of Management Annals*, 10(1), 841–889. 10.5465/19416520.2016.1162013

Batala, B., & Slevitch, L. (2024). Keeping two balls in the air: The bleisure travel experience. *Annals of Tourism Research Empirical Insights*, 5(1), 100115. 10.1016/j.annale.2023.100115

BridgeStreet. (2014). Bleisure report. London. Retrieved from February 7, 2022, from Bridge Street, Global Hospitality http://skift.com/wp-content/uploads/2014/10/BGH-Bleisure-Report-2014.pdf

Caicedo-Barreth, A., Pavón, E. S., & Santos, L. L. (2020). Competitiveness of Guayaquil towards bleisure tourism. *European Journal of Tourism. Hospitality and Recreation*, 10(2), 118–133. 10.2478/ejthr-2020-0010

Carlson Wagonlit Travel. (2016). Combing business and leisure trips: A quantitative look at the bleisure phenomenon. In CWT Solution Group White Paper. available at https:// www.mycwt.com/content/dam/cwt/pdf/insights/20160712-solutions-group-whitepaper-bleisure.pdfretrived on 28th April 2024

Chung, J. Y., Choi, Y. K., Yoo, B. K., & Kim, S. H. (2020). Bleisure tourism experience chain: Implications for destination marketing. *Asia Pacific Journal of Tourism Research*, 25(3), 300–310. 10.1080/10941665.2019.1708760

Cohen, S. A., & Gossling, ¨. S. (2015). A darker side of hypermobility. *Environment and Planning A. Environment & Planning A*, 47(8), 166–1679. 10.1177/0308518X15597124

Cook, D. (2023). What is a digital nomad? Definition and taxonomy in the era of mainstream remote work. *World Leisure Journal*, 65(2), 256–275. 10.1080/16078055.2023.2190608

Correia, A., Kozak, M., & Ferradeira, J. (2013). From tourist motivations to tourist satisfaction. *International Journal of Culture, Tourism and Hospitality Research*, 7(4), 411–424. 10.1108/IJCTHR-05-2012-0022

Crompton, J. (1979). Motivations for a Leisure Vacation. *Annals of Tourism Research*, 6(4), 408–424. 10.1016/0160-7383(79)90004-5

Çulfacı, G., Onursoy, F. M., & Akın, M. H. (2024). Business Travel and Bleisure Tourism A Study on The Travel Motivations of Academics. *GSI Journals Serie A: Advancements in Tourism Recreation and Sports Sciences*, 7(2), 406–423. 10.53353/atrss.1403738

Cunningham, J., Mangematin, V., O'Kane, C., & O'Reilly, P. (2016). At the frontiers of scientific advancement: The factors that influence scientists to become or choose to become publically funded principal investigators. *The Journal of Technology Transfer*, 41(4), 778–797. 10.1007/s10961-015-9400-4

Dickmann, M. (2012). Why do they come to London? Exploring the Motivations of Expatriates to Work in the British Capital. *Journal of Management Development*, 8(31), 783–800. 10.1108/02621711211253240

Doherty, N., Richardson, J., & Thorn, K. (2013). Self-initiated expatriation. *Career Development International*, 18(1), 6–11. 10.1108/13620431311305917

Economist. (2019). The 2019 Bleisure barometer: Asia's best cities for work and recreation. London: The Economist Intelligence Unit.

Egencia & Expedia. (2013). Expedia and Egencia unveil the future of travel report. PR Newswire Association LLC. Retrieved from https://search-proquestcom.zorac.aub.aau.dk/ docview/1496067552?accountid=8144

Expedia. (2018). Unpacking bleisuretraveler trends. Retrieved from https://bit.ly/bleisure-trends

Ezeuduji, I. O. (2024). Bleisure Travel Reimagined: Implications for Research. *Proceedings of the 7th International Conference on Tourism Research*, 7(1), 2-9. 10.34190/ictr.7.1.2194

Fay, D., & Frese, M. (2001). The concept of personal initiative (personal initiative): An overview of validity studies. *Human Performance*, 14(1), 97–124. 10.1207/S15327043HUP1401_06

Gale, T. (2009). Urban beaches, virtual worlds and 'the end of tourism'. *Mobilities*, 4(1), 119–138. 10.1080/17450100802657996

García, M. (2016). Turismo de reunionesen la ciudad de Mar de Plata: Situación actual desde la percepción del Mar del Plata Convention & Visitors Bureau. Universidad Nacional de Mar del Plata.

Global Business Travel Association. (2023). Global Business Travel Industry Forecast Is for Accelerated Rebound, Spending to Reach $1.8 Trillion by 2027. Retrieved from https://www.hospitalitynet.org/news/4117734.html

Goecke, R. (2020). The Evolution of Online Booking Systems. In Xiang, Z., Fuchs, M., Gretzel, U., & Höpken, W. (Eds.), *Handbook of e-Tourism*. Springer. 10.1007/978-3-030-05324-6_27-1

Greenhaus, J. H., & Beutell, N. J. (1985). Sources of conflict between work and family roles. *Academy of Management Review*, 10(1), 76–88. 10.2307/258214

Guo, C., Porshitz, E., & Alves, J. (2013). Exploring career agency during self-initiated repatriation: A study of Chinese sea turtles. *Career Development International*, 18(1), 34–55. 10.1108/1362043131130

Gustafson, P. (2012). Managing business travel: Developments and dilemmas in corporate travel management. Tourism Management, 33(2), 276–284. https://doi.org/.tourman.2011.03.00610.1016/j

Howe-Walsh, L., & Schyns, B. (2010). Self-initiated expatriation: Implications for HRM. *International Journal of Human Resource Management*, 21(2), 260–273. 10.1080/09585190903509571

GSI Journals Serie A Advancements in Tourism Recreation and Sports Sciences. (2024). Business Travel and Bleisure Tourism: A Study on the Travel Motivations of Academics. 10.53353/atrss.1403738

Kim, K., Oh, I. K., & Jogaratnam, G. (2007). College student travel: A revised model of push motives. *Journal of Vacation Marketing*, 13(1), 73–85. 10.1177/1356766706071201

Kluin, J. Y., & Lehto, X. Y. (2012). Measuring family reunion travel motivations. *Annals of Tourism Research*, 39(2), 820–841. 10.1016/j.annals.2011.09.008

Kolb, A. Y., & Kolb, D. A. (2005). Learning styles and learning spaces: Enhancing experiential learning in higher education. *Academy of Management Learning & Education*, 4(2), 193–212. 10.5465/amle.2005.17268566

Lee, T., & Crompton, J. (1992). Measuring novelty in tourism seeking. *Annals of Tourism Research*, 19(4), 732–751. 10.1016/0160-7383(92)90064-V

Leiper, N., Witsel, M., & Hobson, J. P. (2008). Leisure travel and business travel. *Asian Journal of Tourism and Hospitality Research*, 2(1), 1.

Leong, A., Yeh, S. S., Hsiao, Y. C., & Huan, T. C. (2015). Nostalgia as travel motivation and its impact on tourists' loyalty. *Journal of Business Research*, 68(1), 81–86. 10.1016/j.jbusres.2014.05.003

Lichy, J., & McLeay, F. (2018). Bleisure: Motivations and typologies. *Journal of Travel & Tourism Marketing*, 35(4), 517–530. 10.1080/10548408.2017.1364206

Lo, A., & Lee, C. (2011). Motivations and perceived value of volunteer tourists from Hong Kong. *Tourism Management*, 32(2), 326–334. 10.1016/j.tourman.2010.03.002

Lubbe, B. (2019). Business travel: A perspective paper. *Tourism Review*, 75(1), 113–116. 10.1108/TR-05-2019-0178

Lubbe, B. (2019). The economic impact of tourism. *Tourism Management*, 40(2), 211–221. 10.1016/j.tourman.2013.06.003

Martín, E. (2011). *El turismo de negocios: unaactividaden auge. Espacios y destinosturísticosentiempos de globalización y crisis. XII Coloquio de Geografía del Turismo, Ocio y Recreación de la Asociación de GeógrafosEspañoles*. AGE.

Meng, F., Tepanon, Y., & Uysal, M. (2008). Measuring tourist satisfaction by attribute and motivation: The case of a nature-based resort. *Journal of Vacation Marketing*, 14(1), 41–56. 10.1177/1356766707084218

Mercan, R., & Sandıkcı, M. (2024). Bleisure Tourism: Business and Leisure Together. In *Future Tourism Trends Volume 1 (Building the Future of Tourism)*. Emerald Publishing Limited. 10.1108/978-1-83753-244-520241001

Murchie, F. (2014). "Bleisure" - mixing business with leisure. Retrieved from https://www. relocatemagazine.com/articles/4344bleisure-mixing-business-with-leisure

NCR. (2019). National car rental. State of business travel survey fact sheet. Retrieved from www.nationalcar.com/en/blog/2019-state-of-business-travel-survey-fact-sheet.html

OEDC. (2020). OEDC Economic outlook, June 2020. Retrieved from https://www.oecd.org/economic-outlook/june-2020/

Pan, T. J. (2012). Motivations of volunteer overseas and what we learned – The experience of Taiwanese Students. *Tourism Management*, 33(6), 1493–1501. 10.1016/j.tourman.2012.02.003

Paraskevaidis, P., & Andriotis, K. (2017). Altruism in tourism: Social exchange theory vs altruistic surplus phenomenon in host volunteering. *Annals of Tourism Research*, 62, 26–37. 10.1016/j.annals.2016.11.002

Pearce, A. (2015). Internationalisation strategy implemented through Faculty Exchange: Strategic Entrepreneurship in a "new" United Kingdom University. *International Journal of Business Innovation & Research.*, 10(1), 43–64. 10.1504/IJBIR.2016.073243

Pearce, P. L., & Lee, U. I. (2005). Developing the Travel Career Approach to Tourist Motivation. *Journal of Travel Research*, 43(3), 226–237. 10.1177/0047287504272020

Petrenko, A., Ekinil, G., & Provotorina, V. (2023). Organization of bleisure-tourists service as a factor of sustainable development of the tourism sector of the Rostov region. In *E3S Web of Conferences* (Vol. 381, p. 01084). EDP Sciences. 10.1051/e3sconf/202338101084

Phosikham, T. (2010). Heritage sites as tourist attractions: A case study of Luang Prabang, Lao People's Democratic Republic [Master's Thesis, Lincoln University]. Lincoln University Archive. http://hdl.handle.net/10182/2584

Pinho, M., & Marques, J. (2021). Business tourism in Porto: An empirical investigation of its potentialities and development challenges. *International Journal of Tourism Cities*, 7(1), 1–12. 10.1108/IJTC-05-2019-0071

Pizam, A., Neumann, Y., & Reichel, A. (1979). Tourist satisfaction: Uses and misuse. *Annals of Tourism Research*, 6(2), 195–197. 10.1016/0160-7383(79)90146-4

Pizam, A., Uriely, N., & Reichel, A. (2000). The intensity of tourist–host social relationship and its effects on satisfaction and change of attitudes: The case of working tourists in Israel. *Tourism Management*, 21(4), 395–406. 10.1016/S0261-5177(99)00085-0

Ralston, R., Downward, P., & Limsdon, L. (2004). The expectation of volunteers prior to the XVII Commonwealth Games, 2002: A qualitative study. *Event Management*, 9(1/2), 13–26. 10.3727/1525995042781084

Ramaswami, A., Carter, M., & Dreher, G. (2016). Expatriation and career success: A human capital perspective. *Human Relations*, 69(10), 1–29. 10.1177/0018726716630390

Richardson, J. (2006). Self directed expatriation: Family matters. *Personnel Review*, 35(4), 469–486. 10.1108/00483480610670616

Sofronov, B. (2018). Millennials: A new trend for the tourism industry. *Annals of Spiru Haret University.Economic Series*, 18(3), 109–122. 10.26458/1838

Sohaili, N. L. M., Aminudin, N., & Amir, A. F. (2022). Bleisure Motivation Towards Leisure Attraction: A Systematic Literature Review. *International Journal of Academic Research in Business & Social Sciences*, 12(11), 910–922. 10.6007/IJARBSS/v12-i11/15626

Sommet Education. (2022, January 5). Evolution of workspace and rising popularity of "bleisure" post-covid. Hospitality Inspired. https://hospitalityinspired.sommet-education.com/index.php/news-insights/trends-hospitality/evolution-workspace-and-rising-popularity-bleisure-post-covid

Staines, G. L. (1980). Spillover versus compensation: A review of the literature on the relationship between work and nonwork. *Human Relations*, 33(2), 111–129. http://hdl.handle.net/2027.42/67317. 10.1177/001872678003300203

Starĉević, S., & Konjikušić, S. (2018). Why millenials as digital travelers transformed marketing strategy in tourism industry. *International Thematic Monograph Tourism in Function of Development of the Republic of Serbia - Tourism in the Era of Digital Transformation*, University of Kragujevac,221-24. https://ssrn.com/abstract=3280320

Stone, M.J., & Petrick, J.F. (2013). The Educational Benefits of Travel Experiences: A Literature Review, *Journal of Travel Research: A Quarterly Publication of the Travel and Tourism Research Association*, 52(6), 731-744. 10.1177/0047287513500588

The Future Laboratories. (2008). The trend tracker. https://www.thefuturelaboratory.com/trend-tracker

Thorn, K. (2009). The relative importance of motives for self-initiated mobility. *Career Development International*, 14(5), 441–464. 10.1108/13620430910989843

Thynk. (n.d.). Bleisure the new holy grail for revenue generation in hospitality? Thynk. https://thynk.cloud/blog/bleisure-for-revenue-generation

Tsaur, S.-H., & Tsai, C.-H. (2023). Bleisure travel experience: Scale development and validation. *Journal of Travel & Tourism Marketing*, 40(1), 21–37. 10.1080/10548408.2023.2199773

Unger, O., Uriely, N., & Fuchs, G. (2016). The business travel experience. *Annals of Tourism Research*, 61, 142–156. 10.1016/j.annals.2016.10.003

UNWTO. (2017). *Overview of the meetings industry in Asia*. UNWTO.

Uysal, M., & Jurowski, C. (1994). Testing the push and pull factors. *Annals of Tourism Research*, 21(4), 844–846. 10.1016/0160-7383(94)90091-4

Viacava, G., Bresciani, S., & Caputo, A. (2021). COVID-19 and the bleisure travellers: An investigation on the aftermaths and future implications.

Whang, H., Yong, S., & Ko, E. (2016). Pop culture, destination images, and visit intentions: Theory and research on travel motivations of Chinese and Russian tourists. *Journal of Business Research*, 69(2), 631–641. 10.1016/j.jbusres.2015.06.020

World Economic Forum. (2015). The travel & tourism competitiveness report 2015. Geneva: WEF. https://www3.weforum.org/docs/gcr/2015-2016/Global_Competitiveness_Report_2015-2016.pdf

Yadav, S. (2023, June 4). Bleisure is back and transforming the travel and hospitality sector. ET HospitalityWorld. https://hospitality.economictimes.indiatimes.com/news/speaking-heads/bleisure-is-back-and-transforming-the-travel-and-hospitality-sector/100738316

Yoo, H., McIntosh, A., & Cockburn-Wootten, C. (2016). Time for me and time for us: Conference travel as alternative family leisure. *Annals of Leisure Research*, 19(4), 444–460. 10.1080/11745398.2016.1147361

Yoon, Y., & Uysal, M. (2005). An examination of the effects of motivation and satisfaction on destination loyalty: A structural model. *Tourism Management*, 26(1), 45–56. 10.1016/j.tourman.2003.08.016

Zimmerman, K. (2017, June 6). How Millennials Are Being Creative With Their Travel. *Forbes*. https://www.forbes.com/sites/kaytiezimmerman/2017/06/06/how-millennials-are-being-creative-with-their-travel/?sh=5a0e28ce18a8

Zubair, S., Zubair, M., & Anwar, M. (2022). The study of advancement in the tourism and hospitality industry post Covid-19 pandemic.

Chapter 3
Confluence of Business and Leisure:
A Study Towards the Origin and Emergence of Bleisure Tourism in Zillennial Context

M. Johnpaul
https://orcid.org/0000-0002-1133-0588
Central University of Kerala, India

ABSTRACT

In the context of Zillennials—those born in the late 1990s and early 2010s—this study investigates the phenomena of bleisure tourism, which combines leisure travel with business travel. The study explores the socio-economic aspects influencing the travel activities of Zillennials and looks into the causes and origins of this trend. Since technological improvements have made remote employment and flexible scheduling possible, Zillennials are trying to balance work and play. The appeal of bleisure travel among this group is driven by the need for work-life balance, cultural immersion, and experience travel. By illuminating the preferences, attitudes, and decision-making processes of Zillennial bleisure travelers, this study seeks to throw light on their motives and actions. Businesses in the travel sector must comprehend how business and leisure intersect in the context of bleisure tourism in order to customize services that meet the specific requirements and preferences of this growing market.

DOI: 10.4018/979-8-3693-4354-8.ch003

INTRODUCTION

More and more individuals travel for a combination of reasons, including business, pleasure, amusement, or education. Following decades in which business travelers said their work was tedious, laborious, and stressful, they are finally starting to acknowledge that they actually love going on business trips. The practice of "blended travel," which involves business travelers staying longer at their location and/or bringing friends or family, has become more popular in recent years.

Bleisure tourism, a combination of "***business***" and "***leisure***," is the term used to describe travel that combines business with pleasure. Due to changing workplace cultural trends and growing company globalization, the term first emerged in the latter half of the 20th century. Business travel was once primarily perceived as a means of achieving professional goals, with little regard for leisure time. But when work-life balance became more popular and technology made it easier to work remotely, professionals started including leisure time into their business trips, which led to the emergence of the bleisure tourism phenomena.

The roots of leisure travel may be found in the evolving nature of the contemporary labour force. Many professionals now have the option to work remotely thanks to developments in communication technology, which extends their business travels to include leisure time. Furthermore, when businesses realized how important it was to keep happy and satisfied workers, they also started to be more understanding when workers wanted to mix personal time with business travel. The expansion of leisure travel was further propelled by the globalization of commerce. Employees found themselves going to a variety of locations for employment as businesses expanded their operations overseas. Many of the travelers decided to prolong their visits for pleasure because these journeys offered the chance to experience different cultures, foods, and sites.

The travel industry has been significantly impacted by the rise of bleisure tourism. In order to meet the demands of bleisure travelers, hotels, airlines, and travel agencies have modified their product lines to include facilities and packages that combine leisure activities with business conveniences. By marketing its attractions and activities to business visitors wishing to extend their stays, destinations have also profited from the trend.

OBJECTIVES OF THE STUDY

The current study focuses on the following goals and attempts to address the specific questions about leisure travel and the elements that encourage its expansion.

1. To investigate the genesis, growth and development of bleisure travel.
2. To comprehend the portmanteau of "Blessure travel in Zillennial context."
3. To investigate the elements that supports the expansion of leisure travel.

The study aims to investigate several facets of leisure travel and its contemporary advancements in the tourism sector by combining business travel. Those mentioned above are some of the primary objectives that motivate this research.

REVIEW OF LITERATURE

The leisure economy of today has seen the transformation of enjoyable pastimes into profitable ventures. Certain businesses, like Google and Face book, have integrated leisure into their operations. Researchers investigated the issue of "fun at work" across the public, nonprofit, and commercial sectors. It focused on how employees felt about having fun, what they believed was and wasn't pleasurable, and how much they trusted their manager and coworkers. Positive aspects of the workplace, such as group activities, public festivities, humor, gaming entertainment, and chances for personal growth, are included in the leisure economy (Grant et al., 2014). Each sector evaluated the company-wide excursions category and the top ten (out of forty) individual fun events differently, but there were no significant changes in attitudes toward fun across the three sectors. Compared to at least one of the other two groups, public sector individuals found the activities less pleasurable. Employees in all three businesses agreed that food-related activities are fun. Furthermore, attitudes toward having fun were shown to be positively connected with confidence in colleagues and supervisors.

For the participants in the leisure economy, the experience's quality becomes paramount, including several aspects like learning, amusement, and beauty (Pine & Gilmore, 2011). Young people demand more leisure time at work, according to some surveys. Managers should understand this and take steps to maintain a creative and enjoyable work environment in order to retain a productive team (Karl, 2005).

People now frequently use a combination of work and play, or leisure and leisure, to do their tasks. According to Blackshaw (2017), work has evolved into leisure, and leisure eventually turns into a job. The flexibility of time and space as well as more laid-back activities are indicative of leisure. According to other studies, leisure includes emotions like freedom, exhilaration, and relaxation (Kleiber et al., 2011).

Many individuals are distressed about their jobs, thus leisure is essential for finishing a task. Leisure can help decrease stress in work and daily life. So, leisure is crucial in human existence, especially when an individual has a stressful work. Employees who have fun at work are more likely to be trusted by supervisors and service companies. Managers recognize the value of fostering a positive link between staff who like their work and customers who have a nice experience. According to Teodoro et al. (2014), mobile working provides a high degree of leisure in the form of flexibility as it enables people to finish their job by traveling from one site of employment to another (Teodoro et al., 2014).This method of working makes it possible to implement the idea of gamification in the workplace. Business, leisure, and social life are just a few of the areas that have been impacted by gamification, or the application of game principles outside of games.

According to other research, employees' creativity may be impacted by their leisure time (Dahlin et al., 2004; Jeppesen & Lakhani, 2010).Furthermore, individual innovation performance and creativity might be impacted by the advantages of leisure in the workplace (Medaille, 2010).In terms of several dimensions including quantity, distribution of working time, and working location, mobile working is an alternative that enables workers to complete their task outside of the typical constraints in regular work organization (Spreitzer et al, 2017). Flexible work schedules, part-time employment, job sharing, shift work, weekend work, overtime, yearly hours, flexible time, temporary work, flexible leave policies, and working remotely are all examples of mobile work (Berkery et al, 2017). Shifting assignments allows mobile workers to be more efficient and enjoy their professions more. Chevron and Primeau (1996) emphasized the importance of completing task. People that work remotely and move far from the workplace in order to perform their activities are known as mobile workers (Axtell et al., 2008).

The focus is on leisure time since it will increase people's productivity in terms of both time and method. Gamification, or the use of game features in non-gaming contexts, like the workplace, has been shown to improve individual participation, work experience, and job satisfaction (Deterding et al., 2011; Lee & Hammer, 2011; Muntean, 2011).

METHODOLOGY

A multidimensional approach is used in the research to explore the genesis and origin of Bleisure tourism in the context of the Zillennial. In order to comprehend current studies on business and leisure travel patterns as well as the distinctive qualities of the Zillennial population, a thorough literature analysis will be done first. This will give the research's theoretical foundation. Second, a variety of data sources, including books, periodicals, and journal articles that highlight millennials who have traveled for leisure, will be analyzed in order to do a qualitative analysis.

The purpose of these interviews is to learn more about their ideas, experiences, and reasons for mixing work and play while traveling.

Thirdly, using some of the quantitative data sources from the existing sets to explore the growth and impact of Bleisure tourism, quantitative data analysis will be used to examine statistical trends and patterns in Bleisure travel among Zillennials, such as destinations frequented, duration of trips, and expenditure. In order to find any distinctive traits or preferences exclusive to Zillennials, a comparison study will be carried out to compare Bleisure travel patterns of Zillennials with those of other generational cohorts, such as Millennials and Gen Xers.

THE EVOLUTION OF BLEISURE TOURISM CONCEPT

The tourist sector is more advanced than ever, changing daily in ways that were unanticipated. Travellers today have access to a vast array of tourism options, including medical, educational, creative, gastronomic, sustainable, ecotourism, green, cultural, and nautical, to name just a few. However, a new form of tourism known as "bleisure travel" is garnering much interest from practitioners and consumers.

One of the top trend, brand, and futures consulting firms in Europe, The Future Laboratory, is credited with creating the word **"bleisure."** In order to put an end to the old work/life balance and characterize the blurring of business and leisure that has come from people's changing work environments, they invented this phrase. The phrase is increasingly used to refer to the merging of business and leisure travel, as more and more visitors combine business visits with pleasure trips and bring friends or family along to take advantage of the local amenities and customs. "Bizcation" is another term used in corporate travel when referring to an extended work vacation taken for leisure (Zak, Karen ., 2016).

Finding a healthy work-life balance is a new problem brought about by modern living. By enhancing the advantages of the trip for the traveler, leisure travel adds value to the situation. There are undoubtedly financial savings because their employer or business frequently pays the primary traveler's lodging and transportation expenses. However, the appeal extends beyond this: Friday afternoon rushes to the crowded airport turn into leisurely wind-downs after a busy week filled with planned activities. Meanwhile, evenings spent by business travelers alone or watching television become opportunities to discover and enjoy a new destination.

In recent years, significant magazines like The Independent and The Sunday Times have identified bleisure as one of the top travel trends. Though the name "bleisure" is relatively new, combining leisure activities with business travel was seen as early as the 1990s and continued into the early 2000s. According to the National Business Travel Monitor (Sharkey, J., 2001), a significant increase over prior years saw more than two-thirds of regular American business travellers report combining leisure with work travel in 2000. This trend has two parts: one is an increase in the number of cases where spouses or kids accompany business travellers for a few extra days of family time, and the other is an increase in the number of solitary leisure and sports activities that are incorporated into business travel, frequently by younger travellers who are being sent farther from home for extended periods.

The leisure traveler is frequently associated with astute corporate travelers who seek out "less of less" and "more of more". Chris Sanderson, a co-founder of The Future Laboratory, discussed bleisure in an interview (Singh et al., 2022). He claims they are tech-aware, having grown up online and being able to flip between Face book, LinkedIn, and software while doing a task. Their desire for convergence might have a significant influence on hospitality. According to Sanderson, Face book has become the new meeting place for leisure travelers who can click their way out of most problems. They usually book boutique hotels for their work travels. The essence of the bleisure lifestyle is in the liminal spaces between their lives—whether on the train, in a taxi, at the airport, or on the beach. Their definition of work now takes into account their multimedia life rather than the work defining them.

BLEISURE TOURISM'S CURRENT STATUS AND PREDICTED GROWTH, AS WELL AS MARKET OPPORTUNITIES

Opportunities for Investments Developing the Leisure Travel Sector's Future. The leisure tourism sector is constantly creating and implementing new concepts to satisfy the ever-evolving needs of travellers. One of the notable trends in the sector is the growing adoption of "workstations," which mix work and vacation into a single package. Most workplaces include accommodation, a workspace, and recreational facilities. Sustainable and ethical travel practices are also growing in the bleisure tourism sector. Travelers are becoming more conscious of their environmental impact as they look for ethical and environmentally sustainable vacation options. Businesses that can offer sustainable and ethical travel experiences will face increased demand from leisure tourists. The estimated size of the leisure tourism market in the United States in 2023 was US$ 594.51 billion.

Nonetheless, the leisure tourism market is anticipated to reach a valuation of US$ 3,530.53 billion by 2033. The predicted CAGR for the market value of leisure tourism between 2023 and 2033 is 19.5%. Leading Players in the Leisure Travel Industry a share of 8.5% was recorded in 2022. Chance of Travelers seeking bleisure are the target audience for investment possibilities in accommodation, transportation, and other services. Significant Trends Among the newer trends are using workstations and environmentally friendly/ethical travel strategies.

Its travel agency services market has a compound annual growth rate (CAGR) of 11.5% from 2023 to 2033. By 2033, it is anticipated that the market for travel agency services will be worth US$ 454.59 billion. The growing trend of personalized and tailored travel experiences creates new opportunities in the travel industry. One of the anticipated developments in travel agency services is using artificial intelligence (AI) and chatbots in the industry.

In addition, the Travel & Tourism User-Generated Content Market is seen in leisure travel. It saw a 15% CAGR between 2023 and 2033. By 2033, the same Market Value will be worth US$ 211.60 billion. Gaining a competitive edge in the market may be facilitated for new entrants through partnerships with local firms, investments in technology and digital solutions, and sustainable practices. Furthermore, companies who can offer customized experiences and services that meet the particular requirements of bleisure travelers can see rapid development in the years to come. The forecast period for this data is from 2023 to 2033. On the other hand, historical data covering North America, Latin America, Europe, East Asia, South Asia, Oceania, and the Middle East is available from 2018 to 2022.

Factors contributing to this growth include a growing trend of combining business and leisure travel. More digital nomads and remote employees prioritize work-life balance. The industry has also experienced a shift toward more sustainable and ethical travel practices, with an increasing proportion of tourists seeking eco-friendly accommodations and excursions. The expansion of technology has also had an impact on the business, with mobile applications and virtual reality experiences boosting the whole travel experience.

THE MILLENNIAL CONTEXT'S PORTMANTEAU FOR LEISURE TRAVEL

Within the setting of Zillennials—a generation born between the mid-1990s and early 2010s—bleisure tourism—a blend of business and leisure travel—resonates powerfully. In contrast to earlier generations, millennial value experiences over material belongings and strive for a work-life balance. Bleisure travel is an optimal opportunity for individuals to integrate work commitments with recreational pursuits, optimizing their time and elevating their vacation experience.

Zillennials frequently have to travel for work-related events, such as training sessions, conferences, or meetings. They consider these travels more than business trips; they see them as chances to go to new places, experience other cultures firsthand, and make lifelong memories. Zillennials can maximize their travel opportunities while upholding their job obligations by extending their business travels into vacation stays.

Furthermore, Zillennials' beliefs and inclinations—which prioritize flexibility, autonomy, and personal fulfilment—align with bleisure travel. They value being able to customize their travel schedules to fit their interests, whether it means visiting nearby sites, sampling different foods, or going on outdoor excursions. Travelling for pleasure enables millennial to escape the grind of daily existence, refuel, and elevate their emotions.

In the digital age, Zillennials use technology to plan, book, and document leisure activities. They use Smartphone applications, social media platforms, and internet travel tools to study places, book accommodations, and uncover hidden treasures suggested by locals. They also use social media to share their travel experiences, interact with other travelers, and get suggestions from their networks. Bleisure tourism appeals to Zillennials' need for meaningful experiences, work-life balance, and personal fulfillment, making it a popular trend among this generation's travelers.

FACTORS DRIVING THE GROWTH IN BLEISURE TOURISM INDUSTRY

Several variables, such as increased remote work and flexible schedules that allow professionals to prolong business visits for pleasure, are responsible for expanding bleisure tourism. Blending work and play has also become more appealing as the importance of work-life balance has grown. Businesses know the advantages of leisure travel regarding worker happiness and output. The industry's growth is further aided by the availability of specialized services and packages designed for leisure travelers, as well as technological improvements that make booking travel easier. These elements work together to support the rising demand and appeal of bleisure travel. Several vital variables have contributed to the notable pace at which this trend has gathered in recent years.

1. **Improved Socio-economic Conditions**: Socioeconomic issues include financial limitations, flexible work arrangements that allow for remote work and prolonged travel, and a desire for novel experiences, all of which have an impact on millennials' travel habits. Their economic stability impacts their capacity to finance travel, but the gig economy offers flexible schedules that encourage exploration. In addition, social media influences how people view travel as a lifestyle and fuels their demand for authentic, Instagram-worthy experiences. Worries about ethical and sustainable tourism also influence destination selections. In general, the travel choices made by millennials strike a balance between social influences, professional prospects, personal ideals, and economic realities.

2. **Balancing daily work and personal life:** Experts are looking for methods to mix their job and leisure obligations as the importance of work-life balance grows. By combining chances for personal exploration and relaxation with business travel, people may make the most of their time away from the workplace when they travel for leisure.
3. **Advancement in Technological Innovations in** Work Life: Introducing new technologies has changed the nature of employment and allowed for more mobility and flexibility. The increasing prevalence of remote work has allowed people to travel for more extended periods than necessary for business, contributing to the rise of bleisure tourism.
4. **Swifts in Preferences of Millennials and Generation Z:** These younger generations value experiences over material belongings and frequently look for chances to travel to and engage with different cultures. By planning leisure activities into their schedules, leisure travel satisfies their thirst for adventure and helps them get the most out of their work visits.
5. **Cost-effectiveness:** Traveling for both work and pleasure may save money for both businesses and employees. Travelers can save money on transportation and some company-paid expenditure, such as lodging and food during the working leg of the trip, by extending a business trip for leisure activities.
6. **Attractions for Travelers:** Many commercial centers are situated in areas or cities with a wide range of cultural and recreational activities. More and more tourists are drawn to places that provide leisure activities, such as seeing historical sites, savoring regional cuisine, or going on outdoor adventures. The allure of these locations plays a role in expanding leisure travel.
7. **Flexible Corporate rules:** Many businesses are implementing more accommodating travel rules that motivate staff members to mix personal time with work travel. Acknowledging the advantages of employee contentment and retention, these establishments endorse leisure travel as a means of augmenting the total travel encounter and advancing the welfare of employees.
8. **Networking Opportunities:** In addition to letting people relax and rejuvenate, leisure travel offers chances to network outside of official professional environments. Informal conversations at social gatherings or networking conferences can benefit professional relationships and partnerships.
9. **Environmental Consciousness:** Travelers may decide to include many goals into a single trip to reduce their total environmental effect in response to increased concerns about carbon footprints and sustainable travel practices. Travel for pleasure can help achieve these sustainability goals by reducing the number of distinct trips.

The need for a work-life balance, technology advancements that allow for remote work, the inclination of younger generations toward experiential travel, affordability, destination allure, adaptable business policies, networking prospects, and environmental awareness are some factors driving the growth of bleisure travel. Travelling has become more experiential and about balancing work and play. This trend reflects this behaviour change. The leisure travel market is expanding, providing advantages to individuals and companies looking to combine work and play conveniently, while establishments and locations adjust to suit leisure travellers.

SUSTAINABLE AND ECO-FRIENDLY TOURISM METHODS IN THE ZILLENNIAL SETTING

Sustainable and environmentally friendly travel practices are essential for optimizing travel experiences while reducing environmental effect when it comes to bleisure tourism among millennials. Zillennials are dedicated to environmental stewardship and look for creative methods to combine work and play activities while maintaining sustainability.

One way to lower travel-related carbon emissions is to select environmentally friendly modes of transportation, such as bicycles, public transportation, or even electric or hybrid cars. Furthermore, eco-conscious lodgings like eco-lodges, green hotels, or home stays with eco-friendly policies like waste minimization and energy conservation are preferred by Zillennial bleisure visitors. In addition, Zillennials practice responsible consumerism by patronizing neighborhood establishments that support sustainable practices, such as fair-trade markets, artisanal stores, and farm-to-table restaurants. Additionally, they take part in community-based tourism programs that support and protect the legacy of the local community.

In line with Zillennial principles, bleisure tourism that incorporates eco-friendly and sustainable practices also creates a stronger sense of place-based attachment. By implementing these strategies, Zillennials help to save biodiversity, maintain natural resources, and advance sustainable development—all of which help to shape a more environmentally friendly tourism industry going forward.

IMPLICATIONS OF BLEISURE TOURISM IN ZILLENNIAL CONTEXT

Examining the inception and growth of travel for pleasure within the framework of the Zillennial has broad and noteworthy consequences for enterprises and the travel and tourism sectors. First of all, businesses may adjust their offers to appeal to the Zillennial population by comprehending their tastes and habits, which emphasize experiences and work-life balance. Businesses may boost productivity and employee happiness on business trips by including leisure activities, which results in a more engaged workforce. Second, acknowledging the growing popularity of Bleisure travel among millennials presents new business prospects for the travel and tourism sector. Destination marketing companies have the ability to create focused advertising campaigns that emphasize the business and leisure components of their destinations, drawing in millennial tourists looking for a variety of experiences.

In addition, lodging facilities, dining establishments, and other service providers can modify their menus to suit the needs of Bleisure visitors by offering flexible reservation policies, co-working areas, and leisure pursuits tailored to their tastes.All things considered, this study emphasizes how critical it is to recognize and welcome the merging of work and leisure travel, especially for millennials. By doing this, companies and other tourism-related stakeholders may benefit from this trend and raise the standard of travel as well as the prospects for employment in the sector.

CONCLUSION

In summary, the fusion of work and play, embodied by the rise of bleisure travel, is a noteworthy development among millennials. This blending of work commitments with personal interests indicates this generation's changing perspectives on employment, travel, and lifestyle choices.

The emergence of leisure travel may be attributed to evolving technology, evolving work environments, and the pursuit of significant experiences. Influenced by digital connection and remote work options, millennials are more open to bleisure travel to balance work obligations with leisure time. Their beliefs of experiencing living, holistic well-being, and work-life balance align with this trend.

In addition, the growth of bleisure travel highlights broader cultural trends toward flexible work schedules and the value of experiences above material belongings. Zillennials regard travel as a way to express themselves and evolve as people. They look for real connections and cultural immersion when they travel. Enterprises in the travel sector had to acknowledge the importance of leisure travel in the Zillennial framework and modify their products and services correspondingly. Enhancing client happiness and loyalty may be achieved by customizing packages and services to meet the demands and preferences of leisure travellers. Moreover, smooth and integrated bleisure experiences depend on cooperation between the hospitality, transportation, and technology sectors.

Overall, the research on bleisure tourism in the context of the Zillennial shows how work, play, and lifestyle choices interact intricately in modern society. The ongoing evolution of this trend poses a range of challenges and opportunities for businesses and policymakers who aim to cater to the changing demands of contemporary travellers.

FUTURE SCOPE OF THE STUDY

Future investigations on bleisure travel within the Zillennial setting may concentrate on a number of important topics. First, examining the distinct driving forces and actions of millennials when they travel for leisure, including their inclinations for trip locations, activities, and lodging types. The second is examining how social media and technology affect millennials' ability to plan and enjoy Bleisure travel. Third, looking at how workplace rules and companies affect Zillennial employees' ability to travel for pleasure. Fourth, evaluating how leisure travel affects local communities and destinations economically and socio-culturally, especially with regard to sustainability and inclusion. In order to comprehend shifting patterns and preferences, longitudinal studies that trace the development of leisure travel among millennials over time are the last point. These potential lines of inquiry into the future can deepen our understanding of leisure travel in the context of the Zillennial generation and help shape the marketing plans of companies and travel locations that serve this market.

REFERENCES

Axtell, C., Hislop, D., & Whittaker, S. (2008). Mobile Technologies in Mobile Spaces: Findings from the Context of Train Travel. *International Journal of Human-Computer Studies*, 66(12), 902–915. 10.1016/j.ijhcs.2008.07.001

Berkery, E., Morley, M. J., Tiernan, S., Purtill, H., & Parry, E. (2017). On the Up-take of Flexible Working Arrangements and the Association with Human Resource and Organizational Performance Outcomes. *European Management Review*, 14(2), 165–183. 10.1111/emre.12103

Blackshaw, T. (2017). Decentring Leisure: Rethinking Leisure Theory (Book Review). *Annals of Leisure Research*, 20(2), 240–242. 10.1080/11745398.2016.1254798

Chevron, J., & Primeau, M. (1996). The telecommuting innovation opportunity. *Journal of Consumer Marketing*, 13(4), 40–48. 10.1108/07363769610124537

Dahlin, K., Taylor, M., & Fichman, M. (2004). Today's Edisons or Weekend Hobby-ists: Technical Merit and Success of Inventions by Independent Inventors. *Research Policy*, 33(8), 1167–1183. 10.1016/j.respol.2004.06.003

Deterding, S., & Dixon, D. (2011). From Game Design Elements to Gamefulness: Defining "Gamification." Proceedings. The 15th International Academic MindTrek Conference, 9-15. 10.1145/2181037.2181040

Grant, A. M., Berg, J. M., & Cable, D. M. (2014). Job Titles as Identity Badges: How Self-Reflective Titles Can Reduce Emotional Exhaustion. *Academy of Management Journal*, 57(4), 1201–1225. 10.5465/amj.2012.0338

Jeppesen, L. B., & Lakhani, K. R. (2010). Marginality and Problem-Solving Effectiveness in Broadcast Search. *Organization Science*, 21(5), 1–18. 10.1287/orsc.1090.0491

Karl, K., Peluchette, J., Hall-Indiana, L., & Harland, L. (2005). Attitudes toward Workplace Fun: A Three Sector Comparison. *Journal of Leadership & Organizational Studies*, 12(2), 1–17. 10.1177/107179190501200201

Kleiber, D. A., Walker, G., & Mannell, R. C. (2011). a Social Psychology of Leisure (2nd ed.). State College: Venture Publishing, Inc. https://lccn.loc.gov/2011929715

Lee, J., & Hammer, J. (2011). Gamification in Education: What, How, Why Bother? Gamification in Education: What, How, Why Bother? *Academic Exchange Quarterly*, 15(2), 1–5.

Medaille, A. (2010). The Power of Play: Fostering Creativity and Innovation in Libraries. *Journal of Library Innovation*, 1(October), 8–23.

Muntean, C. I. (2011). Raising Engagement in ELearning through Gamification. Proceedings. The 6th International Conference on Virtual Learning ICVL 2011, (1), 323-329.

Pine, J., & Gilmore, J. H. (2011). *The Experience Economy: Past, Present and Future*. Handbook on the Experience Economy., 10.4337/9781781004227.00007

Sharkey, J. (2001). Leisure activities are increasingly being fitted in to help make life on the road less difficult. The New York Times, New York, NY, C6.

Singh, M., Verma, V., Gopal, R., & Aggarwal, P. (2022). Hospitality Education: Past, Present, and Future. Present and Future (June 6, 2022).

Spreitzer, G. M., Cameron, L., & Garrett, L. (2017). Alternative Work Arrangements: Two Images of the New World of Work. *Annual Review of Organizational Psychology and Organizational Behavior*, 4(1), 473–499. 10.1146/annurev-orgpsych-032516-113332

Swaminathan, R. (2022). How Can Resilience Create and Build Market Value? *Journal of Creating Value*, 8(2), 204–218. 10.1177/23949643221125287

Tejedor, B., & Aguirre, A. (1998). Proyecto Logos: investigación relativa a la capacidad de aprender de las empresas españolas. Boletín de estudios económicos, 53, 231.

Teodoro, R., Ozturk, P., Naaman, M., Mason, W., Lindqvist, J., Tech, C., & York, N. (2014). The Motivations and Experiences of the On-Demand Mobile Workforce. Performing Crowd Work, 236-247. 10.1145/2531602.2531680

The Independent. (2009, Dec. 11). Top 10 travel trends in 2010 - look out for "granny chic," "ecoluxe," "bleisure" trips.

The Sunday Times. (2010). Bleisure travel: the best of both worlds.

Umarov, S., Durmanov, A., Kilicheva, F., Murodov, S., & Sattorov, O. (2019). Greenhouse vegetable market development is based on the supply chain strategy of the Republic of Uzbekistan. *International Journal of Supply Chain Management*, 8(5), 864–874.

UNWTO. (2020). El turismo internacional sigue adelantado a la economía global. Ginebra: UNWTO.

UNWTO. (2022). El turismo internacional consolida su fuerte recuperación en medio de crecientes desafíos. Ginebra: UNWTO.

Yang, Z., Yin, M., Xu, J., & Lin, W. (2019). Spatial evolution model of tourist destinations based on complex adaptive system theory: A Southern Anhui, China case study. *Journal of Geographical Sciences*, 29(8), 1411–1434. 10.1007/s11442-019-1669-z

Zak, K. (2016). Maximizing the value of conferences to communities: 'Bleisure Travel' and 'Bizcations' emerge with social media boosts.

Chapter 4
Navigating Bleisure Frontier:
Behavioural Expedition Through a Transtheoretical Lens – A Thematic Study

Sreeparna Bhattacharyya
https://orcid.org/0000-0002-2093-4519
Bharatiya Vidya Bhavan, Institute of Management Science, Maulana Abul Kalam Azad University of Technology, India

Sarani Bhaumik
https://orcid.org/0009-0003-6888-2214
Independent Researcher, India

Sarbari Bhowmick
https://orcid.org/0009-0007-2887-8463
Independent Researcher, India

ABSTRACT

This study investigates the behavior of bleisure travelers, a fusion of business and leisure, in the backdrop of the BANI world. It aims to understand their journey, motivations, challenges, and outcomes, using 16 professionals' experiences using thematic analysis. The study generates eight themes, preparation, pre-contemplation, termination, contemplation, action, maintenance, rejuvenation, and revitalization. The transtheoretical framework by Carlo C. DiClemente and James O. Prochaska since 1983 derived from the first six generated themes. The implications extend to intervention strategies, such as conscious raising, self-revaluation, dramatic relief, emotional arousal, social liberation, stimulus control, and contingency manage-

DOI: 10.4018/979-8-3693-4354-8.ch004

ment in strategising bleisure using the AIDA model. The findings will inform future research directions and strategies in the evolving landscape of bleisure tourism.

1. INTRODUCTION

Travel's significance can be interpreted from a variety of angles. Expanding one's horizons, fostering personal development, and gaining a more profound understanding of the world all require travel. Exposing oneself to diverse cultures, customs, and points of view promotes tolerance and empathy. Travelling allows people to push themselves beyond their comfort zones and improve their problem-solving skills. Discovering new places to visit, foods to try, and ways of living encourages creativity and generates original ideas. Furthermore, travel encourages reflection, aiding people's self-discovery—that is, their understanding of their identity and place in the world. The ability to improve lives, widen perspectives, and foster a more cohesive global community makes travel valuable.

1.1. The Evolution of the Terminology Bleisure

In 2009, writer and silent revolutionist Jacob Strand coined the term "bleisure" at the 'Future Laboratory'. Since 2011, 7% of all work visits have been classified as "bizcations," or prolonging work trips for personal reasons. "Bleisure" is a play on words, fusing the words "business" and "leisure" to draw attention to the growing trend of business professionals incorporating tourism into their travels (The Future Laboratories, 2008). This illustrates how the dynamics of contemporary work-life balance are evolving due to the demand for more flexible corporate cultures and holistic experiences. Bleisure travellers often prolong their business trips to travel to new places, experience the local way of life, or unwind after work.

1.1.1. Leisure Tourism vs. Bleisure Tourism

The main distinction between leisure and bleisure travel is the structure and goal of each. Travelling for bleisure mixes leisure and business purposes into one trip. It begins with business commitments such as conferences or meetings and then progresses to include leisure activities. On the other hand, leisure travel has no business obligations and is entirely focused on personal enjoyment. Travelling for bleisure has a schedule that mixes business obligations with leisure pursuits like sightseeing and dining out.

On the other hand, leisure travel gives travelers greater freedom to prioritize their favorite activities without worrying about meeting deadlines for work-related commitments. Depending on personal preferences and destination attractions, bleisure travel usually entails extending a business trip by a few days for leisure activities. The duration of a leisure trip depends only on the traveler's availability and can range from short getaways to extended vacations. Overall, bleisure travel integrates business and leisure, following a structured plan, while leisure travel focuses solely on relaxation and personal enjoyment without business-related components (Figure 1).

Figure 1. Changes in Tourism Concepts (Authors' Own Creation)

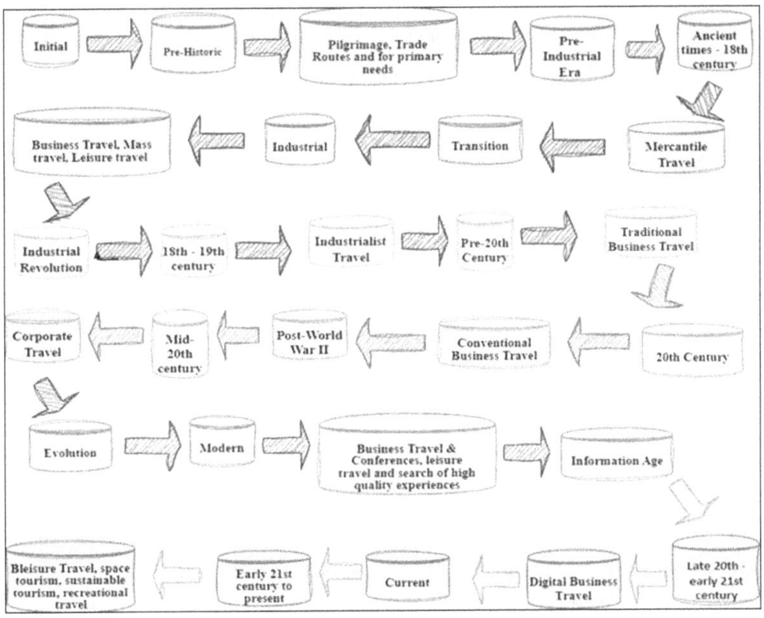

1.1.2. The Role of Bleisure Tourism in Supporting the Economy

By spending money, generating employment, and promoting economic growth, bleisure travellers help local economies grow. Their extended visits and ability to bring friends and family make them important customers for nearby companies. The local economy benefits from this kind of tourism, which boosts activity in the retail, hospitality, and service sectors. Bleisure travel also increases employee satisfaction and can save employers money because tickets are cheaper when they include a

Saturday stay. Destinations should emphasise their distinctive historical, cultural, and natural features to attract tourists. They should also run creative marketing campaigns through various media platforms to increase interest and awareness (Jin & Cheng, 2020; Chung *et al.*, 2020).

1.1.3. Challenges of Bleisure Tourism

1.1.3.1. Bleisure Tourist Perspective

Bleisure tourists may face challenges like 'changing hotel,' 'family pressure,' 'canceling leisure plans,' and 'burdening spouse with kids,' they use several strategies such as 'separating/integrating business and leisure,' 'considerate family,' 'remote work,' 'clarification of travel companions', and 'flexibility and creativity in travel rearrangement.' It may be challenging for workers to distinguish clearly between work and play obligations, which could result in burnout or lower output. It can be challenging to distinguish between personal and business expenses, which can cause disagreements or miscommunications regarding reimbursement. Confusion and inconsistent application of bleisure travel policies can result from unclear guidelines and policies. All this burden of pre-tour, on-tour, and post-tour can be tiresome and contribute to conflicting behavior among tourists.

"Post-travel blues" are the fatigue or tiredness one feels after a trip. Business travellers frequently experience physical and mental health problems like weariness, irritability, and anxiety. Bleisure travellers may feel just as tired or even more so.

1.1.3.2. Service Provider and Company's Perspective

Firstly, convincing an employee to travel repeatedly might be challenging. Managing personal time with professional commitments could result in diversions and lower total output while travelling. Businesses may struggle to monitor and manage spending, which could result in financial inefficiencies or system abuse. When travelling for bleisure, ensuring compliance with corporate governance, tax, and labour laws can be more difficult.

1.1.4. Ways to Overcome Challenges

1.1.4.1. Bleisure Tourist Perspective

How bleisure travelers experience travel in different phases (pre-travel, during, and post-travel) differs from pure business and leisure traveller. Bleisure travelers show unique characteristics in 'planning,' 'family,' and the 'challenges' in the pre-travel phase. For example, when planning the trip, they are 'well-organized,' 'futuristic plan,' and have 'competency in travel arrangements.' Also, they expressed that when they add a leisure component to their business travel, the trip would be 'more complex and need more coordination.' Moreover, the activities they prefer during the travel phase are unique. They would prefer 'short-squeezed,' 'educational,' and 'family-oriented' activities and avoid one-time leisure events.'

However, because bleisure travellers experience less work-family conflict—especially if they travel with their families—they usually reintegrate into their regular schedules more efficiently. Many bleisure travelers use advances in information and communication technology (ICT) to complete tasks remotely, reducing post-trip workload. Thanks to this remote work capability, they can avoid feeling overworked when they return. Most bleisure travellers say they return from their trips feeling more guilt-free and physically tired but mentally rejuvenated.

1.1.4.2. Service Provider and Company's Perspective

It is essential to prevent misunderstandings by clearly defining and conveying the boundaries between work and play—Organise training sessions to teach staff members how to balance work and personal life when on vacation. To prevent disputes, establish clear policies about which expenses are reimbursed. Encouraging management and staff to communicate openly to quickly resolve any issues or concerns. Making sure bleisure travel policies are inclusive and respectful of cultural differences by adjusting them accordingly.

Creating well-organized guidelines that specify the parameters and requirements for bleisure travel, which include acceptable activities and cost control. Establishing mechanisms to track and assess the performance of business travel policies to ensure they are fulfilling the needs of employees and the organization's goals. Developing thorough risk management plans that handle possible security risks and guarantee appropriate insurance coverage for both work and recreation. Utilizing technology to keep tabs on spending, plan travel, and stay productive by using online collaboration platforms.

1.2. Importance of increasing Bleisure Tourism

For enjoyable activities and temporary commitments, bleisure travellers frequently extend their stays from a few days to several weeks. These visitors can be drawn in by offering extensive post-conference programmes that include meals, sightseeing, and outdoor pursuits like biking, hiking, and water sports. After business trips, many people spend five hours online researching local events. Coworking spaces and suites or one-bedroom accommodations enable visitors to continue working after others have left (Ahmad, 2024).

Providing "bleisure" options encourages a healthy work-life balance, lowers employee stress and burnout, and boosts retention and job satisfaction, particularly for younger employees. Travel for bleisure stimulates local economies by creating jobs, promoting prosperity in the community, and raising tourism receipts. It also improves relationships between clients and employees, fostering teamwork and improving business results.

1.4. Scope of the Study

In a BANI (Brittle, Anxious, Non-Linear, Incomprehensible) world, bleisure travel offers relief from modern complexities through immersive experiences. The BANI framework highlights a fragile, anxious, unpredictable, and complex environment that demands flexibility and creativity for competitiveness and innovation. Understanding the behavioral journey of bleisure travelers—from planning to feedback—allows businesses to engage and influence them at crucial touchpoints, enhancing their experience. Identifying behavior causes is critical to effective interventions, as Nietzsche suggests. By knowing bleisure travelers' preferences and decision-making processes, businesses can tailor offerings and marketing to attract and retain this market, boosting customer satisfaction and loyalty. The transtheoretical model (Prochaska & DiClemente, 1970) outlines stages of behavior change, helping businesses understand and influence travel decisions and promoting more bleisure travel.

2. LITERATURE REVIEW

2.1. What Is Bleisure?

To improve the quality of travel, Yoo *et al.* (2016) examined the experiences of travelers who traveled for conferences and meetings and clarified that leisure could be a part of business travel, especially when people travel with partners or coworkers (Shaheer *et al.*, 2021). From the outset, there is an interchange between the terms "business event travelers," "working tourist," "business tourist," and "bleisure tourist." They claimed that while there is not a single kind of bleisure traveler, there is a variety of them with unique passions, purposes, and life situations (Mohd Sohaili *et al.*, 2022). These days, businesses worldwide are adopting and popularising the combination of business and leisure or "bleisure" to achieve their organizational objectives. Traveling for bleisure is becoming increasingly popular. Particularly among Millennials, this market has expanded dramatically (Pinho & Marques, 2021). Although "bleisure" has recently gained popularity, people have historically combined business and leisure travel (Mercan & Sandıkcı, 2024).

The goal of bleisure travel is to persuade business travelers to extend their stay, see more sights, engage in leisure activities, and ultimately spend more money following meetings, conferences, and exhibitions/events (Lichy & McLeay, 2018). Due to work-related stress and a desire to unwind, business travelers tend to spend more time engaging in leisure activities (Expedia, 2018; World Economic Forum, 2016). In other words, it is becoming increasingly important to understand where and when business travelers or MICE (Meetings, Incentive tours, Conventions, and Exhibitions) spend and how much spending affects local and occasionally even foreign businesses. These issues highlight the value created for visitors and the relationships among the value-producing endeavors (Porter, 1985). Experts and researchers have created value chains for this market segmentation to serve the industry better and preserve a competitive advantage for the industry and the tourism destination (Chung *et al.*, 2020).

According to recent data (Expedia, 2018), business travelers still spend roughly half their travel budget on lodging, food, and drink. However, they also spend a quarter of their budget on leisure activities like guided tours, concerts, museums, and sporting events.

Five categories of bleisure travelers were identified by Lichy and McLeay (2018), and each had a distinct motivation: altruistic knowledge sharers, escapers, working vacationers, experiential learners, and trailblazers actively engaged in research.

Tsaur and Tsai (2023) investigated the bleisure travel experience, dividing it into six domains utilizing the experience economy perspective, among the few studies that have been conducted on the subject. According to Huang *et al.* (2022), the "job-related learning experience" entails actively engaging in leisure activities that foster skill development, such as attending exhibitions or participating in community festivals or other cultural events. Sports events, food adventures, and cultural interaction are all enjoyable activities in the "entertainment experience." The term "escapism experience" refers to detaching oneself from reality and relieving stress by engaging in local activities. Engaging in a "sociocultural experience" entail getting to know the people and their customs, including their cuisine. A "prestige experience" is when a traveler's social needs are met while on bleisure travel, and they feel favored or receive special treatment.

Travelers on business frequently schedule their leisure activities far in advance to guarantee they will have the options they want for their leisure time (Batala & Slevitch, 2024).

2.4. Difference With Business Tourist

Because business and bleisure travel have different goals and activities, they are typically viewed as distinct travel experiences (Yoo *et al.*, 2016). This covers travel for business events, partner meetings, conferences, and other professional gatherings made by business owners, executives, workers, and other professionals. The term "bleisure tourism" has changed the perception of travel, which is now usually connected to work and professional obligations. Now, you can enjoy your vacation in addition to conducting business. (Marques & Pinho, 2021).

Travelers who travel for bleisure have different characteristics from those who travel for business or leisure. For instance, "weekend for leisure," "using leisure as a motivation," and "realistic expectations" are just a few characteristics that set bleisure travelers apart from other traveler demographics (Batala & Slevitch, 2024).

2.5. Difference With Leisure

Studies that have already been conducted should concentrate more on tourists who combine leisure and business travel by including non-business activities (Lichy & McLeay, 2017). Travelers on vacation appreciate having the freedom to mix business obligations with leisure and exploration. When scheduling conflicts arise, bleisure travellers prioritize work even though business travel remains the top priority (Batala & Slevitch, 2024). According to earlier studies, business travellers consider their trips work-related obligations and consider their free time a perk (Gustafson, 2013; Unger et al., 2016; Unger & Uriely, 2022). Academics close to retirement, especially those in their senior years, frequently combine work and leisure time by networking and sharing knowledge when they travel abroad (Lichy & McLeay, 2018).

2.5.1. Push Factors

A push factor in tourism is a term that describes factors or incentives from the traveler's home country that "push" them to look for travel opportunities abroad. These elements may include a desire for novel experiences and adventures or a dissatisfaction with one's current situation, such as the need to escape from stressful or routine surroundings. Economic or social motives can also be push factors, such as the desire for better opportunities, education, or healthcare abroad. In essence, push factors motivate travellers to explore places outside their everyday surroundings. They stem from the traveler's home environment.

The push factor plays a significant role in bleisure travel by influencing individuals to seek a combination of business and leisure experiences. These factors originate from the traveler's intrinsic or psychological needs, such as the desire for rejuvenation, self-actualization, and social interaction. For example, individuals may need to escape from routine or stressful work environments (Crompton, 1979), which pushes them to incorporate leisure activities into their business trips. Push factors can also include a desire for personal growth and exploration. Bleisure travelers who view travel as an opportunity for self-improvement or education may be motivated to extend their trips to explore new destinations, cultures, or experiences. Additionally, individuals on bleisure trips may seek opportunities to network, build relationships, or engage in social activities while on business trips, leading them to extend their stays for leisure purposes.

2.5.2. Pull Factors

"Pull factors" refer to outside variables like the attractiveness of the surroundings, the climate, the friendliness of the host community, and available facilities (Correia et al., 2013). Pull factors in tourism are features or draws of a place that entice or "pull" tourists to visit. Natural landmarks, historical and cultural sites, outdoor pursuits, events and entertainment, infrastructure and hospitality, dining and shopping options, accessibility, marketing initiatives, etc., are examples of pull factors. Travelers' perceptions and preferences are shaped by pull factors, which also impact the destinations they choose and their overall travel experiences.

Pull factors are crucial in bleisure travel, drawing travellers to destinations where they can mix leisure and business activities. These elements contribute to a destination's allure, encouraging visitors to prolong their business trips for leisure. They provide tourists with a wide variety of leisure experiences by encompassing a variety of attractions and activities, such as natural wonders, cultural sites, recreational opportunities, and entertainment options. These pull factors allow bleisure travellers to relax, explore, and fully immerse themselves in the local culture outside their work obligations, improving their overall travel experience (Batala & Slevitch, 2024). Furthermore, pull factors affect the destination choice for bleisure travel since travelers looking for a rewarding and pleasurable experience are more likely to be drawn to places with lively attractions and enticing features (Gustafson, 2014). Pull factors are primarily responsible for drawing bleisure travelers and enhancing their experiences, emphasizing the importance of comprehending and taking advantage of them for destination marketing and management.

2.6. Psychological Characteristics

An individual can make some work effective, productive, and efficient if he is aware of the traits typical for him. Cognitive styles form the foundation of learning styles. Studies on these two phenomena rank among the most significant educational advancements because they emphasize the significance of metacognition and meta-learning.

Lichy *et al.* (2018) provide evidence that "Seeking Knowledge and Novelty" are the most cited reasons why bleisure travelers visit leisure attractions. According to the scenario, bleisure tourists will be more inclined to visit if they believe that visiting the leisure attractions will allow them to experience what they have been reading about in a book. The second factor that influenced bleisure travelers' motivation to visit leisure attractions was "escape." Crompton (1979) concurred that bleisure travelers might see or do something out of the ordinary in a new location with new people and desire independence from partners, kids, and coworkers. The third factor influencing bleisure attraction motivation is "Fun and Resting."

Offering bleisure travelers a variety of leisure attractions (historical and cultural sites) will help them unwind after a long day at the office. In comparison to the traditional approach of providing a unique value addition (safe environment, convenience, and full tourist facilities including accessibility, connectivity, online product acquisition, high-quality service, and other innovative aspects) will enable the nation to profit from the largest consumer and foster the requisite loyalty to become known as a bleisure tourism city. Integrating family-friendly and kid-focused activities into a bleisure trip's leisure section can help travelers achieve a better work-life balance, fortify family ties, and compensate for missed time during the trip's business portion, among other advantages (Batala & Slevitch, 2024).

Their cognitive and learning styles shape people's metacognitive potential. "Cognitive style is the manner that information is received and processed that is preferred; it is primarily innate, hard to modify, and not very related to content." By contrast, a person's preferred learning style is complex procedures. Although it starts from an innate basis, it may evolve and get better over time. A person rarely recognizes his preferred learning method, does not grow consciously, or does not conduct a methodical analysis of it. It is not easy to change them, and he may do so on his own or with the assistance of others in his social circle (teachers, schoolmates, parents, etc.). (Abedini, 2021).

2.7. Identification of Bleisure Tourists Based on Plog's Tourist Typology

In recent years, scholars and practitioners have paid increasing attention to leisure travel—"bleisure tourism," defined as the combination of leisure and business travel activities. Plog's tourist typology provides a valuable framework for comprehending the behavioral dynamics of bleisure travelers within the context of tourism typologies. Plog's typology categorizes travelers according to their psychographic traits, particularly their inclination to seek out experiences and destinations they are familiar with or unfamiliar with.

According to Plog's typology, bleisure travellers may display a combination of psychographic traits that fall into the “allocentric” and “psychocentric” extremes of the spectrum. Psychocentric travellers typically seek security, comfort, and familiarity in their travel experiences. In contrast, allocentric travelers are known for their adventurous spirit, openness to new experiences, and preference for foreign places (Plog, 2001). Travellers who combine work-related responsibilities with recreational activities may exhibit a complex mix of these characteristics.

For example, when choosing a place to stay or eat, bleisure travellers may display psychometric tendencies, putting convenience, comfort, and safety first during their business trip. But in their free time, they might develop a more allocentric viewpoint and look for local outdoor activities, unusual culinary experiences, or cultural events. This behavioral duality highlights the intricate relationship between bleisure tourists' leisure preferences and work-related obligations.

Furthermore, according to Plog's typology, bleisure travellers might not neatly fit into a single psychographic category but rather show varied degrees of allocentric and psychocentric tendencies based on contextual factors like individual preferences, trip purpose, and destination characteristics. Therefore, comprehending bleisure travelers via Plog's typology requires a detailed investigation of their behavioral incentives, inclinations, and decision-making procedures during various trip stages. (Figure 2)

Figure 2. Categories of Bleisure Traveller (Authors' Own Creation)

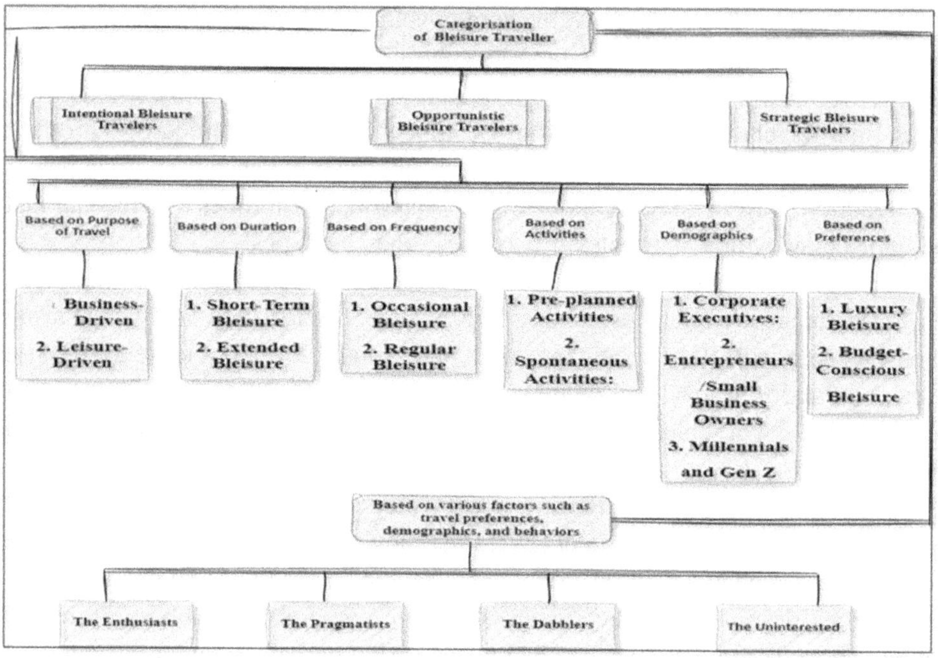

2.8. Significance of the Study

Earlier research focused on the fundamentals of bleisure travel, such as typology, current trends, future potential, competitiveness, experience chain, etc. The primary goal of the current study is to create a route map that meticulously documents the travelers' decisions and actions, incorporating contextual information, identifying potential barriers that may impact these decisions, and, crucially, determining the necessary cues to support the underlying assumptions before, during, and after travel, as well as their proclivity to repeat travel. The study will also analyze modern bleisure travelers' motivations and psychological state.

3. RESEARCH GAPS

Despite the growing popularity of bleisure tourism, significant research gaps still need to be discovered. Current literature often focuses on the benefits and motivations of combining business and leisure travel; however, more studies need to examine bleisure travelers' behavior at different stages, from not getting their professional assignment to the post-travel stage. Understanding each stage's unique characteristics and needs could provide deeper insights into their decision-making processes. There is also lacking detailed studies needed to identify stage-specific motivational drivers and barriers to understand the long-term behavioral outcomes of integrating leisure with business travel, mainly how it affects travelers' overall lifestyle and work-life balance, remain underexplored which guide on how companies perceive and support bleisure travel, including policies, financial implications, and potential impacts on corporate culture. Addressing this gap can provide a more holistic understanding of bleisure tourism and its implications for travelers, organizations, and the travel industry. According to Kluin and Letho (2012), tourists' motivations are difficult to understand due to their fuzziness and complexity, difficulty quantifying an intangible set of factors, and the need for established theories and research.

To put it more clearly, there needs to be more theoretical underpinning to explain the motivations of bleisure travelers who engage in business and leisure activities.

This highlights the necessity for conducting studies to classify different sorts of bleisure travelers according to their travel motivations.

4. RESEARCH QUESTIONS

RQ.1: How do modern travelers prioritize and balance work-related obligations with leisure activities during business trips progressing through stages of change?
RQ.2: What key motivators prompt travelers to consider incorporating leisure elements into their business trips?
RQ.3: What strategies can the travel industry and stakeholders implement to promote and facilitate the integration of bleisure travel into the mainstream travel experience?

5. RESEARCH METHODOLOGY

The proposed research was qualitative. The study explored the experiences of the respondents' bleisure experiences and their motivations, and ongoing interests in bleisure traveling was the aim of the research.

A non-probability purposive sampling technique was used to choose a sample. For open-ended interview questions, a request was made to the 35 professionals by sending a request email explaining the objectives of the study. Out of them, 16 agreed to participate in the face-to-face (in case of distance using Zoom / Google Meet) interview. Each interviewee was chosen based on their interest and availability. Thus, the response rate was $\approx 46\%$.

The structured interviews could address the critical areas of bleisure. The sixteen structured interviews were recorded to explore travelers' mindset behind bleisure and the factors that made them keep traveling places on accepting their business assignments.

All willingly participated in the interview after the aim was explained to them. Anonymity was promised, but no reference was made in the study.

The researchers pitched after building a good rapport and getting introduced to them. Then, the researcher asked the respondents the following five open-ended questions.

- Tell me about your business trips.
- Tell me about the leisure activities during these official trips.
- How do you plan for such trips?
- After your return, how do you feel about the tour?
- Do you want to go on such a tour again?

6. DATA ANALYSIS

The responses were tabulated as codes where a code can be defined as "a code in qualitative inquiry is most often a word or short phrase that symbolically assigns a summative, salient, essence-capturing, and evocative attribute for a portion of language-based or visual data (Saldana, 2013, p3)." These codes were then converted into commonly used concepts in the industry to enable the formation of themes. Word cloud diagrams were created (Figure 3), followed by bar-chart-based graphical generation codes (Figure 4) to assist in categorizing the codes into themes (Figure 5). Word cloud diagrams were created, followed by bar-chart-based graphical generation codes to assist in categorizing the codes into themes. MAXQDA-20 software was used for text analysis, modeling, and graphic display. A word cloud is a visual representation of standard terms among different sources. Cloud, a term with a bigger size, represents a word that has been extensively discussed in multiple pieces of literature (McNaught & Lam, 2010). In this study, it refers explicitly to the concepts that were referenced more frequently. Additionally, the occurrence of terms that the participants repeated is displayed as a frequency table.

Figure 3. The Word Clod (Using MAXQDA-20) (Authors' Own Creation)

Figure 4. The Code-Book (Using MAXQDA-20) (Authors' Own Creation)

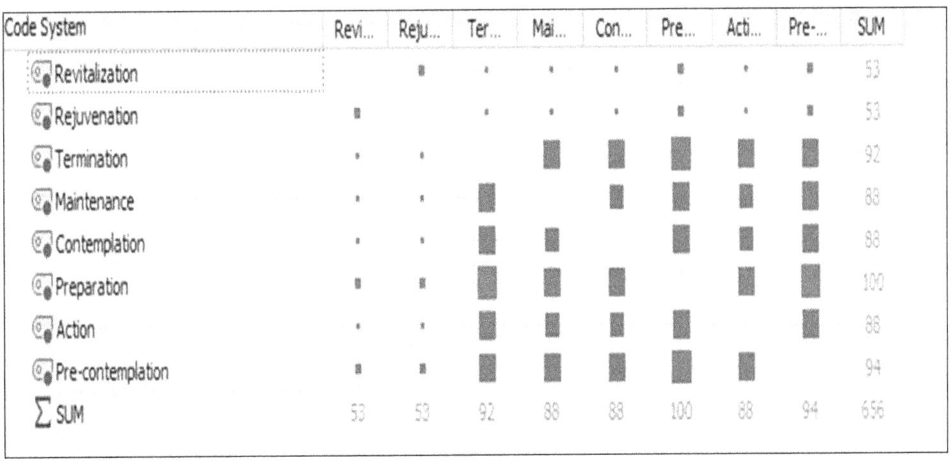

Figure 5. The Themes and Codes Generated through In-Depth Interviews (Using MAXQDA-20) (Authors' Own Creation)

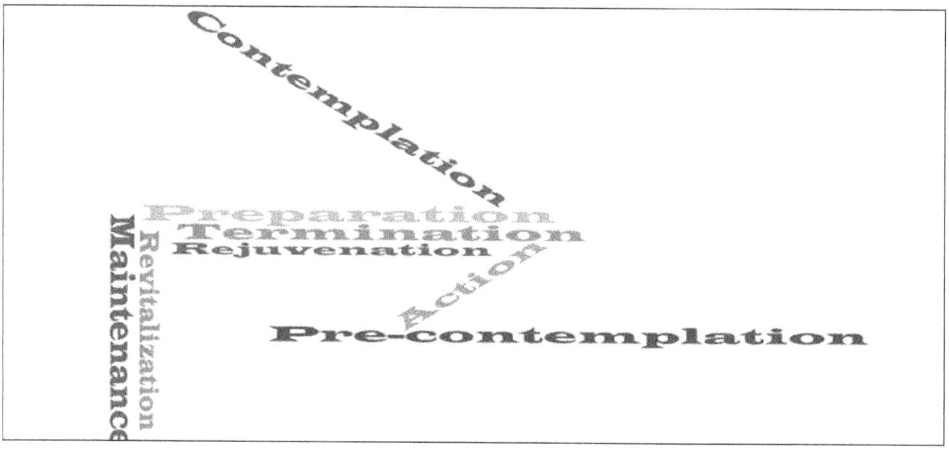

7. FINDINGS

Out of sixteen, thirteen (81.25%) were male. The rest of the respondents (18.75%) were female (Figure 6). The participants' age range varied from 26-30 years (31.25%); 31-35 years (18.75%); and the rest groups till 51-55 years (6.255); and above 60 years (18.75%) (Figure 7). Their professions included Management (37.5%); Mental health Care (6.25%); Engineer et al. (12.55%); and Academicians (18.75) (Figure 8) whose total work experiences were 2-7 years (43.75%); 8-12 years (12.75%); 19-24 years (6.25%); and 25-29 years and above 30 years (18.75%) (Figure 9). Their income ranges were below INR 25,000/, INR 25,001/-35,000/, INR 35,001/-45,000/, and INR 45,001/-55,000/ (12.5%); and above INR 85,001/ (43.75%) (Figure 10). All samples were recruited from PAN India.

Figure 6. Gender Representation of the Respondents (Authors' Own Creation)

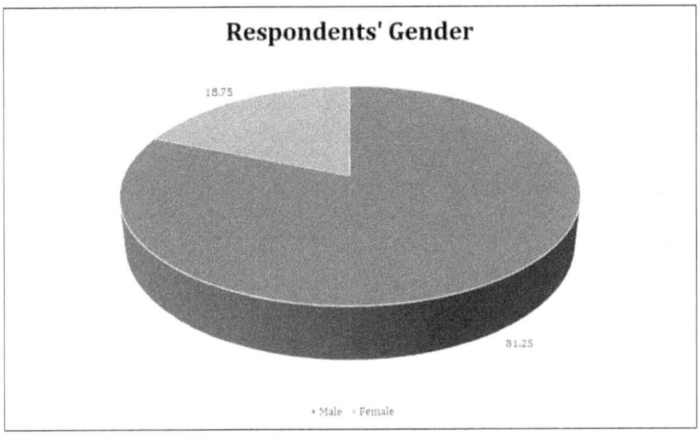

Figure 7. Age Range Representation of the Respondents (Authors' Own Creation)

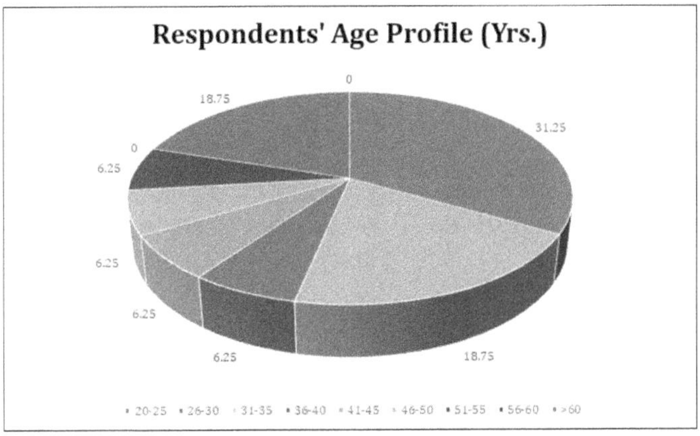

Figure 8. Professions Representation of the Respondents (Authors' Own Creation)

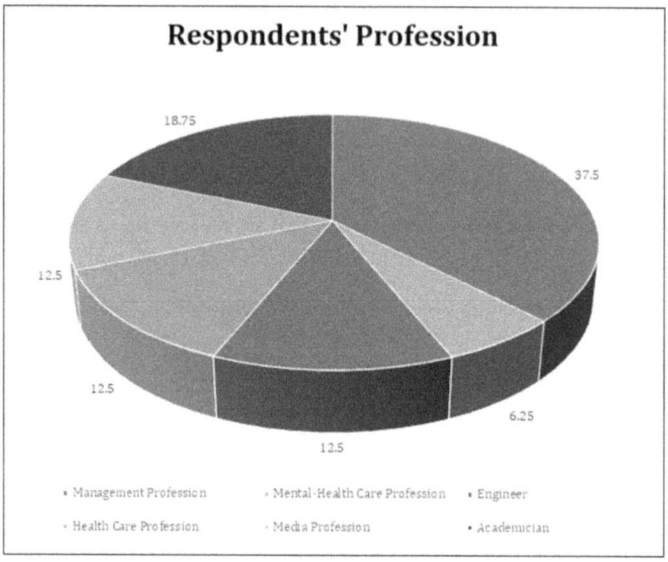

Figure 9. Total Work Experiences (Yrs.) Range Representation of the Respondents (Authors' Own Creation)

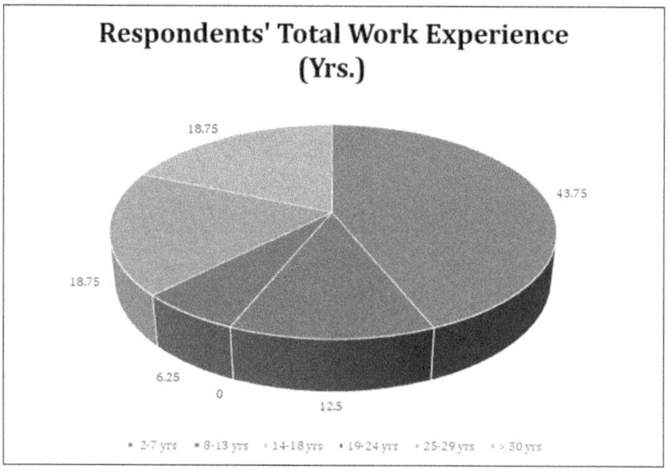

Figure 10: Income Range (INR) Representation of the Respondents (Authors' Own Creation)

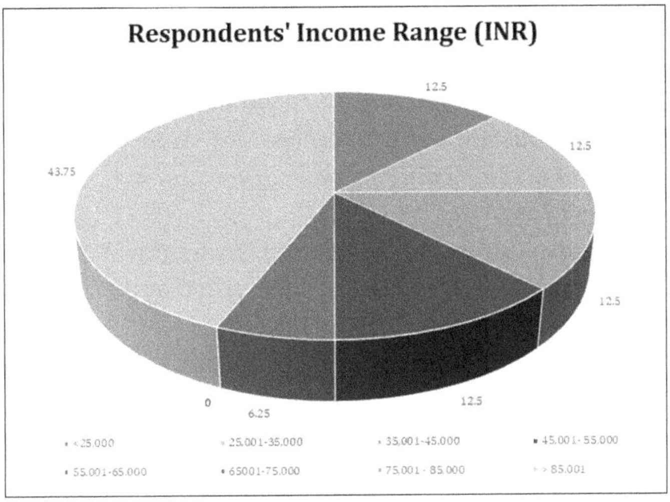

The in-depth interview was conducted with sixteen different top and middle levels professionals (subjects/participants positioned in management, academics, media, technical, health care, and mental health care in reputed organizations) exploring the significant behavioral variables related to changing business travel experiences that influence the economic development of a nation and suitable recommendations to the industry to focus on business travel to manage evolving business environment.

All participants reported they intended to take action, encompassing setting their primary goal, such as business activities, meticulous step-by-step planning, including exploring visiting places and times, times, resource gathering, and readiness assessment to ensure the successful execution of their travel plan. The results of in-depth interviews produced eight themes:

Theme 1: Preparation: Intention to Take Action or Some Steps Taken

Participants said as follows:

Respondent 3: "*Meticulous step-by-step planning is crucial for me. I explore visiting places and manage my time to ensure everything is aligned with my travel objectives.*"

This respondent clearly states they foresee no travel opportunities in the next three months. Their repeated "No No" emphasizes a strong disinterest or lack of awareness regarding bleisure travel. This response indicates that their current focus and priorities lie elsewhere, and the concept of combining business and leisure travel needs to be added to their radar. The absence of upcoming travel plans and the lack of consideration for bleisure travel suggests a mindset that needs to be more open to or in need of such an approach.

Respondent 11: *"Just listen. After attending the meeting, I realized it's not an easy one. I need to make a detailed chalk-out of my business activity......how long it will go, etc. Then I find out how many days I can stay there...hmmm...that I need to make sure and need to accommodate my leave. Then no worry...after that, explore how much I can cover...then finally ......"*

This respondent also dismisses the idea of bleisure travel, stating that it "isn't now on my radar." Their primary focus is on their office work, indicating a commitment to professional responsibilities. The phrase, "see.... If something is assigned to me and at the same time, I need to be also available. Right? " underscores their need to be fully available for work tasks, leaving no room for leisure activities. This respondent prioritizes being responsive and dedicated to work assignments, which prevents them from considering bleisure travel as a viable option.

Theme 2: Pre-Contemplation: No Intention to Taking Action

In their accounts, most participants highlighted all plans made in a vacuum as follows:

Respondent 7: *"At this stage, I don't see the need for any opportunity for travel in the coming three months.... No No.... Bleisure travel hasn't even crossed my mind as something to consider."*

This respondent values detailed, systematic planning to meet their travel objectives. Exploring potential places to visit and managing their time effectively ensures that business and leisure activities are seamlessly integrated. Their emphasis on "meticulous step-by-step planning" indicates a structured approach where they carefully consider each aspect of their trip to align with their overall goals. This method ensures they can enjoy leisure activities without compromising their business responsibilities.

Respondent 16: "*The idea of bleisure travel isn't now on my radar. I'm entirely focused on completing my office work.... see.... If something is assigned to me, I need to be available at the same time. Right?."*

This respondent acknowledges the challenge of enjoying leisure time after business meetings. They stress the need for a detailed plan, starting with mapping out their business activities and understanding the duration of these commitments. They then calculate the remaining days available for leisure, ensuring that their leave is appropriately accommodated. The phrase "then no worry" suggests they can entirely focus on exploring leisure opportunities once these details are sorted.

This response highlights the complexities of balancing work and leisure, indicating a thorough and practical approach to planning.

Theme 3: Termination: No Desire to Return to Prior Negative Behaviour

A third theme is enjoying the trend as follows:

Respondent 10: *"I've moved on from my old habits and have no desire to revert. The positive changes in my life are too significant to give up. This is the most cost-effective way to refresh yourself... .See, if you plan individually, there will be many issues...getting approval for leave...to and from transportation costs... and day expenses...the 70% cost at least saved."*

This respondent emphasizes the substantial positive changes they have experienced, making reverting to old habits unattractive. They provide a practical perspective by pointing out the cost-effectiveness of their new lifestyle. The respondent highlights how planning and executing their activities in a new way saves them significant costs, including leave approvals, transportation, and daily expenses. The financial benefits and streamlined processes reinforce their commitment to maintaining their current lifestyle, as the advantages far outweigh any perceived benefits of their past behaviors.

Respondent 12: *"The benefits of my new lifestyle far outweigh any momentary pleasure from past behaviors. I'm committed to this new path..... hahaha. Now I'm looking for opportunities to go back on a new assignment...I shouldn't immerse myself again in gloomy, monotonous jobs."*

This respondent contrasts their new lifestyle's substantial and lasting benefits with the temporary pleasure of previous behaviors. Their laughter and enthusiasm suggest a positive outlook and a sense of fulfilment with their current path. They proactively seek new and engaging assignments to avoid monotonous and unfulfilling tasks. This proactive approach demonstrates their commitment to staying on their current path, highlighting the importance of continuous growth and engagement to avoid falling back into old habits.

Theme 4: Contemplation: Intentions to Take Action and a Plan Shortly

Participants reflected on the theme as follows:

Respondent 4: *"I'm seriously considering my options and have started to outline steps to move forward. I intend to take action soon. I've been researching and planning on the new place (with giggling), and I aim to implement my plan shortly."*

This respondent emphasizes their serious contemplation of options and proactive planning approach. They have begun outlining steps to move forward and intend to take action soon. Including "with giggling" suggests a sense of excitement or anticipation about their plans. Their research and planning activities indicate a focused effort to prepare for action, particularly about a new place or opportunity. Overall, this response highlights a deliberate and enthusiastic approach to making changes shortly.

Respondent 6: *"I'm in the process of planning my next steps. I know I need to act on both my assignments as well as the old place, and I'm laying the groundwork to make it happen soon."*

This respondent acknowledges the need to act on multiple fronts – both on their assignments and in their current location. They describe themselves as being in the process of planning their next steps, indicating an active engagement in preparing for action. By mentioning the need to act on both assignments and their current situation, they demonstrate a comprehensive approach to addressing their goals. The phrase "laying the groundwork" suggests a deliberate effort to set the stage for future action, indicating a thoughtful and methodical approach to initiating change.

Theme 5: Action: Behaviour Changed for a Short period

Participants considered the theme as follows:

Respondent 2: *"I've started planning my trips and am excited about exploring new places while traveling for work. This shift has brought much happiness, and I'm eagerly looking forward to my upcoming trips."*

This respondent indicates a recent change in their approach to travel by incorporating the exploration of new places into their work trips. The phrase "I've started planning my trips" suggests a deliberate and proactive approach to integrating leisure with business travel. This shift has resulted in a significant increase in their happiness and enthusiasm for future travels. Their excitement about upcoming trips demonstrates how this new behavior has positively influenced their overall outlook on travel.

Respondent 8: *"Just last month, I began booking extra days at my destinations to enjoy sightseeing. This new approach has added a lot of joy to my travel experience. I can't wait for my upcoming adventure as well. "*

This respondent highlights a recent change: booking extra days at their destinations to allow time for sightseeing. By doing so, they have added significant joy to their travel experiences. The recent implementation of this approach ("Just last month") shows that they are in the early stages of this new habit. Their anticipation for future adventures underscores this change's positive impact, enhancing their overall travel satisfaction and eagerness for more experiences.

Theme 6: Maintenance: The Changes Behaviour Continues to be Maintained

Most participants thought about the idea as follows:

Respondent 5: *"I've consistently planned my business trips to include some leisure time for six months. This balance has greatly improved my satisfaction with travel and continues enriching my travel experiences."*

This respondent has maintained a bleisure approach for the past six months, indicating a relatively recent but consistent adoption of this behavior. They have significantly improved their overall travel satisfaction by planning their business trips to include leisure time. The word "consistently" suggests a disciplined and ongoing effort to maintain this balance. The phrase "it continues to enrich my travel experiences" highlights this behavior's sustained positive impact, enhancing their professional and personal travel enjoyment.

Respondent 13: *"Maintaining a mix of business and leisure activities during my travels has been fantastic. I've stuck with this habit for over years, and it's paid off in terms of work-life balance. It's become a natural part of my routine, and I wouldn't have it any other way."*

This respondent has a longer-term commitment to maintaining a bleisure approach, having sustained this behavior for "more than years." Their word "fantastic" conveys strong enthusiasm and satisfaction with the results. They emphasize the significant benefits of work-life balance, indicating that integrating leisure activities during business travel has had a profound and lasting positive effect. The statement "It has become a natural part of my routine, and I wouldn't have it any other way" underscores the deep integration of this behavior into their lifestyle, suggesting it is now an indispensable and highly valued part of their travel habits.

Theme 7: Revitalization: Mind and Body

This is what many people who took part thought about the idea:

Respondent 15: *"I've managed to sustain this approach for quite some time now. It helps me stay productive and rejuvenated, making each trip more enjoyable. This rejuvenating effect of business plus leisure travel is undeniable. After immersing myself in work commitments, taking time for leisure activities restores my energy and creativity.* "

This respondent has successfully maintained a bleisure approach to travel for an extended period. They emphasize the benefits of this strategy in enhancing both productivity and rejuvenation during trips. By combining work commitments with leisure activities, they experience a significant rejuvenating effect, which restores their energy and creativity. This highlights the importance of balance in their travel routine, ensuring optimal performance while enjoying their trips to the fullest.

Respondent 1: *"This traveling strategy has been a game-changer for me. It's like hitting the reset button – I return from trips feeling refreshed and ready to tackle new challenges. I've noticed a significant improvement in my well-being since incorporating ... .Yes, bleisure into my travel routine. It's amazing how a balance of work and leisure can invigorate both mind and body."*

This respondent describes their bleisure travel strategy as transformative, likening it to hitting the reset button. They express how this approach leaves them feeling refreshed and mentally prepared to take on new challenges upon their return. By incorporating leisure into their travel routine, they have noticed a notable improvement in their overall well-being. This highlights the holistic benefits of bleisure travel, not only in terms of physical relaxation but also in invigorating the mind and enhancing overall health.

Theme 8: Rejuvenation: Short Break

Here's what most participants had to say about the idea:

Respondent 9: *"Experiencing bleisure has taught me that true rejuvenation comes from finding balance in our travels. It's about blending work and leisure seamlessly to ensure we return home feeling refreshed and invigorated. It's about freeing ourselves from the stresses of work and embracing the present moment, wherever we may be. "*

This statement underscores the concept of finding an equilibrium between work responsibilities and personal relaxation during travel. By seamlessly integrating work and leisure activities, individuals can immerse themselves fully in the experiences of their surroundings while also fulfilling professional obligations. This balanced approach allows for genuine rejuvenation, as it enables individuals to temporarily disconnect from work-related stressors and focus on the present moment, returning home with renewed energy and enthusiasm.

Respondent 14: *"After incorporating bleisure into my travel routine, I've realized that rejuvenating time isn't a luxury—it's a necessity. It's about prioritizing self-care and well-being amidst our busy schedules. It's not just about the sights we see, but also the moments we take to recharge and reflect on our experiences in a midway short break."*

This explanation highlights the shift in perspective that occurs when individuals prioritize self-care and well-being through bleisure travel. Rather than viewing rejuvenation as an indulgence reserved for special occasions, individuals recognize it as essential to maintaining a healthy work-life balance. Individuals can enhance their well-being and productivity by incorporating short breaks for reflection and recharge during travel experiences. This holistic approach to rejuvenation emphasises the importance of nurturing both mind and body while exploring new destinations (Figure 11) and this phenomenon goes in a cycle (Figure 12).

Figure 11. Psychological Journey of Bleisure Traveller (Authors' Own Creation)

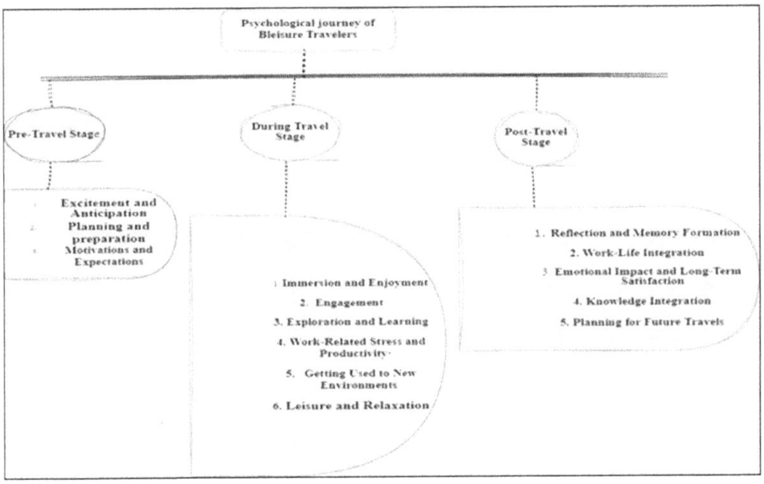

Figure 12. Schematic Representation of the Behavioural Journey of Bleisure Travelers Thorough Transtheoretical Stage of Change Model

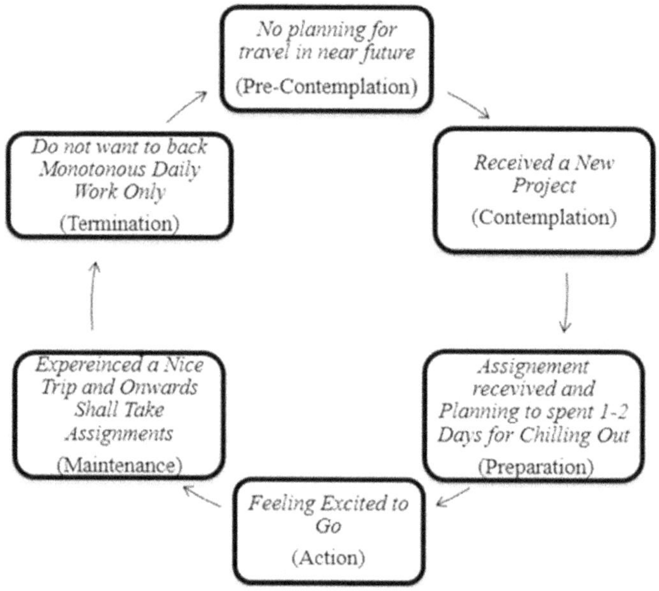

DISCUSSION

After data analysis, the emerging themes are preparation, pre-contemplation, termination, preparation, maintenance, action, rejuvenation, and revitalization. Dann's (1981) push and pull theory, Pearce's (1988) TCL, and Pearce and Lee's (2005) TCP were all influenced by Maslow's (1943) hierarchy of needs, which evolved from a general motivation theory to one that was specifically pertinent to tourism behaviors (Yousaf *et* al., 2018). Recent increases in bleisure (or business leisure) travel have necessitated a greater emphasis on catering to the requirements of corporate travelers who wish to partake in recreational pursuits while away on business. This prompted academicians, in particular, to reconsider business travel as a means to an end, whereas leisure travel could be considered the end in and of itself (Ezeuduji, 2024). Bleisure tourism, i.e., business and leisure, impacts their creativity and highly innovative performance in their workplace (Ardian *et al.*, 2019).

As the previous tourism studies (including bleisure) identified, the attractiveness of tourist spots plays a crucial role in revisiting (Bi *et al.*, 2020; Ünal & Özgürel, 2021).

Business travellers tend to allocate additional time for recreational pursuits, likely due to work-related stress and the need for relaxation (Expedia, 2018; World Economic Forum, 2016). Meanwhile, 60% of business travelers transition into bleisure excursions (Stratos, 2020). According to Gustafson (2014), business travellers often feel a range of emotions when on the road, including stress, excitement, and anticipation of new experiences.

Exhaustion concerning career advancement, a yearning for recreation, and an identity that embraces diversity (Cohen & Gossling, 2015). Business travelers' time constraints (Nan *et al.*, 2020) may lead to engaging them in leisure activities during their business trips.

THEORETICAL FRAMEWORK

Numerous popular ideas of tourist motivation have been condemned on occasion because they are either out of date, invalid, or inapplicable in the continuously evolving tourism sector (Chen et al., 2011; Leong *et al.*, 2015; Whang *et al.*, 2016).

The widely used "push-pull framework" provides the theoretical basis for numerous studies on the motivations behind leisure tourism (Crompton, 1979; Leong et al., 2015; Whang et al., 2016). According to the push-pull theory, most tourists are motivated to travel either by internal causes (Kim *et al.*, 2007) or external forces (Correia *et al.*, 2013; Yoon & Uysal, 2005). This means the 'push forces' are associated with more inward or psychological goals like self-actualization, leisure, recreation, and social contacts.

The attractiveness of the surrounding environment, the quality of the weather, the friendliness of the locals, and other amenities are examples of "pull factors" (Correia et al., 2013).

However, these theories cannot explain how they long for leisure activities. The current study suggested that time pressure is a subjective psychological stressor or chronic trait (Gunthorpe & Lyons, 2004; Kim & Kim, 2008). According to Nan *et al.* (2020), business travelers may experience anxiety or tension due to time constraints, which might interfere with their enjoyment of the location. The more time constraints business travellers face, the more harmful they are likely to feel, leading to mixed emotions.

Alternatively, mixed emotions refer to emotional dissonance between positive and negative feelings (Fong, 2006; Rees *et al.*, 2013). Dissonance theory (Festinger, 1957) suggests that individuals prioritise aligning their thoughts and actions, regardless of cognitive or emotional factors. Mixed emotions can be uncomfortable and cause disharmonious states that stray from consistency preferences (Cacioppo *et al.*,

1997). Emotion-focused and problem-focused coping strategies can reduce emotional dissonance (Van Harreveld *et al.*, 2009). Emotion-focused strategies involve procrastination or downplaying the situation, while problem-focused strategies involve significant effort to make changes. In business tourism, conflicting emotions from time limits and the desire to fully enjoy the site can lead to emotional dissonance. Business travellers may employ one or two coping techniques (emotion-focused and problem-focused) to reduce dissonance. If using a problem-focused method, revisiting the destination during leisure time may be effective.

Therefore, mixed emotions may lead business visitors to revisit their travel destination (Nan *et al.*, 2020). None of the theories can explain business travelers' behavioral journeys when participating in bleisure tourism.

A journey can be defined as a process of traveling from one place to another, typically involving a series of experiences, challenges, personal growth, and discovery. It often represents a transformational or significant passage in one's life, leading to new perspectives and insights. It is a process of moving forward, facing challenges, and experiencing new perspectives. It can also refer to a path or course taken to reach a destination, whether physical or metaphorical. Moreover, a journey must have cyclical means, i.e., a clear beginning and end point, allowing for reflection and growth. This cyclical nature ensures that lessons learned can be applied to future journeys, creating a continuous personal development and discovery cycle. It has a beginning, middle, and end, allowing for growth and transformation. This cyclical nature allows for reflection and learning from past experiences to inform future decisions and actions. It must have a beginning and an end, with the possibility of repeating or continuing. This cyclical nature allows for growth, learning, and transformation throughout the journey.

This can be explained by the Transtheoretical Framework (TTM) - Stages of Change Model of Carlo C. DiClemente and James O. Prochaska's studies since 1983 (DiClemente *et al.*, 1991). TTM suggested that instead of seeing change as a straight line, we should see it as a spiral that winds through the stages (Prochaska *et al.*, 2013). The Transtheoretical Model (TTM) proposes that individuals progress through six distinct stages of change: pre-contemplation (where a participant does not have any intention of taking action), contemplation (where a participant has intentions to take action and a plan to do so shortly); preparation (participant has taken some actions already); action (participant's behavior has been changed for a shorter time); maintenance (participant's changed behavior continues for a longer time); and termination (participant does not want to return prior negative behavior).

8. CONCLUSION

8.1. Theoretical Implications

The Transtheoretical Model (TTM) by Prochaska and DiClemente outlines six behavioral change stages applicable to bleisure tourism decision-making. These stages include pre-contemplation, contemplation, preparation, action, and maintenance (Prochaska & DiClemente, 1983). They assist in recognizing travelers' readiness for bleisure travel, with each stage indicating varying levels of awareness and engagement. For instance, individuals in pre-contemplation may not acknowledge the benefits, while those in contemplation require more information to decide. Intervention strategies aligned with TTM stages can effectively promote bleisure travel. During contemplation, travelers benefit from informational campaigns highlighting rewards like reduced stress. Those in the action stage benefit from logistical support, which facilitates the incorporation of leisure into business trips. Personal, environmental, and behavioral factors influence the progression through the stages. Personal attitudes toward work-life balance, past travel experiences, organizational support, and travel habits play crucial roles. Sustaining bleisure behaviors requires consistent positive experiences, employer support, and routine integration of leisure into business travel. Research can delve into habit formation and reinforcement for long-term adoption. Cultural norms also shape bleisure travel behavior, with cross-cultural studies revealing how these norms influence stage progression. Policy implications involve designing initiatives tailored to each stage, incentivizing bleisure travel, and fostering supportive corporate policies to encourage adoption and maintenance. Overall, TTM provides a structured framework for understanding and influencing bleisure travel behaviors, supporting its growth and sustainability.

8.2. Managerial Implications

The Transtheoretical Model (TTM) offers interventions to support the six stages of change through ten strategies. By incorporating the AIDA advertising model, organizations can effectively promote bleisure travel among employees. Firstly, it captures attention by raising awareness about the concept of bleisure travel and its inclusion in strategic plans, such as the Five-Year Plan or Governmental Policy. Educate staff about the leisure activities and tourist destinations available during business trips to pique their interest (consciousness raising). Next, sustain interest by highlighting the benefits of bleisure travel for work-life balance and job satisfaction. Evoke positive emotions associated with bleisure travel, such as relaxation and cultural immersion (emotional arousal). To foster desire, establish policies that facilitate leisure travel while ensuring work obligations are met. This includes considering safety, accessibility, and recreational resources (policy making). Encourage employees to commit to bleisure travel by making plans that merge leisure and business activities (commitment). Finally, prompt action by recognizing and rewarding employees who successfully incorporate leisure activities into their work schedules, offering incentives like additional vacation days or travel benefits (reward). Promote a work environment that values work-life balance by providing tools for managing workloads efficiently, allowing for leisure time without compromising productivity (stimulus control). Encourage a sense of community among bleisure travelers by fostering networking, peer support, and the exchange of information and experiences (social liberation). By applying these strategies, organizations can create a supportive culture that enhances employee satisfaction and productivity (Sun *et al.*, 2015; Prochaska *et al.*, 2013).

9. LIMITATIONS AND FUTURE RESEARCH DIRECTIONS

The study could not provide a generalized opinion because the data was insufficient. However, the researchers managed to get an insight into the trend with a limited number of data: 16. If the researchers had a wide range of data, 100-150 people, they could have found differences in the findings. Additionally, if the study had been conducted incorporating other theories, then the results could have been diverse.

REFERENCES

Abedini, Y. (2021). Metacognition as a core skill for wise decision-making in higher education: investigating gender differences. *Journal of Applied Research in Higher Education*. 10.1108/JARHE-11-2020-0400

Adhiatma, A., Muna, N., & Fachrunnisa, O. (2019). Business and Leisure "Bleisure" in Organization: Antecedents and Outcomes. *JDM: Jurnal Dinamika Manajemen/ Jurnal Dinamika Manajemen Jurusan Manajemen Fakultas Ekonomi Universitas Negeri Semarang, 10*(2), 216–228. 10.15294/jdm.v10i2.19783

Agenda. (n.d.). World Economic Forum. https://weforum.org/agenda/

Ahmad, S. (2024, May 13). *What is the Importance of Bleisure Travel?*https:// satgurutravel.com/importance-of-bleisure-travel/

BANI: What is it, and how can it help us? (n.d.). Impact International. https://www .impactinternational.com/blog/2023/10/bani-what-it-and-how-can-it-help-u

Batala, B., & Slevitch, L. (2024). Keeping two balls in the air: The bleisure travel experience. *Annals of Tourism Research Empirical Insights*, 5(1), 100115. 10.1016/j. annale.2023.100115

Bi, N., Yin, C. Y., & Chen, Y. (2020). A bittersweet experience! The effect of mixed emotions on business tourists' revisit intentions. *Journal of Travel & Tourism Marketing*, 37(6), 695–710. 10.1080/10548408.2020.1795047

Bleisure Travel: The Challenges & Rewards. (2023b, August 3). https://www.linkedin .com/pulse/bleisure-travel-challenges-rewards

Cacioppo, J. T., Gardner, W. L., & Berntson, G. G. (1999). The affect system has parallel and integrative processing components: Form follows function. *Journal of Personality and Social Psychology*, 76(5), 839–855. 10.1037/0022-3514.76.5.839

Chen, Y., Mak, B., & McKercher, B. (2011). What Drives People to Travel: Integrating the Tourist Motivation Paradigms. *Journal of China Tourism Research*, 7(2), 120–136. 10.1080/19388160.2011.576927

Chung, J. Y., Choi, Y. K., Yoo, B. K., & Kim, S. H. (2020). Bleisure tourism experience chain: Implications for destination marketing. *Asia Pacific Journal of Tourism Research*, 25(3), 300–310. 10.1080/10941665.2019.1708760

Cohen, S. A., & Gössling, S. (2015). A darker side of hypermobility. *Environment & Planning A*, 47(8), 166–1679. 10.1177/0308518X15597124

Correia, A., Kozak, M., & Ferradeira, J. (2013). From tourist motivations to tourist satisfaction. *International Journal of Culture, Tourism and Hospitality Research*, 7(4), 411–424. 10.1108/IJCTHR-05-2012-0022

Crompton, J. L. (1979). Motivations for pleasure vacation. *Annals of Tourism Research*, 6(4), 408–424. 10.1016/0160-7383(79)90004-5

Davidson, R. (2003). Adding Pleasure to Business. *Journal of Convention & Exhibition Management*, 5(1), 29–39. 10.1300/J143v05n01_03

DiClemente, C. C., Prochaska, J. O., Fairhurst, S. K., Velicer, W. F., Velasquez, M. M., & Rossi, J. S. (1991). The process of smoking cessation: An analysis of precontemplation, contemplation, and preparation stages of change. *Journal of Consulting and Clinical Psychology*, 59(2), 295–304. 10.1037/0022-006X.59.2.2952030191

Dieffenbacher, F. S. (2023, September 3). *BANI World: What is it and Why We Need it?* Digital Leadership. https://digitalleadership.com/blog/bani-world/#:~:text=The%20BANI%20effect%20refers%20to

Ezeuduji, I. O. (2024). Bleisure Travel Reimagined: Implications for Research. *International Conference on Tourism Research, 7*(1), 2–9. 10.34190/ictr.7.1.2194

Fong, C. T. (2006). The Effects of Emotional Ambivalence on Creativity. *Academy of Management Journal*, 49(5), 1016–1030. 10.5465/amj.2006.22798182

Gunthorpe, W., & Lyons, K. (2004). A Predictive Model of Chronic Time Pressure in the Australian Population: Implications for Leisure Research. *Leisure Sciences*, 26(2), 201–213. 10.1080/01490400490432127

Gustafson, P. (2013). Business Travel from the Traveller's Perspective: Stress, Stimulation and Normalization. *Mobilities*, 9(1), 63–83. 10.1080/17450101.2013.784539

Huang, X., Chen, M., Wang, Y., Yi, J., Song, Z., & Ryan, C. (2022). Visitors' spatial-temporal behaviour and their learning experience: A comparative study. *Tourism Management Perspectives*, 42, 100951. 10.1016/j.tmp.2022.100951

Kim, J. H., Ritchie, J. R. B., & McCormick, B. (2010). Development of a Scale to Measure Memorable Tourism Experiences. *Journal of Travel Research*, 51(1), 12–25. 10.1177/0047287510385467

Kim, S.-H., Holland, S., & Han, H.-S. (2012). A Structural Model for Examining how Destination Image, Perceived Value, and Service Quality Affect Destination Loyalty: A Case Study of Orlando. *International Journal of Tourism Research*, 15(4), 313–328. 10.1002/jtr.1877

Kluin, J. Y., & Lehto, X. Y. (2012). Measuring Family Reunion Travel Motivations. *Annals of Tourism Research*, 39(2), 820–841. 10.1016/j.annals.2011.09.008

Kraaijenbrink, J. (2022, June 23). What BANI Really Means (And How It Corrects Your World View). *Forbes*. https://www.forbes.com/sites/jeroenkraaijenbrink/2022/06/22/what-bani-really-means-and-how-it-corrects-your-world-view/?sh=3a0d6cbe11bb

Leong, A. M. W., Yeh, S. S., Hsiao, Y. C., & Huan, T. C. T. (2015). Nostalgia as travel motivation and its impact on tourists' loyalty. *Journal of Business Research*, 68(1), 81–86. 10.1016/j.jbusres.2014.05.003

Lichy, J., & McLeay, F. (2017). Bleisure: Motivations and typologies. *Journal of Travel & Tourism Marketing*, 35(4), 517–530. 10.1080/10548408.2017.1364206

Mareš, J. (1998). *Styly učení žáků a studentů*. Portál. https://is.muni.cz/el/sci/podzim2015/XS150/um/02_XS150_Styly_uceni.pdf

McNaught, C., & Lam, P. (2014). Using Wordle as a Supplementary Research Tool. *The Qualitative Report*, 15(3). Advance online publication. 10.46743/2160-3715/2010.1167

Özgürel, G. (2022). A Research on Determining the Destination Quality Perceptions and Intentions to Revisit of Bleisure Tourists: İstanbul Case. www.academia.edu. https://www.academia.edu/91300746/A_Research_on_Determining_the_Destination_Quality_Perceptions_and_Intentions_to_Revisit_of_Bleisure_Tourists_%C4%B0stanbul_Case

Pearce, P. L., & Lee, U. I. (2005). Developing the Travel Career Approach to Tourist Motivation. *Journal of Travel Research*, 43(3), 226–237. 10.1177/0047287504272020

Pinho, M., & Marques, J. (2021, September). The bleisure tourism trend and the potential for this business-leisure symbiosis in Porto. In *Journal of Convention & Event Tourism* (Vol. 22, No. 4, pp. 346-362). Routledge. 10.1080/15470148.2021.1905575

Pisoňová, M. (2015). Creation and Results of a Research Project with a Focus on School Management for Teachers. *Acta Technologica Dubnicae*, 5(2), 14–30. 10.1515/atd-2015-0062

Plog, S. (2001b). Why destination areas rise and fall in popularity: An update of a Cornell Quarterly classic. *The Cornell Hotel and Restaurant Administration Quarterly*, 42(3), 13–24. 10.1016/S0010-8804(01)81020-X

Porter, M. (1985). *The Competitive Advantage: Creating and Sustaining Superior Performance*. Hbs.edu. https://www.hbs.edu/faculty/Pages/item.aspx?num=193

Prochaska, J. O., Norcross, J. C., & DiClemente, C. C. (2013). Applying the Stages of Change. In *Oxford University Press eBooks* (pp. 177–181). 10.1093/med:-psych/9780199845491.003.0034

Rees, C. S., Breen, L. J., Cusack, L., & Hegney, D. (2015). Understanding individual resilience in the workplace: The international collaboration of workforce resilience model. *Frontiers in Psychology*, 6. Advance online publication. 10.3389/fpsyg.2015.0007325698999

Saldana, J. (2021). *The Coding Manual for Qualitative Researchers*. SAGE Publications Ltd - Torrossa. https://www.torrossa.com/en/resources/an/5018667

Shaheer, I., Lee, C., & Carr, N. (2021). Factors motivating working holiday travel: The case of Latin American visitors to New Zealand. *Tourism and Hospitality Research*, 21(3), 330–343. 10.1177/14673584211003630

Sohaili, N. L. M., Aminudin, N., & Amir, A. F. (2022). Bleisure Motivation Towards Leisure Attraction: A Systematic Literature Review. *International Journal of Academic Research in Business & Social Sciences*, 12(11). Advance online publication. 10.6007/IJARBSS/v12-i11/15626

Stanford University Press. (2019). *A Theory of Cognitive Dissonance | Leon Festinger*. Sup.org. https://www.sup.org/books/title/?id=3850

Sun, P., Cárdenas, D. A., & Harrill, R. (2015). Chinese Customers' Evaluation of Travel Website Quality: A Decision-Tree Analysis. *Journal of Hospitality Marketing & Management*, 25(4), 476–497. 10.1080/19368623.2015.1037977

The Future Laboratories. (2008). The trend tracker. https://www.thefuturelaboratory.com/trend-tracker

Thomas, J. (2023, November 23). *77+ Bleisure Travel Statistics [Updated 2022]*. Stratos Jet Charters, Inc. https://www.stratosjets.com/blog/bleisure-travel-statistics/

Tsaur, S. H., & Tsai, C. H. (2023). Bleisure travel experience: Scale development and validation. *Journal of Travel & Tourism Marketing*, 40(1), 21–37. 10.1080/10548408.2023.2199773

Unger, O., & Uriely, N. (2022). The bleisure memories of business travelers. *Annals of Tourism Research*, 97, 103497. 10.1016/j.annals.2022.103497

Unger, O., Uriely, N., & Fuchs, G. (2016). The business travel experience. *Annals of Tourism Research*, 61, 142–156. 10.1016/j.annals.2016.10.003

Unpacking Bleisure Traveler Trends. (n.d.). https://info.advertising.expedia.com/bleisure-travel-trends

Van Harreveld, F., Rutjens, B. T., Schneider, I. K., Nohlen, H. U., & Keskinis, K. (2014). In doubt and disorderly: Ambivalence promotes compensatory perceptions of order. *Journal of Experimental Psychology. General*, 143(4), 1666–1676. 10.1037/a003609924588217

Whang, H., Yong, S., & Ko, E. (2016). Pop culture, destination images, and visit intentions: Theory and research on travel motivations of Chinese and Russian tourists. *Journal of Business Research*, 69(2), 631–641. 10.1016/j.jbusres.2015.06.020

What is Bleisure? Benefits & Challenges | Uber for Business. (n.d.). Uber. https://www.uber.com/us/en/business/articles/what-is-bleisure-travel/

Yoo, H., McIntosh, A., & Cockburn-Wootten, C. (2016). Time for me and time for us: Conference travel as alternative family leisure. *Annals of Leisure Research. Annals of Leisure Research*, 19(4), 444–460. 10.1080/11745398.2016.1147361

Yoon, Y., & Uysal, M. (2005). An examination of the effects of motivation and satisfaction on destination loyalty: A structural model. *Tourism Management*, 26(1), 45–56. 10.1016/j.tourman.2003.08.016

Yousaf, A., Amin, I., & Santos, J. C. (2018). Tourists' Motivations to Travel: A Theoretical Perspective on the Existing Literature. *Tourism and Hospitality Management*, 24(1), 197–211. 10.20867/thm.24.1.8

Chapter 5
Behavioral Reliability on Social Media for Destination Choices in Bleisure Travel

Harjot Kaur
https://orcid.org/0009-0006-5856-4302
Chandigarh University, India

Shikha Sharma
Chandigarh University, India

Sandeep Guleria
Chandigarh University, India

ABSTRACT

Social media has revolutionized the travel industry, becoming an increasingly important aspect of the sector. It has influenced our behavior in every part of our lives, including the way we consume travel content. Tourism is one of the world's most active economic sectors, and social media is a substantial component of it. The age of brochures and billboards in the tourist business has come to an end. Today, the usage of social networking sites may be the most important factor impacting the tourist business. Tourists, in particular, benefit from social media since it enables them to share their most memorable travel experiences with a large number of people. Since travel has always been a popular pastime, the arrival of technology has resulted in a paradigm change in communication and trip planning practices, both of which have been beneficial. This chapter will explore the reliability of social media and how it is utilized to make travel choices in the travel process by the tourist

DOI: 10.4018/979-8-3693-4354-8.ch005

who lives in Chandigarh and prefers business and leisure together.

INTRODUCTION

In the last decade, especially in the early 21st century, the traveling industry experienced a whole new paradigm of leisure in the business. Business and leisure lines became obscure, and a new type of tourism, known as "bleisure travel," began to make its way into practice and research. Bleisure travel is a category that allows guests to resolve business matters and explore new territories visiting in tandem, meaning that guests would have their business meetings for a few days and a small holiday or sightseeing for remaining days. The essence of such a form of inclusiveness in leisure travel is that one can combine his or her visits to a meeting room and to the tourism attraction. Bleisure travel has grown in popularity over time, further expanding the effect it had on a myriad of industry sectors. The concept of bleisure travel combines business and leisure activities into a single trip, where the former is the main goal, and the latter one is of secondary but still great meaning. This long life shows the connection between bleisure traveling and duality, where one has the right to work with himself and, thanks to relaxation, advances commander tasks and vice versa, does future tasks while relaxing.

The term bleisure tourism, which combines the first syllable of "business" and "leisure", refers to the trend of mixing business and leisure experience during one trip. This concept has become increasingly popular in recent years because there is a blurring of differences between business and leisure travel (Economist, 2019; Expedia, 2018). Bleisure marketing promotes the extension of a business person's stay, visiting more sites, engaging in more entertainment and leisure activities and eventually increasing spending after a conference, convention or meeting (Lichy & McLeay, 2017).

According to research, about half of the money allocated to business travelers' expenditures, approximately 50%, is still spent on the traditional components of traveling: accommodation, displacement, food, and drink. However, it should be highlighted that one-fourth of the budget is set aside for non-work related costs: guided trips, concerts, museum and gallery entry, and participation in sporting events (Expedia, 2018).

The growth of bleisure travel is associated with multiple factors explaining certain technological advancements, change workplace conditions, and surrounding society's principles. The opportunities for digital communication and flexible hours allowed professionals to perform their job at a distance and decide on their activities; as a result, people could manage the most suitable time for travel (Kurkland & Bailey, 1999) Additionally, Millennials, one of the most powerful consumer groups, promote experiential consumption and balance between personal and professional affairs through the use of bleisure.

Although still more theoretical than practical, bleisure travel present distinctive challenges and potentials to a range of actors across the travel value chain. From a destination marketing standpoint, there is a need to amend targeting strategies to focus on luring in the type of tourist looking for genuine and holistic business and leisure experiences (Kim et al.,2019). In the same way, an employer's need to ensure employees' welfare and productivity while supporting ship trips is also possible; therefore, the situation is complex (Danna & Griffin, 1999). In the same way, as researchers investigating the motivations, behaviors, and outcomes of bleisure travel, they can contribute to the development of knowledge and best practices in the industry (Sohaili, Aminudin & Amir, 2022).

Considering the intricate nature of bleisure travel and its repercussions for the measures involved in the segment of the travel industry, the primary purpose of this chapter is to overview the phenomenon by analyzing its definition, impetuses, structures, and effects. Ultimately, the presentation will explore the existing literature and empirical observations accompanied by the author's critical reflection to provide a superficial understanding of bleisure travel and its reshaping impact on the contemporary structure of travel experiences.

SOCIAL MEDIA'S SIGNIFICANCE IN TRAVEL DECISION MAKING

Social media platforms have become invaluable in the manner in which people attain information in addition to making decisions and painting experiences in the present digital era. Social media is pivotal in the process of travel decision-making as it acts as the ultimate virtual marketplace where people find inspiration and a point of reference and get the confidence to choose a distinct place as their destination. This factor revolves around the concept of user-generated content and other peer's references making social media critical in affecting the perceptions, attitudes, and buying behaviours of travellers in the end.

Research indicates that social media has a direct impact on every phase of the travel decision-making process, including destination exploration and post-trip introspection (Xiang & Gretzel, 2010). Specifically, digital platforms such as TripAdvisor, Instagram, and Facebook serve as canvases on which travelers display their experiences through images, reviews, and recommendations. Ultimately, these interconnected canvases create a rich tapestry of travel stories that not only entertain but also enlighten potential travelers (Litvin et al., 2018). However, in addition to attracting players, the social media space allows clients to interact with travel destinations, brands, and other tourists, establishing a sense of community and trust that transcends geophysical boundaries (Jalilvand & Samiei, 2012).

Understanding the impact of social media on the travel decision-making process is not only about spreading information. It is also about forming the understanding of accommodation, destination, and experience attractiveness. According to Yo & Gretzel (2011), social media affects how tourists consider a destination's attractiveness, safety, and authenticity through user-made content. Social media mechanisms like tailored news feeds, influencers, and algorithms have plans for travelers. It makes some destinations and experiences more popular, leaving some marginalized (Hudson et al., 2016) . Given the extensive influence that social media has on the travel decision-making process, filming destinations and hospitality sectors should utilize these platforms. Destinations can increase visibility, attractiveness, appeal, and profitability in an overcrowded market by interacting with travelers through social media and producing interesting products (Perles-Ribes et al.,2019).

The segment is particularly important as social media has deeply transformed the digitalization of the travel decision-making process, and one should analyze the ways in which various types of social media may affect the perceptions, preferences, and choices of travelers, providing invaluable knowledge of destination marketing and customer interaction in the digital era.

PURPOSE AND SCOPE

This chapter seeks to evaluate behavioral reliability's and its impact on destination selection in relation to social media's influence on passengers when constructing bleisure travel. Due to bleisure trip's widespread acceptance globally, it is necessary to comprehend the pathway that leads to the selection of a given destination by a given customer. The primary objective of this chapter is to evaluate the reliability of the behavioral indications and the information available on social media's and how it directs their decision-making processes among bleisure travelers. This chapter's aim to assess the reliability and impact of social media content will provide useful insights to passengers, destination markers, and researchers regarding the efficiency and efficacy of using social media as an avenue for planning their respective trips. This chapter will evaluate other relevant topics, including the meaning of behavioral reliability, and the impact of social media on destination selection. In this respect, this chapter will also delve into the implications for destination marketing package by investigating strategies used by destinations to enhance their credibility presence and interactions with bleisure travelers.

The chapter also investigates the affected aspects of bleisure decision-making concerning the social media phenomenon, taking into account the reliability of shared information and outcomes for the field of travel. The analysis can help the relevant parties optimize the possibilities of using social media and ensure that the data obtained by travelers during bleisure trips is reliable and efficient.

BLEISURE TRAVEL

Bleisure travel, the mix of "business" and "leisure" that combines the fulfilment of work-related duties and leisure on vacation, has obtained some additional meaning over the years. Such a notion has recently acquired popularity because working cultures have been reshaping, people have reconsidered their attitudes towards the maintenance of the right work-life balance, and many technological advances have made the development of remote work possible. The following section is a compendium of academic conversation on the subject of the definition and creation of bleisure travel. It addresses critical areas, scholarly perspectives, and study findings.

Scholars define bleisure travel as a specific type of travel that includes both business and leisure. Batala & Slevitch (2024) define bleisure travel as an activity that involves engaging in business and leisure during the same trip. While leisure is secondary to the primary objective involving business interaction, the leisure aspect acts as enrichment. Therefore, this definition proves that business is the cause of the beginning of travel, while leisure provides for more experiences.

Increased flexibility in work arrangements and the erasure of traditional boundaries separating work and leisure were the factors contributing to the emergence of bleisure travel. Prior to the digital era, it was often deemed irrelevant to spend any spare time during a business trip not related to work. However, technological advancements, such as smartphones, laptop computers, and widespread digital platforms providing opportunities to cooperate and work online remotely, have enabled today's business people to work essentially from almost any location (White, M.,2012). As a result, the boundaries of time and necessary locations have been blurred, making the integration of leisure during a business-oriented vacation seamless.

It is also essential that the reasons for bleisure travel and its motivation are considered in order to understand the reasons for the development and prevalence of this phenomenon. In this regard, Pereira, Gupta, and Hussain argue (2019) that travelers' motivation for bleisure is primarily a desire to make the most of their travel experiences, do more during their time away from home, and strive for a better balance between work and personal life (Pereira, Gupta, & Hussain, 2022). In addition, continuous leisure-based decisions are positively influenced by destination appeal, proximity to leisure activities, and flexible work opportunities (Liu et al., 2021).

The birth of bleisure travel holds significant implications for several stakeholders in the travel industry. These include destination marketers, hospitality providers and employers. Destination marketers must change their plans to meet the needs and wants of bleisure tourists. This may include offering various events or activities that appeal to both leisure and business activities (Chung et al., 2020). Moreover, businesses must ensure that they capitalize on the advantages associated with bleisure travel. This includes increased employee satisfaction and retention. However, potential setbacks may also include reduced productivity and work-life balance (Park, Lehto & Kang, 2024).

KEY MOTIVATIONS FOR COMBINING BUSINESS WITH LEISURE

The phenomenon of combining business and leisure, known as bleisure travel, has been vigorously discuss by researchers and professionals in recent years. For a better understanding of what motivates people to join professional and leisure commitments, one should review the causes. The research is aimed to provide a review of the major reasons for business-leisure merging in travel from scientific models and studies to developing perspectives.

Figure 1. Motivations for Bleisure Travel

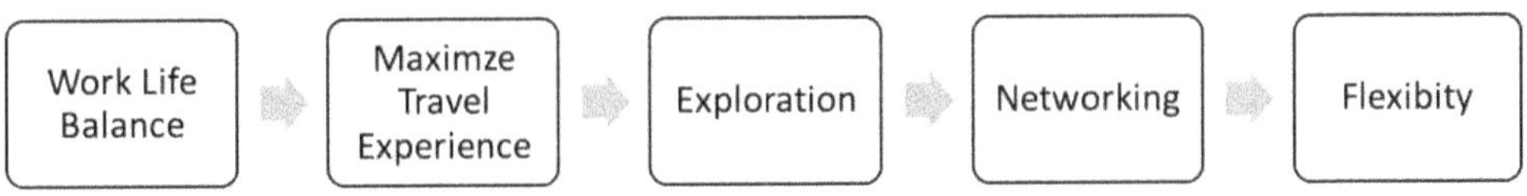

One of the main motivating factors for engaging in bleisure travel is the desire to maintain work-life balance and well-being. As already mentioned, "after a long period of hard work people feel the need to rest and restore their strength". The study (Chen et al., 2016) emphasizes the fact that travelers perceive the trip differently – as relaxation, recovery, and well-being following hard periods of the work process. By marrying work and leisure, people can mitigate the adverse effects of stress from work and maintain equilibrium to their work and personal lives.

The motivation behind bleisure travelers is the desire to maximize their travel needs during the current business travels. This motivation is reflected towards not wanting to waste time during people's visits and, hence, events of combining their work schedules with leisure activities prior to, during, or after completing the assigned tasks (Pinho & Marques, 2021). It is a rational expression towards a trip that people utilize to meet their personal and professional needs hence may lack its own proper form of motivations.

The possibility of exploration and cultural immersion is yet another critical reason for mixing business and pleasure. Most often, bleisure travelers regard their business travels as an opportunity to explore new destinations, immerse themselves in local cultures, and go beyond their professional roles and responsibilities (Xiang & Gretzel, 2010). This approach implies the traveler's autobiographical and experiential involvement with the destination, encouraging genuine relationships and meaningful encounters with its residents.

Bleisure travel is also highly driven by the prospect of relationship building and networking for professionals, primarily focusing on generating business contacts and expanding their professional circle. Busines- related events, including conferences and meetings, that create an informal environment for interaction with clients, coworkers, and professionals within the given field (Asero, Gozzo & Tomaselli, 2016). Blending professional and personal life allows people to establish meaningful relationships and improve their reputation in the industry.

Bleisure travel offers the opportunity for an individual to freely configure his experience according to his specific needs and goals. It is fundamentally different from conventional business trips with a fixed time frame and schedule. Taking a bleisure trip is a call for independence and the right to decide to form your own travelogue (Kachniewska, 2016). They try to find themselves in the interstices of work and interest. Identifying these spaces becomes an important part of everyday life in work and personal life."

SOCIAL MEDIA IN TRAVEL DECISION MAKING

Social media platforms have emerged as important conduits for accessing information and drawing inspiration and influence in making travel decisions. This literature review summarizes the existing studies on the complex roles of social media in shaping travelers' perception, preferences, and behavior. This review will focus on theoretical underpinnings, empirical findings, and managerial and theoretical implications.

Information Seeking and Inspiration: It can be understood from the abovementioned line that social media works as a digital market from where visitors seek inspiration and collect information to determine their travel plans. Based on a study, it is observed that people engage proactively with travel content on social media such as Instagram, Facebook, and YouTube. People look through the photos, videos, comments, suggestions submitted by their friends, famous people, and marketers (Xiang & Gretzel, 2010). The learning and discovering process is critical in defining where to go and developing a travel itinerary.

Peer influence and social proof. Social media's interactive feature greatly amplifies the impact a person's peers and social evidence have on the travel selection process. User-generated content has a solid influence review, rating, and testimonial websites on how passengers perceive destinations, lodging facilities, and experiences (Yoo & Gretzel, 2011). Several studies have proven that social advice has a significant impact on people's choices. Travelers quite frequently use the experiences and advice of others to validate their selection and decrease perceived risk (Litvin et al., 2018).

Engagement and Interaction: Social media allows visitors, The places they are visiting, and brands to communicate and interact directly. This creates the sense of a virtual community. It can be accomplished by allowing travelers to communicate with other users, seek advice, exchange their experience, or receive and share in the form of feedback, comments, likes, shares, or direct messages in real time (Jalilvand & Samiei, 2012). By creating a two-way communication channel, travelers can engage in the decision-making process related to the content, which means they can co-create and curate their travel itinerary collaboratively.

Influencer Marketing and Aspirational Branding. Influencer marketing has become a powerful strategy for brands and destinations to leverage the power of social media stars to impact travel decisions. Travel influencers serve as aspiration referents because they showcase a well-orchestrated photoshoot and perfect lifestyle online, making destinations, accommodations, and experiences appear appealing and persuasive (Hudson et al., 2016). Partnerships with influencers enable organizations to effectively target the right people, create brand awareness, and drive engagement with authentic storytelling and content creation.

User-Generated Content and Authenticity. The most eligible footage from SNS happens to be its realness and trustworthiness of user-generated material. Issues of authenticity are vital to what people think and how they choose to act. Travelers prefer self-generated and shared content because other people and peers make it appear more authentic (Yoo & Gretzel, 2011). Brands and places boosting UGC and real engagement with the audience become more credible, and people are increasingly willing to make choices.

FACTORS AFFECTING TRUST AND RELIABILITY OF SOCIAL MEDIA CONTENT

Trust and reliability are critical variables in determining the credibility and utility of social media content in making travel-related decisions. The present review consolidates previous investigations regarding material that promotes or disqualifies people's trust and reliance on messages conveyed through social media platforms. To do so, a literature review of theoretical foundations, empirical studies, and insights in the tourism and hospitality fields is employed.

The credibility of the sources plays a fundamental role in verifying legitimacy of social media content. People tend to trust more the information provided by the sources they believe are credible, possess authority, and are trustworthy (Hudson et al., 2016). Indeed, Litvin et al. (2018), argue that individuals with a good reputation and history in the traveling sector, such as influencers, brands, and peer groups, are seen to be credible sources of information. Consequently, people are more likely to believe their information.

Furthermore, when the social media material is authentic and transparent, it influences trust in users. The authenticity of the information expressed and how genuine is the experience or recommendation provided is appreciated by the end-users (Yoo & Gretzel, 2011). Adults trust brands and influencers more when they are open about their sponsorships, collaborations, and advertising, for example (Xiang & Gretzel, 2010).

Consistency and accuracy are essential factors that enhance the reliability of the social media content. The users want to rely on the content that is in line with their expectations, past activities, and background knowledge of the destinations and travel experiences. Information that is genuine, recent, and true promotes the trust and belief of the users; on the other hand, the misleading information or that which is found to be untrue weakens the users' trust and reliability of the source (Jalilvand & Samiei, 2012).

The extent to which people interact/engage with social media information can influence the degree of trust they accord to it and credibility perception. The likelihood that the material will be trusted increases if users witness positive involvement, such as likes, shares, commentary, and endorsements from their friends and fellow travelers (Hudson et al., 2016). Constant interaction with content creators and companies has the impact of creating a sense of community or belonging, which again leads to trust and credibility among the followers and the audiences (Yuan & Lou, 2020).

In social media content, social proof also has a significant effect on trust and reliability due to peer recommendations and user-generated content creation. By referencing the experiences, thoughts, and guidance of peers and social groups, users strive to validate their travel choices and diminish instilled risk perceptions (Litvin et al., 2018). In line with findings of Xiang and Gretzel (2010), evaluations, ratings, and testimonials of other travelers contribute to trust and credibility in relationships with travel destinations and experiences.

BEHAVIORAL RELIABILITY IN SOCIAL MEDIA CONTEXT

The behavioral reliability in the context of social media is the perspicuity and trustworthiness of users' actions and information, particularly regarding their influence on decision-making.

The dependability of UGC can fluctuate significantly, even though the content is always part and parcel of the social media experience. Trust in the information derived from UGC is contingent on numerous factors, including the perceptions of skill, source authenticity, and reliability. According to Erkan and Evans (2016), the source credibility of the sharer is defined through his or her perceived expertise and trustworthiness. Travelers often rely on others' assessments and ratings of their own experiences to inform their decisions: easy ways to read and view things, the more trustworthy and credible material becomes more crucial.

Influencers play a very influential role in shaping attitudes and behaviors in social media. Since their operating capacity is perceived as more reliable due to the conclusion of their qualifications and trusted relationships with listeners, their reliability may be accompanied by numerous stipulations arising from commercial interest. Boerman, Willemsen, and Van Der Aa (2017) shed light on the role of transparency in the behavior of influencers: "... participants indicated that Instagram bloggers publishing a disclaimer that their post was sponsored is more honest than if a blogger does not". Indeed, the studies have shown that listeners have more confidence in the source and its reliability when the source disproves commercial interest.

First of all, how real social media material is affects how trustworthy this information is. Users are more likely to believe something that they think is real and unfiltered. According to Djafarova and Rushworth's study (2017), the realism of material posted on social media has a significant impact on people's belief and interaction with it. Those who follow someone are more likely to believe them if they post personal stories, process videos, or create honest reviews.

Several methods help to determine how trustworthy social media materials are. Many times, polls of users, sentiment analysis, and content analysis are used to determine how trustworthy social media information is. According to Mehra, P. (2023). sentiment analysis shows the overall sentiment and trust of UGC using the language people use and their feelings. Similarly, content analysis looks for patterns and themes that predict how trusting people will perceive something.

Despite being crucial, discerning how genuine a person's conduct is on social media is difficult in several areas. Data can seem and vanish due to the users deciding how social media post will transform in any different ways at any time. In addition, phoney ratings, untrue posts, and content affected by the prejudice can also make people more skeptical of something. According to Lazer et al., (2018), both platforms and users should keep continue striving to fend off misinformation and verify that the material is genuine.

Therefore, users and marketers are likely to experience the central consequences of the relevant behavioral reliability aspects. In particular, user's satisfaction, trust, and engagement can be increased due to the application of reliable material on social media, which ultimately contributes to more informed decision-making. As for marketers, their ability to exhibit the reliability of their content on social media can assist in increasing the reputation of their company and the loyalty of its consumers.

SOCIAL MEDIA CAMPAIGNS IN SHAPING DESTINATION CHOICES

Social media campaigns have become a valuable tool that destination marketers could implement to choose various other destinations, get more people to travel to their countries, and strengthen the brand of the country. This literature review is based on theoretical frameworks, empirical studies, and practical evidence in the field of destination marketing and tourism and synthesizes research and case studies already published on the various effects of social media campaigns on forming choices over destinations.

Case studies have demonstrated that influencer partnerships are successful in changing destination decisions as they provide travel experiences that are authentic and appealing to the target customers. For example, Tourism Australia collaborated with popular Instagrammers including @Australia and @Gypsea_lust who shared the nation's landscapes, fauna, and culture with millions of their fans globally, motivating them to travel to Australia. Using the influence of popular influencers, destinations can develop attractive stories that resonate with tourists and impact their destination decisions.

The potential of user-generated content as a strong tool for destination marketers to influence the destination choices through social proof and peer recommendations have become more prominent. An example is the #ShareYourJordan campaign created by the Jordan Tourism Board, in which people were invited to share their pictures and experiences of Jordan. Such evidence of the destination's authenticity generates the impression that other people have already visited it and there is no risk of being disappointed and convinced many potential visitors to visit Jordan. Destinations may use the persuasive force of social proof to affect the choices of the destination and persuade people to visit. This can be achieved by sharing personalized travel experiences of the current tourists.

Destinations can influence guests' choice by incorporating them into destination marketing actively; hence, engaging and interactive social media campaigns successfully affect and change visitors' choice of destination. Powers recommended the "Norway Lights" campaign by Visit Norway that encouraged people to post their experience of the northern lights on Instagram with that hashtag. Consequently, passengers felt a part of a virtual community that share the same enthusiasm for the aurora and unified Norway as the leading country to witness the natural phenomenon. Agreed, destinations can affect passengers' choice by encouraging active engagement and participation, making them feel part of something.

Tourism destination choices in response to targeted social media campaigns with personalized recommendations were shaped by the customization of content to their exact preferences. For example, the Dream Big campaign on Facebook and other platforms by Visit California engaged personalized video content to showcase for each viewer the state's numerous attractions, events, and experiences based on their interests and demographic. In doing so, destinations have the opportunity to engage potential tourists and influence their decision-making by providing personalized and relevant content that matches their travel personality.

To understand the impact of social media campaigns on destination selection and assess the return on investment, it is essential to correctly evaluate and assess the social media initiatives. Based on the case study of campaign of Tourism New Zealand under the programme "100% Pure New Zealand", it is seen that it is essential to assess campaigns based on key performance indicators creating the following data points, i.e. engagement measurement which includes liking, commenting, re-tweeting, sentiment analysis, reach measurements, and conversion rate. While using data analytics and insights, destination organizations can improve their social media campaigns; this will result in better influencing of peoples' travel destination selection and efficient resource management.

STRATEGIES FOR ENHANCING BEHAVIOURAL RELIABILITY ON SOCIAL MEDIA

Behavioral Reliability generally refers to the reliability and credibility of user behavior and content, which significantly influence decision-making processes. Enhancing the dependability of user behavior is necessary in establishing credibility and maximizing the benefits of social media marketing. This literature review considers several methods implemented in various case studies to enhance dependability.

Figure 2. Methods to Enhance Behavioural Reliability on Social Media

Transparency and Authenticity	Consistent Brand Messaging	Engaging with User Feedback	Leveraging Influencer Partnerships	Misinformation
•Transparency and authenticity are crucial for improving the trustworthiness of conduct on social media.	•Ensuring consistency in brand messaging is crucial for generating a sense of dependability on social media platforms.	•Interacting with customer input is crucial for showcasing responsiveness and responsibility on social media.	•Collaborating with influencers can improve behavioral consistency by utilizing the reputation and trustworthiness of these individuals.	•Ensuring the accuracy and credibility of content on social media is crucial for upholding trustworthiness and dependability

Authenticity and transparency are values that users find appealing. According to Kaplan and Haenlein (2010), businesses and influencers contribute to building and retaining trust by sharing their motivations, affiliations, and creative process. Businesses may build trust and credibility by sharing sponsored content while keeping their true colors and remaining authentic.

Furthermore, individuals tend to trust organizations that share their values, tone, and language through various platforms. Delgado-Ballester, Navarro & Sicilia (2012) argue that creating a shared brand experience depends on brand communication, increasing consumer trust. In other words, organizations can gain credibility and develop reliability on social media by maintaining coherence in brand voice and visual representation.

When a business actively listens, responds to promptly, and addresses feedback in public, people are drawn to it. Mangold and Faulds (2009) revealed that participating in user-generated content and effectively reacting positively to negative comments would boost a firm's reliability and credibility. Companies that foster open communication and a strong client focus to their social media pages will continue to gain more reliability and recognition.

To enhance the trust and expand the reach on social media platforms, the organization can engage in partnerships with influencers who promote the same values and have the target audience. Jin and Phua (2014), found out in their research that influencer marketing can "significantly enhance brand trust and credibility by capitalizing on the influencers' authority and experience". Hence, by carefully selecting influencers and creating truthful relationships with them, organizations can further increase their trustworthiness and credibility on social media.

Negative repercussions of the miscommunication happen when companies disseminate the wrong data cause direct impressions and reputation deterioration. To the study by Shao, Ciampaglia, Varol, Yang, and Flammini (2018), found that deploying fact-checking systems and providing users with information on misinformation as well as promoting media literacy substantially decreases the cascade size but the general influence. It means that the organizations better their reputation and trust nationality on the social media channels when actively overview the fake news and inaccurate information.

BEST PRACTICES FOR ENGAGING BLEISURE TRAVELERS

Bleisure travel gives both locations and companies a unique opportunity to engage with passengers who strive to maximize their experiences. To that end, it is also critical for destinations, hotels, and other areas of the traveler's industry to understand and implement the most effective strategies for attracting bleisure tourists as mentioned below.

First effective strategy can be Tailored Experiences and Packages. Experience and package customization that meets bleisure travelers' needs and preferences are essential to win over and retain this niche crowd. The article by Batala & Slevitch (2024) elucidates the importance of customizable options that allow passengers to seamlessly factor in recreational components during work-related traveling. There is an opportunity for destinations and firms to develop customized packages that combine business amenities with leisure offers; for example, it could be extended check-in/check-out times, discounted attraction tickets, coworking environments, and more.

The second strategy is the use of Seamless Booking and Planning Processes. It is essential to get on a course to optimize the booking and planning process to enhance the bleisure travel experience. Bleisure travelers who are time-constrained can use this method to streamline the preparation of excursion activities by providing user-friendly booking platforms and itineraries.

The next strategy is Personalized Recommendations and Concierge Services. Making recommendations and offering to help based on a person's own tastes and needs makes the bleisure experience more enjoyable, as it takes into account the unique likes and dislikes of the traveler. According to Ha & Perks (2005), when using advanced technology like artificial intelligence and machine learning algorithms, companies believe that by using technology, machine leaning, and artificial intelligence can do a better job of providing people with customized dining, entertainment, and sightseeing tips. The results of the research described by Ha & Perks (2005), showed that some tailored recommendations can increase enjoyment and loyalty among travelers.

Another strategy can be Networking and Social Events. By organizing networking occasions and social events, there will be more opportunities for people traveling for buy leisure who will meet local working professionals or other travelers. Business parties, meetups, and cultural events offer fantastic opportunities for networking, exchanging knowledge, and learning about different cultures for people traveling. According to a study by Tussyadiah and Zach (2012), social contacts and networking opportunities are important motivational factors motivating individuals to travel; hence, it is important to integrate social aspects into travel experiences.

Finally, one more approach can be adopted, namely, Flexible Policies and Amenities. It implies the necessity to change the rules and amenities to keep the pace with the demands of bleisure tourists. It is useful to offer flexible cancellation rules, numerous options for staying, as well as amenities tailored to the individuals' needs, including coworking spaces and gyms. The research presented by Mody et al., (2023), reveals that kind of accommodations have a significant effect on bleisure visitors' satisfaction and return.

FUTURE DIRECTIONS IN BLEISURE TRAVEL RESEARCH

There has been increased interest in bleisure travel in light of the evolving desire among passengers to maximize their experiences and efficiency during trips. Despite the growing intrigue of bleisure travel, there are various unexplored and under examined areas. The reasons and characteristics of bleisure travelers calls for an increased research effort to suggest further studies. Despite the indications from prior research on balance between professional and leisure time, the attractiveness of the location, and socialization opportunities, the core motives driving travelers' decisions may require deeper examination. Moreover, longitudinal research focused on the frequency and duration of bleisure travelers' behaviors could indicate the development of motives and their influence on travel strategies.

Apart from these aspects, more investigation is required to reflect on the economic consequences of bleisure tourism for destinations, businesses, and the sector as a whole. On the one hand, informal evidence suggests that bleisure travelers spend more money and have a positive influence on the local economy. On the other hand, the sustainable outcomes based on empirical research may be beneficial. In any case, discovering more about the economic consequences of bleisure tourism may be critical for destination marketing, company strategies, and policy development.

Ultimately, technology enhances leisure and business travelers' lives by allowing them to handle hotels and transportation and offering remote employment tools and digital nomad communities. In the future, it might be interesting to study the impact of emerging technologies on bleisure travelers; this might even encompass the effects of virtual reality, augmented reality, and remote work platforms. In addition, researching how digital nomadism affects destination selections and economies could provide new information on the continuing development of the work-travel lifestyle.

Since sustainability is becoming more important in the tourism industry, an avenue for future research may explore sustainable practices in bleisure travel. The study might examine the environmental, social, and economic impacts of bleisure travel and seek ways to minimize its detrimental effects on the environment. Another direction that research could go is identifying the consumer demand for sustainable travel and understanding the role of destination marketing organizations and companies in promoting sustainability.

CONCLUSION

This chapter has provided a broad examination of bleisure travel, emphasizing its growing prevalence and the crucial need for research to understand its complexities. It has covered a wide array of topics on bleisure travel, from definitions to motivations, economic impacts, technological applications, sustainable practices, and cross-cultural comparisons. The concept of behavioral dependability on social media is observed regarding destination choices for bleisure travel. The factors that influence behavioral dependability include source credibility, user-generated content, social evidence, transparency, and regularity. The best strategies to enchant bleisure tourists entail personalizing approaches, streamlining booking systems, offering tailored suggestions, organizing networking meetings, and presenting accommodating policies and amenities.

Advanced planning is critical for travelers, notably if they are considering bleisure travel. The source of entertainment, including the main entertainment tourism, must be feasible and explored in advance. Before pairing pleasure with the business aspect of the journey, there are several recommendations for the bleisure reader planning. Use social media as a method for finding out the views, reviews, or referrals of those who have previously been there, be it an insta post or snap story. Meet the bleisure concept: interact with increasingly trendy hashtags and establishments in the destination to locate trending and local favorite locations. Look for locations and businesses that specialize in catering to a visitor's personal predilections. This could involve trip plans that can change at the last minute, flexible booking, or securities constructed primarily for bleisure passengers.

The combination of social media and bleisure travel creates a complex, constantly changing situation with serious implications for travelers, destination marketers, and academics. The influence of social media on a bleisure trip cannot be overstated, as it actively shapes the way we communicate, share experiences, and make choices about social media platforms. Social media acts as a powerful tool for inspiration, exploration, and interaction to help visitors gain valuable insight, gather recommendations, and establish linkages with people with common interests. The impact of user-generated content, influencer ties, and destination marketing are powerful actors in influencing opinion and driving the choice of location for bleisure passengers. This influences the necessity to secure the authenticity, openness, and trustworthiness of the content distributed on social media platforms. As travelers become more reliant on social media to create and organize their journeys, destination marketers must maintain their integrity, cultivate confidence, and provide accurate details with their changing bleisure travelers' demands and expectations. The convergence of social media and bleisure travel also provides fresh possibilities for study and learning. The rapidly expanding field of bleisure trips allows scientists to delve more deeply into various aspects, from learning people's motives and behaviors to measuring the financial impacts and implementing sustainability strategies.

Since social media is sure to remain at the forefront in shaping the future, it is important to mention that it will significantly affect the bleisure travel industry. By applying sound practices, encouraging collaboration, and being up-to-date with the current trends, the professionals engaged can make a difference by harnessing the potential of social media and managing bleeding for better travel quality, sustainable tourism, and successful outcomes for passengers and destinations.

REFERENCES

Asero, V., Gozzo, S., & Tomaselli, V. (2015). Building Tourism Networks through Tourist Mobility. *Journal of Travel Research*, 55(6), 751–763. 10.1177/0047287515569777

Batala, B., & Slevitch, L. (2024). Keeping two balls in the air: The bleisure travel experience. *Annals of Tourism Research Empirical Insights*, 5(1), 100115. 10.1016/j.annale.2023.100115

Boerman, S. C., Willemsen, L. M., & Van Der Aa, E. P. (2017). This post is sponsored. *Journal of Interactive Marketing*, 38, 82–92. 10.1016/j.intmar.2016.12.002

Chen, C., Petrick, J. F., & Shahvali, M. (2014). Tourism experiences as a stress reliever. *Journal of Travel Research*, 55(2), 150–160. 10.1177/0047287514546223

Chung, J. Y., Choi, Y., Yoo, B., & Kim, S. (2020). Bleisure tourism experience chain: Implications for destination marketing. *Asia Pacific Journal of Tourism Research*, 25(3), 300–310. 10.1080/10941665.2019.1708760

Danna, K., & Griffin, R. W. (1999). Health and well-being in the workplace: A review and synthesis of the literature. *Journal of Management*, 25(3), 357–384. 10.1177/014920639902500305

Delgado-Ballester, E., Navarro, A., & Sicilia, M. (2012). Revitalising brands through communication messages: The role of brand familiarity. *European Journal of Marketing*, 46(1/2), 31–51. 10.1108/03090561211189220

Djafarova, E., & Rushworth, C. (2017). Exploring the credibility of online celebrities' Instagram profiles in influencing the purchase decisions of young female users. *Computers in Human Behavior*, 68, 1–7. 10.1016/j.chb.2016.11.009

Economist. (2019). The 2019 Bleisure barometer: Asia's best cities for work and recreation. London: The Economist Intelligence Unit. https://www.insidethegames.biz/media/file/135299/ECO056-JP-ANA-Bleisure-Business-and-Leisure-5-ver20190212.pdf

Erkan, I., & Evans, C. (2016). The influence of eWOM in social media on consumers' purchase intentions: An extended approach to information adoption. *Computers in Human Behavior*, 61, 47–55. 10.1016/j.chb.2016.03.003

Expedia. (2018). Unpacking bleisure traveler trends. Retrieved from https://bit.ly/bleisure-trends

Ha, H., & Perks, H. (2005). Effects of consumer perceptions of brand experience on the web: Brand familiarity, satisfaction and brand trust. *Journal of Consumer Behaviour*, 4(6), 438–452. 10.1002/cb.29

Hudson, S., Huang, L., Roth, M. S., & Madden, T. J. (2016). The influence of social media interactions on consumer–brand relationships: A three-country study of brand perceptions and marketing behaviors. *International Journal of Research in Marketing*, 33(1), 27–41. 10.1016/j.ijresmar.2015.06.004

Jalilvand, M. R., & Samiei, N. (2012). The impact of electronic word of mouth on a tourism destination choice. *Internet Research*, 22(5), 591–612. 10.1108/10662241211271563

Jin, S. A., & Phua, J. (2014). Following celebrities' tweets about brands: The impact of Twitter-Based electronic Word-of-Mouth on consumers' source credibility perception, buying intention, and social identification with celebrities. *Journal of Advertising*, 43(2), 181–195. 10.1080/00913367.2013.827606

Kachniewska, M. (2016). Bleisure: business and leisure equilibrium in contemporary hotel chains. Routledge Handbook of Hotel Chain Management, 542–554. https://doi.org/10.4324/9781315752532.ch45

Kaplan, A. M., & Haenlein, M. (2010). Users of the world, unite! The challenges and opportunities of Social Media. *Business Horizons*, 53(1), 59–68. 10.1016/j.bushor.2009.09.003

Kim, H., Joun, H. J., Choe, Y., & Schroeder, A. (2019). How can a destination better manage its offering to visitors? Observing visitor experiences via online reviews. *Sustainability (Basel)*, 11(17), 4660. 10.3390/su11174660

Kurkland, N. B., & Bailey, D. E. (1999). The advantages and challenges of working here, there anywhere, and anytime. *Organizational Dynamics*, 28(2), 53–68. 10.1016/S0090-2616(00)80016-9

Lazer, D. M. J., Baum, M. A., Benkler, Y., Berinsky, A. J., Greenhill, K. M., Menczer, F., Metzger, M. J., Nyhan, B., Pennycook, G., Rothschild, D., Schudson, M., Sloman, S. A., Sunstein, C. R., Thorson, E. A., Watts, D. J., & Zittrain, J. L. (2018). The science of fake news. *Science*, 359(6380), 1094–1096. 10.1126/science.aao299829590025

Lichy, J., & McLeay, F. (2017c). Bleisure: Motivations and typologies. *Journal of Travel & Tourism Marketing*, 35(4), 517–530. 10.1080/10548408.2017.1364206

Litvin, S. W., Goldsmith, R. E., & Pan, B. (2018). A retrospective view of electronic word-of-mouth in hospitality and tourism management. *International Journal of Contemporary Hospitality Management*, 30(1), 313–325. 10.1108/IJCHM-08-2016-0461

Liu, H., Huang, Y., Gao, M., & Stebbins, R. (2021). From serious leisure to devotee work: An exploratory study of yoga. *Leisure Studies*, 41(3), 405–419. 10.1080/02614367.2021.1980087

Mak, A. H. (2017). Online destination image: Comparing national tourism organisation's and tourists' perspectives. *Tourism Management*, 60, 280–297. 10.1016/j.tourman.2016.12.012

Mangold, W. G., & Faulds, D. J. (2009). Social media: The new hybrid element of the promotion mix. *Business Horizons*, 52(4), 357–365. 10.1016/j.bushor.2009.03.002

Mehra, P. (2023). Unexpected surprise: Emotion analysis and aspect based sentiment analysis (ABSA) of user generated comments to study behavioral intentions of tourists. *Tourism Management Perspectives*, 45, 101063. 10.1016/j.tmp.2022.101063

Mody, M. A., Jung, S., Dogru, T., & Suess, C. (2022). How do consumers select between hotels and Airbnb? A hierarchy of importance in accommodation choice. *International Journal of Contemporary Hospitality Management*, 35(4), 1191–1218. 10.1108/IJCHM-12-2021-1551

Okumus, B., & Bilgihan, A. (2014). Proposing a model to test smartphone users' intention to use smart applications when ordering food in restaurants. *Journal of Hospitality and Tourism Technology*, 5(1), 31–49. 10.1108/JHTT-01-2013-0003

Park, S., Lehto, X., & Kang, J. (2024). Balancing Work and Leisure: Unraveling constraints on Work-Leisure integration in Bleisure travel. *International Journal of Hospitality & Tourism Administration*, •••, 1–27. 10.1080/15256480.2024.2344226

Pereira, V., Gupta, J. J., & Hussain, S. (2019). Impact of travel motivation on tourist's attitude toward destination: Evidence of Mediating Effect of destination image. *Journal of Hospitality & Tourism Research (Washington, D.C.)*, 46(5), 946–971. 10.1177/1096348019887528

Perles-Ribes, J. F., Ramón-Rodríguez, A. B., Moreno-Izquierdo, L., & Such-Devesa, M. J. (2019). Online reputation and destination competitiveness: The case of Spain. *Tourism Analysis*, 24(2), 161–176. 10.3727/108354219X15525055915518

Pinho, M., & Marques, J. (2021). The bleisure tourism trend and the potential for this business-leisure symbiosis in Porto. *Journal of Convention & Event Tourism*, 22(4), 346–362. 10.1080/15470148.2021.1905575

Shao, C., Ciampaglia, G. L., Varol, O., Yang, K., Flammini, A., & Menczer, F. (2018). The spread of low-credibility content by social bots. *Nature Communications*, 9(1), 4787. Advance online publication. 10.1038/s41467-018-06930-730459415

Sohaili, N. L. M., Aminudin, N., & Amir, A. F. (2022). Bleisure Motivation towards Leisure Attraction: A Systematic Literature Review. *International Journal of Academic Research in Business & Social Sciences*, 12(11). Advance online publication. 10.6007/IJARBSS/v12-i11/15626

Tussyadiah, I. P., & Zach, F. J. (2012). The role of geo-based technology in place experiences. *Annals of Tourism Research*, 39(2), 780–800. 10.1016/j.annals.2011.10.003

White, M. (2012). Digital workplaces: Vision and reality. *Business Information Review*, 29(4), 205–214. 10.1177/0266382112470412

Xiang, Z., & Gretzel, U. (2010). Role of social media in online travel information search. *Tourism Management*, 31(2), 179–188. 10.1016/j.tourman.2009.02.016

Yoo, K., & Gretzel, U. (2011b). Influence of personality on travel-related consumer-generated media creation. *Computers in Human Behavior*, 27(2), 609–621. 10.1016/j.chb.2010.05.002

Yuan, S., & Lou, C. (2020). How Social Media Influencers Foster Relationships with Followers: The Roles of Source Credibility and Fairness in Parasocial Relationship and Product Interest. *Journal of Interactive Advertising*, 20(2), 133–147. 10.1080/15252019.2020.1769514

Zeng, B., & Gerritsen, R. (2014). What do we know about social media in tourism? A review. *Tourism Management Perspectives*, 10, 27–36. 10.1016/j.tmp.2014.01.001

Chapter 6
Exploring the Future Trends of Bleisure Tourism in Nepal

Narendra Kumar
https://orcid.org/0000-0002-3325-3448
Amity University, Noida, India

Subhadip Majumder
https://orcid.org/0000-0002-1851-2253
Silver Mountain School of Hotel Management, Kathmandu, Nepal

ABSTRACT

The purpose of this research study is to investigate the developing trend of bleisure tourism in Nepal, which is characterised by tourists who combine business and leisure activities together with their vacations. This chapter intends to provide insights into the potential growth and impact of bleisure tourism in Nepal by conducting a thorough analysis of existing trends and future projections using the information gathered from the analysis. The purpose of this chapter is to effectively harness this trend by discussing several reasons that are driving the increase of bleisure travel in the region. The research draws on current literature and statistical data to support its discussion.

INTRODUCTION

Bleisure tourism, an increasingly popular trend in travel, combines business trips with leisure activities. This approach allows business travellers to extend their stays for personal enjoyment, discovering new places and immersing themselves in

DOI: 10.4018/979-8-3693-4354-8.ch006

local culture (Lichy & McLeay, 2018; Mercan & Sandıkcı, 2024; Park et al., 2024). By striking a balance between professional obligations and recreational pursuits, bleisure tourism optimizes travellers' time away from home.

Analysing bleisure tourism in Nepal is vital as it can help the country's tourism sector cater effectively to these travellers' needs. Nepal can attract luxury travellers by understanding their interests and preferences, crafting bespoke vacation packages and experiences. This could potentially boost tourism revenue, create more jobs, and foster broader economic growth. Additionally, exploring bleisure tourism can promote lesser-known areas in Nepal beyond popular tourist spots, fostering diverse and sustainable tourism. Nepal can appeal to luxury travellers seeking unique experiences by offering packages that combine wellness retreats in rural areas with Himalayan adventures. This approach showcases the country's cultural heritage and natural beauty while supporting local communities and preserving traditional lifestyles.

Bleisure tourism also benefits Nepal's economic expansion by creating opportunities for small businesses and innovators in remote areas. Encouraging exploration of lesser-known destinations can distribute income more evenly across the country, alleviate overcrowding in tourist hotspots, and promote sustainable growth. Promoting eco-friendly practices in hotels and organizing cultural exchange events can position Nepal as a leader in ethical and environmentally conscious tourism. A comprehensive tourism development strategy can further boost the local economy while enhancing visitors' appreciation of Nepal's unique cultural and environmental heritage.

OVERVIEW OF TOURISM IN NEPAL

Nepal's multifaceted topography and culturally rich legacy position it as a coveted site for travellers seeking both adventurous escapades and immersive cultural encounters. In the context of burgeoning bleisure tourism, Nepal stands at a pivotal juncture to allure a fresh cohort of tourists inclined towards purposeful and sustainable travel engagements. Embracing principles of responsible tourism could not only distinguish Nepal from its counterparts but also foster positive ramifications on local societies and ecological ecosystems. As conscientious travellers increasingly scrutinize their impact on visited locales, Nepal finds itself in a unique position to exemplify the merits of ethical and sustainable tourism practices.

Situated amidst the Himalayan expanse, Nepal unfolds a captivating tableau of natural splendor, cultural diversity, and spiritual profundity, drawing wanderers from diverse corners of the globe. Revered as the birthplace of Lord Buddha and home to eight of the world's highest peaks, notably Mount Everest, Nepal offers an array of enticements for seekers of adventure, serenity, and spiritual enlightenment.

The tourism sector in Nepal predominantly hinges on its magnificent terrains, serving as playgrounds for adventure aficionados and nature enthusiasts alike. Trails like the Annapurna Circuit and Everest Base Camp Trek allure myriad trekkers annually, proffering breathtaking panoramas of snow-clad peaks, tranquil alpine meadows, and idyllic hamlets. Additionally, Nepal's array of national parks and wildlife reserves, such as Chitwan National Park and Bardia National Park, harbour rare and endangered fauna, rendering it a sanctuary for wildlife aficionados and conservationists.

Cultural heritage constitutes another cornerstone of Nepal's allure, underscored by UNESCO World Heritage Sites like the Kathmandu Valley, Lumbini, and Bhaktapur Durbar Square, which showcase the nation's opulent architectural, religious, and artistic heritage. The kaleidoscopic spectrum of ethnic enclaves, each enshrining its distinct customs, traditions, and festivities, enriches Nepal's cultural fabric, affording travellers an immersive odyssey into the country's living legacy. Moreover, Nepal's spiritual magnetism, stemming from its association with Hinduism and Buddhism, magnetizes pilgrims and seekers worldwide. Sacred enclaves like Pashupatinath Temple, Swayambhunath Stupa, and Lumbini, the birthplace of Lord Buddha, serve as epicentres for spiritual introspection and pilgrimage, engendering cross-cultural dialogue and comprehension. Notwithstanding its prodigious tourism potential, Nepal grapples with assorted challenges that impede the sustainable progression of its tourism sector. Inadequate infrastructural facilities, encompassing roads, airports, and lodging amenities, curtail accessibility to remote precincts and constrain the overall tourist experience. Political volatility and sporadic unrest have further compounded hurdles to tourism development, denting visitor confidence and investment inflows into the sector. Additionally, the delicate equilibrium between tourism expansion and environmental preservation remains a pressing quandary, as unchecked proliferation jeopardizes the immaculate ecosystems and biodiversity of Nepal's natural patrimony. Despite these impediments, Nepal's tourism industry evinces resilience and promise, buoyed by governmental endeavours aimed at propelling sustainable tourism practices, fortifying infrastructure, and diversifying tourism offerings. As Nepal aspires to emerge as a preeminent global tourist hub, strategic planning, collaborative stakeholder engagement, and unwavering commitment to responsible tourism ethos will be imperative in unleashing the full spectrum of economic, social, and cultural dividends accruable from tourism for the nation and its denizens.

UNDERSTANDING BLEISURE TOURISM IN NEPAL

Bleisure tourism, an amalgamation of business and leisure travel, constitutes a burgeoning trend that Nepal stands poised to leverage to attract a broader spectrum of visitors. By acknowledging the potential for travellers to extend their business commitments into leisure sojourns, Nepal can curate packages and experiences catering to both professional responsibilities and recreational pursuits. This not only augments the nation's tourism revenue but also heightens the overall visitor experience, rendering Nepal a more enticing destination for diverse traveller profiles. Embracing bleisure tourism signifies yet another avenue for Nepal to showcase its adaptability and dedication to furnishing varied and gratifying travel prospects.

Bleisure tourism, a portmanteau encompassing "business" and "leisure," denotes the phenomenon wherein travellers amalgamate business-related engagements with recreational or leisurely endeavours during their excursions. This emergent trend mirrors a blurring of demarcations between work and leisure as professionals' endeavour to optimize their travel undertakings by intertwining business obligations with personal inclinations and relaxation.

A distinguishing feature of bleisure tourism resides in its fusion of work and leisure facets within a single travel itinerary (Voll et al., 2023). Business travellers frequently elongate their stays in destination locales to partake in local attractions, pursue recreational activities, or foster familial and social connections. This amalgamation of professional commitments with leisure pursuits empowers travellers to maximize their time away from domicile, metamorphosing ostensibly work-centric excursions into enriching and enjoyable experiences.

Bleisure tourism epitomizes evolving outlooks towards travel and work-life equilibrium in today's interlinked and swiftly paced milieu. With technological innovations facilitating remote labour and flexible scheduling, professionals increasingly seek avenues to meld business travel with leisure endeavours, capitalizing on their journeys as conduits for personal growth and repose. Furthermore, the ascendancy of the gig economy and freelance employment has bolstered the prevalence of bleisure travel, as autonomous contractors and digital nomads relish the autonomy to labour from any locale and explore novel destinations at their own tempo. Discerning the motivations and behaviours of bleisure travellers is pivotal for destination marketers, hospitality purveyors, and tourism stakeholders endeavouring to cater to this burgeoning market segment. Bleisure travellers frequently harbour distinct preferences and priorities vis-à-vis purely leisure or business travellers, accentuating factors such as proximity to conveniences, accessibility to amenities, and opportunities for cultural immersion and discovery (Puerta López et al., 2023; Unger & Uriely, 2022). By tailoring offerings, amenities, and experiences to align with the needs and predilections of bleisure travellers, destinations can fortify their competitiveness and allure within this lucrative market segment. No doubt, bleisure tourism epitomizes a vibrant and evolving trend within the travel sector, emblematic of shifting attitudes towards labour, leisure, and travel. As professionals increasingly endeavour to amalgamate business and leisure elements into their travel escapades, comprehending the motivations and behaviours of bleisure travellers assumes paramount importance for destinations and tourism enterprises to adapt and flourish within an ever-evolving market milieu. By seizing the opportunities engendered by bleisure travel and proffering bespoke experiences tailored to the exigencies of this burgeoning segment, destinations can position themselves as preferred hubs for both business and leisure travellers alike.

DEFINITION AND CHARACTERISTICS OF BLEISURE TOURISM

Bleisure tourism, a neologism derived from the amalgamation of "business" and "leisure," denotes a contemporary phenomenon wherein individuals intertwine leisure activities with their business trips or extend their corporate travels for recreational purposes. This trend signifies a departure from traditional demarcations between professional duties and personal indulgences, underscoring the evolving lifestyles and priorities of modern travellers. Essentially, bleisure tourism erases the boundaries between work-related obligations and individual pursuits, affording travellers the opportunity to harmonize productivity with relaxation and exploration within a singular trip itinerary.

Several salient features distinguish bleisure tourism from conventional business or leisure travel. Firstly, bleisure travellers typically exhibit a penchant for flexibility and autonomy in orchestrating their travel itineraries (Batala & Slevitch, 2024; Caicedo-Barreth et al., 2020). They may strategically coordinate their business engagements to align with weekends or holidays, facilitating seamless transitions between work-related responsibilities and leisure pursuits.

Secondly, bleisure tourism often entails the fusion of work and leisure components within the same travel agenda. Business travellers may designate specific intervals for professional meetings, conferences, or commitments, while concurrently carving out time for sightseeing, dining, or recreational endeavours during their sojourn (Pinho & Marques, 2021). This duality of purpose enables travellers to optimize their time away from their habitual abode by striking a balance between their professional duties and personal interests.

Thirdly, bleisure travellers tend to prioritize convenience and accessibility when selecting destinations and accommodations. Proximity to business hubs, transportation facilities, and tourist attractions assumes paramount importance, as travellers endeavour to minimize transit durations and optimize their overall experience.

Furthermore, amenities and services catering to both work and leisure requisites, such as co-working spaces, fitness amenities, and concierge provisions, are highly coveted by bleisure travellers in pursuit of a seamless and expedient travel experience.

Lastly, bleisure tourism is underpinned by a yearning for enrichment and cultural immersion. Unlike their counterparts in traditional business travel, who may focus solely on work-related undertakings, bleisure travellers are driven by a desire to delve into local culture, gastronomy, and attractions, enriching their travel escapades and fostering a profound connection with the destination (Tsaur & Tsai, 2023; Unger & Uriely, 2022). Cultural excursions, guided tours, and immersive encounters furnish opportunities for bleisure travellers to unwind, rejuvenate, and forge enduring memories beyond the confines of the corporate boardroom or conference venue (Petrenko et al., 2023).

FACTORS DRIVING THE GROWTH OF BLEISURE TOURISM

Bleisure tourism, the blending of business and leisure travel, is experiencing rapid growth worldwide, fuelled by several key factors that cater to the evolving preferences and lifestyles of modern travellers. Understanding these drivers is essential for stakeholders in the tourism industry to capitalize on the opportunities presented by this burgeoning trend.

- *Flexible Work Arrangements:* One of the primary drivers of bleisure tourism is the proliferation of flexible work arrangements, including remote work, telecommuting, and flexible scheduling. As technology enables professionals to work from anywhere with an internet connection, individuals have greater freedom to combine business trips with leisure activities, extending their stays to explore new destinations or spend time with family and friends.
- *Work-Life Balance:* The pursuit of work-life balance is another factor driving the growth of bleisure tourism. With mounting pressures and demands in the workplace, individuals seek opportunities to unwind, recharge, and rejuvenate amidst their busy schedules. Bleisure travel offers a perfect solution, allowing travellers to blend work-related commitments with leisure pursuits, thereby maximizing their time away from home and fostering well-being (Ezeuduji, 2024; Miao et al., 2024).
- *Desire for Exploration and Enrichment:* Bleisure travellers are motivated by a desire for exploration and enrichment, seeking to make the most of their travel experiences by immersing themselves in local culture, cuisine, and attractions (Chung et al., 2020; Park et al., 2024). Business trips often present opportunities for travellers to discover new destinations, experience different

cultures, and broaden their horizons beyond the confines of the conference room or boardroom.

- *Technological Advancements:* Technological advancements play a crucial role in facilitating bleisure travel, providing travellers with access to real-time information, communication tools, and travel booking platforms (Batala & Slevitch, 2024; Orel, 2019). The widespread availability of smartphones, travel apps, and digital platforms enables travellers to research destinations, book accommodations, and plan leisure activities with ease, enhancing the convenience and efficiency of bleisure trips.
- *Changing Corporate Culture:* There has been a notable shift in corporate culture towards promoting employee well-being, satisfaction, and engagement. Employers increasingly recognize the benefits of allowing employees to incorporate leisure activities into business trips, acknowledging the positive impact on morale, productivity, and retention. Companies may encourage bleisure travel through flexible policies, incentives, and perks, contributing to the growth of this trend.

The growth of bleisure tourism is driven by a convergence of factors including flexible work arrangements, the pursuit of work-life balance, a desire for exploration and enrichment, technological advancements, and changing corporate culture (Sohaili et al., 2022). As these drivers continue to shape the travel preferences and behaviours of modern professionals, bleisure tourism is expected to further expand its footprint in the global tourism landscape, presenting opportunities for destinations, hospitality providers, and tourism businesses to cater to the needs and preferences of this growing segment of travellers.

BENEFITS OF INCORPORATING BLEISURE TOURISM IN DESTINATION MARKETING

Bleisure tourism, the amalgamation of business and leisure travel, has emerged as a significant trend reshaping the tourism industry (Ozdemir & Celebi, 2023). In the context of destination marketing, integrating bleisure tourism presents a range of advantages that extend beyond traditional approaches. This paper examines the multifaceted benefits of incorporating bleisure tourism into destination marketing strategies, encompassing enhanced revenue streams, prolonged visitor stays, positive brand associations, and competitive advantages.

- *Enhanced Revenue Streams*

One of the primary benefits of integrating bleisure tourism into destination marketing is the potential for enhanced revenue streams. Research by the Global Business Travel Association (GBTA) indicates that bleisure travellers tend to spend more than those on strictly business trips. By enticing business travellers to extend their stays for leisure purposes, destinations can capture additional spending on accommodations, dining, entertainment, and activities. This influx of expenditure not only benefits local businesses but also stimulates economic growth within the destination.

- Extended Length of Stay

  Moreover, incorporating bleisure tourism facilitates the extension of visitor stays, thereby maximizing the destination's tourism potential. Studies, such as those published in the Journal of Travel Research, reveal that bleisure travellers stay an average of 2.6 nights longer than those solely on business trips. This prolonged duration translates to higher occupancy rates for hotels, increased patronage for local attractions, and a more substantial overall economic impact on the destination (Chung et al., 2020). Consequently, promoting bleisure offerings becomes integral to optimizing the length and depth of visitor experiences.

- Positive Brand Association

  Cultivating positive brand associations is essential in destination marketing, and bleisure tourism offers a unique avenue to achieve this objective. By positioning a location as conducive to combining work and leisure, destinations can convey a message of versatility and vibrancy to prospective travellers. Seamless integration of professional obligations with recreational pursuits enhances the overall visitor experience, leading to heightened satisfaction and positive word-of-mouth recommendations. A destination perceived as accommodating diverse needs is more likely to establish itself as a desirable and memorable location, fostering long-term loyalty and advocacy among visitors.

- Competitive Advantage

  In an increasingly competitive tourism landscape, destinations must differentiate themselves to attract and retain travellers. Incorporating bleisure offerings into destination marketing strategies confers a distinct competitive advantage by catering to the evolving preferences of modern travellers. By highlighting the availability of leisure amenities, cultural experiences, and recreational activities alongside business infrastructure, destinations demonstrate adaptability and responsiveness to emerging trends. This comprehensive approach positions a destination as dynamic and appealing, thereby enhancing its relevance and competitiveness in the global marketplace.

Integrating bleisure tourism into destination marketing strategies offers a plethora of benefits that extend beyond traditional tourism paradigms. From diversifying revenue streams and prolonging visitor stays to fostering positive brand associations and gaining a competitive edge, embracing bleisure tourism enhances the attractiveness and sustainability of destinations. As the travel landscape continues to evolve, destinations that proactively embrace and promote bleisure offerings are poised to thrive in an increasingly dynamic and competitive marketplace.

FUTURE TRENDS OF BLEISURE TOURISM IN NEPAL

As the global prevalence of bleisure travel burgeons, Nepal is poised to witness a surge in demand for accommodations, dining venues, and recreational pursuits tailored to this amalgamated form of travel. To remain competitive and entice bleisure travellers, businesses in Nepal may necessitate adapting their offerings to accommodate the idiosyncratic requisites of this market segment. Furthermore, with the proliferation of flexible work arrangements and remote work options by numerous companies, the prospects for bleisure travel are anticipated to proliferate, rendering Nepal an even more enticing destination for individuals seeking to amalgamate work commitments with leisure activities in a singular trip. On the whole, the outlook for bleisure tourism in Nepal appears auspicious, harbouring the potential to yield substantial economic dividends for the nation's tourism sector. Bleisure tourism, the fusion of business and leisure travel, emerges as a notable trend poised to leave an indelible mark on Nepal's tourism panorama. As the country continues to fortify its infrastructure and allure business travellers, an opportune moment arises to leverage the burgeoning trend of bleisure tourism. This study scrutinizes the future trajectory of bleisure tourism in Nepal, elucidating the potential catalysts, impediments, and opportunities that will delineate its trajectory in the forthcoming years.

Nepal has long been lauded for its opulent cultural heritage, awe-inspiring landscapes, and vivacious tourism offerings. Historically, the nation has magnetized a steady stream of leisure travellers in pursuit of adventure, spiritual enlightenment, and natural splendour. Nonetheless, in recent years, Nepal has also emerged as an emergent hub for business travellers, particularly in sectors such as technology, finance, and development aid. This confluence of business and leisure travel sets the stage for the ascendancy of bleisure tourism in Nepal.

Several factors are poised to propel the proliferation of bleisure tourism in Nepal in the future. Firstly, the country's strategic positioning amid major economic epicentres in Asia, such as India and China, positions it as a compelling destination for business travellers. Additionally, Nepal's burgeoning infrastructure, encompassing enhanced airports, road networks, and telecommunications, augments its allure as a conducive milieu for conducting business endeavours. Moreover, the kaleidoscopic array of leisure offerings, spanning trekking, wildlife safaris, and cultural odysseys, furnishes ample opportunities for business travellers to elongate their stays and immerse themselves in the country's attractions.

Notwithstanding the sanguine prospects, bleisure tourism in Nepal confronts certain hurdles. One such challenge pertains to the imperative for sustained investment in infrastructure development to guarantee seamless connectivity and accessibility across the nation. Additionally, there exists a need for targeted marketing and promotional endeavours to heighten awareness regarding Nepal's potential as a bleisure haven among business travellers. However, these challenges engender prospects for synergistic collaboration between the government, private sector, and tourism stakeholders to foster sustainable growth in bleisure tourism.

Looking ahead, several nascent trends are poised to sculpt the future of bleisure tourism in Nepal. These encompass the ascendancy of digital nomadism; wherein remote workers intertwine business pursuits with travel experiences. Nepal's picturesque vistas, affordable cost of living, and vibrant cultural tapestry position it as an enticing destination for digital nomads in quest of work-life equilibrium. Furthermore, the assimilation of sustainability and responsible tourism practices into bleisure offerings is anticipated to garner traction, consonant with burgeoning consumer preferences for eco-conscious travel experiences.

The future of bleisure tourism in Nepal beckons significant promise, propelled by factors such as strategic positioning, infrastructure amelioration, and diverse leisure offerings. Whilst challenges loom, they proffer opportunities for collaborative and innovative endeavours within the tourism sector. By capitalizing on emergent trends such as digital nomadism and sustainable tourism, Nepal can carve a niche for itself as a preeminent bleisure destination in the region. As the nation evolves and adapts to shifting traveller predilections, bleisure tourism stands poised to exert a pivotal influence on shaping Nepal's tourism landscape in the years ahead.

POTENTIAL GROWTH OF BLEISURE TOURISM IN NEPAL

Nepal, renowned for its majestic Himalayan mountains, rich cultural heritage, and vibrant traditions, has traditionally attracted leisure travellers. However, recent developments, including the rise of business hubs and enhanced infrastructure, are facilitating the emergence of bleisure tourism in the country. This study explores the potential expansion of bleisure tourism in Nepal, examining the driving factors, obstacles, and opportunities involved.

Nepal's strategic location between significant economic centres like India and China positions it favourably for business travel. As Kathmandu, the capital, evolves into a regional business centre, an increasing number of professionals visit for conferences, meetings, and investment prospects. This influx presents an opportunity for Nepal to promote its leisure activities, encouraging visitors to extend their stays for recreational purposes and thereby fostering bleisure tourism.

The country's diverse leisure options, from Himalayan trekking to cultural exploration, provide ample opportunities for blending work with leisure. Adventure activities such as trekking to Everest Base Camp or rafting in the Trishuli River can entice professionals to extend their stays. Moreover, Nepal's cultural heritage sites, including Bhaktapur Durbar Square and Lumbini, offer immersive experiences for bleisure travellers seeking cultural enrichment.

Improvements in infrastructure and connectivity are further facilitating the growth of bleisure tourism in Nepal. Investments in airports, roads, and telecommunications are enhancing accessibility across the country, making it easier for business travellers to explore leisure activities during their stays.

Despite the promising outlook, bleisure tourism in Nepal faces challenges, including the need for targeted marketing and adequate accommodations. However, these challenges also present opportunities for collaboration between the government, private sector, and tourism stakeholders to develop tailored bleisure packages. Nepal is well-positioned to experience significant growth in bleisure tourism due to its strategic location, diverse leisure offerings, and improving infrastructure. By leveraging these strengths and addressing key challenges, Nepal can enhance its appeal as a destination for both business and leisure travellers, tapping into the growing trend of combining work and leisure travel.

OPPORTUNITIES FOR BUSINESSES AND DESTINATIONS TO CATER TO BLEISURE TRAVELLERS

Bleisure tourism represents a burgeoning opportunity for businesses and destinations in Nepal to leverage the amalgamation of business and leisure travel. Tailoring experiences and services to meet the specific needs and desires of bleisure travellers can enhance the competitiveness and allure of businesses and destinations in the market. This segment delves into the diverse opportunities available for businesses and destinations to cater to bleisure travellers in Nepal.

One prominent opportunity for businesses in Nepal is the provision of customized accommodation options tailored to the distinctive requirements of bleisure travellers. This entails offering adaptable booking arrangements, such as extended stays or weekend packages, to accommodate leisure pursuits alongside professional commitments. Moreover, businesses can enrich the leisure aspect of their accommodations by furnishing amenities like wellness facilities, recreational activities, and cultural experiences, facilitating bleisure travellers in unwinding and exploring the locale during their sojourn.

Businesses and destinations in Nepal can also seize the opportunity to amalgamate business and leisure facilities to cater to the multifaceted needs of bleisure travellers. For instance, hotels and conference centres can collaborate with local tour operators to furnish customizable leisure packages that complement business engagements, encompassing team-building activities, sightseeing excursions, or gastronomic escapades. By ensuring seamless transitions between work and leisure endeavours, businesses can heighten the overall satisfaction of bleisure travellers and distinguish themselves within the market.

Nepal's opulent cultural heritage and diverse array of experiential offerings present abundant opportunities for businesses and destinations to entice bleisure travellers. Collabourating with local artisans, cultural entities, and heritage sites enables businesses to curate authentic cultural experiences, such as traditional craft workshops, folk performances, or heritage strolls, immersing bleisure travellers in the local ethos. Furthermore, businesses can tap into the burgeoning demand for experiential travel by proffering unique activities, such as wildlife safaris, mountain treks, or spiritual retreats, showcasing Nepal's natural splendour and adventurous ethos.

Given the ascendancy of remote work and digital nomadism, businesses and destinations in Nepal can harness the escalating demand for digital connectivity and remote workspaces among bleisure travellers. Furnishing high-speed internet access, co-working venues, and business support amenities enables businesses to attract bleisure travellers seeking to amalgamate work with leisure in inspiring locales like Nepal. Additionally, destinations can position themselves as optimal hubs for remote work and digital nomadism, leveraging Nepal's scenic grandeur, reasonable cost of living, and vibrant culture to captivate this burgeoning cohort of bleisure travellers.

CHALLENGES IN IMPLEMENTING BLEISURE TOURISM STRATEGIES

Implementing bleisure tourism strategies in Nepal presents several challenges that businesses and destinations must address to maximize the potential of this emerging trend. Below are some of the key challenges:

- *Limited Awareness and Promotion:* One of the primary challenges in implementing bleisure tourism strategies in Nepal is the limited awareness and promotion of the concept among both businesses and travellers. Many businesses may not be familiar with the concept of bleisure tourism or may not understand how to tailor their offerings to cater to bleisure travellers. Similarly, travellers may not be aware of Nepal's potential as a bleisure destination or may not consider extending their business trips for leisure purposes. Therefore, there is a need for targeted marketing and promotional efforts to raise awareness about bleisure tourism and highlight the unique attractions and experiences that Nepal has to offer.
- *Infrastructure and Connectivity:* Nepal's infrastructure and connectivity pose significant challenges to the implementation of bleisure tourism strategies. While major cities like Kathmandu may have adequate infrastructure to support business activities, rural areas and remote destinations may lack essential facilities and services required to cater to bleisure travellers. Additionally, transportation infrastructure, including roads, airports, and public transportation, may be inadequate or unreliable, making it difficult for bleisure travellers to explore different regions of the country. Improving infrastructure and connectivity is crucial to enhancing the accessibility and appeal of Nepal as a bleisure destination.
- *Seasonal Variability:* Nepal's tourism industry is highly seasonal, with peak tourist seasons coinciding with favourable weather conditions for trekking and outdoor activities. However, business travel may not always align with peak tourist seasons, leading to challenges in balancing demand for business and leisure services throughout the year. Additionally, seasonal variability in weather conditions, such as monsoon rains and harsh winters, can impact the feasibility of outdoor leisure activities and limit the options available to bleisure travellers. Strategies to diversify tourism offerings and attract visitors year-round are essential to overcome this challenge.
- *Regulatory and Legal Frameworks:* Regulatory and legal frameworks in Nepal may present challenges to the implementation of bleisure tourism strategies, particularly for businesses seeking to offer integrated business and leisure services. Licensing requirements, taxation policies, and labour reg-

ulations may differ for businesses operating in the tourism, hospitality, and leisure sectors, creating administrative burdens and compliance challenges. Streamlining regulatory processes and fostering collaboration between government agencies and private sector stakeholders are essential to create an enabling environment for bleisure tourism development.

- *Cultural Sensitivities and Social Norms:* Nepal's rich cultural heritage and diverse traditions add to its appeal as a tourism destination, but they also present challenges in terms of cultural sensitivities and social norms. Business travellers and leisure tourists may have different expectations and preferences when it comes to cultural experiences, dining options, and social interactions. Balancing the need to respect local customs and traditions with the desire to provide memorable experiences for bleisure travellers requires careful consideration and cultural competency. Training programs and cultural awareness initiatives can help businesses and destinations navigate these challenges effectively. While bleisure tourism holds significant potential for Nepal's tourism industry, implementing effective strategies requires addressing various challenges related to awareness and promotion, infrastructure and connectivity, seasonal variability, regulatory frameworks, and cultural sensitivities. By overcoming these challenges and leveraging Nepal's unique attractions and experiences, businesses and destinations can capitalize on the growing demand for bleisure travel and enhance the overall visitor experience.

STRATEGIES FOR PROMOTING BLEISURE TOURISM IN NEPAL

Some potential strategies for promoting bleisure tourism in Nepal could include partnering with local businesses to offer special packages that cater to the needs of bleisure travellers, such as discounted rates on accommodation and transportation. Additionally, marketing campaigns targeted towards business travellers could highlight the unique cultural experiences and outdoor activities that Nepal has to offer, enticing them to extend their stay for leisure purposes. By focusing on creating a welcoming and inclusive environment for bleisure travellers, Nepal can position itself as a top choice for those looking to combine work and play in one unforgettable trip.

MARKETING STRATEGIES TO ATTRACT BLEISURE TRAVELLERS

In recent times, the phenomenon of bleisure travel has garnered considerable attention, presenting an unprecedented opportunity for destinations such as Nepal to attract a novel cohort of travellers who seamlessly integrate business and leisure pursuits during their journeys. To capitalize on this trend, adept marketing strategies are imperative to heighten awareness and promote Nepal as an exemplary bleisure destination. This segment elucidates diverse marketing approaches that businesses and destinations can adopt to entice bleisure travellers to Nepal.

Digital marketing campaigns assume paramount importance in reaching and engaging bleisure travellers, who frequently demonstrate adeptness with technology and rely extensively on digital platforms for trip planning and reservation. Through the utilization of social media platforms, search engine optimization (SEO), and precisely targeted online advertisements, businesses and destinations can spotlight Nepal's distinctive allure, cultural encounters, and recreational offerings to bleisure travellers. Compelling content comprising captivating imagery, immersive videos, and authentic narratives serves to captivate the interest of bleisure travellers and motivate them to prolong their stays in Nepal for leisure pursuits.

The provision of integrated business and leisure packages constitutes another efficacious marketing strategy to allure bleisure travellers to Nepal. By forging collaborations with hotels, conference centres, tour operators, and local attractions, businesses can curate bespoke packages that seamlessly blend business engagements with leisurely pursuits such as sightseeing tours, adventure treks, or cultural immersions. Emphasizing the convenience and value proposition of these packages, along with the seamless transition between professional and leisure experiences, holds appeal for bleisure travellers seeking to optimize their time and experiences in Nepal.

Nepal boasts a plethora of distinctive encounters, ranging from Himalayan treks to exploration of ancient temples and participation in cultural festivities. Marketing these experiences as integral components of the bleisure travel proposition can set Nepal apart from other destinations and entice bleisure travellers in search of authentic and indelible experiences. Employing storytelling and experiential marketing techniques facilitates the showcasing of Nepal's cultural heritage, natural landscapes, and adventurous pursuits, thereby enticing bleisure travellers to extend their stays and uncover the nation's hidden treasures.

Forging partnerships with corporate entities and offering incentives for bleisure travel can serve as an effective marketing tactic to attract business travellers to Nepal. Businesses can collabourate with corporations to promote bleisure travel among employees through the provision of discounts on leisure activities, complimentary upgrades, or exclusive access to cultural events and experiences. Moreover, businesses can extend incentives such as loyalty rewards, corporate discounts, or flexible booking options to incentivize bleisure travellers to select Nepal as their preferred destination for amalgamating business and leisure travel.

Targeted advertising and adept public relations endeavours are imperative for reaching and influencing bleisure travellers actively seeking destinations tailored to their unique preferences and needs. Businesses and destinations can leverage trade publications, industry gatherings, and travel media platforms to showcase Nepal's bleisure offerings and forge alliances with key stakeholders. Engaging travel influencers, hosting familiarization journeys, and participating in industry exhibitions represent effective strategies for generating buzz and enhancing awareness regarding Nepal as a bleisure destination.

Prudent marketing strategies are indispensable for attracting bleisure travellers to Nepal and positioning the nation as a quintessential destination for combining business and leisure travel. Through the leveraging of digital marketing campaigns, integrated business and leisure packages, distinctive experiences, corporate partnerships, targeted advertising, and public relations endeavours, businesses and destinations can underscore Nepal's diverse attractions and encounters, thereby capturing the interest of bleisure travellers in pursuit of authentic and enriching travel experiences. As the trajectory of bleisure travel continues to ascend, investment in innovative marketing strategies stands pivotal for Nepal to capitalize on this lucrative market segment and propel sustainable tourism growth.

COLLABORATION BETWEEN TOURISM STAKEHOLDERS TO PROMOTE BLEISURE TOURISM

Promoting bleisure tourism in Nepal requires a concerted effort and collaboration among various stakeholders within the tourism industry. Firstly, governmental bodies play a pivotal role in fostering an environment conducive to bleisure travel. This involves creating policies and regulations that support both business and leisure activities, such as streamlined visa processes and investment in infrastructure that caters to the needs of modern business travellers while also preserving the country's natural and cultural assets.

Secondly, collaboration with hospitality providers is essential for offering seamless experiences to bleisure travellers (Mercan & Sandıkcı, 2024). Hotels, resorts, and other accommodation providers can adapt their offerings to meet the needs of this niche market segment by providing amenities and services that cater to both work and leisure, such as conference facilities, high-speed internet, and recreational activities.

Thirdly, travel agencies and tour operators can play a crucial role in promoting and facilitating bleisure travel in Nepal. By offering integrated packages that combine business meetings or conferences with leisure activities such as trekking, sightseeing, or cultural experiences, they can appeal to a wider range of travellers and enhance the overall experience.

Furthermore, collaboration with local communities is vital for promoting authentic and immersive experiences for bleisure travellers. Community-based tourism initiatives can provide opportunities for visitors to engage with local culture, traditions, and lifestyles, thereby enriching their travel experiences and contributing to the sustainable development of tourism destinations. Effective collaboration between tourism stakeholders, including governmental bodies, hospitality providers, travel agencies, and local communities, is essential for promoting bleisure tourism in Nepal. By working together, these stakeholders can create a holistic and compelling offering that caters to the needs and preferences of bleisure travellers, ultimately contributing to the growth and sustainability of Nepal's tourism industry.

DEVELOPMENT OF INFRASTRUCTURE AND SERVICES TO CATER TO BLEISURE TRAVELLERS

In order to successfully cater to bleisure travellers in Nepal, it is imperative to develop infrastructure and services that seamlessly blend business and leisure aspects of travel. Firstly, enhancing transportation infrastructure is key to facilitating smooth travel experiences for bleisure travellers. This involves improving connectivity between major business hubs and popular leisure destinations, as well as upgrading transportation modes such as airports, roads, and public transit systems to ensure convenient access to both urban centres and recreational areas.

Secondly, investing in accommodation options that cater to the diverse needs of bleisure travellers is essential. This includes providing a range of lodging choices, from upscale hotels with business facilities to boutique accommodations that offer unique leisure experiences. Additionally, incorporating amenities such as co-working spaces, high-speed internet, and wellness facilities allows bleisure travellers to seamlessly transition between work and relaxation during their stay.

Moreover, developing entertainment and recreational facilities that showcase Nepal's rich cultural heritage and natural beauty is crucial for enhancing the leisure aspect of bleisure travel. This can involve creating leisure zones within urban centres that offer opportunities for shopping, dining, and entertainment, as well as promoting outdoor activities such as hiking, wildlife safaris, and cultural tours in Nepal's scenic landscapes.

Furthermore, investing in technology and digital infrastructure can greatly enhance the bleisure travel experience in Nepal. This includes providing reliable internet connectivity, mobile apps for booking accommodations and activities, and digital platforms for remote work and virtual meetings. Embracing technological innovations not only improves the efficiency of business activities but also enables bleisure travellers to explore and enjoy the destination to the fullest.

The development of infrastructure and services tailored to the needs of bleisure travellers is essential for positioning Nepal as a competitive destination in the global tourism market. By investing in transportation, accommodation, leisure, and technology infrastructure, Nepal can create a compelling offering that attracts a growing number of travellers seeking to blend business and leisure experiences in this culturally rich and naturally diverse destination.

CASE STUDIES

Ten potential case studies of bleisure tourism initiatives in Nepal along with general descriptions that one can further research:

- *Kathmandu Valley Cultural Tour Packages:* Many travel agencies in Nepal offer bleisure packages combining business trips with cultural tours around the Kathmandu Valley. These packages typically include visits to UNESCO World Heritage Sites like Boudhanath Stupa, Pashupatinath Temple, and Bhaktapur Durbar Square.
- *Adventure Sports Integration:* Companies like Himalayan River Operator offer tailored bleisure packages that include white-water rafting or trekking experiences alongside business meetings or conferences. These initiatives showcase Nepal's adventure tourism potential while catering to business travellers.
- *Sustainable Tourism Initiatives in Pokhara:* Some hotels and resorts in Pokhara, a popular tourist destination, have initiated bleisure packages that include eco-friendly activities like nature walks, bird watching, or participation in community-based tourism projects alongside business events.
- *Yoga and Wellness Retreats in the Himalayas:* Several wellness centres and resorts in Nepal's Himalayan region offer bleisure opportunities combining business events with yoga and meditation retreats. These initiatives cater to the growing demand for wellness tourism among business travellers.
- *Corporate Social Responsibility (CSR) Projects in Rural Nepal:* Some corporations partner with local NGOs in Nepal to organize bleisure trips that include volunteering opportunities in rural communities. These initiatives

focus on CSR activities such as building schools, health camps, or promoting sustainable agriculture.

- *Mount Everest Base Camp Trekking Packages:* Travel agencies offer bleisure packages combining business meetings in Kathmandu with trekking adventures to the Everest Base Camp. These initiatives appeal to adventurous business travellers seeking unique experiences in Nepal.
- *Culinary Tours and Cooking Classes:* Hotels and cooking schools in Kathmandu and other cities offer bleisure packages that include cooking classes and culinary tours alongside business events. These initiatives promote Nepali cuisine and cultural exchange among business travellers.
- *Art and Handicraft Workshops in Bhaktapur:* Some boutique hotels and cultural centres in Bhaktapur organize bleisure packages combining business seminars with art and handicraft workshops. These initiatives showcase Nepal's rich cultural heritage and traditional craftsmanship.
- *Environmental Conservation Projects in Chitwan National Park:* Eco-lodges and conservation organizations in Chitwan National Park offer bleisure opportunities combining business conferences with wildlife conservation activities such as jungle safaris, bird watching, or tree planting.
- *Medical Tourism and Wellness Retreats in Kathmandu:* Hospitals and wellness centres in Kathmandu offer bleisure packages combining medical treatments or wellness programs with business meetings or conferences. These initiatives cater to business travellers seeking healthcare services or rejuvenation therapies (Kumar & Sharma, 2019).

CONCLUSION

By studying successful case studies and learning from the experiences of other destinations, Nepal can develop a comprehensive strategy to attract and cater to bleisure travellers. With the right approach and collaboration, Nepal has the opportunity to position itself as a top bleisure travel destination in the Asia-Pacific region, offering a unique blend of business and leisure experiences for visitors to enjoy. Overall, incorporating bleisure tourism into Nepal's tourism industry has the potential to drive economic growth, increase visitor numbers, and diversify the types of travellers coming to the country. By understanding the needs and preferences of bleisure travellers, Nepal can tailor its offerings to cater to this market segment effectively. This strategic approach will not only benefit the tourism industry but also help in showcasing Nepal as a versatile destination that appeals to a wide range of travellers. By capitalizing on the bleisure trend, Nepal can further establish itself as a competitive player in the global tourism market. Nepal Future research on bleisure tourism in Nepal could focus on understanding the specific activities and amenities that bleisure travellers are seeking during their trips. This information can help tourism authorities and businesses in Nepal better tailor their offerings to meet the needs of this growing market segment. Additionally, research could explore the impact of bleisure travel on local economies and communities, providing valuable insights for sustainable tourism development in the region. Overall, further studies on bleisure tourism in Nepal can provide valuable data and insights to support the growth and success of this market segment in the country.

REFERENCES

Batala, B., & Slevitch, L. (2024). Keeping two balls in the air: The bleisure travel experience. *Annals of Tourism Research Empirical Insights*, 5(1), 100115. 10.1016/j.annale.2023.100115

Caicedo-Barreth, A., Pavón, E. S., & Santos, L. L. (2020). Competitiveness of Guayaquil towards bleisure tourism. *European Journal of Tourism. Hospitality and Recreation*, 10(2), 118–133. 10.2478/ejthr-2020-0010

Chung, J. Y., Choi, Y. K., Yoo, B. K., & Kim, S. H. (2020). Bleisure tourism experience chain: Implications for destination marketing. *Asia Pacific Journal of Tourism Research*, 25(3), 300–310. 10.1080/10941665.2019.1708760

Ezeuduji, I. O. (2024). Bleisure Travel Reimagined: Implications for Research. *International Conference on Tourism Research, 7*(1), 2–9. 10.34190/ictr.7.1.2194

Kumar, N., & Sharma, S. (2019). Are they really happy? Insights into the Medical Tourists' Satisfaction in Delhi Hospitals. *African Journal of Hospitality, Tourism and Leisure*, 8(4). www.ajhtl.com

Lichy, J., & McLeay, F. (2018). Bleisure: Motivations and typologies. *Journal of Travel & Tourism Marketing*, 35(4), 517–530. 10.1080/10548408.2017.1364206

Mercan, R., & Sandıkcı, M. (2024). Bleisure Tourism: Business and Leisure Together. In *Future Tourism Trends Volume 1* (pp. 3–15). Emerald Publishing Limited. 10.1108/978-1-83753-244-520241001

Miao, L., Yang, F. X., Im, J., & Zhang, Q. (2024). Flexwork and flextravel. *Annals of Tourism Research*, 106, 103763. 10.1016/j.annals.2024.103763

Orel, M. (2019). Coworking environments and digital nomadism: Balancing work and leisure whilst on the move. *World Leisure Journal*, 61(3), 215–227. 10.1080/16078055.2019.1639275

Ozdemir, G., & Celebi, D. (2023). Bleisure trends: Combining business and leisure travel. *Routledge Handbook of Trends and Issues in Global Tourism Supply and Demand*, 411–420. https://doi.org/10.4324/9781003260790-41/BLEISURE-TRENDS-GOKCE-OZDEMIR-DUYGU-CELEBI

Park, S., Lehto, X., & Kang, J. (2024). Balancing Work and Leisure: Unraveling Constraints on Work-Leisure Integration in Bleisure Travel. *International Journal of Hospitality & Tourism Administration*, 1–27. 10.1080/15256480.2024.2344226

Petrenko, A., Ekinil, G., & Provotorina, V. (2023). Organization of bleisure-tourists service as a factor of sustainable development of the tourism sector of the Rostov region. *E3S Web of Conferences, 381*, 01084. 10.1051/e3sconf/202338101084

Pinho, M., & Marques, J. (2021). The bleisure tourism trend and the potential for this business-leisure symbiosis in Porto. *Journal of Convention & Event Tourism*, 22(4), 346–362. 10.1080/15470148.2021.1905575

Puerta López, M. E., Pindado Martínez, J., & González Alvarado, T. E. (2023). The resilience of corporate tourism: Bleisure, digitalization, and sustainability. *Mercados y Negocios*, 2023(48), 53–74. 10.32870/myn.vi48.7679

Sohaili, N., Aminudin, N., & Amir, A. (2022). Exploring Items for Measuring Behavioural Intention among Bleisure in Malaysia: An Exploratory Factor Analysis. *Article in International Journal of Academic Research in Business and Social Sciences*. 10.6007/IJARBSS/v12-i11/15164

Tsaur, S. H., & Tsai, C. H. (2023). Bleisure travel experience: Scale development and validation. *Journal of Travel & Tourism Marketing*, 40(1), 21–37. 10.1080/10548408.2023.2199773

Unger, O., & Uriely, N. (2022). The bleisure memories of business travelers. *Annals of Tourism Research*, 97, 103497. 10.1016/j.annals.2022.103497

Voll, K., Gauger, F., & Pfnür, A. (2023). Work from anywhere: traditional workation, coworkation and workation retreats: a conceptual review. *World Leisure Journal*, 65(2), 150–174. 10.1080/16078055.2022.2134199

Walia, S., Kour, P., Choudhary, P., & Jasrotia, A. (2023). COVID-19 and the bleisure travellers: An investigation on the aftermaths and future implications. *Tourism Recreation Research*, 48(5), 657–667. 10.1080/02508281.2021.1946653

Chapter 7
Destination Marketing Within the Scope of Bleisure Tourism

Tuğçe Merve Inak Özberk
https://orcid.org/0000-0002-7642-346X
Mugla Sıtkı Kocman University, Turkey

Levent Karadağ
https://orcid.org/0000-0002-0932-8315
Mugla Sıtkı Kocman University, Turkey

ABSTRACT

In this context, destination marketing and development strategies are of critical importance to effectively leverage the potential of bleisure tourism. Effectively promoting tourist attractions in different regions of the world and developing activities that can attract bleisure tourists can enhance the country's competitiveness in this field. The aim of this study is to focus on the growth of bleisure tourism in Turkey and examine destination marketing and development strategies along with local opportunities. While evaluating the opportunities Turkey offers for bleisure tourism, the study also discusses the sector's future growth potential. It examines how Turkey is preparing to become more competitive in bleisure tourism and provides insights into the impact of this trend on the country's tourism industry. In this context, the study aims to make a significant contribution to the growth of bleisure tourism in Turkey and aims to provide practical guidance to researchers, businesses, and tourism professionals.

DOI: 10.4018/979-8-3693-4354-8.ch007

INTRODUCTION

In the last century, tourism has evolved significantly from its original form into a modern structure, becoming a perceived and consumed service. Tourists have reached a broad network of services that not only meet their curiosity, rest, and entertainment expectations but also include intensive business activities. The industrialization process has led to significant changes in the types of tourism, the number of people traveling, and the diversification of transportation means. Particularly, the recognition of social rights has enabled the working class to use their leisure time for travel and relaxation. Globalization and advancements in technology have facilitated easy access for tourists to their desired destinations, contributing to the rapid development of tourism in all areas.

The tourism industry is increasingly gaining importance worldwide. Among its various components, destination marketing is a critical factor influencing tourists' decisions to visit a particular region. In recent years, a phenomenon known as "bleisure" tourism, arising from the combination of business travel and leisure tourism, has been observed (Dragomir et al., 2021). Bleisure tourism refers to the tendency to include leisure activities during business trips and this emerging trend significantly impacts destination marketing strategies (Chung et al., 2020).

Bleisure tourism emerges as a combination of business and leisure travel, allowing tourists to spend their extra time during business trips on vacations or engaging in different activities. Various factors contribute to the emergence of this phenomenon. For example, digital nomads like Generation Y take advantage of technological developments enabling flexible work schedules and mobility, turning their business trips into holiday opportunities. Additionally, individuals seeking to maintain a balance between work and personal life are influenced by the appeal of bleisure tourism (Batala & Slevitch, 2024).

Key features of bleisure tourism include a balance between work and leisure, flexibility, and innovation and exploration (Lichy & Mcleay, 2018). Bleisure tourists aim to combine their business trips with leisure activities to both fulfill their work obligations and find relaxation and enjoyment opportunities. Achieving this balance helps improve both their work performance and personal satisfaction. Furthermore, bleisure tourists seek flexibility in their travel plans, making it easier to transition between work and leisure. Flexible travel plans make their travel experiences more enjoyable. Innovation and exploration refer to bleisure tourists' desire to see new places and experience different cultures. By turning business trips into opportunities, they explore the tourist and cultural activities of destinations during their non-business hours.

LEISURE

The word "Leisure" is derived from the Latin word "Licer," which means to permit or to be permitted (Cordes & Ibrahim, 2003). This term, known as "Leisure" in English (Torkildsen, 1999), is actually a result of good motivation, self-efficacy, engagement in activities, and satisfaction (Chen et al., 2013). According to Herbert (1988), leisure is the time when an individual engages in activities freely and voluntarily according to their own choices.

Leisure refers to the time when we are not busy or working, and it excludes biological or essential social needs (such as eating, drinking, sleeping, shopping, school visits, etc.). It is the period during which we freely decide how to use our time (Brightbill, 1960). After work, commuting, sleeping, and necessary household chores, the remaining time that can be used voluntarily is defined as leisure time (Tribe, 2004).

Leisure time is the period after fulfilling one's professional, familial, and social duties, during which individuals engage in activities such as relaxation, entertainment, skill development, and voluntary participation in social life (Argan, 2013)

The concept of leisure has been discussed throughout history because it offers opportunities for self-development and social inclusion (Torkildsen, 2012). Studies also indicate that the positive use of leisure time contributes to self-fulfillment and mental health (Passmore & French, 2001).

In response to the stresses and challenges of daily life, individuals often engage in leisure activities to feel better, and one of these activities is going on vacation. Relaxation is a primary motivation for tourists (Seabra et al., 2014)

Due to the broad scope of the concept of leisure, it has been categorized from different perspectives. For example, Jensen and Guthrie (2006) classified leisure time into four categories: daily, weekly, annual, and retirement. Hazar (2003) examined leisure based on its purpose: sports, creative, social, and touristic leisure time. Similarly, Torkildsen (2005) argued that categorizing leisure time is beneficial. Torkildsen (2012) further divided leisure into four main categories: leisure as time, leisure as activity, leisure as recreation, and leisure as a lifestyle.

BUSINESS (TRAVEL) TOURISM

Business tourism, or business travel, is a type of travel and tourism that arises from businesspeople conducting business activities away from their place of residence. Types of business-related tourism can be categorized into conference and meeting tourism as well as trade fair tourism (TURSAB, 2024). Business travel involves visits made by employees outside their place of residence for work-related purposes (Aguilera, 2008). Business and commercial travel aims both to discover and procure resources for production and to reach target markets for the trade of produced goods in a competitive global market (Hazar, 2003).

In a world where distances are shrinking, companies are increasingly striving to integrate their services with the global market and maintain this integration. Consequently, business travel to strengthen ties with the world is becoming increasingly important for companies. The time and budgets allocated for these travels are now more significant. According to data published by Statista, business travel expenditures have increased by six to seven percent annually since 2015 (HIS Global, 2020).

Table 1. Visitor Numbers Departing by Purpose of Visit

Year	Total Tourist	Arrivals Business Travel (conferences, meetings, assignments, etc.)
2019	51.860.042	2.096.803
2020	15.826.266	702.027
2021	29.357.463	1.269.750
2022	51.369.026	1.694.697
2023	57.077.440	1.843.800

Kaynak: TUİK, 2024.

Upon examining Table 1, we observe significant changes in the number of tourists visiting Turkey for various purposes over the past five years. Prior to the pandemic, the number of tourists exceeded 50 million, but during the pandemic, this figure dropped to nearly a third of that number, and has since returned to its pre-pandemic levels. These data illustrate how Turkey's tourism sector was impacted by the pandemic and the recovery process it underwent. A similar trend is observed in the number of tourists traveling for business purposes. Before the pandemic, this number exceeded 2 million, but experienced a significant decline during the pandemic and subsequently showed an increase post-pandemic. This underscores the importance of business travel in the tourism sector. Business travelers, particularly those attending meetings, conferences, and short-term assignments, prefer Turkey. These travelers may also wish to take a vacation or explore the destination after their business trips. This situation highlights the importance of making destinations that cater to business travelers equally appealing for vacation purposes.

In the post-pandemic period, the increasing popularity of bleisure (business and leisure) travel is noteworthy. Business travelers often tend to extend their trips for vacation purposes. This necessitates marketing destinations in a way that integrates both business and leisure travel. For instance, offering leisure facilities near convention centers can encourage tourists to extend their stay for leisure purposes after their business commitments.

The pre- and post-pandemic data in Table 1 are crucial for understanding the dynamics of the tourism sector. The decline during the pandemic demonstrates the resilience and recovery capacity of the tourism sector. The recovery in business travel data indicates that Turkey remains an attractive destination for business tourism. This suggests that destination marketing strategies should be revised to adapt to the post-pandemic era.

Furthermore, according to the 2019 report of the United Nations World Tourism Organization (UNWTO), 11% of international tourism participants traveled for business reasons. Business tourism can take various forms: individual business trips, group trips, meetings, incentives, conventions, exhibitions (MICE), team-building, and educational trips, among others. The classification of business tourism, as generally outlined by Nicula and Elena (2014), includes:

- Individual business trips, which are common across many professional fields and involve individuals traveling outside their city for work-related purposes.
- Meeting and conference tourism, which encompasses events organized by companies or associations to facilitate communication among employees, clients, suppliers, shareholders, or other stakeholders.
- Trade fairs and exhibitions, typically organized for product presentations.
- Incentive trips, which are rewards given to employees for outstanding performance.
- Corporate events, which are activities organized by companies to enhance business relationships with their most valuable clients or potential customers.

LEISURE, BUSINESS TRAVEL, AND TOURISM RELATIONSHIP

While in ancient Greece, the concept of leisure was associated with universal values such as goodness, truth, and knowledge (Juniu, 2000), in modern times, the notion of leisure has become closely intertwined with tourism. Examination of the definitions of leisure and tourism demonstrates the interconnectedness of these experiences (Netto, 2009).

Particularly since the 18th century, significant changes have occurred in the realm of work and employment. During this period, leisure time was often perceived as idleness. Concepts like idleness, spending, and aimlessness began to be viewed as sinful. Work, saving, renouncing pleasure, and postponing enjoyment became associated with divine qualities. Additionally, there was a significant increase in working hours, with the emphasis shifting towards increasing production rather than considering workers' rights. Changes also emerged in non-work-related social processes during this period. With the aim of sustaining and increasing production, economic rewards began to be supplemented with social rewards. Consequently, economic reward began to provide workers with the ability to purchase leisure time and pleasure (Juniu, 2000).

At the intersection of the concepts of leisure and tourism lies the notion of recreation. Meyer et al. (1969) define recreation as voluntary participation in physical, mental, and emotional activities during times exempt from obligations. Recreation encompasses activities in which individuals actively or passively engage according to their own desires (Lu & Hu, 2005). In essence, recreation is an experience of renewal, escape from daily routine, revitalization, and change (Jensen & Guthrie, 2006).

Recreational activities can be classified in various ways, including by place, time, type of action, and mode of execution; they can be individual, physical, mental, therapeutic, or purpose-driven. Each recreational activity's category varies according to the individual's expectations and mode of participation. These activities are also classified based on their purposes and functions. They may serve purposes such as relaxation, cultural engagement, social interaction, sports, tourism, and artistic expression (Mull et al., 1997).

Recreational activities, whether active or passive, group or individual, encompass sports, cultural events, exploration of nature and human history, leisure travel, enjoyable events, and informal education. Consistent with the definitions of recreation, recreational activities are expected to provide participants with happiness, satisfaction, creativity, mental balance, character development, competitive ability, mental capacity, freedom, physical and mental fitness, and a broader worldview (Hazar, 2003).

Business tourism plays a crucial role in the initiation and development of tourism movements and has a leveraging effect on the orientation towards other forms of tourism. Numerous activities are conducted within the scope of business tourism, including fairs, exhibitions, and conferences, which hold significant importance within the tourism industry. Visitors participating in business travel movements through these activities represent an important target audience for the tourism industry as they have the potential to benefit from other tourism assets and services at the destination they visit. The most commonly conducted activities within business tourism are fairs and conferences (Walia et al., 2021).

BLEISURE TOURISM

In recent years, bleisure tourism has become a significant travel trend. Although the term “bleisure” has only recently come into use, it was revealed that back in the 2000s, American businesspeople extended their business trips to allocate time for various holiday activities, yet they referred to these trips as "holiday makers" rather than using the term "bleisure" (Chang & Chung, 2018).

It is stated that tourists traveling for business purposes extend their stays to explore the destinations they visit, participate in activities aligned with their interests, and try local cuisines, among other purposes (Cheeyong et al., 2017).

In this tourism concept, the traveler usually indulges in "leisure life" activities during their free time while on a business visit. These trips are often undertaken alone, with colleagues, or with family, where they explore the city, visit museums, and explore historical sites (Tretyakevich, 2015).

A significant characteristic of bleisure travel is the freedom to engage in enjoyable and relaxing activities away from office work (Lichy & McLeay, 2018). While Lichy and McLeay (2018) define bleisure tourists as experiential learners, escapists, working vacationers, altruistic knowledge sharers, and investigative active pioneers, Sardest and Ivanauskas (2019) categorize bleisure tourists into industrial and postmodern bleisure tourists.

DESTINATION AND DESTINATION MARKETING

Destinations are places where tourists spend most of their time and constitute a significant portion of their expenditures. These primary locations where tourist activities are offered typically encompass countries, regions, towns, and similar areas, possessing the potential to attract tourists (Medlik, 2003). A tourism destination refers to places where specific tourist products and services are planned and promoted within specific geographical boundaries, valued by consumers for their unique attributes (Buhalis, 2000).

With the impact of globalization, increased competition between countries and regions further emphasizes the importance of marketing strategies aimed at attracting investors and tourists to destinations. In this context, countries and regional areas increasingly prioritize their roles as tourist destinations and invest significant efforts and resources to enhance their images and attractiveness among consumers (Baker & Cameron, 2008). It can be argued that a significant portion of tourism activities takes place in these destinations.

Destinations are not merely physical places; they also encompass abstract aspects carrying cultural values. Success in tourism destinations relies not only on physical features such as natural beauty and historical monuments but also on social factors like language spoken and the hospitality of the local community (Ross & Iso-Ahola, 1991).

Destination marketing is defined as the process of identifying and satisfying the needs and desires of consumers considering traveling to a specific place (Sharma, 2013). Destination marketing aims to increase visitor numbers through the promotion of a destination (town, city, region, country, etc.). The objectives of destination marketing include promoting the destination at both national and international levels, creating a positive image among target audiences, contributing to the branding of the region, ensuring a competitive advantage over destination competitors, and striving to increase competitiveness (Li et al., 2017).

According to Baker and Cameron (2008), destination marketing encompasses all activities and processes aimed at bringing together buyers and all other parties. It also focuses on responding to consumer demands and competitive positioning. This process involves decisions regarding the marketing mix (product, price, distribution, and promotion), as well as branding and market segmentation.

The profile of tourists traveling for business purposes is evolving, leading to the emergence of the concept of "bleisure" tourism, which combines business and leisure travel. Bleisure tourism represents a segment of tourists who combine business trips with leisure activities, thus spending longer periods in business tourism destinations (Pinho & Marques, 2021).

Bleisure tourism destination marketing strategies should aim to balance the needs of business and leisure tourism segments. These strategies should include appropriate accommodation and meeting facilities for business travelers, as well as cultural, entertainment, and relaxation activities for their leisure time (Pinho & Marques, 2021).

In conclusion, bleisure tourism emerges as an important segment in destination marketing. This type of tourism, resulting from the synthesis of business and leisure tourism, requires destinations to consider the needs of this segment in their marketing strategies (Lichy & McLeay, 2018).

BLEISURE MARKETING, DESTINATION ATTRACTIONS, AND STRATEGIES

Destination marketing aims to increase the tourism potential of a destination by bringing together tourist businesses and service providers. This entails considering a destination as a combination of various tourist products, offering customers an integrated experience within a specific geographic area and time frame (Haris & Leiper, 1995). The tourism status of a destination relies not only on its geographical size or boundaries but also on determining factors such as its ability to attract visitors and meet visitor needs. These factors include attractiveness, accessibility, availability, specific services, activities, and support services (Djurica & Djurica,

2010). Particularly in destination marketing, a wide range of activities is offered to consumers, encompassing the attractive features of the destination (such as marine tourism activities, the region's marine flora and fauna, natural beauty, etc.) (Carvache-Franco et al., 2020a).

Bleisure tourism, a term derived from the combination of "business" and "leisure," refers to the merging of business travel with leisure travel. With the blurred lines between business and leisure tourism, this phenomenon has gained popularity in recent times (Economist, 2019; Expedia, 2018). Bleisure marketing aims to encourage business travelers to visit more tourist sites, engage in additional recreational activities, and spend more money after meetings, conferences, and exhibitions/events (Lichy & McLeay, 2018).

Efforts to encourage business travelers to make additional expenditures beyond convention venues are important for the equitable distribution of economic impact in a destination. Moreover, bleisure marketing helps provide business travelers with multifaceted experiences from various attractions and activities in the destination, rather than just the events they attend (Chung et al., 2020).

Statistics indicate that about half of the expenditures made by business travelers are still allocated to traditional travel expenses (accommodation, transportation, and dining, etc.). However, a quarter of the expenditures are allocated to leisure activities such as guided tours, concerts, museums and galleries, and sports events (Expedia, 2018). Therefore, understanding where and when business travelers or MICE (Meetings, Incentives, Conferences, and Exhibitions) travelers spend their money and how their expenditures impact local businesses (or sometimes global businesses) and local communities has become increasingly important (Ezeuduji, 2024).

Within the context of bleisure marketing, four different types of experiences (entertainment, educational, aesthetic, and escapism experiences) are recommended from an experience economy perspective for bleisure travelers (Pine & Gilmore, 1998). In this theoretical framework, various bleisure experiences can be offered through bleisure marketing practices utilizing destination attractions.

The first area of bleisure marketing involves promoting local attractions that business travelers can visit and participate in during their leisure time. This includes providing information and advertisements. Conference attendees can be provided with voluntary maps and promotional brochures as part of the conference kit, encouraging them to visit local restaurants, cafes, and retail stores (Pine & Gilmore, 1998).

The second area within bleisure marketing is the development of support programs to encourage additional consumption by business travelers. Support programs include factory tours, team-building activities, and themed local tours, often embedded within the main event program. Thus, collaboration with an event organizer is necessary for this type of bleisure marketing. Support programs not only increase participant satisfaction but also contribute to the sustainable growth of the local economy by utilizing local goods and services. Additionally, the importance of local tours and cultural events in creating unique destination experiences should be emphasized. This approach is particularly effective for specific theme-based conferences and professional industry fairs (Chung et al., 2020).

Another area of bleisure marketing is facilitating the access of meeting participants to local businesses and attractions. In this approach, unconventional venues can be considered by event organizers and DMOs. Unique venues not only create unique experiences for delegates but also help increase additional revenues because they typically have their own business models alongside typical business events. Finally, enhancing value and profit sharing with bleisure tourism stakeholders can help achieve the ultimate goal of bleisure marketing. DMOs, local businesses, and event organizers can form partnerships to encourage additional spending by conference and exhibition attendees and to support the ultimate goal of Bleisure marketing (Chung et al., 2020).

Bleisure tourism, as a combination of business and leisure travel, is becoming increasingly popular (Alp & Ayyildiz, 2020). In this type of tourism, people experience holiday experiences by combining business trips with leisure activities. Various attractions influence the destination choices of bleisure tourists, and marketing these attractions requires significant strategy (Mercan & Sandikci, 2024).

Destination attractions are factors that enrich the holiday experiences of bleisure tourists and determine destination preferences. These attractions include natural beauty, cultural and historical heritage, entertainment and shopping opportunities, and sports and recreational facilities. Natural beauty is a significant factor that enhances the attractiveness of bleisure tourists. Natural areas such as beaches, mountains, and lakes in a destination can influence tourists' decisions to extend their business trips or revisit (King et al., 2023).

Cultural and historical heritage also play a significant role in bleisure tourism. Historical buildings, museums, festivals, and other cultural events in a destination can transform business trips into holiday experiences for tourists (Richards & Munsters, 2010). Entertainment and shopping opportunities can also be influential in the destination preferences of bleisure tourists. Restaurants, bars, shopping centers, and nightlife in a destination can make business trips more enjoyable for tourists and encourage them to revisit (Bowie & Buttle, 2004).

Marketing destination attractions is an important strategy for success in bleisure tourism. Effectively promoting a destination's attractions and reaching the target audience can influence tourists' destination choices and increase tourism revenues (Pike, 2008). With the increasing popularity of bleisure tourism, various attractions that influence bleisure tourists' destination choices are emerging. Motivations for combining business travel with holiday experiences are among these attractions

(King et al., 2023). Therefore, an important aspect of bleisure tourism is understanding the motivation factors of bleisure tourists and effectively using these factors in destination marketing.

MOTIVATION FACTORS IN BLEISURE TOURISM FROM THE DESTINATION MARKETING PERSPECTIVE

Bleisure tourism, which combines business and leisure, is gaining increasing popularity. This type of tourism is preferred by individuals aiming to experience a vacation by blending business trips with leisure activities. Besides being an attractive option for both business and leisure travelers, bleisure tourism also presents a significant marketing opportunity for destinations (Pinho & Marques, 2021).

Motivation is defined as the need or condition that directs individuals towards specific activities (Moutinho, 2000). In tourism literature, motivation is a concept used to examine and understand the factors influencing tourists' travel decisions (Meng et al., 2008). Therefore, understanding motivation is important for grasping the internal and external factors determining tourists' travel desires, preferences, and behaviors. These factors may include satisfaction, expectations, personal interests, the quest for experiences, social interaction, and cultural exploration (Crompton, 1979). Motivation in tourism often plays a critical role in marketing strategies and destination management. Thus, understanding motivation in tourism literature is crucial for effective industry management and meeting tourists' needs.

In the context of bleisure tourism, both push and attractive factors influencing travel motivations become particularly prominent. Push motivation factors reflect individuals' personal travel motivations, while attractive motivation factors encompass elements influencing the selection of preferred destinations (Lichy & McLeay, 2018).

Numerous studies in the literature examine destination characteristics (Hsu et al., 2009; Van Der Merwe et al., 2011; Güzel et al., 2020; Carvache Franco et al., 2020a; Carvache Franco et al., 2020b; Solid-Radilla et al., 2021; Carvache Franco et al., 2023). However, research on bleisure tourism and the motivation factors driving business travelers towards bleisure trips is more limited (Lichy & McLeay, 2018; Çetinsöz & Hazarhun, 2020; et al., 2009; Sohaili et al., 2022; Mercan & Sandıkçı, 2024).

To better position and understand bleisure tourism in the industry, it is necessary to identify bleisure tourists' profiles, motivations, and habits. However, there is a scarcity of scientific studies in this field (Alp & Ayyıldız, 2020), and explanations have been made based on the available sources.

Sohaili et al. (2022) systematically reviewed studies on bleisure travel motivations using the PRISMA method across three different databases from 2012 to 2022, namely Google Scholar, WoS, and Scopus. The research found that significant factors motivating bleisure travelers to utilize their leisure time visiting attractions during business trips were identified as *novelty-seeking, escape, entertainment, cultural and historical values, environment and safety, tourist facilities, and convenience* (Sohaili et al., 2022).

Çetinsöz and Hazarhun (2020) conducted interviews with business people working in various industries in different provinces who undertake national or international business trips. As a result of the interviews, it was observed that the driving factors for bleisure travel motivations were identified as the desire *to meet new people, see new places, relax, relieve stress, and have fun*. Additionally, *cultural heritage, shopping, and local food and beverages* were identified as attractive factors for bleisure travel (Çetinsöz & Hazarhun, 2020).

In the study by Lichy and Mcleay (2018), it is noted that bleisure travels occur for various motivations, and participants engage in such trips for reasons such as *discovering new things, sharing experiences and knowledge, finding business partners or resources, among others*. Researchers have identified five different bleisure typologies based on participants' different special interests, personality traits, and motivations, namely *experiential learners, escapers, working vacationers, altruistic knowledge sharers, and research-active trailblazers* (Lichy & Mcleay, 2018).

Following the study by Lichy and McLeay (2018), effective marketing communication strategies targeting bleisure participation should be developed using plans divided into sections that highlight push and attractive motivation factors, as well as tangible and intangible elements guiding each typology. For example, marketing materials aimed at encouraging *experiential learners* should emphasize the benefits of learning new transformative skills as well as the challenges of useful difficulties. *Escapers'* emphasis should be on risk and adventure. Like the traditional tourism industry, vacationing workers are likely to respond positively to messages that emphasize cultural exploration. Information about knowledge transfer opportunities will attract *altruistic knowledge sharers*. *Trailblazers* who are active in research may be interested in joint grant applications and research collaboration opportunities. Different types of *leisure travelers* may be found in other work environments, which may require managers to take different measures to encourage business-related travel if it is advantageous for the organization (Ezeuduji, 2024).

Push motivation factors in bleisure tourism reflect individuals' personal travel motivations, which have been identified in relevant research. These factors include desires such as seeing new places, exploring foreign cultures, meeting new people, relaxing, socializing, relieving stress, having fun, breaking away from daily routines, and self-discovery (Lichy & McLeay, 2018; Çetinsöz & Hazarhun, 2020). These factors are often based on the desire to blend business trips with leisure activities. Here are some significant *push motivation factors* in bleisure tourism (Lichy & McLeay, 2018; Çetinsöz & Hazarhun, 2020; Sohaili et al., 2022; Mercan & Sandıkçı, 2024):

Work-Life Balance: Bleisure tourists are motivated by the desire to achieve a balance between work and leisure. By combining business trips with leisure activities, they can both fulfill their work obligations and find opportunities for relaxation and enjoyment. Achieving this balance aims to enhance both their work performance and maximize their personal satisfaction (Lichy & McLeay, 2018).

Flexibility: The desire of bleisure tourists to create a flexible travel schedule is a significant part of their motivation. Flexibility can manifest in ways such as taking a vacation by adding extra days after a business trip or taking short breaks during business trips. Flexible travel plans facilitate transitions between work and leisure for individuals and make their travel experiences more enjoyable (Batala & Slevitch, 2024).

Novelty and Exploration: Bleisure tourists are motivated by the desire to see new places and experience different cultures. By turning business trips into opportunities, they explore tourist and cultural attractions during their non-working hours. The desire to interact with local cultures and experience different experiences is a fundamental motivating factor in bleisure tourism (Sohaili et al., 2022).

Personal Development: Bleisure tourists tend to view business trips as opportunities for personal development. Experiences such as seeing new places, interacting with different cultures, and learning foreign languages can contribute to individuals' personal and professional development (Lichy & McLeay, 2018). Therefore, the number of bleisure tourists who see business trips not only as a business necessity but also as an opportunity for personal development and exploration is increasing.

The attractive motivation factors in bleisure tourism encompass elements that influence the selection of preferred destinations. In relevant studies, some significant attractive motivation factors specific to bleisure tourism include cultural heritage, local food and beverages, price policy, ease of transportation, safety, climate, natural attractions, cleanliness standards, infrastructure and superstructure conditions, local attitudes towards tourists, service quality, entertainment options, shopping opportunities, special events, food and beverage establishments, and accommodation options (Lichy & McLeay, 2018; Alp & Ayyıldız, 2020; Çetinsöz & Hazarhun, 2020; et al., 2009; Mercan & Sandıkçı, 2024). These factors play an important role in shaping tourists' holiday experiences and influencing destination choices. Here are some significant attractive motivation factors in bleisure tourism (Lichy & Mcleay, 2018; Alp & Ayyıldız, 2020; Mercan & Sandıkçı, 2024):

Location and Accessibility: The location and accessibility of a destination are crucial for bleisure tourists. Destinations easily accessible after business trips and with easy access to tourist attractions become more attractive to bleisure tourists. Additionally, the diversity and ease of transportation options are important factors in bleisure tourists' destination choices (Ezeuduji, 2024).

Touristic and Cultural Attractions: Bleisure tourists are interested in the tourist and cultural attractions of a destination. Places with historical and cultural heritage, natural beauty, and unique experiences attract bleisure tourists. Touristic and cultural attractions are essential attractive factors of bleisure tourism and play a key role in enhancing destinations' competitiveness.

Service Quality and Facilities: Bleisure tourists want access to quality and diverse facilities in accommodation, dining, and other services. The quality of services in a destination enhances tourists' satisfaction and strengthens their intentions to revisit. Additionally, various activities, events, and entertainment options are important factors in bleisure tourists' destination choices (Batala & Slevitch, 2024).

Safety: The safety of a destination is an important factor for bleisure tourists. Destinations that provide a safe environment allow tourists to have a comfortable and peaceful holiday. Safety plays a critical role in tourists' travel decisions and significantly influences destinations' images (Pinho & Marques, 2021).

Motivation factors in bleisure tourism encompass both push and attractive (pull) elements. The desire to blend work and leisure experiences is one of the fundamental push motivation factors for bleisure tourists. Additionally, attractive factors such as location, touristic and cultural attractions, service quality, and safety are essential elements influencing bleisure tourists' destination choices. Bleisure tourism, by integrating business and leisure experiences, will continue to hold a significant position in the tourism industry.

THE IMPACT OF BLEISURE TOURISM ON DESTINATION MARKETING

Bleisure tourism, defined as the blending of business trips with leisure, is a growing trend in tourism. This trend arises from the desire of individuals on business trips to enjoy tourist activities alongside their business endeavors. A study by

McCabe and Stokoe (2004) revealed that combining business travel with leisure can lead to different experiences akin to "the tale of two cities".

Bleisure tourism has significant effects on destination marketing strategies. Various motivation factors influencing destination selection by bleisure tourists shape destination marketing strategies. Understanding these factors allows destinations to develop effective marketing communication strategies targeting bleisure tourists (Chung et al., 2020).

For instance, destinations can attract bleisure tourists by offering flexibility in business trip schedules and adding extra vacation days after business trips (Unger & Uriely, 2022). Additionally, destinations can cater to the needs of bleisure tourists by providing facilities and activities that balance work and leisure. Destinations targeting the motivation of novelty and exploration can attract bleisure tourists by emphasizing tourist and cultural attractions (Chung et al., 2020).

The impact of bleisure tourism on destination marketing has triggered a significant transformation in the travel industry. Traditional tourism promotion and marketing strategies now need to be adapted to meet the needs of bleisure tourists (Pinho & Marques, 2021). Destinations can gain a competitive advantage by offering special packages, events, and promotions targeting bleisure tourism. From this perspective, the impact of bleisure tourism on destination marketing can be summarized as follows:

Innovative Marketing Strategies: Bleisure tourism necessitates the development of new and creative marketing strategies for destination marketers. Kim et al. (2007) obtained significant findings regarding gender differences in travel information search habits online, shedding light on important aspects of online marketing.

Expanded Customer Base: Bleisure tourism creates many potential customers who prefer combining business travel with leisure. This allows destinations to expand their customer base by targeting both business travel segments and vacationers (Pinho & Marques, 2021).

Increase in Longer Stays: Bleisure tourists often extend their business trips into vacations, resulting in longer stays in destinations. Joo and Woosnam (2020) conducted significant research on how local emotional solidarity towards bleisure travel is perceived by the local community.

Sustainable Tourism Opportunities: Bleisure tourism can increase opportunities for sustainable tourism. When tourists extend their business trips, they tend to immerse themselves more deeply in local culture and contribute more to the local economy. This can help balance the environmental and social impacts of tourism (McCabe & Stokoe, 2004).

Opportunities for Local Businesses: Bleisure tourism can create new opportunities for local businesses. Restaurants, shops, tourist spots, and entertainment venues can offer special services and products to meet the needs of these tourists (Kim et al., 2007).

Bleisure tourism has become a significant aspect of the tourism industry as a combination of business and leisure travel. This new tourism trend influences destination marketing strategies, enhancing destinations' competitive advantage. As bleisure tourism continues to gain popularity as a fusion of business and leisure travel, it is crucial for destinations to develop marketing strategies targeting this segment. In this regard, understanding bleisure tourists' motivations and creating destination marketing strategies based on these motivations are vital for destinations to increase tourism revenue and strengthen their competitive advantage (Lichy & McLeay, 2018; Batala & Slevitch, 2024).

A comprehensive literature review indicates that it is possible to evaluate both the positive and negative aspects of the impact of bleisure tourism on destination marketing and to specify ways to enhance or mitigate these effects.

Positive Aspects

Opportunity to Develop Innovative Marketing Strategies: Since bleisure tourism involves the combination of business travel and leisure, destinations need to develop innovative marketing strategies. Especially, digital marketing and promotions via social media platforms can be effective in reaching this tourist segment (Kim et al., 2007). Destinations can organize targeted advertising campaigns online and increase social media activities. By offering packages that integrate business and leisure activities, they can attract these types of tourists.

Expansion of Customer Base: Bleisure tourists are individuals who combine business trips with vacations, allowing destinations to cater to a broad customer base that travels for both business and leisure (Pinho & Marques, 2021). By offering accommodation options suitable for business travel and tourist activities, destinations can attract these tourists. Additionally, attractive vacation packages can be created for participants in conferences and business meetings.

Extension of Stay Duration: Bleisure tourists tend to extend their stay in destinations by combining business trips with vacations. This increases the use of accommodation and other tourist services (Joo & Woosnam, 2020). Providing discounts and special advantages for longer stays can encourage tourists to extend their stay.

Opportunities for Sustainable Tourism: Bleisure tourism allows tourists to experience local culture more deeply and provides long-term contributions to the local economy (McCabe & Stokoe, 2004). By investing in sustainable tourism projects and promoting eco-friendly tourist activities, the environmental benefits of bleisure tourism can be enhanced.

Opportunities for Local Businesses: Bleisure tourists support the economic vitality of local businesses such as restaurants, shops, and tourist attractions by increasing demand (Kim et al., 2007). Local businesses can take advantage of this trend by offering special services and products to bleisure tourists.

Negative Aspects

Pressure on Popular Tourist Areas: Bleisure tourism can exert pressure on tourist infrastructure in popular destinations, leading to the depletion of resources (Chung et al., 2020). To alleviate this pressure, alternative tourist areas can be promoted and various regions can be directed to balance visitor density.

Rising Accommodation and Service Costs: Increased demand can raise accommodation and service costs in destinations, causing economic difficulties for local residents (Unger & Uriely, 2022). By offering affordable accommodation options and balancing service costs, such economic pressures can be reduced.

Environmental Impacts: Intensive tourist activities can have negative effects on natural resources and lead to sustainability issues (McCabe & Stokoe, 2004). Environmental impacts can be mitigated by promoting eco-friendly practices and organizing tourism activities that do not harm nature.

Socio-Cultural Pressures on Local Communities: Bleisure tourism can impose pressures on the lifestyles and cultural values of local communities, leading to socio-cultural changes (Chung et al., 2020). To reduce these pressures, awareness campaigns can be organized to preserve the cultural heritage of the local population, and tourism activities can be designed to respect local values.

Dependency on the Local Economy: Bleisure tourism can make destinations' local economies dependent on tourism revenue and reduce economic diversity (Pinho & Marques, 2021). Strategies to diversify the tourism-dependent economy can be developed to reduce dependency on tourism.

Bleisure tourism has both positive and negative impacts on destination marketing. To enhance the positive effects, innovative marketing strategies should be developed, stay durations should be encouraged, and sustainable tourism opportunities should be supported. To mitigate the negative impacts, environmental effects should be minimized, economic dependency should be reduced, and respect for the cultural values of local communities should be ensured. These approaches will help manage bleisure tourism sustainably and beneficially for destinations.

CONCLUSION AND RECOMMENDATION

Business travelers often extend their trips to relax in the visited destination. This trend is considered a result of the combination of business and leisure travel, termed as "hybrid travel," which encompasses combining tourism with business, medical visits, politics, or migration (Unger & Uriely, 2022). Particularly among Generation Y, the desire to incorporate leisure time into business trips has led to the emergence of the term "bleisure" (Batala & Slevitch, 2024).

Today, bleisure tourism has become a trend in the travel and tourism industry. Bleisure travels have led to the opening of niche markets offering endless opportunities. Bleisure, defined as the combination of business and leisure, involves extending business trips for personal reasons. Especially Tokyo is known as the best business-travel (bleisure) destination in Asia, ranking first among 26 cities in the region. Tokyo, the capital of Japan, and "five-star" business-travel cities are followed by Singapore, Sydney, Hong Kong, and Melbourne (Economist, 2019; Expedia, 2018).

The most intense bleisure travel destinations worldwide are (Economist, 2019; Expedia, 2018):

> ***New York:*** Recognized as the business and cultural capital of the world, New York is a hub of activity and influence. The Financial District in Manhattan, centered around Wall Street, is the heart of global financial markets. For business travelers, it provides an ideal location for significant business meetings and financial transactions. Additionally, it is famous for landmarks like Times Square, a central point for both business and entertainment. Brooklyn is known for its art galleries, boutique stores, and alternative cultural scenes, making it perfect for post-work exploration. Central Park, located in the heart of Manhattan, stands out with its vast green space, natural beauty, walking paths, and museums, attracting both business travelers and tourists.
>
> ***London:*** Known as a metropolis where history, culture, finance, and art converge, London offers a unique blend of experiences. The City of London area is the center of global financial markets and an ideal location for business meetings, hosting the headquarters of financial institutions and corporations. The West End is popular for its theaters, restaurants, and shops, providing cultural activities and entertainment that are perfect for post-work outings. The South Bank, with its art galleries, museums, and festival spaces along the

Thames River, offers a rich cultural experience, making it an excellent choice for cultural activities after a business trip.

Singapore: Singapore stands out as one of Asia's most significant business and trade centers. The city is known for its modern infrastructure, advanced business centers, and high living standards. The Central Business District (CBD) plays a central role in global financial markets, offering an ideal location for business travel. The Marina Bay area is notable for its high-tech skyscrapers and unique natural and architectural structures like Gardens by the Bay. This area is also equipped with luxury hotels, shopping malls, and entertainment complexes, making it a perfect place for relaxation and enjoyment after business engagements. Sentosa Island, located a short distance from the city center, is a holiday paradise with its beaches, golf courses, theme parks, and world-class hotels, offering an ideal escape for relaxation and entertainment.

Sydney: As one of Australia's largest and most dynamic cities, Sydney combines business and leisure seamlessly. Known for its modern business centers and unique natural beauty, the city hosts world-class cultural and artistic events at iconic landmarks such as the Sydney Opera House. Sydney Harbour is one of the city's symbols, offering activities like harbour cruises or a walk on the Harbour Bridge, ideal for relaxation after business. Bondi Beach is perfect for those who wish to surf or simply sunbathe, and its proximity to the city center is a notable advantage.

Hong Kong: Hong Kong is one of Asia's key financial and trade hubs, blending Eastern and Western cultures into a dynamic city. The spectacular view of Victoria Harbour is one of the city's icons and a popular spot for dinner. The Central District is filled with modern skyscrapers, chic restaurants, and luxury shopping centers. Lan Kwai Fong is renowned for nightlife and entertainment, making it an ideal venue for social events after work. Victoria Peak offers some of the best views of the city and is a great option for relaxation and enjoying panoramic cityscapes after business activities.

Melbourne: Considered the cultural capital of Australia, Melbourne is a hub that combines business opportunities with tourist attractions. Boat tours along the Yarra River are perfect for those who want to discover the city's beautiful scenery. Federation Square hosts cultural events and festivals and is one of the relaxing spots in the city center. Melbourne Zoo, with its natural beauty and extensive animal collections, offers a great escape for those looking to unwind from work stress. Eureka Tower, the tallest building in the city, features a 360-degree observation deck, perfect for those wanting to enjoy panoramic views of the city after business meetings.

Dubai: Dubai is one of the most important trade and tourism centers in the Middle East. Dubai Marina and Jumeirah Beach are popular for their luxury hotels, beaches, and entertainment venues, making them ideal for relaxation and enjoying the sea after work. Downtown Dubai is known for iconic structures like the Burj Khalifa, shopping malls, and luxury hotels, making it a perfect choice for prestigious business meetings. Business Bay, with its modern office complexes and transportation network, provides a convenient location for business travel, offering a perfect balance between work and leisure. These destinations offer rich opportunities for both business and leisure travel, facilitating the spread of bleisure tourism. Each is an attractive area for business professionals and tourists alike, providing ideal spots for completing work and then enjoying a pleasant time.

This study focuses on the concept of business tourism or "bleisure" tourism, emphasizing the importance of destination marketing. Literature review and analysis of business tourism destinations show that this emerging trend, resulting from the combination of business and leisure travel, offers unique opportunities for destinations. Business travelers often extend their trips with leisure activities, resulting in longer stays in destinations (Mercan & Sandıkçı, 2024). Therefore, it is essential for destination marketers to develop strategies targeting business tourism, offering various opportunities for tourists to experience both of these aspects simultaneously and encouraging the combination of business travel with leisure tourism. With collaboration and innovative marketing strategies, destinations can maximize the benefits from the business tourism market and increase tourism revenues. However, for these strategies to be successful, local governments, tourism industry stakeholders, and businesses need to collaborate and work together. Based on this point, some strategic recommendations for the development of the business tourism market can be summarized as follows:

Targeted Marketing Strategies: Targeted marketing strategies to develop the business tourism market are important. For example, offering special discounts or organizing special events for business travelers can increase the destination's business tourism potential.

Business Community Collaboration: Offering attractive opportunities for business tourism by collaborating with the local business community. Special agreements with local businesses can be made to provide discounted or special services to business travelers.

Infrastructure Development: Developing infrastructure to meet the needs of business travelers is necessary. This may include the construction of modern conference centers and providing high-speed internet access.

Regional Collaboration: Regional collaboration among business tourism destinations can strengthen marketing and promotion activities. Collaborations between similar business tourism destinations can increase competitiveness.

Effective Communication Strategies: Developing effective communication strategies for business travelers is crucial. This may include providing informative content about business tourism opportunities or communication campaigns that promote the combination of business travel with leisure tourism.

Bleisure tourism indicates significant growth potential in Turkey's tourism industry. Bleisure tourism has rapidly become a growing market segment in the country. The rich history, cultural heritage, and natural beauty of Turkey make it an attractive destination for those looking to turn business trips into enjoyable holiday experiences. This study evaluates the opportunities offered by Turkey in bleisure tourism while discussing the sector's future growth potential. In this context, Istanbul and Antalya stand out as the most developed bleisure destinations in Turkey.

Istanbul: Istanbul is the largest city and cultural capital of Turkey, with a unique geographical position that bridges Asia and Europe. It boasts both historical and modern elements. For business travelers, Istanbul offers ideal facilities for international conferences and meetings. The financial districts, such as Levent and Maslak, are filled with modern hotels and conference centers. Among Istanbul's tourist attractions, historic sites like Sultanahmet Square and Hagia Sophia are popular options for cultural excursions after work. Additionally, Istiklal Street and Taksim Square are central locations for shopping and entertainment. Taking a Bosphorus tour to explore the city's stunning scenery is also a great option for relaxation after business engagements.

Antalya: Antalya, located on the Mediterranean coast in southern Turkey, is famous for its summer tourism. The city offers many luxury hotels, golf courses, and spa centers that perfectly combine business travel with vacation experiences. Antalya's beaches, especially Lara and Konyaaltı, are ideal spots for relaxing and swimming after work. The historic Kaleiçi district, with its narrow streets and historical texture, is like a treasure waiting to be explored. The ancient Aspendos Theater offers a cultural experience with its events. Antalya Harbor and Marina are perfect for yacht trips and marine tourism.

Izmir: The largest city in the Aegean Region, Izmir is an attractive destination for both business and leisure visits. The city is known for its historical landmarks such as Konak Square and the Clock Tower. The Kordonboyu coastal strip in Izmir is a great option for post-work walks and enjoying the sea view. The historic Kemeraltı Bazaar is an ideal place for shopping and tasting local delicacies. Tourist attractions around Izmir include the ancient city of Ephesus, which offers a historical journey with its ancient theater and the Temple of Artemis. Nearby towns like Çeşme and Alaçatı are known for their beaches, windsurfing opportunities, and vibrant nightlife.

Ankara: As the capital of Turkey, Ankara is known for its modern business centers as well as its rich historical and cultural heritage. Anıtkabir, the mausoleum of Mustafa Kemal Atatürk, is one of the city's most important tourist attractions. Ankara Castle offers a panoramic view of the city and provides a space for history enthusiasts to explore. Atatürk Forest Farm is a perfect getaway for those looking to escape work stress with its natural beauty. Ankara is also a significant center for national and international conferences, boasting modern facilities for the business world. The Kocatepe Mosque, with its modern architecture, and CerModern, which hosts contemporary art exhibitions, are notable sites.

Muğla: The Muğla/Bodrum destination on the Aegean coast is famous for its luxury vacation options and historical richness. Bodrum Castle and the Underwater Archaeology Museum are ideal spots for cultural tours after work. Bodrum Marina is a popular port for yachts and luxury boats, serving as a perfect starting point for marine tourism and yacht tours. Bodrum also offers historical sites such as the Ancient Theater and Bodrum Museum, providing visitors with opportunities to explore the past.

Some strategic recommendations to enhance Turkey's potential in bleisure tourism can be summarized as follows:

Identification of Target Audience and Development of Marketing Strategies: Identifying the profiles of bleisure tourists and understanding their interests enables the development of targeted marketing strategies. Highlighting the features of developed bleisure destinations like Istanbul and Antalya can enhance Turkey's attractiveness in bleisure tourism.

Improvement of Accommodation Facilities and Tourist Attractions: Enhancing the quality of accommodation facilities and tourist attractions in Istanbul and Antalya can increase bleisure tourists' satisfaction and repeat visit rates. Particularly in hotel establishments, areas such as lobbies and bars should be redesigned to create environments where bleisure guests can both socialize and work comfortably. Fast internet access, comfortable seating, sockets, printers, etc., should be redesigned throughout the hotel. Travel agencies should have package programs tailored to bleisure tourists. Bleisure tourists should be informed about what they can do in the destinations they visit due to time constraints, and package tours should be prepared for them. These tours should include places to see in the city, events to attend, art centers to visit, museums, historical sites, etc.

Promotion of Local Cuisine and Cultural Events: Promoting local cuisine and cultural events in Istanbul and Antalya encourages bleisure tourists to integrate into the destination and experience local cultures. For bleisure tourists who are away from home for a long time, healthy eating is an important issue. There should be special healthy menu options in hotel restaurants or local restaurants where they can taste traditional dishes.

Development of Activities That Combine Business and Leisure: Developing activities that combine business and leisure in Istanbul and Antalya allows bleisure tourists to spend their time more efficiently. Infrastructure development, such as the construction of modern conference centers and providing high-speed internet access, is crucial to meet the needs of bleisure travelers. With such arrangements, business travelers will extend their stays in the destinations they visit, and they will be encouraged to explore the surroundings more. Travel agencies and tourist guides will provide different programs with special arrangements for them. This will positively affect employment.

As a result, the implementation of these recommendations can help Turkey become more competitive in the field of bleisure tourism and sustain its growth in the tourism industry. Additionally, in the post-pandemic era, the combination of business and leisure travel has become even more common. Business travelers, especially after a period of extended home stays and remote work during the pandemic, tend to turn their trips into vacation opportunities. It is important for Turkey to adapt to this trend and make its destinations suitable for both business and leisure travel. Turkey needs to reevaluate its destination marketing strategies to encourage bleisure tourism. Attractive offers should be presented to business travelers to turn their trips into vacation opportunities. This can include special packages and campaigns for business travelers, cultural events, and tourist tours. Especially in cities with a high volume of business travel, such as Istanbul, Ankara, and Izmir, the expansion of such services will increase the potential to attract both business and leisure tourists.

It is critical for Turkey to make its tourism infrastructure suitable for both business and leisure travel to develop bleisure tourism. Accommodation options such as hotels and resorts near conference centers should be increased, and environmental arrangements should be made to allow business travelers to benefit from vacation facilities. At the same time, strengthening infrastructure elements such as transportation, communication, and security will facilitate travel for bleisure tourists. The economic contribution of business travelers to Turkey is significant. By promoting bleisure tourism, it is possible to encourage business travelers to spend on vacation. This will contribute to increasing tourism revenues and supporting local economies.

Particularly, local small businesses should be encouraged to develop services for bleisure tourists to benefit from them.

In conclusion, strengthening Turkey's destination marketing in the scope of bleisure tourism will increase the number of tourists traveling for both business and leisure, contributing to the sustainable growth of the tourism sector. These strategies will help Turkey enhance its competitive advantage in the tourism sector during the recovery process from the effects of the pandemic.

REFERENCES

Aguilera, A. (2008). Business travel and mobile workers. *Journal of Transportation Research Part A: Policy andPractice, 42*(8), 1109-1116.

Alp, B., & Ayyıldız, A. Y. (2020). A new opportunity in tourism market: Bleisure. *Journal ofTourism & Gastronomy Studies*, 8(1), 336–354. 10.21325/jotags.2020.551

Argan, M. (2013). *Rekreasyon yönetimi*. Anadolu Üniversitesi Web-ofset Tesisleri.

Baker, M. J., & Cameron, E. (2008). Critical success factors in destination marketing. *Tourism and Hospitality Research*, 8(2), 79–97. 10.1057/thr.2008.9

Batala, B., & Slevitch, L. (2024). Keeping two balls in the air: The bleisure travel experience. *Annals of Tourism Research Empirical Insights*, 5(1), 1–10. 10.1016/j. annale.2023.100115

Bowie, D., & Buttle, F. (2004). *Hospitality marketing*. Routledge.

Brightbill, C. K. (1960). *The challenge of leisure*. Prentice-Hall.

Buhalis, D. (2000). Marketing the competitive destination of the future. *Tourism Management*, 21(1), 97–116. 10.1016/S0261-5177(99)00095-3

Carvache, F. M., Perez, O. A., Carvache, F. O., Víquez, P. A. G., & Carvache, F. W. (2020a). The perceived value in ecotourism related to satisfaction and loyalty: A study from Costa Rica. *Geographica Pannonica*, 24(3), 229–243. 10.5937/gp24-25082

Carvache-Franco, M., Carvache-Franco, W., Carvache-Franco, O., Hernández-Lara, A. B., & Buele, C. V. (2020b). Segmentation, motivation, and sociodemographic aspects of tourist demand in a coastal marine destination: A case study in Manta (Ecuador). *Current Issues in Tourism*, 23(10), 1234–1247. 10.1080/13683500.2019.1600476

Carvache-Franco, M., Solis-Radilla, M. M., Carvache-Franco, W., & Carvache-Franco, O. (2023). Push and pull motivations as demand predictors of coastal and marine destinations: A study in Acapulco, Mexico. *Tourism Planning & Development*, 20(6), 1000–1018. 10.1080/21568316.2021.1945673

Çetinsöz, B. C., & Hazarhun, E. (2020). Turizm Endüstrisinde Yeni Bir Trend: Bleisure Seyahatler Ve Motivasyon Unsurları. *Journal Of Recreation and Tourism Research*, 7(4), 500–527. 10.31771/jrtr.2020.75

Chang, L., & Chung, K. (2018). Leisure tourism connection behaviors by life stage and gender. *International Journal of Culture, Tourism and Hospitality Research*, 12(3), 292–309. 10.1108/IJCTHR-03-2018-0036

Cheeyong, K., Kim, J. C., Jung, S. H., & Kim, E. K. (2017). Marine leisure sports based on realistic VR system for Bleisure Busan. *International Journal of Grid and Distributed Computing*, 10(10), 69–78. 10.14257/ijgdc.2017.10.10.06

Chen, Y. C., Li, R. H., & Chen, S. H. (2013). Relationships among adolescents' leisure motivation, leisure involvement, and leisure satisfaction: A structural equation model. *Social Indicators Research*, 110(3), 1187–1199. 10.1007/s11205-011-9979-2

Chung, J. Y., Choi, Y. K., Yoo, B. K., & Kim, S. H. (2020). Bleisure tourism experience chain: Implications for destination marketing. *Asia Pacific Journal of Tourism Research*, 25(3), 300–310. 10.1080/10941665.2019.1708760

Cordes, K. A., & Ibrahim, H. M. (2003). *Applications in recreation and leisure: for today and the future* (3rd ed.). McGraw-Hill.

Crompton, J. L. (1979). Motivation for pleasure vacation. *Annals of Tourism Research*, 6(4), 408–424. 10.1016/0160-7383(79)90004-5

Djurica, M., & Djurica, N. (2010). *Tourism destination marketing management, faculty of tourism and hospitality management in opatija. Biennial International Congress, Tourism & Hospitality Industry, University of* Rijeka, Faculty of Tourism & Hospitality Management, 890-901.

Dragomir, L., Girniceanu, A., & Mazilu, M. (2021). Trends in worldwide tourism in 2020. *Quaestus*, 18, 28–41.

Economist. (2019). The 2019 Bleisure barometer: Asia's best cities for work and recreation. London: The Economist Intelligence Unit.

Expedia. (2018). Unpacking bleisure traveler trends. Retrieved from https://bit.ly/bleisure-trends https://go2.advertising.expedia.com/rs/185-EIA-216/images/Bleisure%20Select%20Meeting.pdf

Ezeuduji, I. O. (2024). Bleisure travel reimagined: Implications for research. *International Conference on Tourism Research, 7*(1), 2-9.

Global, H. I. S. (2020). İş seyahatleri ve küresel seyahat riskleri raporu. Retrieved from https://www.hisglobal.com.tr/uploads/HIS_travel_is_seyahati_ve_kuresel_seyahat_riskleri_raporu_mayis2020.pdf

Güzel, Ö., Sahin, I., & Ryan, C. (2020). Push-motivation-based emotional arousal: A research study in a coastal destination. *Journal of Destination Marketing & Management*, 16, 1–11. 10.1016/j.jdmm.2020.100428

Hacıoğlu, N. (2003). *A. Gökdeniz ve Y. Dinç*. Boş Zaman Ve Rekreasyon Yönetimi-Örnek Animasyon Uygulamaları, Detay Yayıncılık.

Haris, R., & Leiper, N. (n.d.). *Sustainable Tourism: An Australian Perspective.* Butterworth-Heinemann.

Hazar, A. (2003). *Rekreasyon ve animasyon (2. baskı).* Detay Yayıncılık.

Herbert, D. T. (1988). Work and leisure: Exploring a relationship. *Area*, 20(3), 241–252.

Hsu, T. K., Tsai, Y. F., & Wu, H. H. (2009). The preference analysis for tourist choice of destination: A case study of Taiwan. *Tourism Management*, 30(2), 288–297. 10.1016/j.tourman.2008.07.011

Jensen, C. R., & Guthrie, S. (2006). *Outdoor recreation in america* (6th ed.). Human Kinetics. 10.5040/9781492597438

Jiang, Y., Gu, Z., & Law, R. (2020). Understanding bleisure travelers: A systematic literature review. *Journal of Travel Research*, 59(8), 1344–1361.

Joo, D., & Woosnam, K. M. (2020). Measuring tourists' emotional solidarity with one another: A modification of the emotional solidarity scale. *Journal of Travel Research*, 59(7), 1186–1203. 10.1177/0047287519878503

Kim, D. Y., Lehto, X. Y., & Morrison, A. M. (2007). Gender differences in online travel information search: Implications for marketing communications on the internet. *Tourism Management*, 28(2), 423–433. 10.1016/j.tourman.2006.04.001

King, B., Lejealle, C., & Chapuis, J. M. (2023). Educational travellers and destination appeal: Deconstructing intrinsic motivations. *Journal of Vacation Marketing*, 29(1), 38–53. 10.1177/13567667221078241

Le, T. H., Arcodia, C., Novais, M. A., & Kralj, A. (2019). What we know and do not know about authenticity in dining experiences: A systematic literature review. *Tourism Management*, 74, 258–275. 10.1016/j.tourman.2019.02.012

Li, S., Robinson, P., & Oriade, A. (2017). Destination Marketing: The Use of Technology since the Millennium. *Journal of Destination Marketing & Management*, 6(2), 95–102. 10.1016/j.jdmm.2017.04.008

Lichy, J., & McLeay, F. (2018). Bleisure: Motivations and typologies. *Journal of Travel & Tourism Marketing*, 35(4), 517–530. 10.1080/10548408.2017.1364206

Lu, L., & Hu, C. (2005). Personality, leisure experiences and happiness. *Journal of Happiness Studies*, 6(3), 325–342. 10.1007/s10902-005-8628-3

Mccabe, S., & Stokoe, E. H. (2004). Place And Identıty In Tourısts' accounts. *Annals of Tourism Research*, 31(3), 601–622. 10.1016/j.annals.2004.01.005

Medlik, S. (2003). *Dictionary of travel, tourism, and hospitality*. Butterworth-Heinemann.

Meng, F., Tepanon, Y., & Uysal, M. (2008). Measuring tourist satisfaction by attribute and motivation: The case of a nature-based resort. *Journal of Vacation Marketing*, 14(1), 41–56. 10.1177/1356766707084218

Mercan, R., & Sandıkcı, M. (2024). Bleisure tourism: Business and leisure together. In *Future tourism trends volume 1: Tourism in the changing world*. Emerald Publishing Limited.

Meyer, D. H., Brightbill, K. C., & Sessoms, D. H. (1969). *Community recreation a guide to ıts organization* (4th ed.). Prentice Hall.

Moutinho, L. (2000). *Strategic management in tourism*. Cabi. 10.1079/9780851992822.0000

Mull, R. F., Bayless, K. G., Ross, C. M., & Jamieson, L. M. (1997). *Recreational sport management* (3rd ed.). Human Kinetics.

Netto, A. P. (2009). What is tourism? Definitions, theoretical phases and principles. *Philosophical issues in tourism, 37*, 43-62.

Passmore, A., & French, D. (2001). Development and administration of a measure to assess adolescents' participation in leisure activities. *Adolescence*, 36(141), 67–75.11407636

Pike, S. (2012). *Destination marketing*. Routledge. 10.4324/9780080568935

Pine, B. J., & Gilmore, J. H. (1998). Welcome to the experience economy. *Harvard Business Review Press*, 76(4), 97–105.10181589

Pinho, M., & Marques, J. (2021). The bleisure tourism trend and the potential for this business-leisure symbiosis in Porto. *Journal of Convention & Event Tourism*, 22(4), 346–362. 10.1080/15470148.2021.1905575

Richards, G., & Munsters, W. (Eds.). (2010). *Cultural tourism research methods*. Cabi. 10.1079/9781845935184.0000

Ross, G. F., & Iso-Ahola, S. E. (1991). Sightseeing tourists' motivation and satisfaction. *Annals of Tourism Research*, 18(2), 226–237. 10.1016/0160-7383(91)90006-W

Sardest, Z. F., & Ivanauskas, V. O. (2019). Bleisure Tourism'Impact of Employees' Motivations and Quality of life. *Unpublished Master Thesis). Aalborg University, Denmark.*

Seabra, C., Vicente, M., Silva, C., & Abrantes, J. L. (2014). Motivation and involvement in international tourism. *International Journal of Multidisciplinarity in Business and Science*, 2(2), 1–15.

Sharma, S. K. (2013). Destination marketing: An integrated marketing communication approach. *Journal of Management and Marketing Research*, 12, 1–11.

Sohaili, N. L. M., Aminudin, N., & Amir, A. F. (2022). Bleisure motivation towards leisure attraction: A systematic literature review. *Social Sciences*, 12(11), 910–922.

Solis-Radilla, M. M., Carvache-Franco, M., Carvache-Franco, O., & Carvache-Franco, W. (2021). Motivations as predictive variables of satisfaction and loyalty in coastal and marine destinations: A study in Acapulco, Mexico. *International Journal of Tourism Cities*, 7(3), 767–782. 10.1108/IJTC-12-2020-0283

Torkildsen, G. (1999). *Leisure and recreation management*. Spon Press.

Torkildsen, G. (2005). Leisure and recreation management *(fifth edition)*. London And Newyork: Taylor and Francis Group. 10.4324/9780203401651

Tretyakevich, N. (2015). Corporate mobility: Impacts on life domains and implications, (Ph.D), Faculty of Economics Universita della Svizzera İtaliana.

TUİK. (2024). Türkiye istatistik kurumu. Retrieved from. https://data.tuik.gov.tr/Bulten/Index?p=Turizm-Istatistikleri-IV.-Ceyrek:-Ekim---Aralik,-2023-53661#:~:text=Geli%C5%9F%20ama%C3%A7lar%C4% B1na%20g%C3%B6re%20ziyaret%C3%A7iler%2C%20IV.&text=Y%C4%B1l1%C4%B1k%20olarak%20de%C4%9Ferlendirildi%C4%9Finde%20ziyaret%C3%A7ilerin%20geli%C5%9F,ve%20arkada%C5%9F%20ziyareti%22%20amac%C4%B1yla%20geldi, Accessed: 07.05.2024.

TURSAB. (2024). Türkiye sehayat acantaları birliği. Retrieved from. https://www.tursab.org.tr/assets/pdf/tursab-akademi/e-egitim/konu-ozetleri/unite-08.pdf

Ünal, A., & Özgürel, G. (2021). A research on determining the destination quality perceptions and intentions to revisit of bleisure tourists: İstanbul case. *Tourism and Recreation*, 3(1), 1–10.

Unger, O., & Uriely, N. (2022). The bleisure memories of business travelers. *Annals of Tourism Research*, 97, 1–13. 10.1016/j.annals.2022.103497

Van der Merwe, P., Slabbert, E., & Saayman, M. (2011). Travel motivations of tourists to selected marine destinations. *International Journal of Tourism Research*, 13(5), 457–467. 10.1002/jtr.820

Chapter 8
How Technology Is Revolutionizing the Bleisure Experiences of Tourists in Malaysia

Md. Tariqul Islam
https://orcid.org/0000-0002-7367-2989
Taylor's University, Malaysia

Jeetesh Kumar
https://orcid.org/0000-0001-9878-1228
Taylor's University, Malaysia

Rupam Konar
https://orcid.org/0000-0002-3235-3842
Taylor's University, Malaysia

ABSTRACT

This study explores the synergy between technology and bleisure tourism in Malaysia, investigating their combined impact on enriching travel experiences. The chapter aims to uncover insights and implications for the future of bleisure tourism in Malaysia by examining technological advancements, sustainability initiatives, and emerging trends. Findings reveal that technology has democratised travel, making it more accessible and personalised, while sustainability initiatives have promoted responsible tourism practices and environmental conservation. Moreover, emerging technologies such as virtual reality and artificial intelligence offer innovative ways for tourists to engage with destinations and cultural attractions. The study highlights the importance of continued research and collaboration in driving in-

DOI: 10.4018/979-8-3693-4354-8.ch008

novation and sustainability in the bleisure tourism industry, positioning Malaysia as a destination for tourists seeking memorable, responsible, and technologically enhanced experiences.

INTRODUCTION

Bleisure tourism, a fusion of "business" and "leisure," epitomises a contemporary travel trend where individuals merge professional obligations with recreational pursuits, thereby blurring the demarcation between work and play (Miao et al., 2024). This emergent phenomenon has garnered global attention, reshaping conventional business trips into more fulfilling and multifaceted experiences. Technology shapes and enriches bleisure tourism, offering convenience, efficiency, and personalised experiences (Milosh, 2023). In Malaysia, bleisure tourism holds profound significance, fostering growth within its tourism sector and bolstering its economic vitality. This comprehensive introduction will offer an overarching view of leisure tourism, underline the pivotal role of technology in advancing tourism, and illuminate the profound significance of leisure tourism within the Malaysian context.

Bleisure tourism embodies extending business-related excursions to incorporate leisure activities, allowing tourists to explore new locales, immerse themselves in local culture, and unwind from professional commitments (Miao et al., 2024). Historically, business travel was characterised by packed schedules, scant free time, and minimal scope for leisure. However, with evolving work dynamics and an increasing emphasis on work-life equilibrium, many professionals are embracing bleisure travel, considering it a means to intertwine work obligations with leisure pursuits.

Bleisure tourists adeptly leverage technology to seamlessly integrate work and leisure activities (Miao et al., 2024). They often employ mobile applications to secure accommodations, navigate unfamiliar territories and unearth local attractions. Additionally, remote work technology enables professionals to remain connected and productive while moving, further blurring the dichotomy between work and leisure.

The allure of bleisure tourism lies in its ability to furnish a balanced and comprehensive travel experience. Business tourists can optimise their time in a destination by delving into its cultural tapestry, savouring local gastronomy, and engaging in recreational pursuits (Jimenez Ruiz et al., 2024). This amalgamation of work and leisure heightens the travel experience and increases productivity and job satisfaction.

Technology has undergone a paradigm shift in tourism, empowering tourists with unfettered access to information, convenience, and tailored experiences (Pencarelli, 2020). From the initial planning phase to the culmination of the travel journey, technology is indispensable in facilitating every facet of the trip.

Online booking platforms, travel websites, and mobile applications have streamlined the process of researching, planning, and booking travel arrangements (Vayghan et al., 2023). Tourists can seamlessly compare prices, peruse reviews, and secure reservations with minimal effort, thereby obviating the necessity for traditional travel agencies.

Technology perpetuates its role in augmenting the tourism experience throughout the travel phase. Navigation applications furnish real-time directions and traffic updates, ensuring tourists reach their destinations expeditiously (Ye et al., 2023). Furthermore, translation applications obliterate linguistic barriers, enabling tourists to communicate with locals and navigate unfamiliar terrain seamlessly. Moreover, technology engenders personalised and immersive experiences by integrating virtual reality (VR), augmented reality (AR), and interactive mobile applications. Travelers can virtually explore destinations, partake in guided tours, and immerse themselves in cultural showcases, fostering a deeper understanding and appreciation of diverse cultures. Technology engenders efficiency, convenience, and gratification throughout the travel journey, rendering it an indispensable tool for contemporary tourists.

SIGNIFICANCE OF BLEISURE TOURISM IN MALAYSIA

Within the Malaysian context, bleisure tourism holds profound significance for both the tourism sector and the broader economy (Sohaili et al., 2022). As an eclectic and diverse destination, Malaysia boasts an array of attractions, ranging from pristine beaches and verdant rainforests to dynamic urban hubs and rich cultural heritage. Situated strategically within Southeast Asia, Malaysia is a focal point for business and leisure tourists (Sohaili et al., 2022). Endowed with state-of-the-art conference facilities, international airports, and modern infrastructure, Malaysia attracts a steady influx of business tourists from across the globe. Nonetheless, it is not solely business tourists who gravitate towards Malaysia. The country's unique blend of modernity and tradition and its warm hospitality and affordability render it an alluring destination for leisure tourists.

LITERATURE REVIEW

Technological Innovations in Transportation

Technological advancements in transportation have significantly transformed how people move from one place to another. From the convenience of ride-hailing services to the precision of navigation apps and the accessibility of public transportation apps, these innovations have revolutionised the travel experience for individuals around the globe (Iskandar et al., 2020).

Ride-hailing services, also known as transportation network companies (TNCs), have emerged as a convenient and efficient alternative to traditional taxi services (Grahn et al., 2020). Platforms like Uber, Lyft, and Grab have revolutionised urban mobility by connecting passengers with drivers through mobile applications. One of the primary advantages of ride-hailing services is their accessibility and convenience. With just a few taps on their smartphones, passengers can request a ride from anywhere, anytime. This on-demand model eliminates the need to wait for taxis or rely on public transportation schedules, providing greater flexibility and freedom in travel. Moreover, ride-hailing services often offer a range of vehicle options to suit passengers' preferences and needs. Whether it is a standard sedan, a luxury vehicle, or a larger vehicle for group travel, passengers can choose the type of vehicle that best fits their requirements. Additionally, ride-hailing services employ advanced technologies to optimise the efficiency of their operations. Algorithms analyse real-time demand patterns and traffic conditions, enabling drivers to navigate efficiently and passengers to reach their destinations quickly. Despite the numerous benefits, ride-hailing services have faced criticism and regulatory challenges, particularly regarding safety, driver wages, and congestion. However, advancements in technology and regulations continue to address these concerns, ensuring that ride-hailing services remain a valuable component of modern transportation systems.

Moreover, navigation apps have become indispensable for tourists seeking efficient and accurate destination directions (Dickinson et al., 2014). Platforms like Google Maps, Waze, and Apple Maps leverage GPS technology and real-time traffic data to provide turn-by-turn navigation, route optimisation, and traffic alerts. One of the critical benefits of navigation apps is their ability to offer personalised and dynamic routing solutions. These apps can suggest alternative routes to help users avoid delays and congestion by analysing real-time traffic conditions, road closures, and accidents. This saves time and reduces stress and frustration during the journey. In addition, navigation apps have evolved beyond simple directions to offer many additional features and services. Users can find nearby points of interest, such as restaurants, gas stations, and attractions, and access reviews, ratings, and photos to make informed decisions. Some apps even integrate public transportation information, bike routes, and walking directions to provide comprehensive multi-modal navigation options. Another notable aspect of navigation apps is their integration with other technologies and platforms. For example, users can seamlessly share their real-time location with friends and family, coordinate meetups, and track the arrival of delivery services or rideshare vehicles. While navigation apps have undoubtedly enhanced the travel experience for millions of users worldwide, they are not without limitations. Issues such as data privacy, battery consumption, and occasional inaccuracies in mapping data remain areas of concern. Nonetheless, technological advancements and user feedback continue to drive improvements and innovation in navigation app development.

In addition, public transportation apps have revolutionised how commuters navigate and utilise public transit systems in urban areas (Handte et al., 2016). These apps, offered by transit agencies or third-party developers, provide users with real-time information on routes, schedules, fares, and service disruptions for buses, trains, subways, and other modes of public transportation. One of the primary advantages of public transportation apps is their ability to empower users with up-to-date information and trip-planning tools. By accessing detailed route maps, timetables, and service alerts, commuters can make informed decisions about their journeys, such as choosing the most efficient route or deciding when to leave to catch the next bus or train. Public transportation apps often integrate features such as mobile ticketing and fare payment, allowing users to purchase tickets or passes directly from their smartphones. This eliminates the need for physical tickets or cash, streamlines the boarding process, and reduces the risk of fare evasion. Moreover, public transportation apps contribute to improved efficiency and reliability of public transit systems by providing valuable data insights to transit agencies (Ge et al., 2021). By analysing usage patterns, passenger demand, and service performance metrics, agencies can optimise routes, schedules, and resource allocation to meet commuters' needs better. Furthermore, public transportation apps are vital in promoting sustainable mobility and reducing car dependency in urban areas. By providing seamless and user-friendly access to public transit information, these apps encourage more people to choose public transportation as their preferred mode of travel, leading to reduced traffic congestion, air pollution, and greenhouse gas emissions.

Despite the numerous benefits of public transportation apps, challenges such as limited coverage, integration issues with multiple transit systems, and disparities in digital literacy and smartphone ownership among certain demographic groups remain barriers to widespread adoption (Bian et al., 2022). However, ongoing efforts to expand app availability, improve user experience, and address equity concerns are helping to overcome these challenges and make public transportation more accessible and inclusive for all. Technological innovations in transportation, including ride-hailing services, navigation apps, and public transportation apps, have revolutionised how people travel and navigate urban environments. By offering greater convenience, efficiency, and accessibility, these innovations have transformed the travel experience for millions of users worldwide and continue to drive advancements in mobility and urban transportation systems.

Accommodation Enhancements through Technology

In today's digital age, technology has transformed the hospitality industry, revolutionising how accommodations are booked, experienced, and enjoyed by tourists worldwide (Buhalis et al., 2019). From the convenience of online booking platforms to the immersive experiences offered by virtual tours and augmented reality and the innovative features of smart hotels, technology has enhanced every aspect of the accommodation experience.

Online booking platforms have become the go-to method for tourists to search for and reserve accommodations. Websites and mobile applications such as Booking.com, Airbnb, Expedia, and Hotels.com offer users a vast selection of hotels, vacation rentals, and other lodging options, along with detailed descriptions, photos, reviews, and pricing information. These platforms allow tourists to browse and book accommodations from the comfort of their homes or on the go, eliminating the need to visit multiple websites or contact individual hotels directly (Gössling & Lane, 2015). Moreover, online booking platforms often feature advanced search filters and recommendation algorithms that help users find accommodations tailored to their preferences, budgets, and travel dates. Many platforms offer secure payment processing and flexible cancellation policies, giving tourists peace of mind when making reservations.

Virtual tours and augmented reality (AR) have transformed how tourists explore and experience accommodations before booking. Virtual tours allow users to virtually navigate through hotel rooms, lobbies, amenities, and surrounding areas using interactive 360-degree panoramic images or videos (Cha et al., 2023). These immersive experiences give tourists a realistic sense of the layout, design, and ambience of accommodations, enabling them to make more informed booking decisions. Similarly, augmented reality (AR) technology enhances the visualisation of accommodations by overlaying digital information, such as virtual furniture, decor, or amenities, onto real-world environments captured through a smartphone or tablet camera. This lets tourists virtually "try before they buy" and envision themselves staying in a hotel room or vacation rental, enhancing their confidence and satisfaction with their booking choices (Slevitch et al., 2022). Moreover, virtual tours and AR experiences can be accessed through websites, mobile apps, or wearable devices, making them accessible to tourists anytime, anywhere.

Smart hotel features leverage the power of technology to enhance the comfort, convenience, and efficiency of the guest experience. Smart hotel features offer guests a seamless and tailored stay, from keyless entry and in-room automation to personalised services and IoT (Internet of Things) connectivity (Das, 2023). Keyless entry systems, such as mobile vital apps or RFID (Radio Frequency Identification) wristbands, allow guests to bypass traditional check-in procedures and access their rooms using their smartphones or wearable devices, improving security and streamlining the arrival process. In-room automation systems enable guests to control lighting, temperature, entertainment, and other amenities through voice commands or mobile apps, providing a personalised and intuitive experience. Furthermore, smart hotels utilise data analytics and artificial intelligence (AI) algorithms to anticipate guest preferences and deliver personalised recommendations, offers, and services throughout their stay (Das, 2023). Whether recommending nearby restaurants, arranging transportation, or fulfilling special requests, innovative hotel features aim to exceed guest expectations and enhance overall satisfaction.

Technology has revolutionised how accommodations are booked, experienced, and enjoyed by tourists worldwide. From the convenience of online booking platforms to the immersive experiences offered by virtual tours and augmented reality and the innovative features of smart hotels, technology has enhanced every aspect of the accommodation experience. By leveraging advanced technologies, hospitality providers can create more seamless, personalised, and memorable stays for their guests, driving greater satisfaction, loyalty, and revenue in the competitive hospitality industry.

Digital Communication and Information Tools

In today's interconnected world, digital communication and information tools have become indispensable for tourists seeking seamless and convenient experiences (Buhalis et al., 2011). From breaking down language barriers with translation apps to facilitating secure transactions with mobile payment solutions and staying connected with loved ones through social media platforms, these technologies are crucial in enhancing the travel experience.

Translation apps have revolutionised how tourists communicate and interact with people from different linguistic backgrounds (Karusala et al., 2018). Platforms such as Google Translate, Microsoft Translator, and iTranslate enable users to instantly translate text, speech, and images between multiple languages. Whether deciphering street signs, ordering at restaurants, or asking for directions, translation apps provide tourists with a convenient and reliable tool to overcome language barriers and navigate unfamiliar environments. Moreover, many translation apps offer offline functionality, allowing users to access translations even when they do not have an internet connection, making them invaluable companions for international tourists. Additionally, some apps offer advanced features such as real-time conversation translation, voice recognition, and language detection, further enhancing the accuracy and versatility of translation services. Overall, translation apps empower tourists to communicate confidently and effectively in any language, opening up new possibilities for cultural exchange and connection during their journeys.

Mobile payment solutions have transformed how tourists manage their finances and make purchases while on the go. With the rise of digital wallets, contactless payments, and mobile banking apps, tourists can now securely and conveniently pay for goods and services using their smartphones or other mobile devices (Bezovski, 2016). Platforms such as Apple Pay, Google Pay, Samsung Pay, and PayPal offer users a seamless and secure way to store payment information, make transactions, and track spending in real time. Whether booking flights, reserving accommodations, or shopping at local markets, mobile payment solutions enable tourists to streamline their financial transactions and reduce the need to carry cash or multiple credit cards. Moreover, mobile payment technologies continue to evolve, introducing features such as peer-to-peer payments, loyalty rewards, and integration with transportation systems, further enhancing the convenience and utility of digital payment methods for tourists. As mobile payment solutions become increasingly widespread and accepted worldwide, they are poised to become the preferred choice for tourists seeking a fast, secure, and hassle-free way to manage their finances.

Social media platforms have become essential for tourists to share their experiences, connect with others, and discover new destinations and activities. Platforms such as Facebook, Instagram, Twitter, and YouTube serve as virtual travel guides, allowing users to access a wealth of travel inspiration, tips, and recommendations from fellow tourists, influencers, and brands (Dimitriou & AbouElgheit, 2019). Through photos, videos, and personal anecdotes, tourists can showcase their adventures, document their experiences, and inspire others to explore the world. Moreover, social media platforms offer a platform for tourists to connect with locals, seek expert advice, and join online communities dedicated to specific destinations or travel interests. Whether it is sharing travel itineraries, seeking restaurant recommendations, or finding travel companions, social media platforms facilitate meaningful interactions and collaborations among tourists from diverse backgrounds and interests. Furthermore, travel brands and businesses leverage social media platforms to engage with customers, promote their products and services, and cultivate brand loyalty through targeted advertising, influencer partnerships, and user-generated content (Gabelaia & McElroy, 2023). As social media continues to evolve and integrate new features such as live streaming, augmented reality, and virtual reality, it will continue to shape how tourists plan, experience, and share their journeys with the world. Digital communication and information tools enhance modern-day tourists' travel experience (Zheng et al., 2022). Whether it is breaking down language barriers with translation apps, managing finances with mobile payment solutions, or connecting with others through social media platforms, these technologies empower tourists to navigate the world with confidence, convenience, and connectivity. As technology continues to evolve and innovate, it will undoubtedly play an increasingly important role in shaping the future of travel, enabling tourists to explore new destinations, forge meaningful connections, and create unforgettable memories wherever their adventures take them.

Personalised Experiences and Recommendation Systems

Personalised experiences and recommendation systems have become integral components of modern travel, catering to the unique preferences and interests of individual tourists (Wang, 2020). Advanced algorithms, data analytics, machine learning techniques, travel recommender systems, personalised itinerary planning apps, and geo-targeted offers and discounts aim to enhance the travel experience by providing tailored recommendations, curated itineraries, and exclusive deals.

Travel recommender systems leverage user data, historical preferences, and collaborative filtering algorithms to deliver personalised accommodations, activities, and attractions recommendations. Platforms like TripAdvisor, Airbnb, and Netflix analyse user behaviour, search patterns, and ratings to generate customised suggestions matching each tourist's preferences and interests. By considering destination, budget, travel dates, and past experiences, travel recommender systems help users discover new destinations, find hidden gems, and make informed travel plans. Moreover, some recommender systems incorporate social networking features, allowing users to see recommendations from friends, family, and fellow tourists, further enhancing the relevance and credibility of the suggestions. Overall, travel recommender systems empower tourists to explore new horizons, discover unique experiences, and create memorable journeys tailored to their tastes and preferences.

Personalised itinerary planning apps offer tourists a convenient and efficient way to organise and optimise their travel plans (Chiang & Huang, 2015). Platforms like TripIt, Sygic Travel, and Google Trips enable users to create customised itineraries, track reservations, and access real-time information about flights, accommodations, and activities in one centralised hub. These apps automatically generate detailed itineraries by syncing with email accounts, calendars, and booking confirmations and provide personalised recommendations based on user preferences, interests, and available time. Additionally, some itinerary planning apps offer offline access, map integration, and collaborative sharing, allowing users to access their plans anytime, anywhere, and collaborate with travel companions. Whether exploring famous landmarks, trying local cuisine, or embarking on off-the-beaten-path adventures, personalised itinerary planning apps empower tourists to maximise their time, discover new experiences, and create seamless travel experiences tailored to their unique interests and preferences.

Geo-targeted offers and discounts leverage location-based technology and data analytics to deliver targeted promotions, deals, and incentives to tourists based on their current location or travel history (Fong et al., 2015). Platforms like Groupon,

Expedia, and Airbnb use geolocation data, user profiles, and purchase history to offer personalised discounts, special offers, and exclusive experiences tailored to each tourist's preferences and behaviour. By identifying nearby attractions, restaurants, and activities, geo-targeted offers and discounts encourage tourists to explore their surroundings, discover new experiences, and take advantage of exclusive deals available only to them. Moreover, some platforms use push notifications, email alerts, and in-app messages to notify users of relevant offers and promotions in real-time, increasing engagement and conversion rates. Overall, geo-targeted offers and discounts provide tourists with added value, savings, and incentives to enhance their travel experiences and make the most of their journeys.

Personalised experiences and recommendation systems have transformed how tourists discover, plan, and enjoy their journeys (Kabassi, 2010). Whether receiving customised recommendations from travel recommender systems, organising and optimising travel plans with personalised itinerary planning apps or accessing exclusive deals and discounts through geo-targeted offers, these technologies empower tourists to create memorable and fulfilling experiences tailored to their preferences and interests. As technology continues to evolve and innovate, personalised experiences and recommendation systems will play an increasingly important role in shaping the future of travel, enabling tourists to explore new destinations, connect with local culture, and create unforgettable memories wherever their adventures take them.

Enhancing Cultural and Leisure Experiences

Enhancing cultural and leisure experiences through technology has become increasingly prevalent in the travel industry, offering tourists innovative ways to immerse themselves in destinations' rich heritage and vibrant culture. Technology has transformed how tourists engage with and appreciate cultural attractions, from virtual reality (VR) cultural experiences to the gamification of cultural heritage sites and mobile apps for local events and activities.

Virtual reality (VR) cultural experiences offer tourists an immersive and interactive way to explore museums, historical sites, and cultural landmarks from the comfort of their homes or while travelling (Pillai & Sivathanu, 2020). VR technology allows users to don a headset and enter a virtual environment to walk through ancient ruins, examine priceless artefacts, and interact with lifelike representations of historical figures and events. Platforms such as Google Arts & Culture, Oculus Rift, and HTC Vive offer a wide range of VR experiences that transport users to iconic cultural destinations worldwide, providing a deeper understanding and appreciation of different cultures and civilisations. Moreover, VR cultural experiences can be accessed through VR headsets, mobile apps, or web browsers, making them accessible to tourists of all ages and backgrounds (Bekele et al., 2018). By bringing cultural attractions to life in a virtual space, VR technology enables tourists to explore the world's cultural heritage in an immersive and engaging manner, fostering a greater sense of connection and empathy with the past.

The gamification of cultural heritage sites incorporates gameplay, storytelling, and interactivity elements to enhance the visitor experience and encourage deeper engagement with historical and cultural landmarks (Khan et al., 2020). Gamification techniques such as scavenger hunts, augmented reality (AR) challenges, and interactive exhibits transform traditional tourist attractions into dynamic and entertaining experiences that appeal to tourists of all ages (Pillai & Sivathanu, 2020). For example, mobile apps such as Pokémon GO and ARtours guide users on virtual treasure hunts through city streets, parks, and landmarks, where they can discover hidden gems, solve puzzles, and unlock digital rewards. Similarly, heritage sites and museums incorporate gamified experiences such as interactive exhibits, themed trails, and digital storytelling installations to engage visitors and make learning about history and culture more fun and memorable (Othman et al., 2021). By combining technology with gamification, cultural heritage sites can attract new audiences, encourage repeat visits, and foster a deeper appreciation for the significance of historical and cultural landmarks in society.

Mobile apps for local events and activities offer tourists a convenient and personalised way to discover and participate in cultural events, festivals, and recreational activities in destinations around the world (Luxford & Dickinson, 2015). From live music concerts and art exhibitions to food festivals and outdoor adventures, mobile apps provide users with up-to-date information, schedules, and recommendations for local events and activities happening in their vicinity. Platforms such as Eventbrite, Meetup, and TripAdvisor offer comprehensive listings of events, attractions, and experiences tailored to each user's interests, preferences, and location. Moreover, many mobile apps feature social networking, allowing users to connect with like-minded tourists, join group activities, and share their experiences with friends and followers. By harnessing the power of mobile technology, local event apps empower tourists to immerse themselves in the cultural fabric of a destination, discover hidden gems, and connect with local communities in meaningful and authentic ways. Whether attending a traditional dance performance, sampling street food at a night market, or exploring nature trails in a national park, mobile apps provide tourists endless opportunities to explore and experience the rich cultural tapestry of destinations worldwide.

Technology has revolutionised how tourists engage with and appreciate cultural and leisure experiences, offering innovative solutions that enhance immersion, interactivity, and personalisation. Whether through virtual reality (VR) cultural experiences, the gamification of cultural heritage sites, or mobile apps for local events and activities, technology enables tourists to explore the world's cultural heritage in new and exciting ways (Othman et al., 2021). As technology evolves and innovates, cultural and leisure experiences will become increasingly immersive, interactive, and accessible, enriching the travel experience and fostering a deeper appreciation for the diversity and richness of cultures worldwide.

Sustainability and Responsible Tourism Technologies

Sustainability and responsible tourism have become increasingly important considerations in the travel industry as concerns about environmental conservation and social responsibility continue to grow (Mihalic, 2016). In response to these challenges, various technologies have emerged to promote eco-friendly practices, reduce carbon footprints, and support sustainable tourism initiatives.

Eco-friendly transportation options are essential to sustainable tourism, offering tourists environmentally friendly alternatives to traditional modes of transportation such as cars and aeroplanes (Olszewski-Strzyżowski, 2022). Electric vehicles (EVs), hybrid cars, bicycles, and electric scooters are eco-friendly transportation options that help reduce greenhouse gas emissions, minimise air pollution, and alleviate traffic congestion in popular tourist destinations. Moreover, initiatives such as bike-sharing programs, carpooling services, and shuttle buses powered by renewable energy sources provide tourists convenient and affordable ways to explore destinations while minimising their carbon footprint (Gordon, 2023). By embracing eco-friendly transportation options, tourists can contribute to preserving natural resources, protecting fragile ecosystems, and supporting local communities while enjoying sustainable travel experiences.

Carbon footprint calculators enable tourists to measure, track, and offset their carbon emissions associated with travel activities such as flights, accommodation, and transportation (Barret, 2020). These calculators use algorithms and data inputs such as distance travelled, fuel consumption, and energy usage to estimate the carbon dioxide (CO2) emissions generated by individual travel itineraries. Travelers can then use this information to make informed decisions about their travel plans, such as choosing more sustainable transportation options, staying at eco-friendly accommodations, or participating in carbon offset programs. Moreover, some carbon footprint calculators offer personalised recommendations for reducing emissions, educational resources on climate change and sustainability, and links to carbon offset projects that support renewable energy, reforestation, and conservation efforts worldwide. By raising awareness and promoting accountability for carbon emissions, carbon footprint calculators empower tourists to minimise their environmental impact and make responsible choices that contribute to a more sustainable tourism industry.

Sustainable tourism apps and platforms are digital tools that promote environmentally friendly practices, support local communities, and facilitate responsible travel experiences (Bhuiyan et al., 2022). These apps and platforms give tourists access to information, resources, and services, prioritising sustainability and social responsibility. For example, platforms such as Responsible Travel, Ecobnb, and Green Key offer curated listings of eco-friendly accommodations, tours, and activities that adhere to sustainable tourism principles such as resource conservation, waste reduction, and community engagement. Moreover, sustainable tourism apps and platforms often feature user-generated content, reviews, and ratings to help tourists make informed decisions about their travel plans and share their experiences with like-minded individuals. By promoting sustainable tourism practices and supporting responsible travel initiatives, these apps and platforms empower tourists to minimise their environmental footprint, preserve cultural heritage, and promote social equity while enjoying authentic and meaningful travel experiences.

Sustainability and responsible tourism technologies are vital in promoting environmental conservation, social responsibility, and sustainable development in the travel industry (Streimikiene et al., 2021). Whether it is through eco-friendly transportation options, carbon footprint calculators, or sustainable tourism apps and platforms, these technologies empower tourists to make informed decisions, reduce their environmental impact, and support local communities while enjoying memorable and responsible travel experiences. As sustainability continues to be a top priority for tourists and tourism stakeholders alike, adopting and integrating these technologies will be crucial in shaping the future of travel toward a more sustainable and resilient industry.

CHALLENGES AND FUTURE DIRECTIONS

In the ever-evolving landscape of bleisure tourism, challenges and opportunities shape its trajectory. From addressing the digital divide and accessibility issues to navigating data privacy and security concerns and exploring emerging technologies and trends, bleisure tourism's future is dynamic and complex.

The digital divide remains a significant challenge in ensuring equitable access to bleisure travel opportunities. While technology has facilitated connectivity and convenience for many, disparities in access to digital resources persist among different demographic groups and geographic regions. Socioeconomic factors, including income level, education, and infrastructure development, determine individuals' access to technology and the internet (Hargittai et al., 2019). Addressing the digital divide requires concerted efforts from governments, businesses, and civil society to invest in infrastructure, provide digital literacy training, and bridge the gap between urban and rural areas. By promoting digital inclusion and accessibility, stakeholders can ensure that all tourists can participate in bleisure tourism activities and benefit from its advantages.

Tene (2011) stated that data privacy and security concerns loom large in an increasingly interconnected world, where personal information is often shared and stored across various digital platforms and devices. As tourists engage with online booking platforms, mobile apps, and social media platforms to plan and document their bleisure experiences, they entrust their sensitive data to third-party providers. However, data breaches, identity theft, and privacy violations pose significant risks to tourists' personal and financial information. Moreover, the proliferation of location-based services and data-tracking technologies raises ethical questions about surveillance and consent (Abbas et al., 2014). To address these concerns, policymakers must enact robust data protection regulations, and businesses must implement stringent security measures and transparent data practices. Additionally, tourists should exercise caution when sharing personal information online and familiarise themselves with privacy settings and data management tools to safeguard their privacy and security while enjoying bleisure travel.

In addition, emerging technologies and trends promise to reshape the landscape of bleisure tourism and enhance the travel experience for modern-day tourists. Virtual reality (VR), augmented reality (AR), and artificial intelligence (AI) are poised to revolutionise how tourists explore destinations, interact with cultural attractions, and plan their leisure activities. VR and AR technologies offer immersive and interactive experiences that allow tourists to virtually visit museums, historical sites, and natural wonders from anywhere in the world. AI-powered chatbots and virtual assistants provide tourists with personalised recommendations, itinerary suggestions, and real-time assistance, enhancing convenience and efficiency throughout their journey (Pillai & Sivathanu, 2020). Furthermore, blockchain technology has the potential to improve transparency, security, and trust in the travel industry by enabling secure transactions, digital identity verification, and decentralised booking platforms (Banerji et al., 2021). As these technologies mature and become more accessible, they will shape the future of bleisure tourism by offering tourists new ways to explore, connect, and experience the world.

Bleisure tourism presents a unique blend of opportunities and challenges as it continues to evolve in response to changing travel preferences, technological advancements, and global trends. Addressing issues such as the digital divide and accessibility, data privacy and security while harnessing the potential of emerging technologies will be crucial in shaping the future of bleisure tourism and ensuring that it remains accessible, inclusive, and sustainable for all tourists. By embracing innovation, promoting responsible practices, and fostering collaboration across stakeholders, the future of bleisure tourism holds great promise in delivering enriching and memorable experiences for tourists around the globe.

DISCUSSION

The study surrounding the intersection of technology and tourism, particularly in the context of bleisure travel, is multifaceted and dynamic. As outlined in the preceding sections, technology plays a pivotal role in shaping the landscape of modern travel, offering both opportunities and challenges for tourists, businesses, and destination communities.

Digital communication and information tools have revolutionised how tourists plan, book, and experience their journeys (Pencarelli, 2020). Technology has empowered tourists with unprecedented access to information, convenience, and personalised experiences, from online booking and navigation apps to social media and translation apps. However, as highlighted, disparities in access to technology and concerns about data privacy and security persist, posing barriers to digital inclusion and raising ethical considerations about using personal data in the travel industry.

Moreover, the emergence of sustainability and responsible tourism technologies underscores a growing awareness of travel's environmental and social impacts. Eco-friendly transportation options, carbon footprint calculators, and sustainable tourism apps offer tourists tools to make more responsible choices and reduce their environmental footprint. However, challenges such as the digital divide and accessibility issues remain, as not all tourists have equal access to these technologies and resources. Furthermore, the ethical implications of data privacy and security in sustainability initiatives raise questions about transparency, consent, and accountability in collecting and using personal data for sustainability purposes.

Looking to the future, emerging technologies such as virtual reality (VR), augmented reality (AR), and artificial intelligence (AI) hold immense potential to transform the bleisure travel experience (Balasubramanian et al., 2022). VR and AR technologies offer immersive and interactive experiences that allow tourists to explore destinations, interact with cultural attractions, and engage in virtual tourism from anywhere in the world. AI-powered chatbots and virtual assistants provide personalised recommendations, itinerary suggestions, and real-time assistance, enhancing convenience and efficiency throughout the travel journey (Pillai & Sivathanu, 2020). Additionally, blockchain technology has the potential to revolutionise the travel industry by enabling secure transactions, digital identity verification, and decentralised booking platforms, fostering trust and transparency in travel transactions.

The discussion on technology and bleisure tourism is characterised by a complex interplay of opportunities and challenges. While technology can enhance the travel experience, promote sustainability, and drive innovation in the tourism industry, it also presents risks related to digital inclusion, data privacy, and ethical considerations. Moving forward, stakeholders in the travel industry need to embrace responsible practices, prioritise digital inclusion and accessibility, and navigate the ethical implications of emerging technologies to ensure that bleisure travel remains accessible, inclusive, and sustainable for all tourists. By fostering collaboration, innovation, and accountability, the future of bleisure tourism holds great promise in delivering enriching and memorable experiences for tourists worldwide.

Implications for Bleisure Tourism in Malaysia

The findings discussed have several implications for bleisure tourism in Malaysia. As a popular tourist destination known for its cultural diversity, natural beauty, and vibrant urban centres, Malaysia benefits from leveraging technology to enhance the bleisure travel experience. By embracing digital communication and information tools, Malaysian tourism stakeholders can improve the accessibility and convenience of bleisure travel for visitors. Online booking platforms, navigation apps, and translation tools can help tourists easily navigate the country's diverse attractions and engage in leisure activities.

Furthermore, Malaysia can position itself as a leader in sustainable tourism by adopting eco-friendly transportation options, promoting carbon offset initiatives, and supporting sustainable tourism practices. By investing in renewable energy, conservation efforts, and community engagement, Malaysia can attract environmentally conscious tourists and showcase its commitment to sustainability. Additionally, Malaysia can capitalise on emerging technologies such as VR, AR, and AI to offer tourists unique and immersive bleisure experiences. By integrating these technologies into cultural attractions, heritage sites, and leisure activities, Malaysia can differentiate itself as a cutting-edge destination and appeal to tech-savvy tourists seeking memorable and innovative experiences.

Recommendations for Future Research and Industry Practice

There are several recommendations for future research and industry practice in bleisure tourism. Firstly, further research is needed to explore the impact of technology on tourist behaviour, preferences, and satisfaction in the context of bleisure travel. By understanding the motivations and expectations of bleisure tourists, tourism stakeholders can tailor their offerings and experiences to meet the evolving needs of this segment. Additionally, there is a need for more comprehensive data collection and analysis regarding the environmental and social impacts of bleisure travel. Tourism stakeholders can assess sustainability initiatives' effectiveness and identify areas for improvement by measuring and monitoring factors such as carbon emissions, resource consumption, and community engagement.

Furthermore, industry collaboration and knowledge sharing drive innovation and best practices in bleisure tourism. Malaysia can create a supportive ecosystem for technological innovation, sustainability initiatives, and responsible tourism practices by fostering partnerships between government agencies, tourism boards, businesses, and academia. Technology can enhance the bleisure travel experience, promote sustainability, and drive innovation in the tourism industry. By embracing digital communication tools, sustainability initiatives, and emerging technologies, Malaysia can position itself as a leading destination for bleisure tourists, offering unique, memorable, and responsible experiences that showcase the country's cultural heritage, natural beauty, and technological prowess.

CONCLUSION

The exploration of technology's influence on enriching bleisure tourism experiences in Malaysia unveils a multifaceted landscape where innovation intersects with tradition, sustainability intersects with convenience, and personalisation intersects with responsibility. Throughout this chapter, we have delved into how technology is reshaping the bleisure travel experience, from the convenience of online booking platforms to the immersive potential of virtual reality cultural experiences. Let us now reflect on the critical insights gained and the implications for bleisure tourism in Malaysia. Technology has undeniably democratised travel, making it more accessible, convenient, and personalised for a broader range of tourists. Online booking platforms, navigation apps, and translation tools have empowered tourists to explore destinations and engage in leisure activities easily, transcending language barriers and logistical challenges. In Malaysia, where cultural diversity and natural beauty abound, leveraging these digital communication tools can enhance the bleisure travel experience, allowing visitors to immerse themselves in the country's rich tapestry of sights, sounds, and flavours.

Sustainability has emerged as a paramount consideration in the tourism industry, driven by growing environmental awareness and the need to preserve natural resources for future generations. Eco-friendly transportation options, carbon footprint calculators, and sustainable tourism apps offer tourists the tools to make more responsible choices and support sustainable tourism initiatives. In Malaysia, with its lush rainforests, pristine beaches, and diverse ecosystems, embracing sustainable tourism practices is essential for preserving the country's natural heritage and attracting environmentally conscious tourists who seek authentic and eco-friendly experiences. Moreover, emerging technologies such as virtual reality, augmented reality, and artificial intelligence hold immense potential to transform the bleisure travel experience, offering travelers new ways to explore destinations and engage with cultural attractions. By integrating these technologies into cultural sites, heritage trails, and leisure activities, Malaysia can offer immersive and innovative experiences that captivate and inspire visitors while showcasing the country's technological prowess and commitment to innovation. Looking ahead, there are several recommendations for future research and industry practice to enhance the bleisure tourism experience in Malaysia further. Firstly, continued research is needed to understand better the motivations, preferences, and behaviours of bleisure tourists, enabling tourism stakeholders to tailor their offerings and experiences to meet the evolving needs of this segment. Additionally, more comprehensive data collection and analysis are required to assess the environmental and social impacts of bleisure travel and to identify opportunities for improvement and innovation.

Furthermore, industry collaboration and knowledge sharing drive innovation and sustainability in bleisure tourism. Malaysia can create a supportive ecosystem for technological innovation, sustainability initiatives, and responsible tourism practices by fostering partnerships between government agencies, tourism boards, businesses, and academia. By embracing technology, sustainability, and innovation, Malaysia can position itself as a leading destination for bleisure tourists, offering unique, memorable, and responsible experiences that showcase the country's cultural heritage, natural beauty, and technological prowess. Technology can enrich the bleisure travel experience in Malaysia, offering convenience, sustainability, and innovation in equal measure. By leveraging digital communication tools, embracing sustainable tourism practices, and embracing emerging technologies, Malaysia can create a vibrant and inclusive bleisure tourism ecosystem that delights tourists, supports local communities, and preserves the country's natural and cultural heritage for future generations.

REFERENCES

Abbas, R., Michael, K., & Michael, M. G. (2014). Using a social-ethical framework to evaluate location-based services in an internet of things world. *International Journal of Information Ethics*, 22, 42–73. 10.29173/irie127

Balasubramanian, K., Kunasekaran, P., Konar, R., & Sakkthivel, A. M. (2022). *Insights for a Changing World* (Vol. II). Integrating augmented reality (AR) and virtual reality (VR) as marketing communications channels in the hospitality and tourism service sector. *In Marketing Communications and Brand Development in Emerging Markets*. Springer International Publishing.

Banerji, D., Rashideh, W., Arora, B., & Pratihari, A. R. (2021). Application potential of Blockchain technologies in the travel and tourism industry. In *Blockchain Applications in IoT Ecosystem* (pp. 289–299). Springer International Publishing. 10.1007/978-3-030-65691-1_19

Barret, D. (2020). Estimating, monitoring and minimising the travel footprint associated with the development of the Athena X-ray Integral Field Unit: An on-line travel footprint calculator released to the science community. *Experimental Astronomy*, 49, 183–216. 10.1007/s10686-020-09659-832836797

Bekele, M. K., Pierdicca, R., Frontoni, E., Malinverni, E. S., & Gain, J. (2018). A survey of augmented, virtual, and mixed reality for cultural heritage. *Journal on Computing and Cultural Heritage*, 11(2), 1–36. 10.1145/3145534

Bezovski, Z. (2016). The future of the mobile payment as electronic payment system. *European Journal of Business and Management*, 8(8), 127–132.

Bhuiyan, K. H., Jahan, I., Zayed, N. M., Islam, K. M. A., Suyaiya, S., Tkachenko, O., & Nitsenko, V. (2022). Smart tourism ecosystem: A new dimension toward sustainable value co-creation. *Sustainability (Basel)*, 14(22), 15043. 10.3390/su142215043

Buhalis, D., Harwood, T., Bogicevic, V., Viglia, G., Beldona, S., & Hofacker, C. (2019). Technological disruptions in services: Lessons from tourism and hospitality. *Journal of Service Management*, 30(4), 484–506. 10.1108/JOSM-12-2018-0398

Buhalis, D., Leung, D., & Rob, L. R. L. (2011). eTourism: critical information and communication technologies for tourism destinations. *In CABI eBooks* (pp. 205–224). https://doi.org/10.1079/9781845937621.0205

Cha, S. H., Ma, J. H., Seo, J., Kim, J. I., & Han, S. (2023). Empirical comparison of spatial experience between photo-based IVE and real space. *Architectural Science Review*, 66(1), 1–16. 10.1080/00038628.2022.2134089

Chiang, H. S., & Huang, T. C. (2015). User-adapted travel planning system for personalized schedule recommendation. *Information Fusion*, 21, 3–17. 10.1016/j.inffus.2013.05.011

Das, M. P. (2023). Technology and Guest experience: Innovations reshaping hotel management. *International Journal for Multidimensional Research Perspectives*, 1(3), 76–95.

Dimitriou, C. K., & AbouElgheit, E. (2019). Understanding generation Z's travel social decision-making. *Tourism and Hospitality Management*, 25(2), 311–334. 10.20867/thm.25.2.4

Fong, N. M., Fang, Z., & Luo, X. (2015). Geo-conquesting: Competitive locational targeting of mobile promotions. *JMR, Journal of Marketing Research*, 52(5), 726–735. 10.1509/jmr.14.0229

Gabelaia, I., & McElroy, J. W. (2023, October). The Impact of User-Generated Marketing on Creating Greater Audience Connections and Brand Loyalty. In *International Conference on Reliability and Statistics in Transportation and Communication* (pp. 389-403). Cham: Springer Nature Switzerland.

Gordon, A. (2023). The Role of Public Transportation Systems in Promoting Sustainable Mobility in Green Cities. *Advances in Urban Resilience and Sustainable City Design*, 15(6), 1–18.

Gössling, S., & Lane, B. (2015). Rural tourism and the development of Internet-based accommodation booking platforms: A study in the advantages, dangers and implications of innovation. *Journal of Sustainable Tourism*, 23(8-9), 1386–1403. 10.1080/09669582.2014.909448

Hargittai, E., Piper, A. M., & Morris, M. R. (2019). From internet access to internet skills: Digital inequality among older adults. *Universal Access in the Information Society*, 18(4), 881–890. 10.1007/s10209-018-0617-5

Jimenez Ruiz, A. E., Bhartiya, S., & Bhatt, V. (Eds.). (2024). *Promoting Sustainable Gastronomy Tourism and Community Development*. IGI Global. 10.4018/979-8-3693-1814-0

Kabassi, K. (2010). Personalizing recommendations for tourists. *Telematics and Informatics*, 27(1), 51–66. 10.1016/j.tele.2009.05.003

Karusala, N., Vishwanath, A., Vashistha, A., Kumar, S., & Kumar, N. (2018, April). " Only if you use English you will get to more things" Using Smartphones to Navigate Multilingualism. In *Proceedings of the 2018 CHI Conference on Human Factors in Computing Systems* (pp. 1-14).

Khan, I., Melro, A., Amaro, A. C., & Oliveira, L. (2020). Systematic review on gamification and cultural heritage dissemination. *Journal of Digital Media & Interaction*, 3(8), 19–41.

Luxford, A. M. Y., & Dickinson, J. E. (2015). The role of mobile applications in the consumer experience at music festivals. *Event Management*, 19(1), 33–46. 10.3727/152599515X14229071392909

Miao, L., Yang, F. X., Im, J., & Zhang, Q. (2024). Flexwork and flextravel. *Annals of Tourism Research*, 106, 103763. 10.1016/j.annals.2024.103763

Mihalic, T. (2016). Sustainable-responsible tourism discourse–Towards 'responsustable'tourism. *Journal of Cleaner Production*, 111, 461–470. 10.1016/j.jclepro.2014.12.062

Milosh, P. (2023). *Evolving Preferences*. Understanding Contemporary Luxury Hotel Guests. [Bachelor's thesis, Jyväskylä: Jamk University of Applied Sciences]

Olszewski-Strzyżowski, D. J. (2022). Promotional activities of selected National Tourism Organizations (NTOs) in the light of sustainable tourism (including sustainable transport). *Sustainability (Basel)*, 14(5), 2561. 10.3390/su14052561

Othman, M. K., Aman, S., Anuar, N. N., & Ahmad, I. (2021). Improving children's cultural heritage experience using game-based learning at a living museum. *Journal on Computing and Cultural Heritage*, 14(3), 1–24. 10.1145/3453073

Pencarelli, T. (2020). The digital revolution in the travel and tourism industry. *Information Technology & Tourism*, 22(3), 455–476. 10.1007/s40558-019-00160-3

Pillai, R., & Sivathanu, B. (2020). Adoption of AI-based chatbots for hospitality and tourism. *International Journal of Contemporary Hospitality Management*, 32(10), 3199–3226. 10.1108/IJCHM-04-2020-0259

Slevitch, L., Chandrasekera, T., Mejia-Puig, L., Korneva, K., & Akosa, J. S. (2022). Virtual Reality images' impact on cognition and affect in hotel promotions: Application of self-reported and psycho-physiological measures. *Journal of Hospitality and Tourism Management*, 53, 176–187. 10.1016/j.jhtm.2022.10.005

Streimikiene, D., Svagzdiene, B., Jasinskas, E., & Simanavicius, A. (2021). Sustainable tourism development and competitiveness: The systematic literature review. *Sustainable Development (Bradford)*, 29(1), 259–271. 10.1002/sd.2133

Tene, O. (2011). Privacy: The new generations. *International data privacy law, 1*(1), 15-27.

Vayghan, S., Baloglu, D., & Baloglu, S. (2023). The impact of utilitarian, social and hedonic values on hotel booking mobile app engagement and loyalty: A comparison of generational cohorts. *Journal of Hospitality and Tourism Insights*, 6(5), 1990–2011. 10.1108/JHTI-06-2022-0229

Wang, X. (2020). Personalized recommendation framework design for online tourism: Know you better than yourself. *Industrial Management & Data Systems*, 120(11), 2067–2079. 10.1108/IMDS-05-2020-0278

Ye, X., Li, S., Das, S., & Du, J. (2023). Enhancing routes selection with real-time weather data integration in spatial decision support systems. *Spatial Information Research,* 1-9.

Zheng, K., Kumar, J., Kunasekaran, P., & Valeri, M. (2022). Role of smart technology use behaviour in enhancing tourist revisit intention: the theory of planned behaviour perspective. *European Journal of Innovation Management*, (ahead-of-print).

Chapter 9
Co-Working Spaces and Digital Nomadism in the Philippines:
Understanding Bleisure Tourism's Role in Diffusion of Culture

John Ericson Antigua Policarpio
Olivarez College, Philippines

Janice Ley B. Pacete
https://orcid.org/0009-0003-2712-9509
Olivarez College, Philippines

ABSTRACT

The rise of digital nomadism and bleisure tourism is reshaping work and travel paradigms, particularly in Southeast Asian countries like the Philippines. However, there is a dearth of studies that delve into the interplay between co-working spaces, digital nomadism, bleisure tourism, and cultural diffusion in the Southeast Asian context. This chapter employed a qualitative approach, conducting semi-structured interviews with co-working space visitors and owners in the Philippines to understand the dynamics of cultural exchange within these spaces. The findings reveal that co-working spaces foster cultural immersion, knowledge transfer, and professional networking among digital nomads and locals. These spaces serve as conduits for cultural diffusion, where both visitors and locals exchange cultural practices, language, and knowledge. The implications of this chapter underscore the need for co-working spaces to prioritize cultural sensitivity and implement safeguarding measures to ensure responsible and sustainable cultural exchange in the context of bleisure tourism.

DOI: 10.4018/979-8-3693-4354-8.ch009

INTRODUCTION

Throughout the existence of man, mobility has been part of everyone's daily lives. Whether traveling for leisure, business, or any other purpose, human beings are moving from one place to another to fulfill such needs. Maslow (1943) argued a classical point of view that motivated behavior, whether preparatory or consummatory, has spurs out from more than one motivation. In the context of tourism, the purpose of travel may be anchored on more than one motivator. In this case, both conscious and unconscious motivations to travel (Jang et al., 2009) have been evident in every traveler regardless of the purpose of wandering. Thus, there is a strong classical foundation for the existence of the phenomenon of leisure tourism.

Bleisure tourism can easily be stated as the combination of business and leisure travel of a person in a chosen destination or set of destinations. Scholarly arguments highlighted that bleisure travel has blurred lines in terms of the motivation for travel as existing literature on travel motivation has always been strapped on the context of leisure travel (Lichy & McLeay, 2018), neglecting the focus on traveling for business purposes. Research contemporaries in the realm of bleisure travel started exploring this phenomenon in the early 2010's to present (Batala & Slevitch, 2024; Chung et al., 2020; Lichy & McLeay, 2018; Pinho & Marques, 2021a; Tsaur & Tsai, 2023. Bleisure as an experience economy has been seen as a lucrative area of tourism as it focuses on two intertwined purposes of travel (Batala & Slevitch, 2024) and thus, effective destination marketing for bleisure tourist market should be prioritized (Batala & Slevitch, 2024).

In the context of cultural diffusion in tourism, L Kroeber (1940) theorized cultural diffusion in his paper, "Stimulus Diffusion". This theory highlighted that diffusion only happens in pieces and the fragments of culture from the visiting country are diffused towards the host country which may be subjected to change across time, space, nature, and dimension of the cultural piece being diffused. Furthermore, Coşkun (2021) applied cultural diffusion in tourism studies by emphasizing the elements of culture that can be diffused and measured such as art, knowledge, language, poetry, and religion. In his paper, the diffusion exchange also happens between the host and the visitor. Thus, this chapter provides a necessity to understand how cultural diffusion creates an interplay between the bleisure tourism stakeholders of the host community and the digital nomads.

Digital nomadism is a phenomenon in the travel industry as man seeks temporary escape, relaxation, and change of environment while bringing in their work with them. Digital nomads value community characteristics, work environment, convenience, and local tips when choosing a destination (Chevtaeva, 2021). However, challenges of bleisure travel for digital nomads have been identified clearly by Chevtaeva (2021) and this includes limited availability of co-working spaces, the inevitable noise of the community, high rental prices, and lack of privacy.

Moving forward with co-working spaces as an essential element of this chapter, co-working spaces are defined as a temporary work environment that provides a range of services to cater to business professionals, both coming from the host community and the visitors (Merkel, 2022). In recent years, co-working spaces have evolved from serving local business professionals, micro and small business owners, and freelancers to a more complex market segment such as domestic and international bleisure tourists (Fuzi, 2015; Merkel, 2022; Rukmana et al., 2023). Supporting this chapter is the contemporary work of Orel, 2019) where he emphasized the relationship between co-working spaces and digital nomadism in five co-working spaces in Europe. He argued the importance of co-working spaces in the enhancement of the digital nomad's productivity, socialization, and well-being. Though there is evidence of contemporary works on digital nomadism and co-working spaces, there is a dearth of studies that focus in the context of these variables towards bleisure tourism and diffusion of culture. Also, a few studies in the same context are evident in Southeast Asian studies.

This book chapter will attempt to discuss the relationship between Co-working spaces and digital nomadism in a Southeast Asian context. The Philippines was chosen as the locale of this paper because there is a significant growth of bleisure travel evidenced by the increasing demands on tourism destination-based co-working spaces for both local and international visitors. Apart from studying its relationship, this book chapter will also attempt to contextualize bleisure travel and cultural diffusion in a social space like co-working spaces frequented by digital nomads. A sample of key informants coming from both the visitors and co-working space owners will be interviewed to gather relevant responses that may be useful in drawing the results, discussion, and subsequently, the output of this chapter.

LITERATURE REVIEW

The succeeding part of this chapter is devoted to uncover previous works conducted to identify the need for the conduct of the current study. Sections includes Digital nomadism and the Philippine tourism landscape, Bleisure tourism: beyond the laptops and beaches, Cultural diffusion: a digital nomadic influence, and the Future of Bleisure tourism development in the Philippines.

Digital Nomadism and the Philippine Tourism Landscape

The current state of Philippine tourism reflects significant growth in international tourist arrivals and visitor receipts, with a focus on sustainable development (Aquino & Porter, 2022). This is evident in the across the year-on-year increase of foreign visitors arrival statistics of the country before and after the COVID 19 pandemic. The growth of Philippine Tourism, however, was temporarily halted by the COVID 19 pandemic (Susilo & K. Santos, 2023) which in turn made a huge paradigm shift in the industry as it refocuses with new and sustainable tourist market segments that will contribute to the growth of the industry post-pandemic.

In a study conducted by (Capistrano & Notorio, 2020) where they have analyzed presidential speeches from 1987 to 2019 to understand strategic directions and action programs influencing tourism planning, their findings revealed three major drivers of the country's tourism: tourism policy, tourism development, and prospects for the future of the industry. The latter highlighted that former president Rodrigo Duterte said in his State of the Nation Address that there is a need to prioritize tourism roads for better tourism accessibility. With all of these governmental initiatives that are currently materializing in the country, The Philippines tend to open up to a more sophisticated and more demanding type of tourists in our country.

The current tourism landscape of the country is best defined and supported with the increasing positive online reviews that enhances the image of the country (QUIAOIT & FURUYA, 2022). This supports the idea on the readiness of the country to accept more complex type of visitors which includes digital nomads.

Digital nomads are defined as individuals who has the ability and the capacity to live and work on multiple and frequently changing locations (Litchfield & Woldoff, 2023). (Litchfield & Woldoff, 2023) also elaborated the different factors influencing digital nomad lifestyle such as their flexibility in work and living locations, the push and pull factors in digital nomadistic choice, the innovation in virtual work, and the separation from the traditional lifestyle. Another interesting study that supports the definition of digital nomadism comes from (Cook, 2023) where he categorized digital nomads into five distinct characteristics: freelance digital nomads, business owners, salaried digital nomads, experimental digital nomads, and armchair digital nomads. Along the lines of these digital nomad categories, it is imperative that they all share the same characteristics of performing temporary movement and settlement on a certain location over a period of time. Hence, digital nomads can be considered as an emerging tourist market with longer average length of stay in a destination, higher spending capacity, and performs multi-destination visitation in a certain country.

(Hensellek & Puchala, 2021) provided four recurring elements digital nomadism in their paper. These are digital work, flexibility, mobility, and identity and community. These four elements supports the fact that Philippines, like most Southeast Asian countries is considered to be a potential destination for digital nomads. Flexibility and Mobility across different provinces of the Philippines is highly evident with the improvements in the tourism roads of the country and a variety of tourism destinations that the country can offer ranging from nature-based attractions, historical sites, gastronomical flairs, sun & beach destinations, mountains and highlands, and even the urban landscape. Identity and community is also unique in the country as Philippines is considered to be a melting pot of cultures deeply rooted from the historical influences received by the country from its former colonizers. Filipinos are also regarded for the distinct hospitality and a sense of communal living which is best for digital nomads to have a cultural experience in the country.

Bleisure Tourism: Beyond the Laptops and Beaches

While digital nomadism is considered to be a special niche tourist market, the activities done by these digital nomads are considered to be in the context of Bleisure Tourism (Mohd Sohaili et al., 2022). Bleisure tourism is simply put as the combination of both essential elements of business and leisure travel done in a tourism space by a visitor who independently obtain its purpose of visitation (Mohd Sohaili et al., 2022). Factors that should be considered by the destination in motivating bleisure tourists includes the following:

1. Seeking knowledge and novelty – traveling to a new and unfamiliar destination provides the opportunity for the visitor to obtain new knowledge in terms of the geographical setting of the place, the cultural identity of the people, the social patterns and norms, and even the historical value of the place which may be evident on both tangible and intangible aspects of the destination.
2. Escape – this is viewed from the supporting Crompton & McKay (2002) on the context of performing new things and doing activities while seeking autonomy from their spouses, family, friends, and usual people that they share their daily lives with.
3. Fun and Resting – Bleisure tourists seeks work-life balance from different cultural landscape.

On the other hand, destination qualities as a motivators of bleisure tourists (Mohd Sohaili et al., 2022) are identified as follows:

1. Cultural and Historical sites – bleisure tourists looks at cultural and historical sites as a component of new knowledge and also a form new experience after accomplish a day's work.
2. Safety – considered as a special added value of the tourism destination for bleisure tourists. These type of tourist usually brings in high-valued gadgets and tools along with them so they can still accomplish their work while in a destination. A good security system and a safe space is really a motivator of travel for them.
3. Convenience – there is a need for the destination to provide accessible travel components to the bleisure tourist. The need for a seamless movement from the accommodation to the attractions should be present. The presence of ancillary services and establishments should also be in the desired destination such as convenient stores, money changers, banks, hospitals, and visitor centers.

Bleisure tourism happens mostly in millennials (Pinho & Marques, 2021a) due to the fact that there is an existence of a symbiosis between the purpose of business and leisure travel as perceived by this fast-moving generation of travelers. This rising trend of shared purpose of tourism was amplified by social media content consumptions of the millennials that leads them the desire to travel more while accomplishing their work or building their own businesses along the way(Vargas-Sánchez et al., 2020).

Cultural Diffusion: A Digital Nomadic Influence

Cultural diffusion, as evidenced in the by the adoption of internet, has significantly influenced digital nomadism (Nath & Murthy, 2004). This is due to the fact that digital nomads are often influenced highly by what they see within the four corners of their computer screen which in turn converts the desire to travel into an actualized movement. Culture as depicted in travel websites and booking sites are actually used as a promotional component that drives tourists to visit the destination for themselves. Digital nomadism also focuses on connectivity and productivity even in a leisure-like environment (Bozzi, 2020). In this sense, the culture of work is also being diffused on the host destination in return. Culture of remote work has been integrated in the local destination which can lead to locals seeking opportunities for remote work stint as well.

The social interaction between the bleisure tourist and the host community is highly evident in a convergence space like co-working spaces, cafes, and restaurants where digital nomads are often seen working while on a leisure environment (Bozzi, 2020). Digitial nomadism also diffuse the concept of professionalization of remote work across the local destination (Aroles et al., 2019).

On the other hand, a concern of digital nomadism in a local destination as studied by Green (2020) showcased the cultural disruption as a factor of diffusion varied in two different levels. The first one is a radical expression that is evoked the sense of breaking free from the traditional lifestyle of the locals. This imbibed the expression of flexibility, fluidity, and newness. On the other hand, a subtle disruption occurs in the context of understanding of self, place, and mobility. This article strikes the balance on the positive and negative perspectives of digital nomadism in the context of cultural diffusion among locals and visitors.

Future of Bleisure Tourism Development in the Philippines

In light with recent developments in the Philippine tourism industry, bleisure tourism is still considered a niche market segment whereby a plethora of concerns and dearth of studies are still in question (Aquino & Porter, 2022). The need for further studies to uncover the potential of bleisure tourism in the country and to provide empirical findings is indeed a concern of this thriving niche type of tourism activity (Susilo & K. Santos, 2023).

With the growing studies in the context of bleisure tourism in the western academics, there is also a need for Asian academics to keep up and establish strong theoretical foundation in this tourism study area (Mohd Sohaili et al., 2022).

METHODS

This book chapter incorporated a qualitative study approach wherein the authors conducted a semi-structured interview to several visitors of co-working spaces and the owners as well. The goal is to establish the evidence of cultural diffusion among the visitor and locals as they share an interaction opportunity in the study locale.

The questions are focused on understanding their choice of using a co-working space as part of their bleisure activity, their typical perspective of a co-working space as a work and leisure environment, the type of interactions that they experienced in a co-working space, and the local cultural elements that they have acquired in staying in a co-working space. For the owner of the co-working space, a separate question focused on the features of the co-working space, intentions to incorporate bleisure elements in the co-working space, trends or patterns in among the digital nomads who uses co-working spaces, and identified cross-cultural interactions that occurred in the co-working space. Observations are also done in order to witness actual occurrences of cultural diffusion in a co-working space.

The data was treated using thematic analysis to relate the narratives on the existing body of knowledge on bleisure tourism and cultural diffusion. The emerging themes are derived from the categories which are aligned with the significant statements mentioned by the informants during the interview. The significant statements were analyzed and were anchored on contemporary studies on bleisure tourism, digital nomadism, and cultural diffusion. The data is presented in a repertory grid for better visual appreciation of the qualitative data. The presented data are further analyzed and interpreted to develop a discourse on the current learnings on the role of bleisure tourism in diffusion of culture. Further study implications are also provided in the discussion section of the book chapter.

RESULTS AND DISCUSSION

For the purpose of this book chapter, the findings are spread into four aspects; the choice of using co-working spaces for bleisure activity, their typical perspective of a co-working space as a work and leisure environment, the type of interactions that they experienced in a co-working space, and the local cultural elements that they have acquired in staying in a co-working space.

Table 1. Repertory Grid of Co-Working Spaces and Digital Nomadism in The Philippines: Understanding Bleisure Tourism's Role in Diffusion of Culture

Theme	Category	Significant Statements
Motivation	Work-Life Balance	"Sweet spot between work and play," "Maintain a bit of structure," "Balance between work and play," "Blending work with relaxation and leisure activities is key." (Mohd Sohaili et al., 2022)
	Community & Connection	"Sense of community and belonging," "Instant connection with like-minded individuals," "Fostering a sense of community and cultural exchange," "Networking and collaborating with fellow professionals," "Bringing together people from diverse backgrounds... where ideas flourish, connections are made, and lasting memories are created." (Pinho & Marques, 2021)
	Safety & Comfort	"Secure and comfortable environment," "Focus on my work without worrying," "Conducive environment for productivity." (Mohd Sohaili et al., 2022)
Co-Working Space Design	Hybrid Environment	"Hybrid, a bit of both worlds," "Professional atmosphere conducive to productivity," "Relaxed, almost resort-like vibe." (Aroles et al., 2019)
	Amenities & Features	"High-speed Wi-Fi, ergonomic chairs, meeting rooms," "Tropical garden, yoga studio, and even a pool." (Aroles et al., 2019)

continued on following page

Table 1. Continued

Theme	Category	Significant Statements
Interactions	Cultural Exchange	"Filipinos are incredibly warm and welcoming... strong emphasis on community," "Learned to appreciate... shared meals, casual conversations," "Impromptu language lessons to shared meals featuring traditional Filipino dishes." (Susilo & K. Santos, 2023)
	Professional Networking	"Bounce ideas off each other, sometimes collaborate," "Exchanged ideas, collaborated on projects," "Networking opportunities and collaborations." (Aroles et al., 2019)
Cultural Immersion	Local Experiences	"Exploring local attractions and immersing themselves in the culture," "Shared meals featuring traditional Filipino dishes," "Cooking classes, traditional dance performances, and even language exchange sessions." (Bozzi, 2020)
	Learning & Appreciation	"Picked up a few Tagalog phrases," "Gaining valuable insights into Filipino culture and business practices," "Appreciate the value of shared meals, casual conversations," "Opportunities for our members to learn about Filipino culture and connect with the local community." (Coşkun, 2021)
Gender	Female Empowerment	"Being a woman has opened doors to unique networking opportunities and collaborations," "Women-focused workshops and events." (Özoğul Balyali, 2024)

The table presented above show the thematic analysis presented in a repertory grid on the responses from interviewees in regard to the topic of co-working spaces and digital nomadism in the Philippines: understanding bleisure tourism's role in diffusion of culture. The themes that have emerged from the conversation were about motivation, co-working space design, interaction, cultural immersion, and gender. Each emerging themes are discussed below:

Motivation

Digital nomads are drawn to co-working spaces in the Philippines for a blend of work-life balance, community, and safety. As the informants highlighted, the Philippines as a bleisure tourism destination is a "sweet spot" for both leisure and business activities. In an urban landscape like the Metro Manila, co-working spaces are usually located near commercial areas like malls and shopping centers, as well as in a global city like in Taguig City where a plethora of activities can be done right after their done working. In the provinces, co-working spaces are often placed within the commercial area of a tourist attraction. This is for easy access to the beach or to any natural attraction after a day of working or whenever they need a breather.

Bleisure activities done in a co-working space also build a bit of structure. The informant meant that since business travelers need to focus on scheduled task at hand, they may inject a concept of structured workflow during the day for some serious work while they are in a leisurely environment. This brings in a newer perspective in doing serious work or attending meetings while on a vacation. It has been viewed that online meetings and deep work done in a more relaxed environment helps us to be more focused and more creative in accomplishing a task.

Co-working spaces are considered a melting pot of different cultures which makes it more interesting for bleisure tourists to choose co-working spaces over the usual cafes and bars. Co-working spaces here in the country offers activities wherein all customers can converge and socialize. Some co-working spaces offers free seminars and networking activities which basically becomes a way to increase social interaction among its clients.

Safety is another component where bleisure tourists are motivated to choose co-working spaces. Bleisure tourists and digital nomads are often carrying expensive gadgets with them as they travel and perform bleisure related activities. It is imperative that establishments match comfort with a stricter security to ensure the safety of the customers and their belongings. The prevailing theme puts high emphasis on balancing work with leisure aligns with the growing "bleisure" tourism trend.

Co-Working Space Design

The appeal of co-working spaces to digital nomads lies in their hybrid nature, which combines professional amenities with leisure features (von Zumbusch & Lalicic, 2020). Aesthetic appeal and functionality of the entire co-working facility matters the most to these type of consumers. Incorporating a mix of modern and indigenous elements in the establishment can bring in a new feel and a sense of originality to the place. Here in the Philippines, interiors are often designed to match the tropical climate of the country through the use of light materials, utilizing open spaces and natural lights, and installing air-conditioning system to ensure comfort of the working guests. This design philosophy resonates with the evolving preferences of digital nomads, who seek spaces that foster both productivity and relaxation (Chevtaeva, 2021).

The presence of amenities like tropical gardens, yoga studios, and pools reinforces the bleisure concept and enhances the overall experience (Lee et al., 2019). Augmenting the space design is an essential aspect of the experience of the visitors. By adding convergence zone where working guests can take time to meet fellow digital nomads and network opportunities with each other is imperative. Co-working spaces are considered to be social spaces. Adding up activities bring in added value to the visitors. This balance between work and leisure is crucial for digital nomads, who often merge their work and travel experiences (Orel, 2019). The hybrid design of these spaces, combining professional amenities with leisure features, is crucial in attracting and retaining digital nomads.

Interactions

The spaces facilitate both professional networking and cultural exchange, enriching the experiences of both local and foreign participants. Cultural exchanges between foreign and local guests are evident in the cultural knowledge transfer instances such as learning basic local greetings and phrases. Foreign co-working space renters are also reciprocating it by teaching locals their language. Cultural knowledge transfer is superficially evident through actions and words conveyed by the participants in a co-working environment.

Apart from that, another cultural learning experience for the foreign visitors is through their taste buds. Philippines offer unique and a wide variety of culinary wonders that both locals and foreign visitors enjoy. More often than not, co-working spaces with cafes or restaurants in the country creates unique gastronomical flairs that is originally Filipino. For some foreign visitors, it is a new adventure but for some who are not adventurous enough, an option of "close-to-home" dishes with Filipino influence is also offered.

One great thing about co-working spaces is the provision for professional networking opportunities (Aroles et al., 2019; Bozzi, 2020). Consequently, it has been noted that co-working spaces are a good avenue for business owners and professionals to network with other digital nomads and bleisure tourists to either offer their products and services, create new business ventures, collaborate with each other, or even hire them instantly for projects that they can venture out. An informant also mentioned that there are even specific social media and messaging groups intended for foreign digital nomads in the country where they can get the best suggestions on where to work and what to do after working in a certain space.

Cultural Immersion

Co-working spaces act as conduits for cultural immersion, enabling digital nomads to learn and appreciate Filipino customs and traditions. As mentioned on the previous section, learning new language through social interaction between locals and foreign visitors is an evidence of cultural knowledge transfer. Amazingly, foreign and local co-working space renters have the best opportunity to learn more about other people's culture. One noticeable observation is that foreign guests are amazed on the Filipinos' ability to speak English fluently and that they have not problems with the language barrier. On the other hand, Filipinos are also happy to know that foreign visitors get to learn the basic greetings and gestures quickly.

Co-working spaces located in the metro are often a stone's throw away from different cultural and historical attractions. This gives the foreign guests a chance to visit those sites anytime their schedule permits. They either go on their own or arrange visits together with Filipinos they were able to meet in the co-working space.

Multiculturalism is existent in this kind of convergent space. Co-working spaces invites people to share their way of life more than beyond their professional demeanor. After all, bleisure travel allows visitors to incorporate a considerable amount of time to let their hair down and have fun in the destination.

Another noticeable part is the interest of the digital nomads and bleisure tourists on the local community. They are open for discussions, collaborations, and immersive activities where they can build strong and friendly relationship bonds with the locals. The Filipinos, on the other hand, shows their hospitality towards the foreign guests and ensuring that they feel comfortable in their share spaces.

Gender

Female digital nomads find co-working spaces in the Philippines particularly empowering and inclusive, offering unique opportunities for networking and collaboration. Female informants tend to choose the Philippines for bleisure activities simply because of the beautiful natural attractions. Over the past decade, women in tourism has been greatly increasing. The concept of solo female traveler has also been a profound market in the country. This is an interesting feat amidst the concerns on safety and security of the tourist in the country on a general perspective. Event female local remote workers are also a fond visitor of these co-working spaces especially those that are near the metropolis for a quick getaway while fulfilling their daily tasks.

DISCUSSION

Co-working spaces are essentially growing in numbers as remote work and bleisure travel continues to strike a paradigm shift on how work and leisure activities can be done at a fraction of time (Lee et al., 2019). With this, a shift in community development has been seen to change its trajectory as more foreign visitors visit destinations and stay longer to experience the place, get newer perspective of things while ensuring that they can attend to their corporate tasks on time. Communities have greater role in diffusing local cultures to its guests while foreign visitors are subliminally diffusing their origin's culture towards the locals. A responsible sociocultural interaction should always be considered by establishments that forges convergence between people. Taking in the fact that local cultures should be respected, followed, and free from any modifications. On the other hand, reciprocating respect on foreign cultures is also necessary and openness to learn new things should be upheld by the local host community.

Achieving work-life balance is the main goal of every digital nomads practicing bleisure tourism (Pinho & Marques, 2021b). Visiting variety of destination in order to disrupt self, place, and mobility seems to be the action intended in the context of bleisure tourism activity (Green, 2020). Cultural appreciation and cultural knowledge transfer happens subsequently with every activities of this niche type of tourist segment, so it is indeed important to consider strong cultural roots are planted heavily on communities who are willing to engage in bleisure tourist markets as these tourist segment highly values authenticity as an augmented experience on their bleisure activities.

Infrastructure-wise, the Philippines may have been a choice for bleisure tourism however, concerns on internet connectivity seems to be an on-going national concern. Not all of the 7,641 islands have stable and fast internet connection and bleisure tourists's top-most priority is their connectivity. That is why bleisure tourism activities done by most digital nomads are in the tourist-dense destinations in the country. Either on urban jungles or on mainstream tourist destination where internet connection is at its best and co-working spaces are being institutionalized, bleisure tourist market in the country are seen to be flocking in this sector. The need to further improve the internet connectivity across the entire country needs to be prioritized if a destination like the Philippines want to lead the pack in bleisure tourism.

Another area to look at in terms of co-working space development is the focus on gender-based activities that can be done in the establishments. With the rising number of solo female bleisure travelers, there is a need to adapt on the needs of these female travelers. From the essential ones like clean restrooms, private workspaces, vending machines for female hygiene essentials, and stricter establishment security up to the more complex and resource-demanding activities, co-working spaces should re-align their focus to attain a sustainable market share on these emerging tourist segment.

To visualize the concept of co-working spaces on bleisure tourism, the authors suggest this framework (figure 1):

Figure 1. Bleisure Tourism Development on Co-Working Spaces Framework

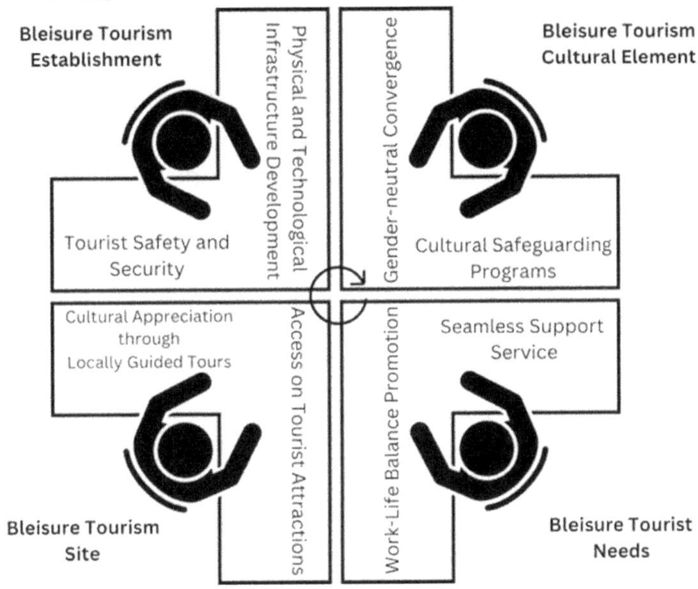

In this framework, four major areas of bleisure tourism development are seen to be a potential driver for co-working spaces. These are the bleisure tourism establishments themselves, bleisure tourism cultural element, Bleisure tourist needs, and Bleisure tourism site. Each of these areas have components in order to establish co-working spaces to be ready for digital nomads practicing bleisure tourism activities.

1. Bleisure Tourism Establishment

This quadrant focuses on the foundational elements necessary for developing and sustaining bleisure tourism. It includes two main components:

Physical and Technological Infrastructure Development: This component underscores the importance of robust infrastructure, including high-speed internet, modern co-working spaces, and reliable transportation systems. For digital nomads, access to cutting-edge technology and infrastructure is crucial. The Philippines, with its burgeoning tech hubs and co-working spaces, has the potential to attract digital nomads by ensuring that these facilities meet international standards.

Tourist Safety and Security: Safety and security are paramount for any tourist destination. Ensuring the well-being of bleisure tourists involves both physical safety measures, such as secure accommodation and safe transportation, and digital security measures, like secure internet connections and data protection. The Philippine government and private sector must collaborate to provide a secure environment that instills confidence in international visitors.

For bleisure tourism establishments themselves, the focus is on the development of the physical space which include areas for private and deep work sessions and convergence zones for meeting and networking opportunities. The physical establishment also needs to ensure high speed internet connectivity, provisions for office work essentials such as printers, office desks, standing desks, telephone lines, and snack areas.

2. Bleisure Tourism Cultural Element

This quadrant highlights the cultural dimensions of bleisure tourism, which are essential for fostering cultural exchange and safeguarding heritage. It comprises:

Gender-Neutral Convergence: This component advocates for inclusivity and equality in the tourism and workspace environments. Ensuring that co-working spaces and tourism services are accessible and welcoming to all genders promotes a culture of equality. This inclusivity is essential for attracting a diverse group of digital nomads who seek environments where they feel safe and respected.
Cultural Safeguarding Programs: These programs are designed to protect and promote local cultures. Initiatives may include preserving historical sites, supporting local arts and crafts, and educating tourists about the cultural significance of various practices. By safeguarding cultural heritage, the Philippines can offer a unique and enriching experience to bleisure tourists, enhancing their appreciation of the local culture.

On bleisure tourism cultural element, there is a need to integrate gender-neutral convergence program. In order to ensure that there is an active cultural knowledge transfer present across the co-working space, coming up with different activities that can be shared by all customers regardless of their profile and personality matters. That includes shared professional activities like in-house professional development seminars, shared leisure activities such as lounge areas where everyone can chitchat and grab some snacks, and others.

Another valuable aspect of this area is the implementation of cultural safeguarding program. Apart from the visual representations, and physical manifestation of cultural elements in the co-working space design, it is also important for the establishment to provide cultural safeguarding programs. This include educating the visitors with the right interpretation and meaning of any cultural components. May it be tangible or intangible.

Some suggestions in safeguarding local culture is by providing information to the visitors. This includes infographics, posters, and signages that shows every cultural element and its meaning. Co-working spaces can also include multi-lingual interpretation on signages and contents visible inside the establishment. Restaurant menus should use multi-language description too.

3. Bleisure Tourism Site

The third quadrant focuses on the actual destinations and activities that bleisure tourists engage in. It includes:

> **Cultural Appreciation through Locally Guided Tours**: Offering locally guided tours allows tourists to experience the culture from an insider's perspective. These tours can be curated to highlight the history, traditions, and contemporary lifestyle of the local community. Engaging local guides not only provides employment opportunities but also ensures that the cultural narrative is authentic and respectful.
>
> **Access on Tourist Attractions**: Ensuring easy access to tourist attractions is crucial. This involves developing infrastructure such as roads, signage, and transportation services that facilitate the movement of tourists. Accessible attractions enable bleisure tourists to seamlessly transition from work to leisure activities, maximizing their overall experience.

As discussed across this chapter, we have identified that there are two main needs of digital nomads performing bleisure tourism activity. Those are promotion of work-life balance and seamless support service from the co-working space. As mentioned, the main goal of a digital nomad is achieving the balance between work life and personal life. Hence, it is necessary that co-working spaces embrace this culture of remote work with high emphasis on leisure component in order for the visitors to enjoy their free time either after or in between work hours. And so, while they are also in their deep work mode, digital nomads need to focus on their task at hand hence, a strong support service must be present in the co-working space. Co-working spaces may hire or assign dedicated secretarial services as an added value for these digital nomads.

4. Bleisure Tourist Needs

The final quadrant addresses the specific needs and expectations of bleisure tourists. This includes:

Seamless Support Service: Providing seamless support services is critical for enhancing the bleisure experience. This can include concierge services, travel assistance, and business support services like meeting rooms and office supplies. Efficient and responsive support services ensure that tourists can focus on both their work and leisure activities without unnecessary interruptions.
Work-Life Balance Promotion: Promoting a healthy work-life balance is essential for attracting and retaining bleisure tourists. This involves creating environments where tourists can easily switch between work and relaxation. Facilities such as wellness centers, recreational activities, and flexible workspaces contribute to a balanced lifestyle, which is a key draw for digital nomads.

Finally, in terms of co-working space location, it is imperative that a bleisure tourism site is adjacent or at least accessible to the bleisure tourists. Co-working spaces in the urban space may locate their business near museums, historical sites, or parks and plaza for a quick or event immersive cultural appreciation opportunity for the foreign and local digital nomads. For provincial destinations, setting up their co-working spaces near the beach, mountain resort, or even in farms can be a huge advantage for the digital nomads to flock in the establishment. A better appreciation of the place needs someone who is experienced in handling guided tours. Co-working spaces may partner with travel agencies or local guides to offer excursion trips that can be availed at the most convenient time of the digital nomad. All these efforts can contribute to development of a destination as bleisure tourist friendly destination.

The conceptual model highlights the interconnection and synergy between these four quadrants. The success of bleisure tourism in the Philippines relies on the harmonious integration of these elements. For instance, robust infrastructure (Establishment) enhances accessibility to tourist attractions (Site), while cultural safeguarding programs (Cultural Element) enrich the experience of locally guided tours (Site). Similarly, seamless support services (Tourist Needs) and a work-life balance (Tourist Needs) are contingent upon the availability of physical and technological infrastructure (Establishment).

IMPLICATIONS FOR THE PHILIPPINES

The Philippines stands at a unique crossroads where it can leverage its rich cultural heritage, natural beauty, and emerging tech hubs to become a premier destination for bleisure tourists. The following implications are derived from the conceptual model:

Economic Growth

By attracting digital nomads and bleisure tourists, the Philippines can stimulate economic growth. These tourists contribute to the local economy through extended stays, spending on accommodation, food, and leisure activities. Additionally, the establishment of co-working spaces and related infrastructure generates employment and promotes entrepreneurship. Digital nomads often document their experiences through social media, blogs and other online platforms. These portrayals can attract more tourists and investors further boosting the economy.

Cultural Preservation and Promotion

Bleisure tourism provides a platform for cultural exchange and preservation. By engaging tourists in cultural safeguarding programs and locally guided tours, the Philippines can promote its heritage while fostering global understanding and appreciation. This not only benefits the local communities but also enriches the tourists' experience, creating a lasting impact. Through encouraging teamwork, advocating for sustainable tourism methods, and transforming shared workspaces into centers of cultural activity, the Philippines has the opportunity to capitalize on this movement to reinforce cultural heritage, facilitate cultural interactions, and safeguard the ongoing development of its distinct cultural melting pot.

Infrastructure Development and Connectivity

The need for advanced infrastructure to support bleisure tourism drives investment in technological and physical development. High-speed internet, modern co-working spaces, and efficient transportation systems are critical for attracting digital nomads. Investments in fiber optic networks, wireless technologies and affordable data plans is a leverage. These developments also benefit the local population, enhancing overall quality of life and positioning the Philippines as a modern, forward-thinking destination.

Inclusivity and Equality

Promoting gender-neutral convergence and inclusivity within the bleisure tourism framework ensures that the Philippines is seen as a welcoming destination for all. This inclusivity attracts a diverse group of tourists, fostering a global community that values equality and respect. It also sets a standard for other destinations, promoting best practices in inclusivity and tourism management.

REFERENCES

Aquino, R. S., & Porter, B. A. (2022). Contemporary Issues in Tourism Management in the Philippines. *Perspectives on Asian Tourism*, (Part F190), 3–19. 10.1007/978-981-19-4497-0_1

Aroles, J., Granter, E., & de Vaujany, F. X. (2019). 'Becoming Mainstream': The Professionalisation and Corporatisation of Digital Nomadism. *New Technology, Work and Employment*, 35(1), 114–129. 10.1111/ntwe.12158

Batala, B., & Slevitch, L. (2024). Keeping two balls in the air: The bleisure travel experience. *Annals of Tourism Research Empirical Insights*, 5(1), 100115. Advance online publication. 10.1016/j.annale.2023.100115

Bozzi, N. (2020). #digitalnomads, #solotravellers, #remoteworkers: A Cultural Critique of the Traveling Entrepreneur on Instagram. *Social Media + Society*, 6(2). Advance online publication. 10.1177/2056305120926644

Capistrano, R. C., & Notorio, P. A. (2020). A content analysis of the future of tourism through the presidential state of the nation address in the Philippines (1987-2019). *Journal of Tourism Futures*, 7(1), 131–146. 10.1108/JTF-05-2020-0075

Chevtaeva, E. (2021). Coworking and Coliving: The Attraction for Digital Nomad Tourists. In *Information and Communication Technologies in Tourism 2021* (pp. 202–209). Springer International Publishing. 10.1007/978-3-030-65785-7_17

Chung, J. Y., Choi, Y. K., Yoo, B. K., & Kim, S. H. (2020). Bleisure tourism experience chain: Implications for destination marketing. *Asia Pacific Journal of Tourism Research*, 25(3), 300–310. 10.1080/10941665.2019.1708760

Cook, D. (2023). What is a digital nomad? Definition and taxonomy in the era of mainstream remote work. *World Leisure Journal*, 65(2), 256–275. 10.1080/16078055.2023.2190608

Coşkun, G. (2021). Cultural diffusion theory and tourism implications. *International Journal of Geography and Geography Education (IGGE)* (Vol. 43). https://orcid.org/0000-0002-5200-6370

Crompton, J. L., & McKay, S. L. (2002). Motives of visitors attending festival events. *Annals of Tourism Research*. Advance online publication. 10.1016/S0160-7383(97)80010-2

Fuzi, A. (2015). Co-working spaces for promoting entrepreneurship in sparse regions: The case of South Wales. *Regional Studies, Regional Science*, 2(1), 462–469. 10.1080/21681376.2015.1072053

Green, P. (2020). Disruptions of self, place and mobility: Digital nomads in Chiang Mai, Thailand. *Mobilities*, 15(3), 431–445. 10.1080/17450101.2020.1723253

Hensellek, S., & Puchala, N. (2021). *The Emergence of the Digital Nomad: A Review and Analysis of the Opportunities and Risks of Digital Nomadism*. 10.1007/978-3-030-62167-4_11

Lee, A., Toombs, A. L., & Erickson, I. (2019). Infrastructure vs. Community: Co-spaces Confront Digital Nomads' Paradoxical Needs. *Extended Abstracts of the 2019 CHI Conference on Human Factors in Computing Systems*. 10.1145/3290607.3313064

Lichy, J., & McLeay, F. (2018). Bleisure: Motivations and typologies. *Journal of Travel & Tourism Marketing*, 35(4), 517–530. 10.1080/10548408.2017.1364206

Litchfield, R. C., & Woldoff, R. A. (2023). Digital nomads: curiosity or trend? *Handbook of Virtual Work*, 186–196. 10.4337/9781802200508.00018

Maslow, A. H. (1943). A Theory of Human Motivation. In *Originally Published in Psychological Review* (Vol. 50). www.excelcentre.net

Merkel, J. (2022). *Coworking Spaces as destinations and new stakeholders in hospitality ecosystems*. https://www.researchgate.net/publication/361794319

Mohd Sohaili, N. L., Aminudin, N., & Amir, A. F. (2022). Bleisure Motivation Towards Leisure Attraction: A Systematic Literature Review. *International Journal of Academic Research in Business & Social Sciences*, 12(11). Advance online publication. 10.6007/IJARBSS/v12-i11/15626

Nath, R., & Murthy, N. R. V. (2004). A Study of the Relationship Between Internet Diffusion and Culture. *Journal of International Technology and Information Management*, 13(1). Advance online publication. 10.58729/1941-6679.1247

Orel, M. (2019). Coworking environments and digital nomadism: Balancing work and leisure whilst on the move. *World Leisure Journal*, 61(3), 215–227. 10.1080/16078055.2019.1639275

Özoğul Balyali, T. (2024). Female digital nomads' destination experiencescape perspective. *Worldwide Hospitality and Tourism Themes*, 16(3), 282–293. Advance online publication. 10.1108/WHATT-03-2024-0051

Pinho, M., & Marques, J. (2021). The bleisure tourism trend and the potential for this business-leisure symbiosis in Porto. *Journal of Convention & Event Tourism*, 22(4), 346–362. 10.1080/15470148.2021.1905575

Quiaoit, M., & Furuya, H. (2022). Analysis of travel reviews on the philippine tourism experience by word2vec model. *Doboku Gakkai Ronbunshu, 77*(5), I_253-I_268. 10.2208/jscejipm.77.5_I_253

Rukmana, G. M., Amin, K., Rahmah, A. H., Sabtohadi, J., Bisnis, F. E., Politik, D., Muhammadiyah, U., Timur, K., Brida, P., & Kartanegara, K. K. (2023). Existence of co-working space to support local industries in Samarinda. *Jurnal Scientia, 12*. https://infor.seaninstitute.org/index.php

Susilo, D., & Santos, , M. C. (2023). Digital Marketing Communication for Promoting Philippines Tourism. *International Journal of Research and Review*, 10(6), 209–220. 10.52403/ijrr.20230625

Tsaur, S. H., & Tsai, C. H. (2023). Bleisure travel experience: Scale development and validation. *Journal of Travel & Tourism Marketing*, 40(1), 21–37. 10.1080/10548408.2023.2199773

Vargas-Sánchez, A., Fotiadis, A., Manuel Alcaraz, J., Castellanos-Verdugo, M., Manuel Hernández-Mogollón, J., Pierre Levy-Mangin, J., Manuel Berbel-Pineda, J., José Martínez-López, F., Riquel-Ligero, F., Miguel Rodríguez-Antón, J., Francesc Valls-Giménez, J., Abbate, T., Aguas, P., Jere Jakulin, T., Morvillo, A., Nigro, C., Allee, J., Chung-chi Wu, S., Jafari, J., & Sheldon, P. (2020). A critical review of literature in the rising tide of social media towards promoting tourism. *Enlightening Tourism: A Pathmaking Journal, 10*(2), 270–305. 10.33776/et.v10i2.4887

von Zumbusch, J. S. H., & Lalicic, L. (2020). The role of co-living spaces in digital nomads' well-being. *Information Technology & Tourism*, 22(3), 439–453. 10.1007/s40558-020-00182-2

Chapter 10
Addressing the Challenges and Proposing Solutions to Bleisure Travelers:
Insights From IT Professionals

Muhammad Lukman Baihaqi Alfakihuddin
https://orcid.org/0000-0003-1260-7136
Sampoerna University, Indonesia

Angelina Priscilla Tan
https://orcid.org/0009-0004-4044-2222
Sampoerna University, Indonesia

ABSTRACT

This chapter investigates the challenges encountered by Bleisure travelers, individuals who combine business travel with leisure activities, through a comprehensive review of existing literature, surveys, and interviews conducted with Bleisure travelers, particularly IT professionals, due to their unique expertise. This study aims to provide insights into the obstacles faced by this segment of travelers and offer practical solutions to enhance their experiences. Key challenges identified include time constraints, balancing work and leisure, managing expenses, navigating unfamiliar destinations, and maximizing leisure opportunities within limited schedules. In light of the conclusions, this chapter presents strategies and recommendations including careful itinerary planning, leveraging technology for time operation, optimizing trip prices, adopting stress relief methods, and exploring destination-specific resources. By addressing these challenges, Bleisure travelers can optimize their experience,

DOI: 10.4018/979-8-3693-4354-8.ch010

achieve outstanding work-life balance, and derive maximum pleasure.

1. INTRODUCTION

The emergence of Bleisure traveling has significantly shifted how professionals integrate business and leisure activities during their excursions. While providing opportunities for enrichment, business travel also presents challenges that must be addressed to enhance the overall experience. Conventionally, studies of travel motivation have primarily concentrated on leisure, overlooking the evolving geography of business trips (Lichy & McLeay, 2017). Research has shown that contemporary business travelers have increasingly prioritized leisure experiences, seeking enjoyment alongside their work commitments (Wee et al., 2022). The term "leisure" has gained prevalence, indicating an integration of business and rest (Chen, 2017). Considering the post-COVID-19 technological advancements, the business trip's necessity and nature have been altered, hence, impacting the future trajectory of leisure experiences (Spanaki et al., 2021).

Bleisure travelers frequently face the challenge of balancing their work commitments with leisure activities due to the limited time available during their business trips (Lichy & McLeay, 2017). Achieving such a balance requires optimal time allocation for both productivity in business engagements and enjoyment in the Bleisure experience (Lichy & McLeay, 2017). Balance between work and leisure is crucial as research suggests that leisure satisfaction can impact one's quality of life and overall well-being (H. M. Kong et al., 2021) with leisure activities reducing negative feelings (Adetola et al., 2021).

The perspectives of IT professionals are particularly crucial in addressing the challenges faced by Bleisure travelers, as these experts possess a unique understanding of the technological tools and innovations that can enhance the Bleisure experience. IT professionals can provide invaluable insights into the deployment of digital solutions that streamline travel planning, improve connectivity, and facilitate a seamless transition between work and leisure activities. Their expertise can lead to the development of apps and platforms that offer real-time itinerary adjustments, virtual meeting capabilities, and personalized recommendations for leisure activities, thus ensuring that Bleisure travelers can maximize their limited time effectively. Furthermore, IT professionals can identify and mitigate cybersecurity risks associated with remote work during travel, ensuring that business data remains secure while travelers enjoy their leisure time.

To effectively address challenges faced by Bleisure travelers, strategies are imperative, encompassing meticulous planning, technology use, and effective stakeholder communication, demonstrating the need for travelers to cultivate an adaptable mindset to navigate unanticipated disruptions in their excursion (Sohaili et al., 2022), with adaptability emphasizing the significance of rigidity and visionary strategies in managing certainties (Elshaer & Saad, 2021). The implementation of such practices in one's travel routines can assist travelers in enhancing their overall satisfaction, optimizing their experiences, and balancing their work and leisure commitments effectively. However, there remains a notable gap in the literature regarding guidance on overcoming associated challenges. While time constraints, work-life balance issues, and fiscal considerations are recognized as obstacles, more comprehensive frameworks are required. As engaging stakeholders such as travelers, businesses, and policymakers, is pivotal for comprehending and addressing issues in the travel industry (Reynolds et al., 2006), it is essential to consider insights from different stakeholders. Understanding the motivations and topologies of leisure travelers allows the formulation of strategies that enrich trip experiences and foster sustainable models in the tourism sector (Griffin et al., 2019).

The objectives of this research are to identify the specific challenges faced by Bleisure travelers and propose actionable solutions to enhance their overall experience. Insights from IT professionals are utilized to develop digital tools and strategies that facilitate a seamless integration of business and leisure activities during travel. Additionally, the research aims to address gaps in the existing literature by offering comprehensive frameworks and practical approaches tailored to the needs of Bleisure travelers.

2. METHODOLOGY

2.1. Research Design

This study employed a qualitative research design to explore the challenges faced by Bleisure travelers and strategies to overcome them. The qualitative methodology allows for an in-depth understanding and exploration of complex phenomena, such as integrating business and leisure travel, by utilizing interviews, observations, and document analysis, to provide insights into the experience of Bleisure travelers and practical approaches for addressing their challenges.

2.2. Data Collection

Data collection methods for this study include structured and unstructured interviews, observations, and document analysis. These approaches offer multiple perspectives and sources of information, enhancing the validity and comprehensiveness of the study. Interviews provided first-hand accounts of travelers' experiences, while document analysis supplemented these methods by examining relevant materials such as travel itineraries and policies. Data was collected from November 2023 to January 2024 in Bali Island, Indonesia. Bali is an island province of Indonesia, renowned for its unique culture, stunning landscapes, and vibrant tourism. Situated between Java and Lombok, Bali is one of Indonesia's 17,000 islands and covers an area of about 5,780 square kilometers. Given the extended data-gathering period from November 2023 to January 2024, participants were interviewed in batches to manage the logistics of data collection effectively and to allow for a more organized and systematic approach to gathering information.

2.2.1 Interviews and Observation

Structured interviews were conducted with Bleisure travelers to systematically explore their challenges and coping strategies. Questions covered various aspects of Bleisure travel, including time management, financial constraints, and cultural adaptation. Meanwhile, unstructured interviews allowed for deeper exploration of individual experiences and perspectives, providing rich qualitative data.

Interviewing Bleisure travelers in their travel environments provided valuable insights into their behaviors and interactions. Field notes captured observations of travelers balancing work and leisure activities and their responses to challenges encountered during their travel. Observations offered real-time context and complemented interview data. Twenty-four people have been interviewed for this research, in three groups consisting of IT Consultants, Graphic Designers, and Web Developers.

2.2.2 Document Analysis

Documents such as travel itineraries, expense reports, and travel policies were analyzed to understand the organizational context and constraints faced by Bleisure travelers, providing additional insights into the challenges and strategies employed by travelers and organizations in facilitating travel.

2.3. Participants

The study included Bleisure travelers from diverse professional backgrounds and travel experiences, who were all of Indonesian nationality, selected through purposive sampling based on their engagement in Bleisure travel and willingness to share their experiences, ensuring the representation of various demographics and travel contexts.

2.4. Procedures

After participant selection, structured interviews were conducted to gather baseline data on participants' travel experiences and challenges. Subsequent unstructured interviews allowed for deeper exploration of specific themes and experiences. Furthermore, observations were scheduled during participants' Bleisure trips to capture real-time behaviors and challenges, with document analysis conducted concurrently with data collection to provide additional context.

2.5. Data Analysis

Transcripts of interviews and field notes from observations were analyzed using thematic analysis to identify patterns and themes related to challenges and coping strategies in Bleisure travel. Document analysis was conducted to triangulate findings and provide additional context, with data organized around key themes and interpreted to generate insights into practical approaches for overcoming challenges faced by Bleisure travelers.

There were two groups of Questionnaires, one regarding the obstacles faced during Bleisure and one regarding strategies for Bleisure, as shown below:

1. Have you encountered any challenges or obstacles while engaging in Bleisure travel? If so, please describe them.
2. Can you share any strategies or techniques you use to overcome obstacles during Bleisure travel?

3. RESULTS AND DISCUSSION

3.1 Demographic Profile of Respondents

Table 1. Demographic Profile of Respondents

Measure	Item	Count	Percentage (%)
Gender	Male	14	48.28%
	Female	15	51.72%

continued on following page

Table 1. Continued

Measure	Item	Count	Percentage (%)
Profession	IT Consultant	11	37.93%
	Graphic Designer	9	31.05%
	Web Developer	9	31.05%
Education	Bachelor's degree	14	38.89%
	Master's degree	12	33.33%
	High School	3	25.00%
Age	> 18 to ≤ 25	4	13.79%
	≥ 26 to ≤ 35	12	41.38%
	≥ 35 to ≤ 45	9	31.03%
	≤ 45 or above	4	13.79%

Table 1 presents the demographic breakdown of respondents, indicating that the sample comprises nearly equal proportions of males and females, with a majority having professions as IT consultants, graphic designers, and web developers. Additionally, respondents are primarily distributed across age brackets with the highest percentage falling between 26 to 35 years old.

Table 2. Summary of Respondent

Respondent	Occupation	Code	Origanility
Repondent 1	It Consultant	P1-C1	Jakarta, Indonesia
Repondent 2	Web Designer	P2-W1	Malang, Indonesia
Repondent 3	Graphic Designer	P3-G1	Surabaya, Indonesia
Repondent 4	It Consultant	P4-C2	Jakarta, Indonesia
Repondent 5	Web Designer	P5-W2	Makasar, Indonesia
Repondent 6	Graphic Designer	P6-G2	Jakarta, Indonesia
Repondent 7	It Consultant	P7-C3	Semarang, Indonesia
Repondent 8	Web Designer	P8-W3	Surabaya, Indonesia
Repondent 9	Graphic Designer	P9-G3	Surabaya, Indonesia
Repondent 10	It Consultant	P10-C4	Jakarta, Indonesia
Repondent 11	Web Designer	P11-W4	Jakarta, Indonesia
Repondent 12	Graphic Designer	P12-G4	Jakarta, Indonesia
Repondent 13	It Consultant	P13-C5	Pontianak, Indonesia
Repondent 14	Web Designer	P14-W5	Bandung, Indonesia
Repondent 15	Graphic Designer	P15-G5	Medan, Indonesia

continued on following page

Table 2. Continued

Respondent	Occupation	Code	Origanility
Repondent 16	It Consultant	P16-C6	Bandung, Indonesia
Repondent 17	Web Designer	P17-W6	Surabaya, Indonesia
Repondent 18	Graphic Designer	P18-G6	Palembang, Indonesia
Repondent 19	It Consultant	P19-C7	Jakarta, Indonesia
Repondent 20	Web Designer	P20-W7	Jakarta, Indonesia
Repondent 21	Graphic Designer	P21-G7	Bekasi, Indonesia
Repondent 22	It Consultant	P22-C8	Depok Indonesia
Repondent 23	Web Designer	P23-W8	Jakarta, Indonesia
Repondent 24	Graphic Designer	P24-G8	Makasar, Indonesia

Table 2 outlines the occupations and origins of 24 respondents, comprising IT Consultants, Web Designers, and Graphic Designers from various Indonesian cities, including Jakarta, Surabaya, and Bandung. Each respondent is uniquely coded for easy reference, such as P1-C1 for the first IT Consultant from Jakarta and P24-G8 for the 24th respondent, a Graphic Designer from Makasar.

Table 3. Summary of Challenges to Bleisure Travel

Theme	Description	Example
Time constraints	Difficulty managing time effectively	"I often find myself struggling to manage my time effectively." *(P2-W1)*
Work-life balance	The transition between work and leisure	"Transition between work and play modes." *(P5-W2)*
Unfamiliar destinations	Limited time to explore a new place	"Limited time to explore the destination." *(P8-W3)*
Financial constraints	Increased expenses	"Increased expenses." *(P11-W4)*

Table 3 outlines challenges to Bleisure travel, identifying challenges such as time constraints, work-life balance issues, unfamiliar destinations, and financial constraints. Examples illustrate difficulties in managing time effectively, balancing work and leisure, limited exploration time in new places, and increased expenses associated with such trips.

Table 4. Solution for the Challenges to Bleisure Travel

Solution	Description	Example
Time constraints	Utilize digital tools for organization	"I have found it helpful to utilize digital tools and apps for communication." (P14-W5)

continued on following page

Table 4. Continued

Solution	Description	Example
Work-life balance	Establish boundaries between work and leisure	"I set specific times for work and play to maintain a healthy balance." ((P16-C6)
Unfamiliar destinations	Use travel guides for destination information	"Use travel guides to learn about the area." (P21-G7)
Financial constraints	Practice financial mindfulness	"Carefully assessing my expenses. " (P23-W8)

Table 4 outlines solutions for common challenges faced by Bleisure travelers. These solutions include utilizing digital tools for time management, establishing boundaries for work-life balance, using travel guides for unfamiliar destinations, and practicing financial mindfulness to overcome financial constraints.

3.2. Discussion

In this study, document analysis was conducted as part of the qualitative methodology to provide additional context and corroborate the findings from interviews and observations. Documents such as travel itineraries, expense reports, and travel policies were meticulously examined to understand the organizational context and constraints faced by Bleisure travelers. This analysis aimed to uncover underlying patterns and institutional factors influencing Bleisure travel, supplementing the primary data gathered through interviews and observations. Despite its integral role in the methodology, the presentation of results and discussion primarily focused on the insights derived from direct interactions with participants, leading to an underrepresentation of the document analysis findings. Future iterations of the study could benefit from a more balanced integration of document analysis results to enrich the understanding of the challenges and strategies associated with Bleisure travel.

3.2.1. Challenges of Bleisure Travel

3.2.1.1. Challenge of Time Constraints

Bleisure travel, the integration of business and rest during trips, presents challenges for travelers. One of the primary challenges faced by Bleisure travelers is time constraints. Business travel generally involves tight schedules and limited free time, leaving little room for leisure activities. The fast-paced nature of business trips can cause fatigue and burnout, underscoring the need for travelers to effectively manage their time for rest (Gustafson, 2012) by balancing professional obligations with the desire to maximize available leisure time.

> "Time constraints have been a notable challenge for me during Bleisure travel." (P1-C1)
> "When I try to combine business and leisure activities in one trip, I often find myself struggling to manage my time effectively." (P2-W1)
> *"It's difficult to balance work and wanting to rest and explore in a new environment. I have to attend meetings and conferences for work, but I also want to spend time traveling and relaxing in a new location." (P3-G1)*

Additionally, travelers who excel at integrating business and leisure activities require smart products and services tailored to their contemporary cultural norms. Offering attractions that seamlessly combine business and leisure can enhance destinations, such as Thailand, for incentive trips (Choi et al., 2020). Hence, it is essential to comprehend the motivations and preferences of Bleisure travelers to create guides that meet their needs effectively.

3.2.1.2. Challenge of Work-Life Balance

Bleisure travelers are professionals who merge work obligations with leisure activities (Chung et al., 2020). This integration of business and relaxation is common in many business trips, often influencing event-hosting decisions based on available leisure options (Campos et al., 2016).

Studies have shown that rest participation can reduce negative feelings and enhance well-being, underscoring the importance of balancing work and leisure. Moreover, sharing rest activities can provide emotional affirmation, fostering positive feelings of accomplishment and value (Elbaz et al., 2020). Furthermore, Bleisure has been linked to heightened creativity and productivity, particularly when combining business with leisure aspects (Adhiatma et al., 2019). Thus, balancing work and rest is critical for reducing work-related stress and perfecting overall health (Rose & Williams, 2015).

However, balancing work commitments with leisure can be discouraging, requiring individuals to navigate a delicate equilibrium between professional obligations and particular enjoyment (Anable & Gatersleben, 2005), with the pressure to stay connected to work through technology further complicating the achievement of work-life balance during Bleisure trips (Reichenberger, 2017).

> "One significant challenge I've faced is finding the correct balance between attending meetings or finishing chores and creating time for leisure and exploration." (P4-C2)
> "It can be challenging to transition between work and play modes, particularly when work obligations appear to follow you everywhere." (P5-W2)

> "Unexpected work emergencies or deadlines can arise, disrupting your plans and causing stress." (P6-G2)

3.2.1.3. Challenge of Unfamiliar Destinations

Navigating unfamiliar destinations can be daunting, particularly when time is limited, and travelers need more knowledge about the destination and face language barriers, cultural differences, and unfamiliar customs (Lichy & McLeay, 2017). Insufficient preparation and research beforehand may hinder leisure travelers from fully immersing themselves in the leisure aspects of their trip, potentially causing them to miss out on enriching experiences (Patsy et al., 2023).

> "One of the biggest problems I experienced while engaging in Bleisure travel was navigating unknown areas." (P7-C3)
> "Since Bleisure travel combines business and leisure activities, there's often limited time to explore the destination thoroughly." (P8-W3)
> "I sometimes found myself feeling a bit lost or overwhelmed in a new city, unsure of where to go or what to do during my free time." (P9-G3)

Research has shown that business travelers increasingly combine business travel with leisure activities, a trend reflected in Bleisure (Alfakihuddin, 2023). This blending of business and leisure has gained prominence in the travel industry, indicating a shift towards incorporating leisure into business trips. Business travelers attending conventions and exhibitions have shown a growing interest in leisure, seeking pleasure through activities like food exploration and cultural experiences during their passages (Wee et al., 2022).

3.2.1.4. Challenge of Financial Constraints

Financial constraints can pose a significant challenge for travelers, particularly when engaging in combined business and rest activities. The fiscal charges associated with accommodation, dining, entertainment, and transportation for leisure activities can strain a traveler's budget if not planned for in advance (Tan, 2020). Managing finances becomes crucial to ensure the affordability of leisure hobbies without compromising the overall trip experience. Studies have shown that income is vital in determining individuals' capability to go on leisure activities and trips (Bjerkan & Øvstedal, 2018; Connolly, 2023; Gross & Huang, 2013). In this case, individuals with advanced fiscal strength have further opportunities to access care and support during travels, which can be particularly important for people with disabilities (Bjerkan & Øvstedal, 2018).

> "One of the most prominent obstacles has been financial constraints." (P10-C4)
> "Balancing work and leisure activities during travel can sometimes lead to increased expenses, especially when trying to enjoy additional leisure activities beyond the scope of a typical business trip." (P11-W4)
> "The cost of extending my stay or upgrading accommodations for leisure purposes can sometimes exceed my budgetary limits." (P12-G4)

Moreover, factors such as household income, comfort and convenience of trip modes, service situations, widespread constraints, and the presence of children or aged persons in a family impact the affordability of travel (Rastogi et al., 2015). Low airfares have been shown to attract new users who previously could not afford air trips, thereby increasing travel frequency (Chen, 2017). Additionally, the growth of disposable incomes for rest trips has contributed to the demand for affordable accommodation, especially in the economic sector (Gross & Huang, 2013).

3.2.2. Proposed Solutions for the Challenges of Bleisure Travel

3.2.2.1 Solution for Time Constraints

Innovative time management technologies can be useful in finding answers to the problem of time restrictions in Bleisure travel. These technologies are designed to make scheduling easier, increase efficiency, and provide time for leisure within busy work schedules. Bleisure travelers can better integrate their work obligations with their desire for leisure and exploration by utilizing technology and strategic preparation (Adhiatma et al., 2019).

> "Utilizing time management tools has significantly improved my pleasure travel experiences." (P13-C5)
> "Apps that help me organize my schedule and prioritize tasks have been a game changer for me when combining work and Leisure trips." (P14-W5)
> "By using time tracking software, I can better allocate my time during business trips, allowing me to enjoy leisure activities without compromising work responsibilities." (P15-G5)

Furthermore, travelers looking for smooth transitions between work and play might have their needs met by incorporating smart technologies into hospitality services (Rastogi et al., 2015). These contemporary amenities, which range from mobile check-ins and virtual event platforms to individualized concierge services, improve the Bleisure experience overall. By creating experiences that are customized to the tastes of Bleisure travelers, destination management companies may profit from this trend and increase the allure of their destinations for both business and pleasure (Reichenberger, 2017).

3.2.2.2. Solution for Work-Life Balance

Technology possesses a significant role in modern travel experiences. For instance, real-time travel time and information reliability can influence routing decisions for travelers, particularly truck drivers (X. Kong et al., 2018). Thus, demonstrating that providing accurate and timely information can impact travel behavior and decision-making processes.

> "Clear communication helps when you're juggling work and play on your trips." (P16-C6)
>
> "Effective communication is key when overcoming obstacles during Bleisure travel." (P17-W6)
>
> "When you're blending business and leisure travel, being able to communicate well is crucial for tackling any hurdles." (P18-G6)

Moreover, technological advancements, particularly post-COVID-19 epidemic, have reshaped competition dynamics in the hostel sector (Spanaki et al., 2021). The rise of remote working conditions has accelerated, potentially reducing the need for future business trips and prompting changes in the hospitality industry (Spanaki et al., 2021). Furthermore, blockchain technology is anticipated to disrupt the hospitality and tourism sectors by potentially disintermediating the industry, affecting pricing, inventory management, and client data access (Kizildag et al., 2019).

Additionally, communication with stakeholders, such as employers, associates, and guests, is crucial as setting clear expectations regarding availability and pre-communicating planned leisure activities can help ensure that work commitments are met without disruptions. Negotiating flexible work arrangements, such as remote work options or acclimated meeting schedules, also offers the freedom to enjoy leisure activities without compromising professional responsibilities (Allen et al., 2012; Groen et al., 2018; Hornung et al., 2008; Kossek & Kelliher, 2022).

Research indicates that flexible work arrangements, including personalized schedules, flextime, and remote work options, can positively impact various aspects of work, such as reducing hand issues, increasing work engagement, and enhancing job satisfaction (Farida, 2020; Hidayah et al., 2021; Sunaryo et al., 2022). Moreover, these arrangements have been associated with a fairer distribution of workloads, the ability to work longer hours when needed, improved work-life balance, and overall well-being. Flexible work arrangements are essential for addressing work-family conflict and promoting work-life balance, enabling better control over work schedules and reducing conflicts between work and personal lives (Brewer, 1998; Choo et al., 2016; Gerdenitsch et al., 2015). Research has highlighted that both formal and informal Work-Family Programs play a significant role in supporting workers in effectively managing their work and personal responsibilities (Wharton et al., 2008).

3.2.2.3. Solution for Unfamiliar Destinations

It is recommended that Bleisure travelers acquaint themselves with the local language, customs, and cultural norms to facilitate interactions with locals and enrich their overall travel experience. Leveraging online resources, travel guides, and recommendations from locals or colleagues can offer valuable insights into the destination, enabling Bleisure travelers to make well-informed decisions about their leisure activities (Rachmat et al., 2023).

> "I've learnt to overcome this obstacle by conducting prior research, depending on local advice, and being open to spontaneous inquiry." (P19-C7)
> "I check websites, read blogs, and look at forums to learn about things like local customs, how to get around, and what problems I might run into." (P20-W7)
> "I use travel guides to learn about the area and find out about cool things to see and do." (P21-G7)

Understanding travelers' acceptance of trip information enhances their overall trip experience. Research frameworks grounded on the technology acceptance model can establish connections between travelers' intention to accept travel information, trust in travel information, perceived usefulness, perceived ease of use, and other affiliated variables. This understanding can help explain, predict, and increase travelers' acceptance of trip information, enhancing their trip experiences (Carlson Wagonlit Travel, 2016).

3.2.2.4. Solution for Financial Constraints

Financial planning and budgeting are essential in mitigating additional costs related to leisure activities during business trips. Setting a realistic budget, researching cost-effective accommodation and dining options, and utilizing discounts and loyalty programs are recommended (Brower et al., 2020). Engaging in free or low-cost leisure activities, such as visiting public parks or museums, can also enhance the travel experience without overspending (Brower et al., 2020).

> "I find helpful for overcoming obstacles during Bleisure travel is meticulous Financial Planning and budgeting." (P22-C8)
> "By carefully assessing my expenses and setting a realistic budget for work-related and leisure activities." (P23-W8)

"Ensure that I have enough resources to address any unexpected challenges." (P24-G8)

Studies indicate that loyalty programs also can significantly impact client satisfaction and loyalty across different disciplines, including tourism and hospitality (Khairawati, 2019). Loyalty programs offering lower prices and discounts can impact client behaviour, encouraging repeat business. Moreover, online brand communities have been considered precious tools for building brand loyalty and enhancing client commitment (Hur et al., 2011).

4. CONCLUSION

In essence, the increasing popularity of merging business with leisure travel presents unique challenges for travelers. The primary challenge revolves around effectively balancing work commitments with relaxation time. Successful navigation of these challenges relies on careful planning, efficient time management, and adaptability. Utilizing technology such as timetable apps can aid in optimizing schedules, while maintaining clear communication with employers is essential for negotiating flexible work arrangements and managing finances during travel. Additionally, embracing cultural immersion and online exploration can enrich the Bleisure experience, with fiscal planning and loyalty programs contributing to the affordability of travel. Moreover, developing tailored interventions can significantly improve the Bleisure experience, foster sustainability in tourism, and enhance overall traveler satisfaction worldwide.

5. LIMITATIONS

This study primarily focuses on the challenges faced by Bleisure travelers and the strategies they employ to overcome these challenges, without considering potential differences in experiences based on factors such as industry, socioeconomic status, and cultural background. Moreover, the study predominantly relies on qualitative methodologies, limiting the generalizability of the findings and providing only a partial understanding of Bleisure travel dynamics. Longitudinal data, which could offer insights into how Bleisure travel preferences evolve over time and in response to external factors such as global events and technological advancements, are notably absent. Further research using diverse methodologies and continuous data collection is necessary to achieve a comprehensive understanding of Bleisure travel intricacies and develop tailored solutions that cater to the diverse needs of Bleisure travelers.

This study holds significant implications for HR professionals, particularly in managing work-life balance and enhancing employee satisfaction. To enhance overall employee well-being and productivity, HR professionals must acknowledge and address the challenges arising from the increasing integration of business and leisure activities during travel. The study underscores the importance of effectively managing time between work and leisure commitments, as well as the need for implementing flexible work arrangements that provide resources for trip planning and budgeting, while promoting open communication about work availability expectations during leisure travel. By supporting employees in achieving a harmonious balance, organizations can boost employee engagement and performance, thereby contributing to overall workforce effectiveness.

6. RECOMMENDATIONS FOR FURTHER RESEARCH

The increasing popularity of Bleisure trips presents an intriguing area for future study, focusing on addressing the challenges professionals encounter while balancing work and leisure activities. As business and leisure become more intertwined, it is crucial to grasp the dynamics of time management, financial constraints, and navigating foreign destinations to enhance Bleisure experiences. Future research should aim to develop comprehensive frameworks and practical solutions tailored to the needs of Bleisure travelers. Utilizing qualitative research techniques such as observations, interviews, and document analysis can provide valuable insights into the experiences of business and leisure travelers, as well as offer practical solutions for their challenges. Additionally, in the ever-evolving landscape of business and travel, collaborations with stakeholders such as travelers, companies, and policymakers are vital for developing sustainable solutions. Researchers play a pivotal role in improving the overall travel experience and fostering a harmonious balance between work and leisure commitments by addressing gaps in the literature and incorporating stakeholder perspectives.

COMPETING INTERESTS

The authors of this publication declare there are no competing interests.

FUNDING

This research received no specific grant from any funding agency in the public, commercial, or not-for-profit sectors. Funding for this research was covered by the author(s) of the article.

REFERENCES

Adetola, O. J., Aghazadeh, S., & Abdullahi, M. (2021). Perceived Environmental Concern, Knowledge, and Intention to Visit Green Hotels: Do Perceived Consumption Values Matter? *Pakistan Journal of Commerce and Social Science*, 15(2).

Adhiatma, A., Muna, N., & Fachrunnisa, O. (2019). Business and leisure "bleisure" in organization: Antecedents and outcomes. *Jurnal Dinamika Manajemen*, 10(2), 216–228. 10.15294/jdm.v10i2.19783

Alfakihuddin, M. L. B. (2023). Dampak dari Pemasaran Hijau dan Iklan Hijau pada Niat Beli Produk Kecantikan pada Generasi Z. *SEIKO: Journal of Management \& Business, 6*(2).

Allen, T., Johnson, R., Kiburz, K., & Shockley, K. (2012). Work—family conflict and flexible work arrangements: Deconstructing flexibility. *Personnel Psychology*, 66(2), 345–376. 10.1111/peps.12012

Anable, J., & Gatersleben, B. (2005). All work and no play? the role of instrumental and affective factors in work and leisure journeys by different travel modes. *Transportation Research Part A, Policy and Practice*, 39(2–3), 163–181. 10.1016/j.tra.2004.09.008

Bjerkan, K., & Øvstedal, L. (2018). Functional requirements for inclusive transport. *Transportation*, 47(3), 1177–1198. 10.1007/s11116-018-9939-7

Brewer, A. (1998). Work design, flexible work arrangements and travel behaviour: Policy implications. *Transport Policy*, 5(2), 93–101. 10.1016/S0967-070X(98)00003-1

Brower, J., LaBarge, M., White, L., & Mitchell, M. (2020). Examining responsiveness to an incentive-based mobile health app: Longitudinal observational study. *Journal of Medical Internet Research*, 22(8), e16797. 10.2196/1679732773371

Campos, A., Fanjul, M., & Moital, M. (2016). Segmenting the business traveler based on emotions, satisfaction, and behavioral intention. *Psychology & Marketing, 33*(2), 82–93. 10.1002/mar.20856

Carlson Wagonlit Travel. (2016). *Combing business and leisure trips: A quantitative look at the bleisure phenomenon.*

Chen, H. (2017). A pilot study of business travelers' stress-coping strategies. *Tourism and Hospitality Research*, 19(2), 252–258. 10.1177/1467358417740747

Choi, G., Kim, J., Sawitri, M. Y., & Lee, S. K. (2020). Ecotourism {Market} {Segmentation} in {Bali}, {Indonesia}: Opportunities for {Implementing} {REDD}+. *Land (Basel)*, 9(6), 186. 10.3390/land9060186

Choo, J., Desa, N., & Asaari, M. (2016). Flexible working arrangement toward organizational commitment and work-family conflict. *Studies in Asian Social Science*, 3(1). Advance online publication. 10.5430/sass.v3n1p21

Chung, J. Y., Choi, Y. K., Yoo, B. K., & Kim, S. H. (2020). Bleisure tourism experience chain: Implications for destination marketing. *Asia Pacific Journal of Tourism Research*, 25(3), 300–310. 10.1080/10941665.2019.1708760

Connolly, F., & Gärling, T. (2023). The relationships between income, life satisfaction and emotional well-being in european countries differing in wealth. *International Journal of Psychology*, 58(6), 594–604. 10.1002/ijop.1293537572010

Elbaz, A., Salem, I., Elsetouhi, A., & Abdelhamied, H. (2020). The moderating role of leisure participation in work—Leisure conflict for the reduction of burnout in hotels and travel agencies. *International Journal of Tourism Research*, 22(3), 375–389. 10.1002/jtr.2342

Elshaer, I., & Saad, S. (2021). Entrepreneurial resilience and business continuity in the tourism and hospitality industry: The role of adaptive performance and institutional orientation. *Tourism Review*, 77(5), 1365–1384. 10.1108/TR-04-2021-0171

Farida, U. (2020). The effect of flexible working arrangements on work engagement of online motorcycle taxi drivers. *Psychological Research and Intervention*, 3(2), 92–99. 10.21831/pri.v3i2.42196

Gerdenitsch, C., Kubicek, B., & Korunka, C. (2015). Control in flexible working arrangements. *Journal of Personnel Psychology*, 14(2), 61–69. 10.1027/1866-5888/a000121

Griffin, J., Youm, Y., & Vivari, B. (2019). Stakeholder engagement strategies after an exogenous shock: how philip morris and r. j. reynolds adapted differently to the 1998 master settlement agreement. *Business & Society, 60*(4), 1009–1036. 10.1177/0007650319870818

Groen, B., Triest, S., Coers, M., & Wtenweerde, N. (2018). Managing flexible work arrangements: Teleworking and output controls. *European Management Journal*, 36(6), 727–735. 10.1016/j.emj.2018.01.007

Gross, M., & Huang, S. (2013). The domestic development experience of a hotel firm with chinese characteristics. *Cornell Hospitality Quarterly*, 54(2), 211–224. 10.1177/1938965512466286

Gustafson, P. (2012). Travel time and working time: What business travellers do when they travel, and why. *Time & Society, 21*(2), 203–222. 10.1177/0961463X12444057

Hidayah, A., Singh, J., & Hussain, I. (2021). Impact of flexible working arrangements in the public sector in Indonesia. *International Journal of Human Resource Studies*, 11(2), 38. 10.5296/ijhrs.v11i2.18458

Hornung, S., Rousseau, D., & Glaser, J. (2008). Creating flexible work arrangements through idiosyncratic deals. *The Journal of Applied Psychology*, 93(3), 655–664. 10.1037/0021-9010.93.3.65518457493

Hur, W.-M., Ahn, K., & Kim, M. (2011). Building brand loyalty through managing brand community commitment. *Management Decision*, 49(7), 1194–1213. 10.1108/00251741111151217

Khairawati, S. (2019). Effect of customer loyalty program on customer satisfaction and its impact on customer loyalty. *International Journal of Research in Business and Social Science, 9*(1), 15–23. 10.20525/ijrbs.v9i1.603

Kizildag, M., Doğru, T., Zhang, T., Mody, M., Altin, M., Ozturk, A., & Ozdemir, O. (2019). Blockchain: A paradigm shift in business practices. *International Journal of Contemporary Hospitality Management*, 32(3), 953–975. 10.1108/IJCHM-12-2018-0958

Kong, H. M., Witmaier, A., & Ko, E. (2021). Sustainability and social media communication: How consumers respond to marketing efforts of luxury and non-luxury fashion brands. *Journal of Business Research*, 131, 640–651. Advance online publication. 10.1016/j.jbusres.2020.08.021

Kong, X., Eisele, W., Zhang, Y., & Cline, D. (2018). Evaluating the impact of real-time mobility and travel time reliability information on truck drivers' routing decisions. *Transportation Research Record: Journal of the Transportation Research Board*, 2672(9), 164–172. 10.1177/0361198118797508

Kossek, E., & Kelliher, C. (2022). Making flexibility more i-deal: advancing work-life equality collectively. *Group & Organization Management, 48*(1), 317–349. 10.1177/10596011221098823

Lichy, J., & McLeay, F. (2017). Bleisure: motivations and typologies. *Journal of Travel & Tourism Marketing, 35*(4), 517–530. 10.1080/10548408.2017.1364206

Patsy, E., Alfakihuddin, M. L. B., Butar Butar, N. A., & Nethania, P. (2023). Corporate action on plastic pollution (the body shop case study). *Jurnal Ekonomi*, 12(2), 1350–1355.

Rachmat, Z., Rukmana, A. Y., Nurendah, Y., Ashari, D. R. W., Donoriyanto, D. S., Bait, J. F., & Kasmita, M. (2023). *Strategi Bisnis Digital dan Implementasinya*. Get Press Indonesia.

Rastogi, R. M. H., & Patil, A. (2015). Segmentation analysis of domestic tourists — A case study. *KSCE Journal of Civil Engineering*, 19(5), 1509–1522. 10.1007/s12205-015-0673-9

Reichenberger, I. (2017). Digital nomads – a quest for holistic freedom in work and leisure. *Annals of Leisure Research*, 21(3), 364–380. 10.1080/11745398.2017.1358098

Reynolds, S., Schultz, F., & Hekman, D. (2006). Stakeholder theory and managerial decision-making: Constraints and implications of balancing stakeholder interests. *Journal of Business Ethics*, 64(3), 285–301. 10.1007/s10551-005-5493-2

Rose, T., & Williams, D. (2015). Nurse leadership: The importance of balancing work with leisure. *Nurse Leader*, 13(3), 60–62. 10.1016/j.mnl.2014.08.004

Sohaili, N., Aminudin, N., & Amir, A. (2022). Bleisure motivation towards leisure attraction: A systematic literature review. *International Journal of Academic Research in Business & Social Sciences*, 12(11). Advance online publication. 10.6007/IJARBSS/v12-i11/15626

Spanaki, M., Παπαθεοδώρου, A., & Παππάς, N. (2021). Tourism in the post covid-19 era: Evidence from hotels in the north east of England. *Worldwide Hospitality and Tourism Themes*, 13(3), 357–368. 10.1108/WHATT-01-2021-0013

Sunaryo, S., Sawitri, H., Suyono, J., Wahyudi, L., & Sarwoto, S. (2022). Flexible work arrangement and work-related outcomes during the COVID-19 pandemic: Evidence from local governments in Indonesia. *Problems and Perspectives in Management*, 20(3), 411–424. 10.21511/ppm.20(3).2022.33

Tan, W. (2020). Destination selection: Influence of tourists' personality on perceived travel constraints. *Journal of Vacation Marketing*, 26(4), 442–456. 10.1177/1356766720942556

Wee, H., Kamarulzaman, N., & Anas, M. (2022). MICE industry survival: A systematic literature review. *International Journal of Academic Research in Business & Social Sciences*, 12(11). Advance online publication. 10.6007/IJARBSS/v12-i11/15622

Wharton, A., Chivers, S., & Blair-Loy, M. (2008). Use of formal and informal work–family policies on the digital assembly line. *Work and Occupations*, 35(3), 327–350. 10.1177/0730888408316393

Chapter 11

Exploring the Synergy Between Bleisure Travel and Information Technology in India:
Current Status and Challenges

Mridula Mishra
https://orcid.org/0009-0007-2144-7556
Amity University, Noida, India

Nitish Kumar
https://orcid.org/0000-0002-2236-0766
Amity University, Noida, India

ABSTRACT

Bleisure tourism in India is experiencing a notable upswing, driven by various factors contributing to its improvement. The country's growing prominence as a global business hub, rich cultural heritage, and diverse leisure offerings make it an attractive destination for travelers seeking a blend of work and leisure experiences. The major cities in India got renowned for their business infrastructure, are also home to vibrant cultural attractions, historical landmarks, and natural wonders, enticing business travelers to extend their stays for leisure purposes. Moreover, advancements in transportation, digital connectivity, and accommodation options cater to the needs of Bleisure travelers, facilitating seamless transitions between work and leisure activities. In this chapter with increasing recognition of the benefits of blending business with leisure, the challenges will also be observed. These challenges, hurdles, and issues inviting the delay in this direction would be discussed while

DOI: 10.4018/979-8-3693-4354-8.ch011

focusing on the solution approach, especially emerging Indian cities in this context.

INTRODUCTION

Bleisure tourism in India presents a unique opportunity for business travelers to blend work with leisure, explore the country's rich cultural heritage, indulge in culinary delights, and rejuvenate amidst serene landscapes, contributing to a fulfilling travel experience. As the trend continues to gain momentum, businesses and travel industry stakeholders can tap into this growing market segment by offering tailored services and experiences to meet the evolving needs of Bleisure travelers (Lichy & McLeay, 2017). India boasts a rich cultural heritage and diverse tourist attractions ranging from historical monuments like the Taj Mahal and Red Fort to vibrant festivals, colourful markets, and serene natural landscapes. Bleisure travellers often take advantage of their business trips to explore these attractions. Apart from traditional tourist destinations, India is witnessing the emergence of new leisure destinations catering to the tastes of modern travellers. Cities like Jaipur, Udaipur, Goa, and Kerala offer a blend of luxury, adventure, and cultural experiences, making them ideal for bleisure travellers. Bleisure travel offers professionals the chance to network with local counterparts, attend industry events, or explore potential business collaborations in a more relaxed setting outside of formal meetings (Chung et al., 2020). Bleisure tourism, a portmanteau of "business" and "leisure," refers to the practice of combining business travel with leisure activities. This trend has gained significant traction globally as professionals seek to make the most of their business trips by incorporating elements of leisure travel into their itinerary. Planning for tourism in India commenced post the nation's independence, with Sir John Sargent chairing the committee in 1945. However, it wasn't until the 1980s that the tourism sector began to flourish, becoming a significant source of employment, revenue, foreign exchange, and recreational activities. This growth was spurred by crucial initiatives undertaken by the government at the time. The inaugural Tourism Policy of 1982 aimed to foster sustainable tourism, promoting social and economic inclusivity while enhancing India's global standing. Subsequently, during the Eighth Five Year Plan (1992-1997), there was a pronounced push for increased private sector involvement to bolster tourism planning. The introduction of the National Tourism Policy in 2002 marked a turning point, catalysing exponential growth, particularly in business tourism (Unger & Uriely, 2022).

India has long been a tourism hub, exemplified by historical figures like the Chinese traveler Hiuen Tsang, and rooted in pilgrimage traditions. Local economies in tourism-dependent regions benefit significantly from heightened tourist expenditures, not only financially but also by preserving and promoting indigenous culture and heritage. Visitor spending often translates into deeper engagement with the local history, fostering a sense of belonging and encouraging repeat visits. India's proactive efforts in tourism development are evident, with the sector playing a pivotal role in the nation's economic landscape (Khoo-Lattimore & Yang, 2018). As per the World Travel and Tourism Council (WTTC), the travel and tourism sector contributed Rs 15.7 trillion to the Indian economy in 2022. Despite challenges posed by the pandemic, foreign tourist arrivals have quadrupled post-pandemic, underscoring the sector's resilience and potential.

To further bolster the tourism industry, the Central Government has drafted a new Tourism Policy for 2023, aiming to revitalize the sector. This draft proposes granting industry status to tourism, thereby incentivizing investments. Additionally, recognizing hotels as integral infrastructure elements underscores the emphasis on business tourism, strengthening key stakeholders in the sector (Frochot et al., 2024).

LITERATURE REVIEW

The history of business tourism in India traces back to ancient times, with evidence of trade and commerce attracting merchants and travelers from distant lands. However, the structured development of business tourism gained momentum in the modern era.

During the colonial period, India's strategic location made it a significant hub for international trade and commerce. Cities such as Bombay (now Mumbai), Calcutta (now Kolkata), and Madras (now Chennai) emerged as key trading centres, attracting businessmen, traders, and colonial administrators from Europe and beyond. The British Raj facilitated the establishment of commercial infrastructure such as trading posts, warehouses, and banking institutions, further promoting business-related travel to India (Ohlan, 2017).

After gaining independence in 1947, India embarked on a path of economic development and industrialization. The government introduced policies to encourage foreign investment and trade, leading to an increase in business-related travel to the country. The establishment of industrial zones, special economic zones, and export processing zones attracted multinational corporations, business delegations, and investors, driving the demand for business tourism services.

In the latter half of the 20th century, India's economic liberalization policies, initiated in the early 1990s, ushered in a new era of economic growth and globalization. The opening up of the Indian economy resulted in increased foreign direct investment, expansion of multinational corporations, and a surge in international trade. Business travel to India surged as companies sought opportunities for investment, partnerships, and market expansion in sectors such as information technology, pharmaceuticals, manufacturing, and services. With the advent of technology and globalization, bliesure tourism in India gained even more prominence. Major business hubs started offering more recreational and leisure options, catering to the needs of bliesure travellers. The rise of boutique hotels, serviced apartments, and co-working spaces also facilitated the growth of bliesure tourism (Rijal et al., 2021). As India's business landscape evolved, so did the nature of business travel. Professionals began extending their business trips to include leisure activities. The growing trend of remote work and flexible schedules further fuelled the rise of bliesure tourism. India's diverse geography and cultural heritage made it an attractive destination for combining business with leisure.

The government played a pivotal role in promoting business tourism by improving infrastructure, facilitating visa procedures, and organizing trade fairs, business conferences, and investment summits. Cities like Delhi, Mumbai, Bangalore, Hyderabad, and Chennai emerged as major business destinations, equipped with world-class hotels, conference centres, and exhibition venues to cater to the needs of business travellers (Gunasekar et al., 2017). Today, business tourism continues to thrive in India, supported by advancements in transportation, communication, and technology. The country's growing stature as a global economic powerhouse, coupled with its rich cultural heritage and diverse tourist attractions, ensures that India remains an attractive destination for business travellers from around the world (Becker, 1962).

BLEISURE TOURISM IN INDIA

History: Bliesure tourism in India has evolved significantly over the years, reflecting changes in the global travel landscape and the country's economic development. While there isn't a specific historical account dedicated to bliesure tourism in India, its roots can be traced back to the growth of India's business and leisure travel sectors.

Bliesure tourism, a blend of business and leisure travel, is gaining traction in India. Not only the after effect of Covid19, with the rise of remote work and flexible schedules, professionals are increasingly combining business trips with leisure activities specially in those cities which are counted vibrant in IT sectors. India, with its diverse cultural heritage, scenic landscapes, and bustling cities, offers a rich tapestry of experiences for bliesure travelers. Major business hubs like Mumbai, Delhi, Bangalore, and Hyderabad are not only centers of commerce related activities but also boast numerous tourist attractions (Astina et al., 2021). Additionally, serene getaways such as Goa, Kerala, and the states situated in Himalayan region specially Dehradun, Shimla etc. provide ample opportunities for relaxation and leisure activities. The growth of bliesure tourism in India reflects the changing preferences and lifestyles of modern travelers, making it an important segment of the country's tourism industry. The following depicts that how fast Indian hotel industry is moving which is one of the major components of bleisure tourism (Bandyopadhyay et al., 2008).

Top Cities: Many cities are leading in Bleisure tourism in India. These are the following cities which are currently leading in field of bleisure tourism –

1. **Mumbai:** Mumbai is financial capital of India, is a hub for business and commerce. It is home to the Bombay Stock Exchange (BSE) and the Reserve Bank of India (RBI). The city hosts numerous international conferences, trade shows, and business events.
2. **Delhi:** Delhi, the capital city, is a prominent center for government and commerce. It houses government offices, multinational corporations, and major industries. The city's strategic location and excellent infrastructure make it a preferred destination for business travelers.
3. **Bangalore** (Bengaluru): Bangalore, known as the Silicon Valley of India, is a major technology hub. It is home to numerous IT companies, startups, and research institutions.
4. **Hyderabad:** Hyderabad is another important city for business tourism, particularly in the IT and pharmaceutical sectors. It is home to major tech parks, research centers, and multinational corporations. The city's HITEC City and Financial District attract a significant number of business travelers.
5. **Chennai:** Chennai is a major industrial and commercial center in South India. It has a strong presence in the automobile, manufacturing, and IT sectors. The city hosts various business events, trade fairs, and conventions.
6. **Pune:** Pune is known for its thriving automotive and manufacturing industries. It is home to several multinational corporations and research institutions. The city's business-friendly environment and modern infrastructure attract business travelers from around the world.

These cities offer a range of accommodation options, conference facilities, transportation services, and recreational activities, making them ideal destinations for business travelers in India.

Leading Players: These are the different companies working in the field of bleisure tourism in India –

a) **MakeMyTrip:** MakeMyTrip is one of India's leading online travel companies, offering a wide range of services including flights, hotels, holiday packages, and corporate travel solutions. They cater to both business and leisure travelers.

b) **Cleartrip:** Cleartrip is another popular online travel company in India, offering services such as flight and hotel bookings, holiday packages, and activities. They provide solutions for both business and leisure travelers.

c) **Yatra.com:** Yatra.com is a prominent online travel agency in India, offering a variety of travel-related services including flight and hotel bookings, holiday packages, and corporate travel solutions. They cater to both business and leisure travelers.

d) **Thomas Cook India:** Thomas Cook India is a leading travel and tourism company offering a wide range of services including travel packages, foreign exchange, travel insurance, and corporate travel solutions. They provide customized bliesure travel packages.

e) **Cox & Kings:** Cox & Kings is one of the oldest and most well-known travel companies in India, offering a wide range of services including tours, travel packages, and corporate travel solutions. They provide personalized bliesure travel experiences.

f) **SOTC Travel:** SOTC Travel is a popular travel company in India, offering a variety of travel services including tours, travel packages, and corporate travel solutions. They specialize in creating customized bliesure travel experiences.

g) **Club Mahindra Holidays:** Club Mahindra Holidays is a leading vacation ownership company in India, offering a range of holiday options including domestic and international travel packages, holiday memberships, and corporate travel solutions. They cater to both business and leisure travelers.

h) **OYO Workspaces:** OYO Workspaces is a part of OYO Hotels & Homes, offering coworking spaces, business centers, and corporate accommodations for business travelers. They provide flexible work and stay options for bliesure travelers.

i) **Airbnb:** Airbnb is a global online marketplace for lodging and tourism experiences. In India, Airbnb offers a wide range of accommodations including homes, apartments, and villas, catering to both business and leisure travelers.

j) **Travel Triangle:** Travel Triangle is an online marketplace for travel packages and holiday planning. They offer customized travel packages for both business and leisure travelers, including bliesure travel experiences.

These tourism companies leverage advanced technology to provide users with a seamless booking experience, personalized recommendations, real-time updates, and secure payment options. Each company has its unique features and offerings, catering to the diverse needs of travellers in India (Lipsa & Dash, 2024) .

The following list describes the comparison among them based on their use of IT –

Table 1. Different IT Equipped Bleisure Tourism Companies

S. No.	Name of the Tourism Company	Platform Availability	Corporate Group Services	Secure Services	Role of IT in Website / App
1	MakeMyTrip	Website / App	Yes, Corporate oriented Bleisure Services	Yes, in Transactions	Personalized Recommendation
2	Cleartrip	Website / App	No Information	Yes, in Transactions	Dynamic Booking system based on AI and Machine Learning technology.
3	Yatra.com	Website / App	Corporate travel management platform for businesses	Yes, Secure Booking Provided.	User history based and preferences analyzed by website.
4	Thomas Cook India	Website / App	Yes, with Customized solutions	Yes, in Transactions	Personalized Recommendation with specific filters.
5	Cox & Kings	Website / App	Corporate travel management platform for businesses with dedicated Team.	Yes, in Transactions	It offers personalized recommendations, detailed itineraries
6	SOTC Travel	Website / App	Customized travel packages	Yes, in Transactions	It offers personalized recommendations, detailed itineraries
7	Club Mahindra Holidays	Website / App	Yes, with Customized solutions	Yes, in Transactions	Personalized Recommendation with specific filters.
8	OYO Workspaces	Website / App	booking coworking spaces and dedicated business accommodations	Yes, in Transactions	Provides personalized trip planning.
9	Airbnb	Website / App	Yes, with Customized solutions	Yes, in Transactions	Personalized Recommendation with specific filters.
10	Travel Triangle	Website / App	Yes, with Customized solutions	Yes, in Transactions	Personalized Recommendation with specific filters.

CONSTITUENTS OF BLEISURE TOURISM

The impact of Information Technology (IT) on bleisure tourism (business + leisure) has been significant, transforming the way professionals combine work and leisure during their travels. These are the following elements which forms the bleisure tourism in any country –

1. **Accessibility and Convenience:** IT has made it easier for business travelers to plan and manage their trips efficiently. Online booking platforms and mobile apps allow travelers to seamlessly book flights, hotels, and other services from anywhere, at any time. This accessibility and convenience enable business travelers to seamlessly extend their trips for leisure purposes without the hassle of separate arrangements (Lichy & McLeay, 2017b).

Role of IT: Information Technology (IT) plays a crucial role in tour planning, offering numerous tools and platforms that simplify the process for travelers. Here's how IT facilitates tour planning:

1. **Online Research and Booking:** Information Access: IT enables travelers to access vast amounts of information about destinations, accommodations, activities, and transportation options.
2. **Online Booking Platforms:** Travelers can use online booking platforms and travel websites to research destinations, compare prices, and book flights, hotels, rental cars, and activities.
3. **Mobile Apps:** Mobile apps provide travelers with convenient access to booking platforms, allowing them to plan and book their trips from anywhere, at any time.
4. **Trip Customization and Personalization:** Travelers can store and access important travel documents such as passports, visas, and tickets electronically, reducing the risk of loss or theft.
5. **Customized Recommendations:** IT allows travel companies to gather and analyze data about traveler preferences, interests, and past behaviors.
6. **Personalized Itineraries:** Based on this data, travel companies can offer personalized recommendations and create customized travel itineraries that cater to the specific needs and interests of individual travelers.
7. **Tailored Experiences:** Travelers can choose from a wide range of options for accommodations, activities, dining, and transportation, allowing them to tailor their trip to their preferences and budget.
8. **Real-Time Updates and Notifications:** Real-Time Information: IT provides travelers with real-time updates and information about flight schedules, delays, cancellations, and gate changes.
9. **Alerts and Notifications:** Travelers receive alerts and notifications via email, SMS, or mobile apps, keeping them informed about any changes to their travel plans.
10. **Weather and Traffic Updates:** IT also provides travelers with real-time information about weather conditions, traffic congestion, and road closures, allowing them to plan their travel routes accordingly.

2. **Personalization:** IT has enabled travel companies to gather and analyze vast amounts of data about traveller preferences, behaviour, and booking patterns.using this data, travel companies can offer personalized recommendations and customized travel packages that cater to the specific needs and interests of bliesure travellers. Personalization enhances the bliesure travel experience by providing tailored recommendations for leisure activities, dining options, and sightseeing based on the traveller's interests and preferences (Gößling et al., 2020).

Role of IT: Information Technology (IT) plays a crucial role in personalization in tourism by leveraging data and technology to tailor travel experiences to the specific preferences and interests of individual travellers. These followings are the different segments where IT is creating a big impact –

1. **Data Collection and Analysis:** In this category, IT plays a important by improvising in different ways -

a) User Profiles: IT allows travel companies to collect and analyse data about travellers' preferences, interests, demographics, and past behaviours.

b) Behavioural Data: By tracking users' interactions with their platforms, travel companies can gather valuable insights into their preferences and behaviours.

c) Third-party Data: Travel companies can also integrate third-party data sources such as social media, location data, and user reviews to enrich user profiles which are collected from different sources and as well as from social media.

d) Personalized Recommendations: Content is also being researched for better recommendation and penetration for better data collection from different engines.

e) Dynamic Content: Based on the data collected, IT enables travel companies to deliver personalized recommendations and offers to users.

2. **Recommendation Engines:** Travel companies use recommendation engines powered by machine learning algorithms to suggest relevant destinations, accommodations, activities, and experiences to users.
3. **Contextual Recommendations:** Recommendations are tailored to factors such as travel history, search history, demographics, location, and current trends.
4. **Customized Travel Itineraries:** IT allows travellers to create customized travel itineraries that match their interests, preferences, and budget.
5. **Flexible Booking:** Travelers can choose from a wide range of options for accommodations, activities, dining, and transportation, allowing them to tailor their trip to their specific needs.

6. **Real-time Updates:** Travelers receive real-time updates and notifications about their itinerary, including changes to flight schedules, hotel reservations, and activities.

Information Technology plays a central role in personalization in tourism by leveraging data and technology to tailor travel experiences to the specific preferences and interests of individual travellers. IT enables travel companies to collect and analyse data, deliver personalized recommendations, create customized travel itineraries, target marketing and advertising messages, enhance the user experience, and collect feedback and reviews to continuously improve their offering.

7. **Design and Customization of Travel Plan:** IT can help tourists to design a better plan. Summarizing many research articles, here are the different ways where IT can play a major role –

a) **Destination Research:** Travelers can use online travel portals to research destinations, attractions, and activities.

b) **Travel Blogs and Forums:** IT enables access to travel blogs, forums, and review websites where travellers can gather information, tips, and recommendations from fellow travellers.

c) **Virtual Tours:** Some websites and apps offer virtual tours of destinations, allowing travellers to explore attractions and landmarks from the comfort of their homes.

d) **Navigation Apps:** Travelers can use navigation apps to find directions, navigate public transportation systems, and explore new destinations.

e) **Ride-Sharing Apps:** IT enables access to ride-sharing apps, allowing travellers to book rides and taxis easily, especially in unfamiliar cities.

f) **Public Transportation Information:** Some apps provide real-time information about public transportation schedules, routes, and fares.

8. **Marketing Management and Advertisement:** Information Technology (IT) plays a crucial role in advertising business tourism by providing innovative tools and platforms to reach and engage with target audiences effectively. IT enables businesses in the tourism sector to create targeted and personalized advertising campaigns that highlight the unique attractions and amenities of a destination for business travelers. Firstly, IT allows businesses to gather and analyze data about potential business travelers, including their demographics, preferences, and past booking behaviors. This data enables businesses to create highly targeted advertising campaigns that resonate with the specific needs and interests of their target audience.

Businesses can use these platforms to reach potential business travelers through targeted ads, sponsored content, and promotional offers. IT also enables businesses to create personalized advertising experiences for business travelers by delivering relevant content based on their preferences and browsing history. This personalized approach helps businesses to capture the attention of potential travelers and increase engagement with their advertising campaigns (Pham et al., 2024).

9. **Analysis of Feedback and Reviews given by Customers:** IT tools use natural language processing (NLP) algorithms to analyse the sentiment of guest reviews and feedback and Hotels can use IT to identify common keywords and themes in guest reviews, helping them to understand guest preferences, concerns, and areas for improvement (Weng, 2024). Similarly, IT allows hotels to identify trends and patterns in guest feedback over time, helping them to track performance and measure the impact of changes and improvements. Here the different ways where IT helps significantly –

a) Online Review Platforms: IT allows hotels to collect guest feedback from various online review platforms such as TripAdvisor, Google Reviews, and Booking.com.

b) Surveys and Feedback Forms: Hotels can use IT to create and distribute online surveys and feedback forms to guests via email, mobile apps, or on-site kiosks.

c) Social Media Monitoring: IT enables hotels to monitor social media channels for mentions, comments, and reviews from guests.

d) Alerts and Notifications: Hotels can set up alerts and notifications to be notified of new reviews, negative feedback, or trends that require immediate attention.

e) Benchmarking: IT enables hotels to benchmark their performance against competitors and industry standards, helping them to identify areas where they can improve.

f) Product and Service Development: IT provides hotels with valuable insights into guest preferences and trends, helping them to tailor their products and services to meet the needs of their guests more effectively.

FACTORS SHAPING THE BLEISURE TOURISM

There are several factors which affect bleisure tourism directly or indirectly. Few of them are listed below -

1. **Work From Anywhere Culture**: When Covid hit the world last year, many companies had to close their offices and work remotely. Now, after a year, people are slowly adapting to the work from anyway culture.

This promotes a better work-life balance as employees can adjust their work schedule according to their needs. Taking short breaks, ensuring a sleep-wake pattern, taking care of yourself, investing time in hobbies and spending time with family all affect blazer trips (Coffey et al., 2024).

2. **Improved Connectivity:** Transportation has been an integral part of the tourism industry; transportation connects tourists to various tourist attractions. Better connectivity and communication, improved tourism services. Nowadays technological innovation has given birth to high-speed trains like "Vande Bharat". India has many domestic and international airports that allow tourists to fly directly to their desired destinations. Regional airports and short-haul flights such as "UDAAN seva" offer cheaper air tickets and enhance intra-state and inter-state connectivity.
3. **Millennials and Gen Z:** Millennials (Generation Y) were born in the early 1980s and mid-1990s. They grew up during the rise of the internet and technology. They are comfortable with digital devices, social media, and online communication. They also value social causes and environmental sustainability. They prioritize work-life balance and seek flexible work arrangements. **Generation Z** was born roughly from the mid-1990s to the early 2010s. Gen Z grew up entirely in the digital age, with smartphones, social media, and instant access to information. They know how to find balance between work and personal life, so they generally take the interest in bleisure tourism.
4. **Destination Appeal:** The more successful tourism destinations in the world are those which appeal to a wide range of tourist attractions. Large cities, such as Mumbai, Delhi, Kolkata, Chennai and Bangalore are successful because they have a varied appeal. Bleisure travellers must visit certain destinations for meetings, conferences and other reasons hence bleisure traveller will be more interested in the ease of travelling to the destination and the facilities for business meetings and the attractions of the destination. The range of attractions, the history and culture of the cities, easily accessible, a range of business accommodation and the offices of many top companies and the choice of transport routes all help to make these destinations appealing.
5. **Corporate Policies focusing Health and Wellness:** Bleisure travel allows professionals to combine work and leisure, it potentially reducing stress and promoting better work-life balance. Employees who can extend business trips for leisure activities may experience improved mental health and job satisfac-

tion. Beleisure Travel has evolved and prolonged to compress all manner of experiences that boost travellers' mental and physical health. Taking the time for leisure during business trips is important for personal well-being. Overall, engaging in sightseeing, outdoors, or wellness, allows travellers to rejuvenate their minds and bodies.

6. **Event and Conference Locations and Cost Efficiency:** Cost efficiency encourages bleisure travel, many business travellers select luxury hotels, and they stay at the same hotel for both the business and leisure purpose, it stands to reason that they would be more economical. The hotels also providing discount for the repeat visit of the bleisure traveller. According to Booking.com, people will accept a job with a lower salary if it offers more business trips. This means companies don't spend much extra while improving staff morale and attracting better talent. Mostly business traveller has a departure date on a Monday or a Tuesday which can drive up airfare on those days. In turn, allowing business travellers to extend trips for leisure could lead to them flying on less popular and less expensive days. Tickets are often cheaper when they stay over Saturday.
7. **Infrastructure development**: Another crucial factor contributing to the growth of bleisure tourism is the development of infrastructure and accessibility. The availability of efficient transportation systems, such as airports, railways, and well-maintained roads, makes it easier for individuals to reach different destinations. Additionally, the presence of a reliable and modern accommodation sector, including hotels, guest houses, and resorts, plays a significant role in attracting bleisure tourists (Elias, 2024). Before 2014, India had only 74 airports, but since then, the number has nearly doubled, reaching 149. This significant increase in airport infrastructure has been accompanied by a remarkable surge in passenger numbers. Prior to the COVID-19 pandemic, the number of passengers grew from one crore to 14.5 crore, demonstrating a substantial rise in air travel. Even in 2023, despite the challenges posed by the pandemic, the number of passengers further increased to 15.20 crore, indicating the sustained growth and potential of the aviation sector in India. The following graph shows the booming of aviation industry which acts a backbone for bleisure tourism. The following figure 1 shows the scenario -

Figure 1. Depiction of Growth of Indian Aviation Industry in Last 10 Years

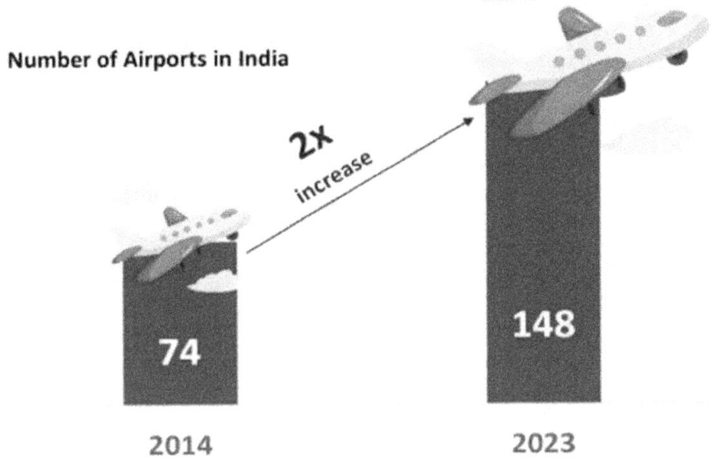

8. **Marketing and Promotion:** Effective marketing and promotion strategies plays a vital role in attracting tourists and driving tourism growth. Destination marketing organizations, travel agencies, and online platforms like social media (Blogs, LinkedIn, Facebook, Instagram, YouTube) plays a crucial role in showcasing the attractions and unique offerings for the bleisure travellers. Engaging and convincing marketing campaigns, coupled with favourable online reviews and recommendations, world of mouth marketing gives the significant impact for promoting bleisure tourism in India.
9. **Emotional / Psychological / Religious Factors**: Being away from home and family during business travel can further impact their mental health, making the business suffer ultimately. Currently Varanasi city is emerging as a major zone for bleisure tourism where many religious but new infrastructures have been raised to cater the leisure-based services i.e. Rudraksh Auditorium as shown below in figure 2.

Figure 2. Different Views of Rudraksh Auditorium in Varanasi UP, India

10. **Technology and Innovation:** Technology enables travelers to access information easily. From booking flights and hotels online to using navigation apps like Google Maps, travelers can plan and execute their trips more efficiently. Electric cars and buses are becoming more common, reducing greenhouse gas emissions and improving air quality. Big data analytics and AI help optimize tourism operations. They can predict travel trends, manage crowd flow, and enhance personalized experiences for tourists. AI-powered chatbots assist travelers with real-time information and recommendations.
11. **Duration and Frequency: Frequent Traveler Vs Short Break:** The bleisure travel contributes to the economic growth of cities by stimulating tourism. Thus, when travellers extend their stays to enjoy leisure activities, they spend into the local economy. This tourism revenue supports job creation and overall prosperity in destination communities.
12. **Readiness of Digital Infrastructure:** Digital infrastructure plays a pivotal role in the development of bleisure tourism in India in this context Ministry of Tourism has been taken different efforts to promote tourism digitally like: A multi-lingual 'Incredible India' website and mobile application assist international and domestic tourists to access information about various tourism destinations and attractions in the country, Ministry of Tourism has set up a platform namely

National Integrated Database of Hospitality Industry (NIDHI) for registration and classification of tourism service providers namely Tour Operators, Hotels and other Tourism Service Providers. It also provides for classification and approval of hotels and other tourism service providers. Ministry is implementing two flagship schemes namely SWADESH DARSHAN and PRASHAD and scheme data has been digitized and progress monitored through portal and dashboards, The Ministry of Tourism houses a 24x7 Toll Free Multi-Lingual Tourist Info-Helpline on the toll-free number 1800111363/ short code 1363 in 12 Languages including Hindi and English to facilitate and assist domestic and foreign tourists in terms of information relating to Travel in India and to provide a sense of safety and security, States have also set up their tourism portals and mobile apps for showcasing tourist attractions, tourist guides, hotels, adventure activities etc. ASI is working on an India heritage app prototype for geo-mapping of heritage monuments and creation of a tourist app. A research report found that, on average, Indian business travelers go on at least seven business trips a year, with more than half of these trips being extended for leisure purposes (Ramanjulu, 2024). The following figure 3 shows the different domain which helped the digital india alternatively strengthing the digital experience in tourism industry.

Figure 3. Domain Which Helped the Digital India

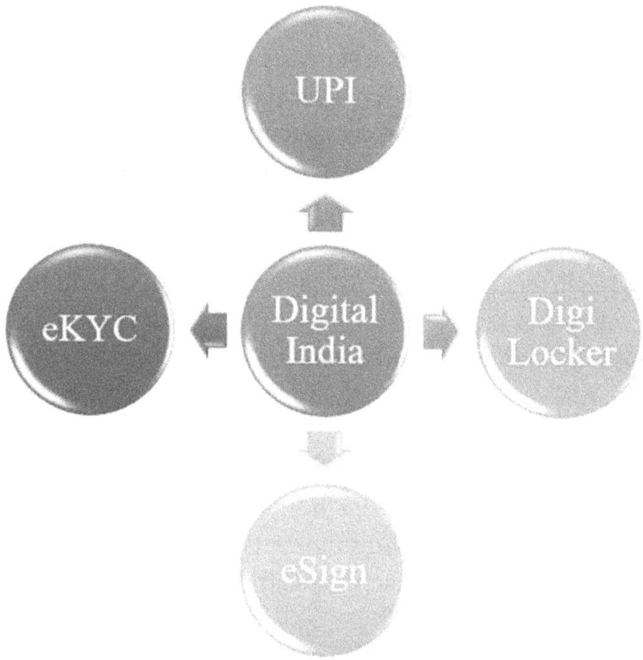

CITIES AND THEIR CAPITAL IN TERMS OF BLEISURE TOURISM

Bleisure tourism will is the future of tourism and mostly in all leading metro of India, it is booming and certainly from the below table, it is evident that these cities are providing the good factor for bleisure based tourism (Geng et al., 2024). The following table presents the list of cities which have both the essential component of bleisure tourism –

Table 2. Depiction of Two Major Elements of Bleisure Tourism in India

S. No.	Leading Cities	Availability of Major Business	Attraction of Leisure
1.	Mumbai	1. Reliance Industries Limited 2. Tata Group 3. Aditya Birla Group 4. Mahindra Group 5. Larsen & Toubro Limited (L&T) 6. HDFC Bank 7. State Bank of India (SBI) 8. ICICI Bank 9. Infosys 10. TCS (Tata Consultancy Services)	1. Gateway of India: Iconic landmark and popular tourist spot overlooking the Arabian Sea. 2. Marine Drive: Also known as the Queen's Necklace, it is a popular promenade along the Arabian Sea. 3. Juhu Beach: Famous for its lively atmosphere and street food. 4. Elephanta Caves: UNESCO World Heritage Site located on Elephanta Island, known for its ancient cave temples. 5. Sanjay Gandhi National Park: A sprawling park with dense forests, hiking trails, and the Kanheri Caves.
2.	Hyderabad	1. Tata Consultancy Services (TCS) 2. Infosys 3. Tech Mahindra 4. Wipro Limited 5. Cognizant Technology Solutions 6. Tata Consultancy Services (TCS) 7. Infosys 8. Tech Mahindra 9. Wipro Limited 10. Cognizant Technology Solutions	1. Charminar: Iconic monument and mosque located in the heart of the city. 2. Golconda Fort: Historic fort known for its architecture and sound & light show. 3. Ramoji Film City: The world's largest integrated film city and a popular tourist attraction. 4. Hussain Sagar Lake: Artificial lake with a large monolithic statue of Buddha in the middle. 5. Nehru Zoological Park: One of the largest zoos in India, home to a variety of exotic animals. 6. Salar Jung Museum: Art Museum with a vast collection of sculptures, paintings, and antiques.
3.	Chennai	1. Wipro Limited 2. HCL Technologies 3. Hyundai Motor India Limited 4. Ford India Private Limited 5. Renault Nissan Automotive India Private Limited 6. Royal Enfield (Eicher Motors) 7. Ashok Leyland	1. Marina Beach: One of the longest urban beaches in the world, known for its scenic beauty and bustling atmosphere. 2. Marina Lighthouse: Offers a panoramic view of the city and the Bay of Bengal from the top. 3. Kapaleeshwarar Temple: An ancient Hindu temple dedicated to Lord Shiva, known for its Dravidian architecture. 4. Santhome Cathedral Basilica: A Roman Catholic minor basilica built over the tomb of St. Thomas the Apostle. 5. Fort St. George: The first English fortress in India, now houses the Tamil Nadu Legislative Assembly and other official buildings.

continued on following page

Table 2. Continued

S. No.	Leading Cities	Availability of Major Business	Attraction of Leisure
4.	Delhi	1. Bharti Airtel Limited 2. Vodafone Idea Limited 3. Tata Communications 4. Reliance Jio Infocomm Limited 5. Maruti Suzuki India Limited 6. Hero MotoCorp 7. Honda Cars India Limited 8. Tata Motors 9. Escorts Limited 10. Bharat Petroleum Corporation Limited 11. Oil and Natural Gas Corporation (ONGC) 12. GAIL (India) Limited 13. Petronet LNG Limited	1. India Gate: Iconic war memorial and popular leisure spot, especially in the evenings. 2. Red Fort: UNESCO World Heritage Site known for its stunning architecture and historical significance. 3. Qutub Minar: UNESCO World Heritage Site and the tallest brick minaret in the world. 4. Humayun's Tomb: UNESCO World Heritage Site, a beautiful example of Mughal architecture. 5. Lotus Temple: Bahá'í House of Worship known for its distinctive lotus flower-like shape.
5.	Gurugram	1. HCL Technologies 2. Tata Consultancy Services (TCS) 3. Infosys 4. Wipro Limited 5. Cognizant Technology Solutions 6. Maruti Suzuki India Limited 7. Hero MotoCorp 8. Honda Cars India Limited 9. Tata Motors 10. Escorts Limited	1. Kingdom of Dreams: Entertainment destination featuring live shows, theatrical performances, and cultural attractions. 2. Sultanpur Bird Sanctuary: Nature reserve known for birdwatching, especially during the winter migration season. 3. Ambience Mall: One of the largest shopping malls in India, offering a wide range of shopping, dining, and entertainment options. 4. Cyber Hub: Dining and entertainment hub with a wide range of restaurants, cafes, bars, and entertainment options. 5. Leisure Valley Park: Urban park with lush greenery, jogging tracks, and recreational facilities.

continued on following page

Table 2. Continued

S. No.	Leading Cities	Availability of Major Business	Attraction of Leisure
6.	Pune	1. Larsen & Toubro Limited (L&T) 2. Escorts Limited 3. Eicher Motors Limited 4. BHEL (Bharat Heavy Electricals Limited) 5. NTPC Limited 6. Vodafone Idea Limited 7. Tata Communications 8. Reliance 9. Jio Infocomm Limited 10. Bharat Forge 11. Kirloskar Group 12. Thermax 13. Cummins India 14. Forbes Marshall 15. Serum Institute of India 16. Lupin Limited 17. Cipla 18. Emcure Pharmaceuticals 19. Sun Pharmaceutical 20. Mercedes-Benz India	1. Shaniwar Wada: Historic fortification and palace known for its architectural grandeur and historical significance. 2. Aga Khan Palace: Historic palace with beautiful gardens, now a museum dedicated to Mahatma Gandhi. 3. Sinhagad Fort: Historic fortress located atop a hill, offering panoramic views of the surrounding landscape. 4. Osho International Meditation Resort: Meditation center offering various meditation techniques, wellness programs, and spiritual practices. 5. Pataleshwar Cave Temple: Rock-cut cave temple dedicated to Lord Shiva, known for its ancient architecture.

LIST OF HOTELS PROVIDING BLEISURE FACILITIES

Table 3. List of Emerging Cities With Their Hotel Names for Bleisure Tourism

S. No.	Cities	Leading Hotels in Bleisure Tourism
1.	Delhi	1. Andaz 2. Crowne Plaza Delhi. 3. InterContinental 4. The Grand New Delhi 5. ITC Hotel Maurya Sheraton & Towers 6. Jaypee Vasant Continental 7. Maidens Hotel 8. Radisson Hotel Delhi 9. Taj Palace Hote 10. The Ambassador Hotel

continued on following page

Table 3. Continued

S. No.	Cities	Leading Hotels in Bleisure Tourism
2.	Mumbai	11. The Emerald 12. Hilton Towers, Mumbai 13. St. Regis (Warli) 14. Inter-Continental 15. The Grand Mumbai 16. ITC Hotel Grand Central Sheraton & Towers 17. ITC Hotel Grand Maratha Sheraton & Towers 18. Taj Lands 19. Taj President 20. Taj Wellington Mews, Mumbai
3.	Chennai	21. ITC Grand Chola 22. Le Royal Meridien 23. Taj Connemara 24. Taj Coromandel 25. The Park
4.	Gurgaon	26. The Oberoi 27. Trident Hilton, Gurgaon
5.	Bangalore	28. ITC Hotel Windsor Sheraton & Towers 29. St. Mark's Hotel 30. Taj Residency, Bangalore 31. The Grand Ashok Bangalore 32. The Leela Palace Kempinski, Bangalore 33. The Oberoi 34. The Park 35. The Taj West End
6.	Pune	36. Taj Blue Diamond Pune 37. The Oakwood
7.	Ahmadabad	38. Cama Hotel 39. Fortune Landmark 40. Taj Residency
8.	Kolkata	41. ITC Hotel Sonar Bangla Sheraton & Towers 42. Park Palace Hotel 43. Taj Bengal
9.	Hyderabad	44. ITC Hotel Kakatiya Sheraton & Tower 45. Taj Banjara 46. Taj Deccan 47. Taj Krishna
10.	Goa	48. Fort Aguada Beach Resort 49. Taj Exotica 50. Taj Holiday Village, Goa.

CURRENT TRENDS IN INDIA

Bleisure trips refer to combining business travel with leisure activities. This can be done by adding sightseeing and relaxation to the itinerary once the business goals have been met. Encouraging this type of travel can increase the number of employees willing to travel for work (Rasoolimanesh et al., 2024). These trips can serve as a much-needed break to refresh and rejuvenate employees.

There are different types of activities includes in bleisure tourism in India.

1. **Providing all the amenities:** Work trips are undertaken for business purposes like client meetings, conferences, seminars etc. Business travelers need certain special amenities like Wi-Fi, meeting rooms, seminar halls and more to stay connected.
2. **All-Inclusive Spa Retreat**: This package includes **all-stay spa access**, granting guests unlimited use of spa facilities during their stay. Guests can choose from a range of professional massage options.
3. **Fitness and Wellness**: The hotel can organize popular fitness classes like **yoga** and **meditation** to enhance the overall well-being of bleisure travellers.
4. **City Exploration Package**: This package encourages guests to explore the city beyond business hours. It includes guided city tours, tickets to local attractions (museums, historical sites, or art galleries), and recommendations for trendy restaurants and cafes.
5. **Customization**: Tailor the package based on the guest's interests, whether they prefer cultural experiences, culinary adventures, or outdoor activities.
6. **Extended Weekend Getaway**: It is deal for business travellers who can extend their stay over the weekend. It includes a discounted rate for the extra nights, complimentary breakfast, and access to nearby recreational facilities (such as golf courses or beach clubs, water sports activities).
7. **Cultural Engagement Package**: It includes tickets to theatre performances, art exhibitions, or music concerts. Arrange private tours to historical landmarks or workshops on traditional crafts. It also includes taste of local Cuisine.
8. **Family-Friendly Bleisure**: Females are more likely than male to take bleisure trips hence it includes family-friendly amenities such as kids' clubs, babysitting services, and family suites. It also offers family-oriented activities like movie nights, treasure hunts, or poolside games.
9. **Home-sharing on work trips:** Read books, watch movies, garden, or engage in hobbies.

10. **Digital Innovation by Hospitality Industry:** Hotels are also adapting to cater to the needs of bleisure travellers, who seek to combine work with leisure activities, often extending their business trips to enjoy local attractions and experiences.

CHALLENGES FOR BLEISURE TOURISM

The challenges of blending business and leisure travel, commonly known as bleisure tourism, include:

1. **Balancing Work and Leisure:** Finding the right balance between work obligations and leisure activities can be challenging, as travellers may struggle to effectively manage their time.
2. **Increased Expenses:** Combining business and leisure travel often results in higher expenses due to additional leisure activities and extended stays.
3. **Work-Life Balance:** Maintaining a healthy work-life balance becomes more complex when business trips are extended for leisure purposes, potentially leading to increased stress and burnout.
4. **Logistical Issues:** Coordinating business meetings or conferences with leisure activities requires careful planning and may present logistical challenges.
5. **Productivity Concerns:** There is a risk that leisure activities during business trips may distract travellers from their work responsibilities, potentially impacting productivity.
6. **Tax and Insurance Implications:** Determining which expenses are tax-deductible and understanding insurance coverage can be complicated when combining business and leisure travel (Srivastava, 2024).

CONCLUSION

Business tourism in India is experiencing steady growth, driven by the country's expanding economy and increasing globalization. Not only India is emerging as a major economy in Asian region, but India has improved its many segments for domestic tourists also so this situation where India is emerging as a key player in the global market, there has been a rise in international business events, conferences, and trade shows held in the country. Additionally, the Indian government's initiatives to promote the tourism sector, along with improvements in infrastructure and connectivity, have further boosted the business tourism industry. Looking ahead, the future of business tourism in India appears promising, with continued investments in infrastructure, the development of world-class convention centres, and the expansion of the hospitality sector expected to attract more business travellers to the country. Moreover, the trend of blending business and leisure travel, known as leisure travel, is gaining popularity, presenting new opportunities for growth in the business tourism sector.

REFERENCES

Astina, I. K., Sumarmi, S., & Kurniawati, E. (2021). Tourism in coastal areas: its implication to improve economic and culture acculturation (case study in goa China Beach, Malang). *Geo Journal of Tourism and Geosites*, 37(3), 740–746. 10.30892/gtg.37302-704

Bandyopadhyay, R., Morais, D. B., & Chick, G. (2008). Religion and identity in India's heritage tourism. *Annals of Tourism Research*, 35(3), 790–808. 10.1016/j.annals.2008.06.004

Becker, G. S. (1962). Investment in Human Capital: A Theoretical analysis. *Journal of Political Economy*, 70(5, Part 2), 9–49. 10.1086/258724

Chung, J. Y., Choi, Y., Yoo, B., & Kim, S. (2020). Bleisure tourism experience chain: Implications for destination marketing. *Asia Pacific Journal of Tourism Research*, 25(3), 300–310. 10.1080/10941665.2019.1708760

Coffey, J. K., Shahvali, M., Kerstetter, D. L., & Aron, A. (2024). Couples vacations and romantic passion and intimacy. *Annals of Tourism Research Empirical Insights*, 5(1), 100121. 10.1016/j.annale.2024.100121

Elias, S. (2024). Economic impact of tourism in developing countries. *Indian Scientific Journal of Research in Engineering and Management*, 08(04), 1–5. 10.55041/IJSREM30010

Frochot, I., Montémont, V., & Violier, P. (2024). *Post-Covid hypermobile tourist practices facing environmental challenges*. Mondes Du Tourisme., 10.4000/tourisme.6689

Geng, Y., Zhang, X., Juan, G., Yan, Y., & Chen, L. (2024). Bibliometric analysis of sustainable tourism using CiteSpace. *Technological Forecasting & Social Change. Technological Forecasting and Social Change*, 202, 123310. 10.1016/j.techfore.2024.123310

Gunasekar, S., Patri, R., & Narayanan, B. (2017). International Tourist arrival in India. *Foreign Trade Review*, 53(1), 12–28. 10.1177/0015732516681882

Khoo-Lattimore, C., & Yang, E. C. L. (2018). Asian Youth tourism: contemporary trends, cases and issues. In *Perspectives on Asian tourism* (pp. 1–13). 10.1007/978-981-10-8539-0_1

Lichy, J., & McLeay, F. (2017). Bleisure: Motivations and typologies. *Journal of Travel & Tourism Marketing*, 35(4), 517–530. 10.1080/10548408.2017.1364206

Lipsa, S., & Dash, R. K. (2024). A seven-year analysis of the tourism sector of India with a prediction model—A case study of smart tourism. *Smart Tourism*, 5(1), 2526. 10.54517/st.v5i1.2526

Ohlan, R. (2017). The relationship between tourism, financial development and economic growth in India. *Future Business Journal*, 3(1), 9–22. 10.1016/j.fbj.2017.01.003

Pham, H. C., Duong, C. D., & Nguyen, G. T. (2024). What drives tourists' continuance intention to use ChatGPT for travel services? A stimulus-organism-response perspective. *Journal of Retailing and Consumer Services*, 78, 103758. 10.1016/j.jretconser.2024.103758

Ramanjulu, D. (2024). Detours and delays: Navigating the pandemic's impact on India's transport sector and tourism. *EPRA International Journal of Economic and Business Review*, 22–27. 10.36713/epra16460

Rasoolimanesh, S. M., Chee, S. Y., & Ragavan, N. A. (2024). From Mindset to Practice: How employees' attitudes impact tourism businesses' sustainability practices. *International Journal of Hospitality & Tourism Administration*, 1–31. 10.1080/15256480.2024.2344224

Rijal, S., Badollahi, M. Z., & Haryanto, B. (2021). *Tourism turbulance*. Advances in Economics, Business and Management Research/Advances in Economics, Business and Management Research. 10.2991/aebmr.k.211223.009

Srivastava, U. K. (2024). A study of global trade war and its impact on Indian economy. *International Journal for Multidisciplinary Research*, 6(2), 14813. Advance online publication. 10.36948/ijfmr.2024.v06i02.14813

Unger, O., & Uriely, N. (2022). The bleisure memories of business travelers. *Annals of Tourism Research*, 97, 103497. 10.1016/j.annals.2022.103497

Weng, Y. (2024). Explore how to refine social media marketing strategies and shape consumer travel preferences: An in-depth study on Airbnb. *Advances in Economics. Management and Political Sciences*, 74(1), 68–74. 10.54254/2754-1169/74/20241499

Chapter 12
Mobile Apps for Enhanced Bleisure Tourism Experiences: Exploring the Prospects and Challenges

Priyakrushna Mohanty
https://orcid.org/0000-0001-6933-2757
Christ University, India

Rashmiranjan Choudhury
https://orcid.org/0000-0001-6956-8057
Jain University (Deemed), India

Indu Ranga
https://orcid.org/0000-0002-8946-050X
Christ University, India

G. Nagarjuna
https://orcid.org/0000-0002-5908-1883
Christ University, India

ABSTRACT

Mobile applications play a pivotal role in enabling and enhancing bleisure travel experiences. These apps offer solutions for communication, itinerary planning, transportation booking, and leisure discovery, reflecting the evolving expectations of modern travelers for efficiency, flexibility, and customized experiences. Despite their benefits, challenges such as data privacy concerns and information overload persist. Looking ahead, the future of bleisure travel is poised for further transformation

DOI: 10.4018/979-8-3693-4354-8.ch012

through advances in mobile technology, including augmented reality and artificial intelligence. However, a research gap exists in understanding the full spectrum of mobile apps catering to bleisure tourists' needs. This chapter aims to address this gap by classifying mobile apps for bleisure tourism, exploring their advantages, and identifying challenges and opportunities for innovation. By doing so, it seeks to contribute to a deeper understanding of the role of mobile technology in shaping the landscape of bleisure tourism in the digital age.

INTRODUCTION

A significant development in the travel industry in recent years has been the merging of business and leisure travel, otherwise known as the "bleisure" travel. This phenomenon is a reflection of the shifting perspectives of contemporary professionals, who are increasingly looking to balance job obligations with travel opportunities for leisure and exploration (Batala & Slevitch, 2024). Professionals are no longer restricted to typical office settings due to the advent of globalisation and remote work, which allows them to extend business visits to include leisure activities or incorporate work duties into holidays (Floričić & Pavia, 2021). The evolution of travel behaviour is embodied by leisure tourism, which reflects the shifting dynamics of work, leisure, and lifestyle preferences in modern society. Travelling for business and pleasure was traditionally seen as two different activities, with professionals keeping their personal and professional lives apart. But since the emergence of "bleisure" tourism, tourists are adopting a more all-encompassing attitude to travel, erasing the distinction between work and recreation, and attempting to strike a balance between business and personal interests while away from home (Chung et al., 2020).

Simultaneously, the swift progress in technology, especially the extensive utilisation of smartphones and mobile applications, has completely transformed the way people organise, reserve, and take pleasure in travel (Lee & Jan, 2022). With their many features that simplify travel planning, boost efficiency, and enable leisure exploration, mobile apps have become as essential tools for travellers (Kim et al., 2023). Mobile applications are essential for bleisure tourism because they facilitate the smooth integration of work and explore new destinations. They offer solutions for remote work communication, itinerary planning, reserving transportation, and leisure discovery. Numerous variables, such as the growing significance of work-life balance, the emergence of remote work and flexible work schedules, and the growing acceptance of travel as a means of personal fulfilment and enrichment, are responsible for this mentality shift. Apart from professional goals, leisure travellers are driven by a desire to discover new places, become fully immersed in other cultures, and have life-enhancing experiences.

Beyond simple convenience, mobile app adoption in bleisure travel signifies a fundamental shift in people's travel mindset, placing an emphasis on efficiency, flexibility, and customised experiences (Lim et al., 2022). Travellers who are travelling for pleasure can make the most of their trip experiences, whether they are attending business meetings, visiting new places, or just relaxing and rejuvenating, by utilising mobile technology to maximise productivity and optimise time. The future of travel in the digital era is expected to be shaped by the growing significance of mobile apps in enabling smooth, joyful, and rewarding bleisure travel experiences, as the lines between work and leisure continue to blur.

There are numerous mobile apps that improve productivity for leisure travellers by organising activities, managing reservations, and combining plans (Respatyanti, 2019). These solutions maximise productivity during travels by streamlining organisation, facilitating informed decision-making, and saving time. Furthermore, applications such as Uber and Google Maps help with booking and navigation for transportation; they provide turn-by-turn navigation and real-time ride-hailing for easy travel between locations. Additionally, websites like Yelp and Localeur enhance free time by offering carefully chosen suggestions for genuine cultural discovery. Even with their advantages, problems like data privacy and information overload still exist, which may prevent them from being widely used by leisure travellers.

In terms of future development and innovation, the potential of mobile apps in leisure travel appears promising. Mobile apps are expected to advance in sophistication, usability, and customisation to meet the specific requirements of leisure travellers as technology develops further. The bleisure travel experience might be completely transformed by cutting-edge technologies like augmented reality, artificial intelligence, and personalised recommendations. These elements would provide immersive experiences and tailored solutions that improve productivity, leisure exploration, and overall enjoyment (Floričić & Pavia, 2021).

While the integration of mobile apps in bleisure tourism has garnered attention for its potential to enhance traveler experiences, there remains a notable research gap regarding the comprehensive understanding of the diverse range of mobile applications available for this emerging trend. Existing studies have primarily focused on the general usage of mobile technology in travel or specific functionalities of individual apps, often overlooking the holistic landscape of mobile apps tailored specifically for bleisure travelers (see Lim et al., 2022). Consequently, there is a need for research that systematically categorizes and evaluates mobile apps catering to the multifaceted needs of bleisure tourists. By addressing this research gap, scholars can provide valuable insights into the classification, functionalities, and effectiveness of mobile apps in facilitating seamless integration of work and leisure elements during travel.

In light of this research gap, this article aims to achieve three primary objectives. Firstly, it seeks to conduct a comprehensive classification of mobile apps for bleisure tourism, categorizing them based on their functionalities and target user segments. Secondly, it aims to explore the advantages of using mobile apps for bleisure tourism, highlighting their role in streamlining travel logistics, enhancing productivity, and enriching leisure experiences. Lastly, the article investigates the challenges of mobile apps in bleisure tourism, identifying barriers to adoption and potential areas for innovation and improvement. By addressing these objectives, this research aims to contribute to a deeper understanding of the role and impact of mobile technology in shaping the landscape of bleisure tourism in the digital age.

LITERATURE REVIEW

Evolution of Bleisure Tourism

The concept of bleisure tourism is not new to the industry as it has been practised since the late 20th century and got popularised in the last two decades with the rapid proliferation of technology (Sohaili, Aminudin, & Amir, 2022). Bleisure tourism is the blend of business and leisure travel where the prior activity is business while the secondary is leisure travel. In the 1990s business travellers rarely extend their stay to explore some leisure activity in the visited destination because of the corporate policies and regulations (Mercan & Sandıkcı, 2024). Gradually the scenario has observed a trend shift with the advent of technology. After the 2000s, when mobile devices and high-speed internet became widespread the gap between business and leisure narrowed and it allowed business travellers to plan with leisure trip while connected to the business remotel .

The shift of work culture also influenced the evolution of bleisure tourism. The corporate sector started to embrace flexible work hours, remote working, and telecommuting has diminished the huddles across business and travel (Lichy & McLeay, 2018). The pandemic situation also influenced the belief of business firms about the possibilities of remote and flexible work environment. In the evolution of bleisure tourism the changing preference of the millennial workforce cannot be ignored. For this dominating workforce the bleisure trip provides an opportunity of personal enrichment and professional exposure with leisure in return the organisation gets business accomplishment and professional loyalty. Through the ever-changing situation, the corporate world changed its attitude for bleisure travel. Several corporates have changed their policies and regulations to support bleisure activities in order to achieve the employee job satisfaction and maximizing productivity (Hussain, Singh, Mohanty, & Gavinolla, 2023).

Though technology influences bleisure tourism, Covid-19 pandemic has accelerated its growth and development (Mohanty, Dhoundiyal, & Choudhury, 2022). Adopting remote work policies business firms provided flexibility to work from remote locations. After the pandemic, the desire for business and leisure intensified as it became a new practice. Travel tourism and its allied industries have come up with significant changes to cater for the new form of tourism. Looking forward to the growth of bleisure tourism the prospects and challenges needs special attention from the concerned corporate sector and the tourism industries.

Mobile Application and Business

Mobile applications have been considered as the compact version of the website or any remote access point to the central server (Desideria & Bandung, 2020). The wide applicability of the mobile application brought a significant change to almost every industry. In present era, effective use of mobile applications ensures the business growth and sustainability (Rakshit, Islam, Mondal, & Paul, 2021). In the competitive market, mobile applications offer an advantage and improve the visibility and reach of the business organisation. Monitoring and field-based operation need regular inspection where the mobile application stand out as best tool in several businesses (Alghizzawi, Habes, Al Assuli, & Ezmigna, 2024).

Mobile applications have turn into a facilitating tool for both business and leisure activities. The integration of mobile applications has simplified the whole process like planning and management, supporting at local operation, offers personalisation and customisation through seamless connectivity (Mohanty, Shreya, & Choudhury, 2021). The use of mobile applications in business operations is not only beneficial to the organisation in several ways, but it also influences the tourism business. Mobile applications provide services like booking and customisation according to any uncertain changes in the business activities, also alerting the other parties regarding the same. All-time access to itineraries and minor business information makes mobile applications a more valuable asset for the business traveller. The benefits of the mobile applications need to be explored along with the challenges to integrate in the future business activities.

Figure 1. Framework for Mobile Application Enhanced Bleisure Tourism (MAEBT)

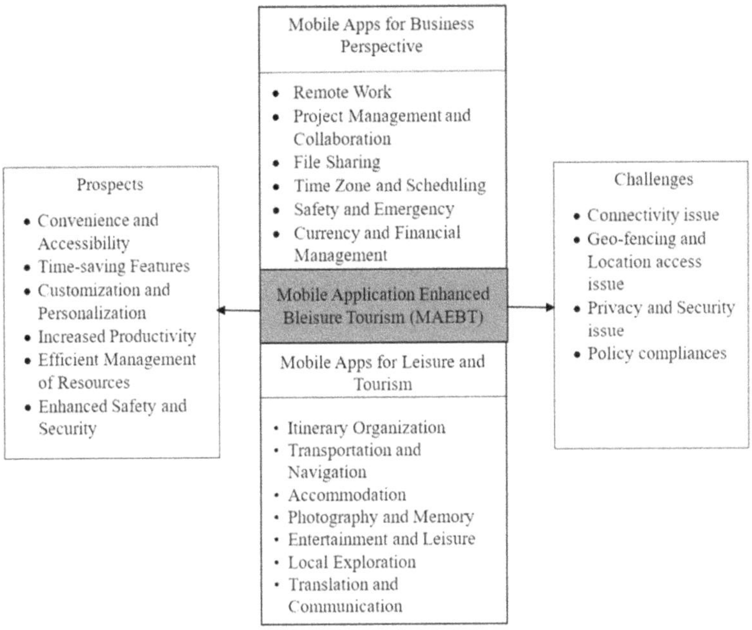

METHODOLOGY

The present study utilised a methodical technique to compile pertinent literature and perform thematic content analysis in order to discern recurrent themes (Vaismoradi et al., 2013). First, a thorough search was done to find papers about mobile apps in bleisure tourism using scholarly databases including Scopus, Web of Science, and Google Scholar. Keywords such as “Mobile apps” or “Mobile Applications”, “Travel technology”, “Smart Tourism”, and “Bleisure Tourism” were employed to retrieve relevant articles. These keywords were strategically selected to target literature specifically focusing on the intersection of mobile applications and bleisure tourism. A total of 17 papers that satisfied the study's inclusion requirements were found through this search. The articles were analysed using thematic content analysis after the literature retrieval procedure to find important recurrent topics about the use of mobile apps in bleisure travel. A qualitative research technique called thematic content analysis is used to find, examine, and interpret patterns or themes in a dataset. The obtained articles' material was rigorously coded and categorised in this study's thematic content analysis to extract pertinent themes and insights.

The analysis method comprised data categorization, interpretation, and coding, among other iterative processes. To find recurring themes, patterns, and trends regarding the use of mobile apps for leisure travel, articles were reviewed and examined. The themes were then arranged into categories that made sense to help with the synthesis and interpretation of the data. The overall goal of the technique used in this study was to systematically compile pertinent literature and use thematic content analysis to analyse it in order to find major recurrent themes about the use of mobile apps in leisure travel. This method made it easier to comprehend the subject matter completely and gave insightful information about how mobile apps may improve leisure travel.

In order to support the research findings given that there wasn't enough scientific literature, sources from the grey literature were also consulted (Benzies et al., 2006). Reports, theses, conference proceedings, and other materials created by organisations or individuals outside of customary academic publishing routes are referred to as grey literature. This multi-pronged strategy guaranteed a thorough investigation of the subject, including reports or insights from the sector as well as academic research. Through the integration of many information sources, the study sought to offer a comprehensive comprehension of how mobile applications might improve leisure travel, consequently boosting the examination and interpretation of significant themes and discoveries.

CLASSIFICATION OF MOBILE APPLICATIONS FOR BLEISURE TRAVELLERS

Based on their features and objectives, mobile applications used by leisure travellers can be divided into multiple categories. Several popular categories and instances of mobile applications utilised by leisure travellers worldwide are as follows:

From Business Perspective

Remote Work Communication

A key component of bleisure travel is *remote work communication*, which allows travellers to remain connected and productive while on the move (Batala & Slevitch, 2024). Mobile apps like Zoom, Slack, and Microsoft Teams are essential for enabling smooth communication and teamwork amongst distant teams. Microsoft Teams provides chat, video conferencing, file sharing, and interaction with other

Microsoft Office applications, making it a complete platform for communication during remote work. Microsoft Teams facilitates efficient communication and collaboration between geographically dispersed teams through features like threaded conversations, channels for team discussions, and document collaboration. As a result, it's a great option for leisure travellers who need to manage work-related tasks and projects. Similarly Slack, which is popular due to its real-time messaging features, customisable channels, and interfaces with numerous third-party apps, distant teams may work together on projects in an organised and effective way by exchanging data and communicating. Furthermore, Zoom is well-known for its video conferencing features, which include screen sharing, webinar capabilities, and high-quality audio and video. These features make it simple for leisure travellers to hold virtual meetings, seminars, and presentations while on the road. Regardless of their location or time zone differences, these remote work communication applications enable leisure travellers to be productive, stay in touch with clients or colleagues, and efficiently manage work-related duties and responsibilities.

Project Management and Task Collaboration

In order to efficiently plan and coordinate work-related activities while balancing leisure interests, project management and task cooperation are crucial elements of bleisure tourism (ÇETİNSÖZ & HAZARHUN, 2020). Travellers looking to combine business and pleasure can benefit greatly from mobile software like Asana and Trello, which provide remote teams with strong project management, task tracking, and assignment collaboration capabilities. Asana is an all-inclusive platform for project planning and task management, enabling users to create tasks, assign responsibilities, set deadlines, and monitor progress in real time. Asana's features, which include customisable project boards, task dependencies, and team collaboration tools, make it easier to manage projects effectively and guarantee that work-related activities are finished on time, even when travelling. Similar to this, Trello is well known for its visual project management methodology. It does this by employing cards, lists, and boards to arrange work and processes in a flexible and understandable way. To track progress, users can make boards for various projects, add tasks as cards, and move them via lists that they can customise. Trello helps leisure travellers keep organised, prioritise projects, and work efficiently with team members regardless of their location or time zone variations. Features like due dates, checklists, and file attachments help. Travellers who combine business and pleasure may stay productive, handle work-related obligations, and plan a well-balanced mix of work and leisure activities while on the road by utilising these project management and task collaboration tools.

Document Collaboration and File Sharing

The management of workflow and smooth communication for remote teams is made possible by document collaboration and file sharing, which are essential components of bleisure travel (Benckendorff et al., 2019). Two well-known services that provide strong options for file sharing and document collaboration are Dropbox and Google Drive. Version control and real-time collaboration are made possible by Google Drive, which lets users create, store, and share documents, spreadsheets, and presentations on the cloud. Similar to this, Dropbox enables users to access and share files from any location by offering safe cloud storage and file synchronisation. Travellers who combine business and pleasure can work together on projects, exchange crucial documents, and maintain productivity while on the road by utilising these technologies.

Time Zone Management and Scheduling

The handling of time zones and scheduling are essential components of leisure travel, particularly for individuals who are balancing professional obligations in multiple locations (Lichy & McLeay, 2018). Travellers may easily manage time zone differences and schedule meetings with the use of mobile applications like World Time Buddy and Calendly. With the help of World Time Buddy's visual time zone converter and scheduler, users can compare different time zones at once and choose times for meetings that work for everyone's schedules. By enabling users to specify their availability preferences and share customised scheduling links with coworkers or clients, Calendly streamlines the appointment scheduling process.

Safety and Emergency Assistance

While juggling business and leisure activities, bleisure travellers may find themselves traversing foreign areas. In these situations, travel safety and emergency help are critical considerations. Apps for smartphones like Safeture and TravelSafe offer useful information to keep travellers aware and ready for emergencies (Bąk & Borkowski, 2015). Travellers can receive real-time warnings from Safeture about potential hazards like natural disasters, political upheaval, or health advisories, as well as safety advice and emergency help services. Similar to this, TravelSafe offers a global database of embassy connections, medical facilities, and emergency service numbers—essential tools for travellers who may encounter unforeseen circumstances while travelling. Bleisure travellers may ensure a safer and more secure travel experience by using these apps to reduce risks, make educated decisions, and obtain assistance when needed.

Currency Conversion and Financial Management

Aside from safety concerns, currency conversion and money management are crucial components of leisure travel (Gunn et al., 1993). When travelling, mobile apps like Trail Wallet and XE Currency make it easier for travellers to handle their money. With the use of historical charts, currency conversion tools, and live exchange rates, XE Currency helps travellers stay on top of exchange rate swings and make well-informed foreign exchange decisions. Comparably, Trail Wallet is a trip expense tracker that provides insights into savings and travel expenses while assisting users in creating budgets, monitoring spending, and managing funds in many currencies. Travellers on a bleisure trip can ensure a hassle-free and seamless journey by using these applications to manage currency conversions, keep an eye on spending, and practise financial restraint.

From Leisure and Tourism Perspective

Itinerary Organization

In bleisure travel, itinerary organisation is essential since it enables travellers to effectively manage their calendars and move between business and leisure activities with ease (Sherry, 2015). This process is made much simpler by mobile apps like Kayak Trips, TripIt, and Travefy,. In order to guarantee seamless travel experiences, Kayak Trips provides travellers with a comprehensive platform to organise all of their trip arrangements, including flights, lodging, and activities. Real-time updates and notifications are also provided. Another well-liked option is TripIt, which gathers travel itinerary information automatically by reading confirmation emails and consolidating it all into a single, conveniently accessible dashboard. TripIt helps travellers stay organised during their travels by streamlining itinerary management with features like flight status updates and mobile notifications. Conversely, Travefy is notable for its collaborative trip planning features, which let users make and share comprehensive plans with other travellers, making group coordination and communication easier. By offering centralised access to crucial trip information and enabling efficient planning and coordination, these itinerary organisation applications not only improve efficiency and productivity for leisure travellers but also contribute to a smooth and joyful travel experience.

Transportation Booking and Navigation

Booking and navigating transportation is a crucial aspect of bleisure travel, allowing visitors to effortlessly transition between work and leisure while discovering new places (Huettermann et al., 2019). Uber and Google Maps are two examples of mobile applications that offer practical solutions for booking and navigating. Uber provides easy on-demand ride-hailing services to travellers worldwide, enabling them to track the real-time location of their driver. Uber offers bleisure travellers navigating metropolitan surroundings freedom and dependability by offering alternatives for many vehicle kinds and payment ways. In addition, Google Maps provides accurate mapping, real-time traffic updates, and navigation to facilitate efficient traveller navigation by foot, vehicle, or public transportation to new places. Google Maps improves the travel experience by offering thorough navigation help and local insights for leisure travellers. Features like turn-by-turn instructions, offline maps, and local business information are just a few examples of how the app works.

Accommodation Booking

Another important component of bleisure travel is arranging accommodations, as guests look for convenient and pleasant housing alternatives that meet both their business and leisure demands (Osakwe, 2023). Mobile apps like Booking.com and Airbnb provide a variety of lodging options catered to the tastes of leisure travellers. Booking.com offers a large selection of lodging alternatives, including hotels, apartments, and vacation rentals, along with features like flexible booking options, user ratings, and real-time availability. Travellers can book distinctive lodgings and activities hosted by locals through Airbnb, providing a more customised and genuine vacation experience. Booking.com and Airbnb offer a range of options to suit different budgets, preferences, and places. This allows travellers who are travelling for pleasure to have a comfortable and pleasurable stay.

Photography and Memory Keeping

Memorabilia and photography are important tools for preserving the special memories from leisure travel (Cardell, 2017). Using mobile apps like Google Photos and Instagram is essential for capturing and saving these moments. Instagram is a popular social networking site where leisure travellers may post images and videos from their travels, creating a visual journal of their experiences and connecting them with friends, coworkers, and other travellers. Instagram's features, such as filters, captions, and stories, improve the storytelling element of leisure travel by enabling users to instantly share their experiences with a worldwide audience. Similarly,

Google Photos gives users a centralised platform to preserve and easily access their travel memories across devices by offering cloud storage and organisation tools for storing, editing, and sharing images and videos. Google Photos makes it easier to preserve and relive travel experiences with features like automatic backup, facial recognition, and album creation. This guarantees that treasured memories are always accessible. Additionally, social media platforms such as Facebook and Twitter serve as invaluable tools for sharing cherished travel memories, fostering connections with friends and family, and inspiring others to embark on similar journeys (Choudhury & Mohanty, 2018).

Entertainment and Leisure Activities

Bleisure tourism necessitates entertainment and leisure activities that provide visitors a chance to unwind, enjoy the cultural and recreational offerings of their destination, and rest. Mobile apps like Eventbrite and Bookmyshow offer easy ways to find and reserve events and activities in your area. Travellers seeking to organise leisure activities based on their interests and preferences can do so using Bookmyshow's extensive database of movie screenings, concerts, theatre productions, and other entertainment possibilities. Similar to this, Eventbrite offers a platform for finding and scheduling festivals, events, and cultural encounters in destination locations, giving leisure travellers the chance to fully immerse themselves in the entertainment and culture of the area. Bookmyshow and Eventbrite improve the leisure component of bleisure travel by offering services like event listings, ticket purchase, and personalised suggestions. These tools help visitors make the most of their free time and have unforgettable experiences while travelling.

Local Discovery and Exploration

In order to fully engage with the culture and attractions of their destination, bleisure travellers must engage in local discovery and adventure. Yelp and Localeur are two examples of mobile applications that offer useful resources for finding hidden gems and having genuine local experiences. Localeur provides hand-picked suggestions from locals in cities all around the world, offering insider knowledge on the greatest eateries, pubs, stores, and off-the-beaten-path attractions. Bleisure travellers may explore destinations like a local and find unique experiences beyond popular tourist destinations with Localeur's features like personalised suggestions and user reviews. Similarly, Yelp helps bleisure travellers identify top-rated places and make educated dining and entertainment decisions by providing user-generated reviews and ratings for nearby businesses, including cafes, restaurants, bars, and attractions. Yelp's features, which include search filters, images, and business information, make it easier for travellers to discover hidden gems and make lasting memories while travelling. Yelp also improves the leisure side of bleisure travel.

Language Translation and Communication

In bleisure travel, language translation and communication are crucial for overcoming linguistic and cultural hurdles (Aydın & Özgürel, 2021). Mobile options for language study and communication abroad are offered by programmes like Google Translate and Duolingo. With its text translation, voice recognition, and video translation capabilities covering more than 100 languages, Google Translate helps vacationers overcome language obstacles and have successful conversations with locals. Google Translate improves cultural immersion and real-time communication on vacations with features like conversation mode and offline translation. Similarly, travellers can brush up on language skills and enhance communication ability while on the go with Duolingo's interactive language courses and quizzes for learning foreign languages. Duolingo makes language learning enjoyable and approachable for leisure travellers, enabling them to interact with locals and thoroughly enjoy the cultural diversity of their location through gamified learning activities and personalised learning paths.

UNVEILING THE MOTIVES: MOBILE APP USAGE IN BLEISURE TRAVEL

Convenience and Accessibility

For bleisure travellers, mobile apps provide unmatched accessibility and convenience, completely changing the way they organise, schedule, and oversee their travels. Travellers can access a multitude of travel-related services, resources, and information at any time and from any location with only a few finger tips (Madeira et al., 2021). The days of laborious paper maps, printed itinerary books, and drawn-out phone conversations to reserve lodging or travel are long gone. Instead, travellers may effortlessly manage every aspect of their trip from the palm of their hand by using smartphone apps.

Mobile apps are more than just convenient; they provide travellers the freedom to plan their travels as they see fit, taking into account their schedules and preferences. Mobile apps offer immediate access to vital travel tools and services, such as finding nearby eateries, monitoring flight statuses, and reserving last-minute hotel rooms. Moreover, the smooth amalgamation of diverse features in a solitary application streamlines the journey encounter by obviating the necessity of managing distinct platforms or websites. All things considered, the ease and accessibility that mobile apps provide for bleisure travel simplify the planning process, boost productivity, and enable travellers to enjoy the most comfortable and convenient travel experience possible.

Time-Saving Features

Due to their time-saving capabilities, mobile applications have revolutionised the way travellers plan and organise their travels, making them invaluable for bleisure travel (Arora et al., 2019). With the abundance of tools and features these apps provide, users may travel more easily and swiftly while completing jobs quickly and effectively. Travellers can avoid the time-consuming procedures often involved in trip preparation, like making hotel reservations, looking up locations, and creating itineraries, by using smartphone apps.

Real-time updates and notifications are among the most important time-saving features of mobile applications (Sia et al., 2023). When there are modifications to airline itineraries, hotel reservations, or gate assignments, travellers are immediately notified, giving them the opportunity to quickly adjust their arrangements. Additionally, mobile apps provide smooth interaction with various travel-related platforms and services, giving consumers access to a wide range of alternatives from a single interface. Travellers can save time and effort by booking flights, hotels, rental cars, and activities from a single app, rather of having to visit various websites or platforms.

Furthermore, user-friendly design and intuitive interfaces are common in mobile apps, which facilitate travellers' ability to locate the information or services they require fast. With a few clicks, users may obtain pertinent information about neighbouring attractions, food recommendations, and transit alternatives. In general, the time-saving capabilities of mobile apps for leisure travel make travel more effective and pleasurable by enabling users to make the most of their time while seeing new places or taking care of business obligations with the least amount of effort.

Customization and Personalization

When it comes to bleisure travel, mobile applications provide unmatched personalisation and customisation capabilities that enable visitors to customise their experiences to suit their interests and tastes. These applications combine cutting-edge technology and data analytics to offer users individualised services, insights, and recommendations that improve their trip experience as a whole (Briliana & Prasetio, 2018).

The ability to customise travel recommendations and itineraries based on user choices is a crucial component of customisation and personalisation in mobile apps. Travellers can input their hobbies, dietary restrictions, preferred accommodations, and more through user profiles and preferences settings. This enables apps to offer personalised recommendations for activities, dining alternatives, and attractions. This degree of personalisation guarantees that visitors can discover locations and activities that suit their own interests and preferences, increasing their level of contentment and happiness all around.

Personalised alerts, messages, and reminders are also frequently included in mobile apps to keep travellers informed and involved during their trip. These customised features enhance and simplify the travel experience by informing customers about forthcoming events, making recommendations based on past choices, and delivering special offers and discounts. Mobile applications for leisure travel enable travellers to make the most of their journeys with the least amount of work and the greatest amount of happiness by customising content and services for each user.

Increased Productivity

Travellers' productivity is greatly increased by mobile apps, which enable users to combine business and leisure activities while on the road, revolutionising bleisure travel. Travellers can stay connected and productive no matter where they are with the abundance of productivity tools and features these applications offer (El-Sofany & Abou El-Seoud, 2023). These tools and features are intended to improve efficiency, organisation, and cooperation.

Platforms for remote business communication and collaboration are a major way that mobile apps boost productivity when travelling for leisure. With the use of apps like Slack, Microsoft Teams, and Zoom, team members can collaborate, share files, and communicate in real time, which helps workers be productive even when they're not in the office. Travellers may now efficiently complete work-related tasks while on the go with the help of these apps, whether they are sharing papers, participating in virtual meetings, or working together on projects.

Additionally, smartphone apps save travellers a great deal of time and effort by streamlining trip logistics and preparation. With the help of apps like TripIt, Kayak Trips, and Travefy, travellers can easily manage their calendars and streamline their vacation plans by providing all-inclusive solutions for itinerary management, hotel booking, and activity scheduling. By offering notifications, reminders, and real-time updates, these apps help travellers keep informed and organised, which maximises their productivity and efficiency when travelling (El-Sofany & Abou El-Seoud,

2023). Overall, bleisure travellers may efficiently mix business commitments and leisure activities thanks to the increased efficiency provided by mobile apps, making the most of their trip experiences without compromising productivity.

Efficient Management of Resources

Travellers who go on vacation for leisure may now manage their resources more effectively thanks to mobile apps, which have completely changed how people plan travel arrangements and make the most of their time, money, and energy while on the road. With the abundance of tools and features these applications provide, travellers can plan their schedule, reserve transportation, handle their finances, and navigate with ease (Igor et al., 2021). This allows them to maximise their vacation experience while putting in the least amount of work. Travellers can optimise their schedules and prevent needless delays or disruptions by using platforms like TripIt, Kayak Trips, and Travefy, which centralise itinerary information and offer real-time updates and reminders. Furthermore, applications such as XE Currency and Trail Wallet provide real-time currency rates, conversion tools, and expense tracking capabilities, enabling travellers to efficiently handle their funds and make well-informed spending decisions while on the move.

Additionally, smartphone apps simplify the booking and routing of transportation, providing easy-to-use solutions for planning transportation, navigating to new places, and planning the best routes. Travellers can move around their destinations more quickly and spend less time on transportation with the help of applications like Uber and Google Maps, which offer features like real-time ride-hailing, turn-by-turn navigation, and local transit information. In general, bleisure travel benefits from the effective resource management made possible by mobile apps. This allows travellers to make the most of their time, money, and energy while also guaranteeing a smoother and more pleasurable trip (Hussein & Ahmed, 2022).

Enhanced Safety and Security

Due to their numerous capabilities and features that help reduce risks and provide a safe travel experience, mobile apps are essential for enhancing the safety and security of leisure travellers (Díaz-Parra et al., 2023). With services like Safeture and TravelSafe providing fast information about potential threats like natural catastrophes or political instability, these applications offer real-time travel alerts and updates. Travellers can make educated decisions about their route and take the required safety procedures to minimise any risks by remaining informed through these notifications. These apps also include useful resources and assistance services, such as medical assistance and emergency contact information, which allow travellers get help and support quickly in case of problems and improve their overall safety and security (Ramos et al., 2024).

In order to keep travellers informed and connected throughout their journeys, smartphone apps incorporate features like GPS tracking, location sharing, and check-in capabilities. Because of this connectivity, travellers may stay in touch with friends, family, or coworkers, which gives them and their loved one's comfort and peace of mind. Travellers on a leisure trip can improve their personal safety and security and make their trip more secure overall by utilising technology. All things considered, smartphone applications are essential for enhancing the security and safety of leisure travellers since they offer helpful tools and assistance for navigating any dangers and crises while on the road.

NAVIGATING OBSTACLES: CHALLENGES OF MOBILE APP USE IN BLEISURE TRAVEL

As the term 'bleisure' suggests addition of both business and leisure aspects it makes the travel purpose more complicated. The bleisure traveller has to manage the work obligations and vacation in same trip which need special care of each component. Though bleisure travel has transformed through the use of mobile applications still several challenges hinder in the whole process and need corrective attentions.

Connectivity Issue

Bleisure travellers transit between different scene of locations for the purpose of business and leisure which may raise the issue of connectivity. The reliability issues cannot be neglected using external access wifi or mobile data services for the mobile app use (Shrivastava et al., 2021). In several leisure destinations or remote locations may have limited internet connectivity further limiting the use of mobile apps. Further, during the foreign bleisure travel in connectivity aspects the issues related to internet data access cannot be ignored. Several business activities like email access and remote conferencing may be disrupted as well, and leisure activities may be affected because of connectivity issues, which can further lead to customer dissatisfaction (Valsaraj et al., 2021).

Geo-Fencing and Location Access Issue

The travel applications mostly work on real-time location access for effective use of resources. Although the travel app benefits a lot convincing a bleisure traveller for consistent use of it seems like a hurdle. Privacy concerns, geo-fencing and the reluctant use of location tracking contribute to the lower acceptance of travel applications during business travel (Garcia, 2023).

Privacy and Security Issue

Bleisure travel involves a lot of crucial information of the traveller, organisation and more rover related to the business. Any security breach in the app-based management system can lead to financial and personal loss to the organisation and individual traveller (Shrivastava et al., 2021). Information like personal details, transaction information, travel and leisure arrangements need extra security to avoid unauthorised access.

Policy Compliances

More often the travel policies are cost centric for the service provider. The travel apps as products of the organisation have limitations to avail of the service provided by that specific organisation. Though the services and facilities are more convenient, bleisure travellers hesitate to use the apps because it binds them to avail of the limited services without any choice (Stoecklin et al., 2016). The policy compliance also tracks the travel expenses through a corporate travel management system which also restricts the bleisure traveller to adopt the app-based management system.

IMPLICATION AND CONCLUSION

This study has a numerous implication in the managerial as well as in state policy planning. The findings can help in planning of business destinations while emphasizing the leisure aspects. As the young generation are more inclined towards technology their preference need to be considered while designing bleisure tourism based applications. Social media integration, gamified experience and bleisure rewards are few implications in that regard. Though bleisure tourism is not new to the industry but it has less practiced hence mobile application based platform can improvise the business travel along with leisure activities. Companies that offer intuitive, feature-rich apps can differentiate themselves by enhancing the customer experience through streamlined booking processes, personalized recommendations, and seamless integration of business and leisure activities. From the employee's perspective app based bleisure travel can provide them with job satisfaction by providing reward-based programs through the mobile application.

In conclusion, this study has achieved its three primary objectives, providing valuable insights into the role and impact of mobile technology in shaping the landscape of bleisure tourism in the digital age. Through a comprehensive classification of mobile apps for bleisure tourism, categorizing them based on functionalities and target user segments, the study has elucidated the diverse array of tools available to bleisure travelers. From a business perspective, major findings highlight the significance of mobile apps in facilitating remote work communication, project management, document collaboration, time zone management, safety assistance, and financial management. These findings underscore the crucial role of mobile technology in enabling seamless integration of work and leisure activities, thereby enhancing the overall bleisure travel experience from a business standpoint.

From a leisure and tourism perspective, the study identified key functionalities of mobile apps such as itinerary organization, transportation booking, accommodation booking, photography, entertainment, local discovery, and language translation. These findings underscore how mobile apps enrich leisure experiences by providing convenient access to essential travel services and resources, enabling travelers to explore destinations, capture memories, and immerse themselves in local cultures with ease. Additionally, the study highlighted the advantages of using mobile apps in bleisure tourism, including convenience, time-saving features, customization, increased productivity, efficient resource management, and enhanced safety and security.

By addressing these objectives, the research contributes to a deeper understanding of how mobile technology enhances the bleisure travel experience, offering insights into the benefits and challenges associated with mobile app usage in this context. Moving forward, continued research and innovation in mobile technology are essential to further enhancing the bleisure travel experience and meeting the evolving needs of travelers in the digital age. Ultimately, by leveraging the advantages of mobile apps and addressing challenges, stakeholders in the tourism industry can create more seamless, personalized, and enriching bleisure travel experiences for travelers around the globe.

REFERENCES

Alghizzawi, M., Habes, M., Al Assuli, A., & Ezmigna, A. A. R. (2024). Digital Marketing and Sustainable Businesses: As Mobile Apps in Tourism. In Hamdan, A., & Aldhaen, E. S. (Eds.), *Artificial Intelligence and Transforming Digital Marketing* (pp. 3–13). Springer Nature Switzerland. 10.1007/978-3-031-35828-9_1

Arora, N., Malik, G., & Chawla, D. (2019). Factors Affecting Consumer Adoption of Mobile Apps in NCR: A Qualitative Study. *Global Business Review*, 21(1), 176–196. 10.1177/0972150919876748

Aydın, Ü., & Özgürel, G. (2021). A research on determining the destination quality perceptions and intentions to revisit of bleisure tourists: İstanbul case. *Tourism and Recreation*, 3(1), 1–10.

Bąk, M., & Borkowski, P. (2015). Applicability of ICT solutions in passenger transport - case studies from different European backgrounds. *Transport*, 30(3), 372–381. 10.3846/16484142.2015.1079552

Batala, B., & Slevitch, L. (2024). Keeping two balls in the air: The bleisure travel experience. *Annals of Tourism Research Empirical Insights*, 5(1), 100115. 10.1016/j.annale.2023.100115

Benckendorff, P. J., Xiang, Z., & Sheldon, P. J. (2019). *Tourism information technology*. CABI. 10.1079/9781786393432.0000

Benzies, K. M., Premji, S., Hayden, K. A., & Serrett, K. (2006). State-of-the-Evidence Reviews: Advantages and Challenges of Including Grey Literature. *Worldviews on Evidence-Based Nursing*, 3(2), 55–61. 10.1111/j.1741-6787.2006.00051.x17040510

Briliana, V., & Prasetio, A. B. (2018). Some antecedents and effects of using mobile apps in tourism marketing. Proceedings of the 7th International Conference on Entrepreneurship and Business. 10.1080/08989575.2017.1337993

Çetinsöz, B. C., & Hazarhun, E. (2020). Turizm endüstrisinde yeni bir trend: Bleisure seyahatler ve motivasyon unsurları. *Journal of Recreation and Tourism Research*, 7(4), 500–527.

Choudhury, R., & Mohanty, P. (2018). Strategic Use of Social Media in Tourism Marketing: A Comparative Analysis of Official Tourism Boards. *Atna Journal of Tourism Studies, 13*(2), 41-56. https://doi.org/https://doi.org/10.12727/ajts.20.4

Chung, J. Y., Choi, Y.-K., Yoo, B.-K., & Kim, S.-H. (2020). Bleisure tourism experience chain: Implications for destination marketing. *Asia Pacific Journal of Tourism Research*, 25(3), 300–310. 10.1080/10941665.2019.1708760

Desideria, G., & Bandung, Y. (2020). User efficiency model in usability engineering for user interface design refinement of mobile application. *J. ICT Res. Appl*, 14(1), 16–33. 10.5614/itbj.ict.res.appl.2020.14.1.2

Díaz-Parra, O., Fuentes-Penna, A., Marroquín-Gutiérrez, F., Rodríguez-Lara, B. M., Salgado Ramírez, J. C., Trejo-Macotela, F. R., & Aguilar-Ortiz, J. (2023). Smart Tourism: Technologies to Improve Tourism. In Ruiz-Vanoye, J. A. (Ed.), *Management, Technology, and Economic Growth in Smart and Sustainable Cities* (pp. 83–96). IGI Global., 10.4018/979-8-3693-0373-3.ch005

El-Sofany, H. F., & Abou El-Seoud, S. (2023). The Effectiveness of Tourism in KSA Using Mobile App During COVID-19 Pandemic. *Artificial Intelligence and Online Engineering*.

Floričić, T., & Pavia, N. (2021). Linkage of leisure with remote work and digital nomadism in tourist accommodation facilities. 6th International Scientific Conference ToSEE-Tourism in Southern and Eastern Europe 2021: ToSEE–Smart, Experience, Excellence & ToFEEL–Feelings, Excitement, Education, Leisure (ToSEE 2021). 10.1504/IJTMKT.2023.127322

Gunn, R. W., Carberry, D. P., Frigo, R., & Behrens, S. (1993). Shared services: major companies are re-engineering their accounting functions. *Management Accounting (USA), 75*(5), 22-35. https://link.gale.com/apps/doc/A14836435/AONE?u=anon~54b151d2&sid=googleScholar&xid=979f5a55

Huettermann, M., Thimm, T., Hannich, F., & Bild, C. (2019). Requirements for future digital visitor flow management. *Journal of Tourism Futures*, 5(3), 241–258. 10.1108/JTF-03-2019-0023

Hussain, S., Singh, A. M., Mohanty, P., & Gavinolla, M. R. (2023). Next generation employability and career sustainability in the hospitality industry 5.0. *Worldwide Hospitality and Tourism Themes*, 15(3), 308–321. 10.1108/WHATT-01-2023-0011

Hussein, S., & Ahmed, E. (2022). Mobile Application for Tourism: The Case of Egypt. *International Journal of Customer Relationship Marketing and Management*, 13(1), 1–29. 10.4018/IJCRMM.290415

Igor, K., Alexander, K., Mikhail, G., Catherine, A., & Pandey, B. (2021). Mobile Application Based Intelligent Role of Information Technologies in Tourism Sector. *International Journal of Aquatic Science*, 12(2), 2706–2731.

Kim, S.-E., Kim, H., Jung, S., & Uysal, M. (2023). The Determinants of Continuance Intention toward Activity-Based Events Using a Virtual Experience Platform (VEP). *Leisure Sciences*, 1–26. 10.1080/01490400.2023.2172116

Lee, T.-H., & Jan, F.-H. (2022). Development and Validation of the Smart Tourism Experience Scale. *Sustainability (Basel)*, 14(24), 16421. 10.3390/su142416421

Lichy, J., & McLeay, F. (2018). Bleisure: Motivations and typologies. *Journal of Travel & Tourism Marketing*, 35(4), 517–530. 10.1080/10548408.2017.1364206

Lim, X.-J., Cheah, J.-H., Morrison, A. M., Ng, S. I., & Wang, S. (2022). Travel app shopping on smartphones: Understanding the success factors influencing in-app travel purchase intentions. *Tourism Review*, 77(4), 1166–1185. 10.1108/TR-11-2021-0497

Madeira, S., Branco, F., Gonçalves, R., Au-Yong-Oliveira, M., Moreira, F., & Martins, J. (2021). Accessibility of mobile applications for tourism—Is equal access a reality? *Universal Access in the Information Society*, 20(3), 555–571. 10.1007/s10209-020-00770-3

Mercan, R., & Sandıkcı, M. (2024). Bleisure Tourism: Business and Leisure Together. In *Future Tourism Trends Volume 1: Tourism in the Changing World* (pp. 3-15). Emerald Publishing Limited.

Mohanty, P., Dhoundiyal, H., & Choudhury, R. (2022). Events tourism in the eye of the COVID-19 storm: Impacts and implications. In *Event Tourism in Asian Countries* (pp. 97–114). Apple Academic Press. 10.1201/9781003161134-6

Mohanty, P., Shreya, V., & Choudhury, R. R. (2021). Information and Communications Technology for Overtourism Management: An Exploration. In *Overtourism, Technology Solutions and Decimated Destinations* (pp. 81-98).

Osakwe, S. (2023). Travelling Arrangements and Requirements in Corporate Organisations. *Innovative Journal of Arts and Social Sciences, 5*(5), 31-43.

Rakshit, S., Islam, N., Mondal, S., & Paul, T. (2021). Mobile apps for SME business sustainability during COVID-19 and onwards. *Journal of Business Research*, 135, 28–39. 10.1016/j.jbusres.2021.06.00534751197

Ramos, C. M., Costa, T., Severino, F. S., & Calisto, M. L. (2024). *Social Media Strategies for Tourism Interactivity*. IGI Global. 10.4018/979-8-3693-0960-5

Respatyanti, Y. R. (2019). *Enhancing the Information Availability of Indonesia's Tourism Destinations Through A Travel App.* Victoria University of Wellington. https://openaccess.wgtn.ac.nz/ndownloader/files/31689896

Sherry, L. (2015). A method for quantifying travel productivity for corporate travel managers. *Journal of Air Transport Management*, 42, 118–124. 10.1016/j.jairtraman.2014.09.012

Shrivastava, J., Srivastava, K. A., Kumar, M., & Yadava, R. L. (2021, April 29-30). 2021). Android Application Development Based Tourist Guiding Mobile Application Using Java & XML Coding. 2021 IEEE International Conference on Nanoelectronics, Nanophotonics, Nanomaterials, Nanobioscience & Nanotechnology (5NANO). 10.1108/JHTI-02-2022-0087

Sohaili, N. L. M., Aminudin, N., & Amir, A. F. (2022). Bleisure Motivation Towards Leisure Attraction: A Systematic Literature Review. *Social Sciences*, 12(11), 910–922.

Stoecklin, M. P., Singh, K., Koved, L., Hu, X., Chari, S. N., Rao, J. R., . . . Schales, D. L. (2016). Passive security intelligence to analyze the security risks of mobile/BYOD activities. *IBM Journal of Research and Development, 60*(4), 9:1-9:13. 10.1147/JRD.2016.2569858

Vaismoradi, M., Turunen, H., & Bondas, T. (2013). Content analysis and thematic analysis: Implications for conducting a qualitative descriptive study. *Nursing & Health Sciences*, 15(3), 398–405. 10.1111/nhs.1204823480423

Valsaraj, B. P., More, B., Biju, S., Payini, V., & Pallath, V. (2021). Faculty experiences on emergency remote teaching during COVID-19: A multicentre qualitative analysis. *Interactive Technology and Smart Education*, 18(3), 319–344. 10.1108/ITSE-09-2020-0198

Chapter 13
Influence of Social Media Influencers on Bleisure Travel in Jammu and Kashmir

Chetna Sharma
Department of Mass Communication, Sharda University, Greater Noida, India

ABSTRACT

The emergence of bleisure travel as a trending concept has propelled Jammu and Kashmir's appeal among travellers, with social media influencers and travel agencies adeptly showcasing the region's potential for blending business and leisure experiences through social media platforms like Instagram. Through innovative approaches and engaging content, the use of social media has not only reshaped travel narratives but also contributed to the sustainable growth of tourism in the region. By leveraging the visual appeal and wide reach of social media, influencers, travel agencies, and tourism authorities have successfully promoted tailored travel packages, highlighted adventure tourism, and showcased the region's infrastructure and amenities. In conclusion, this research illuminates the transformative power of digital platforms in influencing destination preferences and experiences, leading to a clearer knowledge of the growing relationships between social media influencers and emerging travel trends.

DOI: 10.4018/979-8-3693-4354-8.ch013

1. INTRODUCTION

Situated amidst the majestic Himalayas, Jammu and Kashmir stand as a breathtaking territory within India, bordered by Pakistan to the West and China to the East. Historically known for its amazing landscapes, rich cultural heritage, and political complexities, Jammu & Kashmir has always attracted attention from tourists, scholars, and journalists alike. However, the advent of social media has provided locals with a platform to showcase the beauty and diversity of their land to the world, thereby reshaping perceptions and narratives. J&K's awe-inspiring landscapes, this Union Territory has captivated the world's attention, despite enduring political unrest hindering its progress. Amidst the persistent political turmoil in Jammu and Kashmir, the travel industry in the region is experiencing a notable transformation. Despite the challenges posed by the political situation, there's a discernible shift in how Jammu and Kashmir is being perceived and marketed as a travel destination, particularly for business trips.

One significant factor driving this change is the emergence of social media as a powerful platform for showcasing the beauty and allure of the region. With stunning landscapes, serene lakes, and snow-capped mountains, Jammu and Kashmir has always been a paradise for travellers. However, in the past, the negative narrative surrounding the region's political instability often overshadowed its tourism potential. Now, social media platforms such as Instagram, Facebook, and Twitter are playing a pivotal role in reshaping the perception of Jammu and Kashmir (Giri, 2023). Influencers, travel bloggers, photographers and travel agencies are sharing stunning images and captivating stories of their experiences in the region, showcasing its natural beauty and cultural richness. These visually appealing posts could not only attract leisure travellers but also catch the attention of business travellers seeking unique destinations for corporate events, conferences, and retreats.

The rise of social media influencers in Jammu & Kashmir is a testament to the region's untapped potential in the digital age. These influencers, often local residents, have leveraged their platforms to offer a glimpse into the everyday life and extraordinary beauty of Jammu & Kashmir. By doing so, they have managed to shift the focus from political instability to the region's natural and cultural wealth. Their posts, which range from serene shots of Dal Lake to adventurous treks in the Himalayas, serve as powerful tools in changing the narrative and drawing in visitors who might have previously been deterred by the region's political reputation.

Influencers play a crucial role in the tourism ecosystem by providing authentic and relatable content. Unlike traditional marketing campaigns, influencer-generated content is perceived as more genuine and trustworthy (Helme, 2023). Followers are more likely to be influenced by someone they feel a connection with, someone who provides a personal touch to their recommendations. This authenticity is particularly important for Jammu & Kashmir, where potential visitors may have concerns about safety and accessibility. By sharing their own positive experiences, influencers can alleviate these concerns and inspire confidence in prospective travellers.

According to a report by *Business Standard,* Jammu and Kashmir is among the most preferred destinations for solo travellers. It also states that according to research by India's largest travel-focused financial platform- fintech SanKash, almost "35 per cent" of solo travellers prefer Jammu and Kashmir for vacationing, followed by Manali (25 per cent) and Shimla (14 per cent). Local businesses and tourism authorities in Jammu and Kashmir are leveraging social media to promote tailored travel packages and special offers targeted at business travellers. An article published by CNBC TV on March 22, 2024, entitled "*Jammu and Kashmir seeing a tourism boom, here's why*" states that J&K had an unparalleled upsurge in tourism in contrast to the number of guests from prior years. The agency reported that over 21.1 million tourists visited the region in 2023, setting new records for the local economy.

Table 1. Data Showing the Total Number of Tourists Visited J&K in Recent Years

Year	Total no. Toursists Visited J&K
2023	21.1 Million
2022	18.8 Million
2021	11.3 Million
2020	3.4 Million

Source: J&K Tourism Department

The Jammu and Kashmir Tourism Department other than local influencers is making significant strides in positioning the region as one of the premier tourism destinations in the world. Recognising the immense potential of the region's natural beauty and cultural heritage, the department has embarked on a multifaceted approach to enhance tourism infrastructure, promote local attractions, and attract visitors from across the globe. Central to this strategy is the harnessing of social media platforms like Instagram to showcase the diverse and breathtaking landscapes of Jammu and Kashmir.

Figure 1. Instagram Post

Source: @jktourismofficial and @incredibleindia (Instagram)

In a captivating collaboration between Jammu & Kashmir Tourism and Incredible India, an enticing Instagram post has been shared to beckon travellers to immerse themselves in the timeless beauty of the Mughal Garden and Nishat Bagh. The post, adorned with vibrant imagery and evocative storytelling, paints a picturesque scene of lush gardens, inviting viewers to embark on a journey through the enchanting landscapes of Kashmir. The Mughal Garden and Nishat Bagh stand as testaments to the grandeur and opulence of the Mughal Empire.

Figure 2. Instagram Post

Source: @jktourismofficial and @incredibleindia (Instagram)

The Instagram post shared by @jktourismofficial and @incredibleindia offers a glimpse into the enchanting beauty of Jammu & Kashmir's Gurez Valley, nestled amidst the pristine landscapes of Jammu and Kashmir. The image transports viewers to a world of untouched natural splendour, where mountains loom majestically over lush green valleys through the picturesque terrain. By sharing stunning images and evocative storytelling, @jktourismofficial and @incredibleindia aim to inspire wanderlust and encourage travellers to add Gurez Valley to their bucket list of must-visit destinations. Through their collaborative efforts, they showcase the diversity and beauty of Jammu and Kashmir, inviting travellers to embark on a journey of exploration and discovery in one of India's most breathtaking regions.

Figure 3. Instagram Post

Source: @jktourismofficial (Instagram)

Another Instagram post by @jktourismofficial offers a mesmerizing glimpse into the winter wonderland of Kashmir Valley, blanketed in a pristine layer of snow. The image captures the ethereal beauty of the region, where snow-capped trees rise majestically against a backdrop of azure skies, and every surface is adorned with a delicate frosting of white inviting travellers to embrace the magic of winters in Kashmir.

The efforts of Jammu and Kashmir (J&K) Tourism to attract tourists through Instagram have been both strategic and impactful, leveraging the platform's visual appeal and wide reach to showcase the region's stunning landscapes, rich cultural heritage, and diverse attractions.

According to the report by The Economic Times, published in the year 2022, J&K has received investment proposals from various business houses to the tune of about Rs 56,000 crore while sanctions have been granted to proposals worth Rs 38000 crores. The Jammu and Kashmir administration is working to boost the income of the local population.

In addition to showcasing the natural beauty of Jammu and Kashmir, the tourism department is also utilizing Instagram as a platform to promote adventure tourism, cultural festivals, culinary delights, and handicrafts unique to the region. By collaborating with local influencers, travel bloggers, and photographers, they are able to reach a wider audience and create buzz around upcoming events and attractions.

One of the key initiatives of the tourism department is to leverage the visual appeal of the region by curating captivating content on Instagram. Since the writing of this research paper Jammu and Kashmir Tourism Department has one lakh ninety thousand (190K) followers on their Official Instagram account (@jktourismofficial). Through stunning photographs, engaging videos, and compelling stories, the department is showcasing the picturesque valleys, serene lakes, majestic mountains, and vibrant culture of Jammu and Kashmir to a global audience. These posts not only highlight popular tourist destinations such as Srinagar, Gulmarg, and Leh-Ladakh but also shed light on lesser-known gems tucked away in remote corners of the region. The tourism department is actively engaging with travellers on Instagram by responding to queries, providing travel tips, and sharing user-generated content. This interactive approach not only fosters a sense of community among travellers but also helps in addressing any concerns or misconceptions about visiting Jammu and Kashmir.

In parallel with its social media efforts, the tourism department is also investing in infrastructure development, hospitality training, and marketing campaigns to enhance the overall tourist experience in Jammu and Kashmir. By adopting a holistic approach that combines digital outreach with on-the-ground initiatives, the department aims to position Jammu and Kashmir as a must-visit destination for travellers seeking unparalleled beauty, adventure, and cultural immersion. Focussing on Travel agencies, they are capitalizing on the allure of Instagram to promote bleisure travel in Jammu and Kashmir, enticing tourists with the perfect blend of business and leisure experiences. Bleisure travel, a growing trend among modern travellers, combines business trips with leisure activities, allowing individuals to make the most of their time in destinations like Jammu and Kashmir.

Through Instagram, travel agencies curate visually stunning feeds that showcase the region's breathtaking landscapes, cultural heritage, and diverse experiences, enticing both business travellers and leisure seekers alike. By posting captivating images of snow-capped mountains, serene lakes, vibrant markets, and historical landmarks, travel agencies create a compelling narrative that highlights the potential for memorable bleisure experiences in Jammu and Kashmir.

Figure 4. Instagram Post

Source: @fayyaztravels (Instagram)

The above photograph captures the essence of Jammu and Kashmir's fascinating view. Shared by a travel agency (fayyaztravels) on Instagram, this captivating image beckons tourists to explore the mesmerizing landscapes of the region. Against a backdrop of azure skies, towering snow-capped mountains stand sentinel, their peaks glistening in the golden light of the sun. As a travel destination, this photograph encapsulates the allure of Jammu and Kashmir, offering a glimpse into the region's awe-inspiring beauty and adventure opportunities. Whether it's trekking through pristine mountain trails, embarking on scenic drives along winding roads, or simply soaking in the tranquillity of the Himalayan landscape, Jammu and Kashmir promises an unforgettable journey for travellers seeking to connect with nature and experience the wonders of the great outdoors.

Figure 5. Instagram Post

Source: @outlooktraveller (Instagram)

The Instagram post by Outlook Traveller magazine serves as a beacon of exploration, inviting travellers to embark on a unique journey to the Samba district of Jammu and Kashmir, where border tourism along with homestay offers a glimpse into the region's rich history and cultural heritage. Through its Instagram post, Outlook Traveller magazine shines a spotlight on border tourism in the Samba district, encouraging travelers to venture beyond their comfort zones and embrace the spirit of adventure. It's a call to explore the unknown, to forge connections across borders, and to discover the beauty and resilience of the human spirit in one of India's most fascinating regions. Also Staying in homestays not only provides travelers with a more intimate and authentic experience but also directly benefits the local community by providing income opportunities for small-scale farmers and artisans. It's a win-win situation that promotes sustainable tourism and fosters cross-cultural understanding and appreciation.

Figure 6. Instagram Post

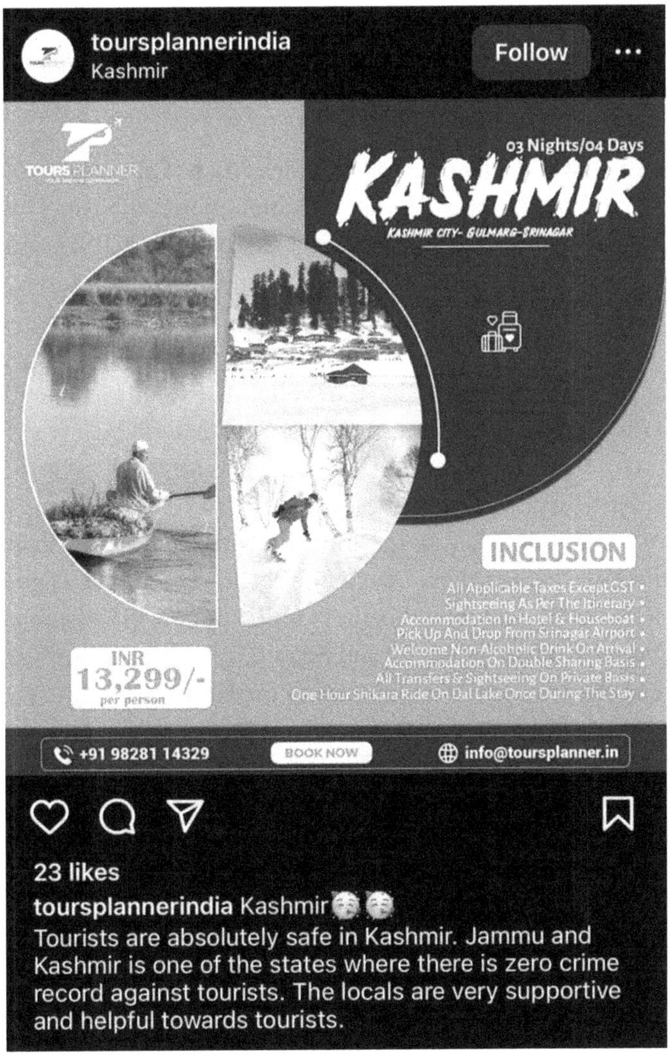

Source: @toursplannerindia (Instagram)

The advertisement post shared by @toursplannerindia encapsulates the allure of Jammu and Kashmir while also addressing the crucial question on the minds of many potential travellers in the Caption: Is it safe to visit? Overall, the Instagram post by @toursplannerindia serves as a compelling advertisement for tour packages to Jammu and Kashmir, highlighting accommodation, pick up and drop services and above all, its safety as a travel destination. It's a testament to the resilience of the region and the enduring spirit of hospitality that continues to draw travellers from around the world.

One of the key strategies employed by travel agencies is to highlight the region's infrastructure and amenities that cater to both business and leisure travellers. From luxury hotels with state-of-the-art conference facilities to boutique accommodations nestled amidst scenic surroundings, Jammu and Kashmir offers a range of options to suit different preferences and budgets. Travel agencies leverage Instagram to showcase these accommodations, emphasizing their convenience, comfort, and accessibility for bleisure travellers.

In addition to promoting accommodation options, travel agencies use Instagram to spotlight a variety of leisure activities and attractions that business travellers can enjoy during their downtime (Ringer & Greg, 2016). Whether it's embarking on a scenic trek in the Himalayas, exploring ancient temples and monasteries, or indulging in local cuisine and shopping experiences, Jammu and Kashmir offers a plethora of opportunities for leisure exploration. Through visually compelling posts and engaging captions, travel agencies inspire business travellers to extend their stay and immerse themselves in the destination's cultural richness and natural beauty (Platon, 2023). Travel agencies leverage Instagram's storytelling features such as Stories and IGTV to provide insider tips, recommendations, and firsthand experiences that resonate with bleisure travellers. By sharing real-time updates, behind-the-scenes glimpses, and curated itineraries, travel agencies create a sense of excitement and anticipation, encouraging travellers to combine business obligations with leisure pursuits for a truly memorable experience in Jammu and Kashmir. Travel agencies also collaborate with influencers, bloggers, and industry professionals who embody the bleisure travel lifestyle, showcasing their experiences and insights through Instagram posts and collaborations. By tapping into the influence of these individuals, travel agencies can reach a wider audience of bleisure travellers who are seeking inspiration and guidance for their next trip to Jammu and Kashmir.

Overall, Instagram serves as a powerful platform for travel agencies to promote bleisure travel in Jammu and Kashmir by showcasing the region's beauty, culture, and diverse experiences to a global audience. Through visually appealing content, strategic storytelling, and influencer collaborations, travel agencies can attract business travellers seeking to enrich their work trips with memorable leisure experiences, ultimately contributing to the growth and sustainability of tourism in the region.

2. BLEISURE TRAVEL: STRATEGIES FOR PROMOTING TOURISM

The convergence of business and leisure travel, commonly known as 'bleisure' travel, has gained significant traction in recent years (Lehto et al., 2024). Bleisure travel refers to the blending of business and leisure activities during a single trip. This emerging trend offers travellers the opportunity to combine work-related obligations with personal exploration and relaxation (Batala et al., 2024). The rise of social media platforms has transformed the way individuals seek, plan, and experience travel, with influencers playing a pivotal role in shaping travel aspirations and choices (Liu et al., 2019).

Bleisure travel, a portmanteau of “business” and “leisure,” has emerged as a trending concept in the travel industry, reflecting a shift in how professionals approach their work-related trips (Matsushita, 2023). This hybrid travel style seamlessly blends business obligations with leisure activities, allowing travellers to maximize their time away from home by mixing work and pleasure (Park et al., 2024). In the fast-paced world of modern business, professionals often find themselves travelling to various destinations for meetings, conferences, or other work-related commitments. Traditionally, these trips have been perceived as solely focused on business, with little room for leisure activities. However, the rise of bleisure travel represents a departure from this conventional mindset, offering travellers the opportunity to extend their stay and explore the destination beyond the boardroom. At its core, bleisure travel is about striking a balance between work and relaxation, leveraging the flexibility of modern work arrangements to integrate leisure experiences into business trips (Miao et al., 2024).

Whether it's extending a weekend after a conference or adding a few extra days to explore a new city, bleisure travellers seek to make the most of their time on the road. One of the key benefits of bleisure travel is the ability to turn a mundane business trip into a memorable and rewarding experience (Schänzel et al., 2005). Instead of rushing from one meeting to the next, bleisure travelers can take advantage of their free time to immerse themselves in the local culture, indulge in culinary delights, or explore iconic landmarks. This blending of work and leisure not only enhances the overall travel experience but also provides an opportunity for personal enrichment and growth (Wearing, 2001).

Moreover, bleisure travel can have positive effects on productivity and well-being. Research has shown that incorporating leisure activities into business trips can reduce stress, boost morale, and increase job satisfaction (Cheng et al., 2022). By allowing travellers to decompress and recharge in a new environment, bleisure travel can enhance creativity and foster a sense of work-life balance.

The growing popularity of bleisure travel has been driven by several factors, including changing attitudes towards work, advances in technology, and the rise of remote work. With more professionals embracing flexible work arrangements, there is greater freedom to tailor travel itineraries to suit personal preferences and interests. Additionally, the proliferation of digital tools and platforms has made it easier than ever to stay connected and productive while on the go, enabling travellers to seamlessly transition between work and leisure activities (Rainoldi et al., 2024).

From a business perspective, bleisure travel can also be advantageous. Offering employees the opportunity to combine business trips with leisure time can serve as a valuable incentive, attracting top talent and enhancing employee retention. Bleisure travellers often spend more money and stay longer at their destinations, providing a boost to the local economy (Caffyn, 2012). However, bleisure travel is not without its challenges. Balancing work commitments with leisure activities requires careful planning and time management. It's essential for bleisure travelers to prioritize their workload, communicate effectively with colleagues, and set realistic expectations about their availability. Additionally, navigating corporate travel policies and expense reimbursement procedures can sometimes be complicated, requiring clear guidelines and open communication between employers and employees. Bleisure travel represents a modern and flexible approach to business travel, allowing professionals to blend work and leisure seamlessly. By embracing this hybrid travel style, travellers can enjoy enriching experiences, enhance productivity, and achieve a healthier work-life balance. As the trend continues to gain momentum, bleisure travel is poised to reshape the way we think about business travel in the years to come.

3. STRATEGIES FOR PROMOTING BLEISURE TRAVEL

Promoting bleisure travel requires a multifaceted approach that caters to the needs and preferences of both business and leisure travelers (Kwan & Tong, 2023). Here are some strategies that destinations, travel companies, and employers can implement to capitalize on this growing trend:

a. **Develop Integrated Travel Packages:** Destinations and travel companies can create travel packages that specifically cater to bleisure travelers. These packages can include business-friendly amenities such as high-speed internet, conference facilities, and meeting spaces, along with leisure activities such as guided tours, cultural experiences, and wellness programs. By bundling these elements together, travelers can enjoy a seamless experience that caters to both their professional and personal needs.

b. **Enhance Local Experiences:** To attract bleisure travelers, destinations should focus on enhancing local experiences that are unique and appealing. This could involve promoting local festivals, culinary tours, historical sites, and outdoor activities. Highlighting these attractions in marketing campaigns can entice business travelers to extend their stay and explore the local culture.
c. **Leverage Technology:** Technology plays a crucial role in facilitating bleisure travel. Travel companies and destinations can develop mobile apps and online platforms that provide real-time information about local attractions, events, and dining options. Additionally, offering virtual tours and augmented reality experiences can help travelers plan their leisure activities in advance.
d. **Collaborate with Employers:** Employers can play a significant role in promoting bleisure travel by offering flexible travel policies that encourage employees to combine business trips with leisure time. This could include providing additional paid time off for bleisure travel, covering a portion of leisure expenses, or offering travel rewards programs that incentivize bleisure trips.
e. **Promote Wellness and Work-Life Balance:** Highlighting the wellness benefits of bleisure travel can resonate with health-conscious travelers. Destinations and travel companies can promote wellness retreats, spa packages, and outdoor activities that help travelers relax and rejuvenate. Emphasizing the importance of work-life balance in marketing campaigns can also appeal to professionals looking to integrate leisure into their business trips.
f. **Tailor Marketing Campaigns:** Effective marketing campaigns should target specific demographics and industries that are more likely to engage in bleisure travel. For example, targeting tech industry professionals, who often have flexible work arrangements, with advertisements showcasing the benefits of bleisure travel can drive interest and bookings. Utilizing social media influencers and travel bloggers to share their bleisure experiences can also boost visibility and attract a wider audience.
g. **Offer Incentives and Discounts:** Providing incentives and discounts for bleisure travelers can encourage longer stays and increased spending. This could include offering discounted rates for extended stays, special deals on local attractions and dining, or loyalty programs that reward repeat bleisure travelers.
h. **Foster Public-Private Partnerships:** Collaboration between public and private sectors can enhance the appeal of a destination for bleisure travelers. Public entities, such as tourism boards, can work with private companies, such as hotels and tour operators, to create comprehensive marketing campaigns and develop infrastructure that supports bleisure travel.
i. **Measure and Analyze Trends:** Collecting data on bleisure travel trends can help destinations and travel companies better understand the needs and preferences of this segment. Analyzing data on traveler demographics, spending patterns,

and preferred activities can inform targeted marketing strategies and product offerings.

Bleisure travel represents a modern and flexible approach to business travel, allowing professionals to blend work and leisure seamlessly. By embracing this hybrid travel style, travelers can enjoy enriching experiences, enhance productivity, and achieve a healthier work-life balance. As the trend continues to gain momentum, implementing effective strategies to promote bleisure travel will be essential for destinations, travel companies, and employers looking to capitalize on this growing market.

4. INFLUENCER CULTURE AND TRAVEL TRENDS

The emergence of social media Influencers in Jammu & Kashmir represents a fascinating intersection of technology, culture, and entrepreneurship (Parry et al., 2023). In recent years, social media platforms have become powerful tools for individuals to express themselves, share their experiences, and influence others. This phenomenon has not spared the scenic region of Jammu & Kashmir, where a new generation of influencers is making its mark (Chan, 2024). Social media influencers, with their vast reach and persuasive capabilities, have become instrumental in influencing consumer behaviour across various industries, including travel. Their authentic content, engaging storytelling, and curated experiences resonate with audiences, inspiring them to explore new destinations and experiences. They play a significant role in promoting bleisure travel destinations by leveraging their platforms to showcase the unique blend of business and leisure experiences that these places offer. With their ability to reach a wide audience and engage followers through compelling content, influencers serve as powerful advocates for destinations seeking to attract bleisure travellers (Laczkovich, 2018).

One of the primary ways social media influencers promote travel places is by sharing their own first-hand experiences (Kiralova & Pavliceka, 2015). Through captivating photos, videos, and personal anecdotes, influencers provide an authentic glimpse into the destination, highlighting its attractions, accommodations, and activities that cater to both business and leisure travellers. Whether it's attending a conference at a state-of-the-art convention centre or exploring hidden gems and local hotspots during downtime, influencers showcase the versatility and appeal of bleisure destinations.

Influencers also play a crucial role in shaping perceptions and generating buzz around bleisure travel places (Tomazos, 2022). By curating visually stunning content and crafting compelling narratives, influencers capture the imagination of their followers and inspire them to consider bleisure travel as a viable option for their next trip. Their endorsements and recommendations carry weight with audiences, influencing their travel decisions and encouraging them to explore destinations that offer a perfect balance of work and leisure opportunities.

Social Media Influencers collaborate with destination marketing organizations, tourism boards, and hospitality brands to create sponsored content and promotional campaigns that highlight the benefits of bleisure travel (Javits, 2019). These partnerships enable influencers to amplify their reach and visibility, reaching new audiences and attracting attention to bleisure destinations through targeted marketing efforts. By strategically leveraging influencer partnerships, destinations can effectively position themselves as desirable places for bleisure travellers to visit.

Influencers also engage with their followers in meaningful ways, providing valuable insights, tips, and recommendations for maximizing the bleisure travel experience. Through interactive Q&A sessions, live streams, and behind-the-scenes glimpses, influencers foster a sense of community and dialogue around bleisure destinations, helping travellers plan and navigate their trips more effectively. By sharing practical advice and insider tips, influencers empower their followers to make the most of their bleisure travel experiences and create lasting memories.

Social Media Influencers also contribute to the ongoing conversation about bleisure travel by participating in industry events, conferences, and panel discussions. Their thought leadership and expertise in travel trends and consumer behaviour help shape the narrative around bleisure travel and elevate its profile within the broader travel industry. By advocating for the benefits of bleisure travel and sharing best practices, influencers contribute to the growth and development of this emerging travel segment.

To delve deeper into the role of social media influencers in promoting bleisure travel, it's essential to explore specific strategies and approaches they employ (Sigala & Gretzel, 2017). Influencers utilize a variety of content formats to engage their audiences and highlight the unique aspects of bleisure destinations. High-quality visuals, such as stunning photographs and professionally edited videos, are instrumental in capturing the attention of followers and showcasing the beauty and appeal of a location. These visuals often highlight key attractions, luxurious accommodations, and unique experiences that blend work and leisure seamlessly.

Narrative storytelling is another powerful tool in an influencer's arsenal (Mueller Correa & Marina, 2022). By sharing personal anecdotes and experiences, influencers create relatable and authentic content that resonates with their audience. For instance, an influencer might recount their experience of attending a business conference in the morning and then unwinding with a scenic hike or a cultural tour in the afternoon. Such stories not only showcase the possibilities of bleisure travel but also inspire followers to consider similar experiences for their own trips.

Engagement with followers is a critical component of an influencer's strategy. Influencers often use interactive features on social media platforms, such as polls, Q&A sessions, and live streams, to connect with their audience and provide personalized recommendations. This interaction helps build a sense of community and trust, as followers feel valued and heard. Moreover, influencers can address specific questions and concerns about bleisure travel, offering practical advice that enhances the overall travel experience.

Partnerships with local businesses and tourism boards are mutually beneficial for influencers and destinations (Ingrassia et al., 2022). By collaborating with influencers, destinations can leverage their reach and credibility to attract a wider audience. These partnerships often involve sponsored trips, where influencers are invited to experience and promote the destination's offerings. In return, influencers receive compensation and exclusive content opportunities, which further enrich their social media profiles and attract more followers.

For destinations like Jammu & Kashmir, which are rich in natural beauty and cultural heritage, influencers can play a pivotal role in showcasing lesser-known attractions and experiences. By highlighting the unique aspects of the region, such as its picturesque landscapes, vibrant festivals, and traditional crafts, influencers can help position Jammu & Kashmir as an ideal bleisure travel destination. This approach not only boosts tourism but also supports local economies by promoting small businesses and artisans.

The impact of social media influencers extends beyond just attracting tourists; they also contribute to the overall perception and reputation of a destination. Positive reviews and endorsements from trusted influencers can significantly enhance a destination's image, making it more appealing to potential travelers. Conversely, negative feedback can also influence perceptions, highlighting the importance of maintaining high standards of service and hospitality (Tham et al., 2020).

As the travel industry continues to evolve, the role of social media influencers is likely to expand further. The rise of new platforms and technologies, such as virtual reality and augmented reality, presents exciting opportunities for influencers to create immersive and interactive content. These technologies can provide followers with a virtual taste of the destination, allowing them to explore and experience its offerings from the comfort of their homes. Such innovations can further enhance the appeal of bleisure travel and attract a tech-savvy audience.

In addition to their promotional efforts, influencers also play a role in advocating for sustainable and responsible travel. Many influencers use their platforms to raise awareness about environmental and social issues, encouraging their followers to travel responsibly and support sustainable practices (Baltezarevic et al., 2022). By promoting eco-friendly accommodations, local conservation efforts, and community-based tourism initiatives, influencers can contribute to the long-term sustainability of bleisure destinations.

Social media influencers are key players in the promotion of bleisure travel destinations. Through their authentic storytelling, engaging content, and strategic partnerships, they inspire and influence travellers to explore the unique blend of business and leisure that these destinations offer. As the influence of social media continues to grow, the role of influencers in shaping travel trends and consumer behaviour will only become more significant. By leveraging the power of social media influencers, destinations like Jammu & Kashmir can attract a diverse and engaged audience, driving tourism growth and creating memorable travel experiences for bleisure travellers.

5. INSTA-INFLUENCER'S IMPACT ON USER ENGAGEMENT

5.1. Inspirational Content Creation

Social media influencers create aspirational and relatable content that showcases the seamless integration of work and leisure activities. Through captivating visuals, personal anecdotes, and practical tips, influencers highlight the benefits and possibilities of bleisure travel, encouraging followers to consider this travel style for their next trip (Roblin & Matthew, 2017).

5.2. Authentic Recommendations

Influencers often share authentic reviews, recommendations, and first-hand experiences of leisure-friendly destinations, accommodations, and activities. Their genuine insights and honest evaluations provide valuable guidance to travellers seeking to optimise their bleisure travel experiences (Setiani et.al., 2024).

5.3. Personalized Travel Experiences

Influencers tailor their content to cater to diverse audience preferences, offering personalized travel recommendations and itineraries that align with individual interests, budgets, and schedules (Soliman et. al., 2023). This personalized approach enhances the appeal of bleisure travel, making it more accessible and appealing to a broader audience.

5.4. Destination Discovery

Social media influencers play a crucial role in introducing followers to new and lesser-known bleisure travel destinations (Qazi & Baig, 2024). By showcasing hidden gems, off-the-beaten-path attractions, and unique experiences, influencers inspire travellers to explore beyond popular tourist hotspots and discover hidden treasures in different regions.

5.5. Building Trust and Credibility

Influencers establish trust and credibility among their followers through consistent and authentic content creation. By sharing their personal experiences, engaging with their audience, and being transparent about sponsored partnerships, influencers build strong relationships with their followers, making their recommendations and suggestions more influential and persuasive (Lou & Yuan, 2019).

5.6. Cultural Immersion

Through their content, influencers provide insights into local cultures, traditions, and lifestyles, enriching the bleisure travel experience (Nunes, 2019). By participating in cultural activities, interacting with locals, and showcasing authentic cultural experiences, influencers encourage travellers to immerse themselves fully in the destination's cultural fabric, fostering cross-cultural understanding and appreciation.

5.7. Sustainable Tourism Advocacy

Influencers advocate for sustainable tourism practices and responsible travel behaviour, promoting eco-friendly accommodations, conservation initiatives, and community-based tourism activities. By raising awareness about environmental and social issues, influencers encourage travellers to make ethical and sustainable choices during their bleisure trips, contributing to the preservation of natural and cultural heritage (Tomazos, 2022).

6. CONCLUSION

The impact of Instagram as a social media platform on bleisure travel cannot be overstated. With its visually immersive interface and global reach, Instagram has become a powerful tool for shaping consumer perceptions, preferences, and behaviours, particularly in the travel industry. As Instagram users continue to evolve and adapt their strategies to meet the changing needs and expectations of their audiences, their influence on the bleisure travel landscape is expected to grow exponentially. Instagram's emphasis on visual storytelling allows users to showcase the unique blend of business and leisure experiences that destinations like Jammu and Kashmir offer. This paper reveals that through captivating visuals, influencers and travel brands can highlight the modern amenities, conference facilities, and opportunities for networking amidst picturesque surroundings, effectively positioning Jammu and Kashmir as a desirable destination for corporate travel. Instagram's interactive features such as Stories, Reels, and IGTV enable users to provide real-time updates, behind-the-scenes glimpses, and curated itineraries that resonate with bleisure travellers. By sharing practical advice, insider tips, and firsthand experiences, influencers and travel brands inspire their followers to consider bleisure travel as a rewarding and enriching way to combine work and leisure. In addition to showcasing the region's tourism potential, the Jammu and Kashmir Tourism Department's use of Instagram and other social media platforms plays a pivotal role in fostering a sense of excitement and curiosity among travellers eager to explore this enchanting land. By highlighting not only the natural and cultural treasures of Jammu and Kashmir but also its modern infrastructure and connectivity, the department is effectively attracting visitors from around the world. Despite occasional disruptions due to political unrest, advancements in infrastructure and connectivity are contributing to the growth of business tourism in the region. Improved road networks, upgraded airports, and efforts to enhance internet connectivity are making it easier for business travellers to access and navigate Jammu and Kashmir, further bolstering its appeal as a bleisure travel destination. In conclusion, Instagram's influence on bleisure travel, combined with the efforts of the Jammu and Kashmir Tourism Departments to showcase the region's tourism potential, is driving significant growth in business tourism. With its visually engaging content and strategic use of social media, Jammu and Kashmir is emerging as a sought-after destination for travellers seeking to blend work and leisure seamlessly.

7. CHALLENGES AND FUTURE PROSPECTS

While the rise of social media influencers has brought many benefits to Jammu & Kashmir, it is not without challenges. One of the primary concerns is the sustainability of increased tourism. The region's fragile ecosystem and limited infrastructure can be strained by a sudden influx of visitors. It is essential for both influencers and local authorities to promote responsible and sustainable tourism practices to ensure that the natural beauty and cultural heritage of Jammu & Kashmir are preserved for future generations. Another challenge is the need for continued investment in infrastructure and services to support the growing tourism industry. Improved transportation, accommodation, and communication facilities are crucial to providing a positive experience for visitors. Local authorities and businesses must work together to address these needs and ensure that the region can accommodate and benefit from increased tourism.

The political instability in the region remains a significant challenge. While social media influencers have managed to shift the narrative to some extent, the underlying issues still pose a threat to sustained tourism growth. Ensuring safety and stability will be key to maintaining and increasing tourist numbers. Despite these challenges, the future prospects for tourism in Jammu & Kashmir are promising. The ongoing efforts of social media influencers to promote the region are likely to continue driving interest and visitation. With the right strategies and investments, Jammu & Kashmir can establish itself as a premier travel destination, known not only for its stunning landscapes but also for its rich cultural heritage and welcoming hospitality.

To achieve this, a collaborative approach involving influencers, local businesses, government authorities, and the community is essential. By working together, they can develop comprehensive tourism policies that emphasize sustainability, safety, and cultural preservation. Furthermore, initiatives like eco-tourism and cultural tourism can be promoted to attract tourists who are interested in more than just scenic beauty, thereby ensuring a diverse and resilient tourism industry. While the path ahead may be fraught with challenges, the potential for growth and prosperity in Jammu & Kashmir's tourism sector is immense. The strategic use of social media, combined with thoughtful planning and investment, can transform the region into a global tourism hotspot, benefiting both its economy and its people.

Also, future research should explore the long-term effects of influencer marketing on bleisure travel trends, examining how sustained campaigns influence travel patterns and destination popularity over time. Additionally, the role of emerging technologies like virtual reality (VR) and augmented reality (AR) in enhancing the bleisure travel experience warrants investigation. These technologies could revolutionize trip planning and immersive destination previews, offering new marketing avenues. Ethical considerations and challenges in influencer marketing, such as transparency, authenticity, and sponsorship disclosure, are crucial areas for study. Understanding best practices for ethical conduct and their impact on consumer trust will be vital for the industry's integrity. Furthermore, research should examine how influencer trust and authenticity affect bleisure travelers' decision-making, focusing on the perceived credibility of content and influencer-audience relationships. The impact of social media algorithms and platform-specific features on the reach and effectiveness of influencer campaigns also needs exploration. Finally, cross-cultural studies could provide insights into regional and demographic differences in travel preferences and social media usage, helping tailor more inclusive and effective marketing strategies. These research areas will guide more ethical and impactful influencer marketing in the bleisure travel industry.

REFERENCES

Baltezarević, R., Baltezarević, B., & Baltezarević, V. (2022). The role of travel influencers in sustainable tourism development. *International Review (Steubenville, Ohio)*, (3-4), 125–129. 10.5937/intrev2204131B

Batala, B., & Slevitch, L. (2024). Keeping two balls in the air: The bleisure travel experience. *Annals of Tourism Research Empirical Insights*, 5(1), 100115. 10.1016/j.annale.2023.100115

Caffyn, A. (2012). Advocating and implementing slow tourism. *Tourism Recreation Research*, 37(1), 77–80. 10.1080/02508281.2012.11081690

Chan, E. Y. (2024). Digital Consumer Behavior. In *Consumer Behavior in Practice: Strategic Insights for the Modern Marketer* (pp. 127–144). Springer Nature Switzerland. 10.1007/978-3-031-50947-6_7

Cheng, S. C., & Kao, Y. H. (2022). The impact of the COVID-19 pandemic on job satisfaction: A mediated moderation model using job stress and organizational resilience in the hotel industry of Taiwan. *Heliyon*, 8(3), e09134. 10.1016/j.heliyon.2022.e0913435342829

Giri, P. (2023). *Social Media and Emerging Public Sphere: A Study of Northeast India* (Doctoral dissertation).

Helme, E. (2023). The role of authentic communication on perceived information credibility in influencer marketing.

Ingrassia, M., Bellia, C., Giurdanella, C., Columba, P., & Chironi, S. (2022). Digital influencers, food and tourism—A new model of open innovation for businesses in the Ho. Re. Ca. sector. *Journal of Open Innovation*, 8(1), 50. 10.3390/joitmc8010050

Jammu & Kashmir seeing a tourism boom, here's why. (2024, March 22). *CNBC TV18. Com.* Retrieved May 11, 2024, from https://www.cnbctv18.com/videos/economy/jammu-and-kashmir-seeing-a-tourism-boom-here-why-19349801.htm

Jammu & Kashmir to see major boost in business, tourism investment. (2022, November 26). The Economic Times. Retrieved May 12, 2024, from https://travel.economictimes.indiatimes.com/news/destination/states/jammu-kashmir-to-see-major-boost-in-business-tourism-investment/95780265

Javits, O. (2019). *Social media influencers in destination marketing. A case study of Visit Tampere, Finland* (Master's thesis).

Kiráľová, A., & Pavlíčeka, A. (2015). Development of social media strategies in tourism destination. *Procedia: Social and Behavioral Sciences*, 175, 358–366. 10.1016/j.sbspro.2015.01.1211

Kwan, M., & Tong, L. (2023). Exemplifying Exceptional Hospitality: Creating Unforgettable Home Away From Home Experiences For a Diverse Range of Discerning Guests- A Case Study of Intercontinental Zhuhai Hotel. *Gulf Journal of Advance Business Research*, 1(1), 44–59.

Laczkovich, I. (2018). Social Media Influencers in the Travel Industry: an analysis.

Lehto, X. Y., Kirillova, K., Wang, D., & Fu, X. (2024). Convergence of boundaries in tourism, hospitality, events, and leisure: Defining the core and knowledge structure. *Journal of Hospitality & Tourism Research (Washington, D.C.)*, 48(3), 407–419. 10.1177/10963480221108667

Liu, H., Wu, L., & Li, X. (2019). Social media envy: How experience sharing on social networking sites drives millennials' aspirational tourism consumption. *Journal of Travel Research*, 58(3), 355–369. 10.1177/0047287518761615

Lou, C., & Yuan, S. (2019). Influencer marketing: How message value and credibility affect consumer trust of branded content on social media. *Journal of Interactive Advertising*, 19(1), 58–73. 10.1080/15252019.2018.1533501

Matsushita, K. (2023). How the Japanese workcation embraces digital nomadic work style employees. *World Leisure Journal*, 65(2), 218–235. 10.1080/16078055.2022.2156594

Miao, L., Yang, F. X., Im, J., & Zhang, Q. (2024). Flexwork and flextravel. *Annals of Tourism Research*, 106, 103763. 10.1016/j.annals.2024.103763

Mueller Correa & Marina. (2022). *Social Media Storytelling: A New Zealand Study of the Use of Narratives to Engage with the Public* (Doctoral dissertation, Auckland University of Technology).

Nunes, L. (2019). *Sustaining a digital online influence through personal branding: a case study of travel bloggers*. University of Johannesburg.

Parry, R. W. A., Saxena, S., Ahmad, S. I., & Basheer, I. (2023). Investigating Consumer Purchase Intentions and Social Media Advertising Attributes Among Generation-Z: An Empirical Study in the Region of Jammu and Kashmir. Top of Form. *The Journal of Research Administration*, 5(2), 8965–8979.

Park, S., Lehto, X., & Kang, J. (2024). Balancing Work and Leisure: Unraveling Constraints on Work-Leisure Integration in Bleisure Travel. *International Journal of Hospitality & Tourism Administration*, 1–27. 10.1080/15256480.2024.2344226

Platon, O. E. (2023). Using Instagram Marketing: Creating the Perception of a Tourism Destination Experience and Influencing the Travel Decision-Making Process. *Challenges of the Knowledge Society*, 669-676.

Qazi, S., & Baig, S. (2024). Promoting Tourism via Instagram: A Study of Instagram Users and the Role of Tourism Companies in Pakistan. Journalism. *Politics & Society*, 2(01), 1–20.

Rainoldi, M., Ladkin, A., & Buhalis, D. (2024). Blending work and leisure: A future digital worker hybrid lifestyle perspective. *Annals of Leisure Research*, 27(2), 215–235. 10.1080/11745398.2022.2070513

Ringer, G. (2016). *Social media travel in Caribbean island destinations*. L'Harmattan.

Roblin & Matthew, (2017). Blogs for The Digital Agency etravelseo. com–Online Travel Marketing.

Schänzel, H. A., Smith, K. A., & Weaver, A. (2005). Family holidays: A research review and application to New Zealand. *Annals of Leisure Research*, 8(2-3), 105–123. 10.1080/11745398.2005.10600965

Setiani, S. S., Setiawati, E., Suryono, C., Yen, Y. F., Dewi, R. P., Khalim, A., & Irawan, J. A. (2024). Optimization Integrated Marketing Communication Model as Strategic Approach to Boost Cirebon Business Leisure. *International Journal Of Accounting, Management, And. Economic Research Journal*, 2(1), 33–44.

Sigala, M., & Gretzel, U. (Eds.). (2017). *Advances in social media for travel, tourism and hospitality: New perspectives, practice and cases*). 10.4324/9781315565736

Soliman, M., & Al Balushi, M. K. (2023). Unveiling destination evangelism through generative AI tools. *ROBONOMICS: The Journal of the Automated Economy*, 4(54), 1.

Surge in solo travel; J&K, Manali preferred travel destinations: Report. (2023, July 2). *Business Standard*. https://www.business-standard.com/india-news/surge-in-solo-travel-j-k-manali-preferred-travel-destinations-report-123070200268_1.html

Tomazos, K. (2022). Social media influencers and tourism sustainability: the good, the irritating, and the desperate. In *Handbook of innovation for sustainable tourism* (pp. 250–273). Edward Elgar Publishing.

Tham, A., Mair, J., & Croy, G. (2020). Social media influence on tourists' destination choice: Importance of context. *Tourism Recreation Research*, 45(2), 161–175. 10.1080/02508281.2019.1700655

Wearing, S. (2001). *Volunteer tourism: Experiences that make a difference*. Cabi. 10.1079/9780851995335.0000

Compilation of References

Abbas, R., Michael, K., & Michael, M. G. (2014). Using a social-ethical framework to evaluate location-based services in an internet of things world. *International Journal of Information Ethics*, 22, 42–73. 10.29173/irie127

Abedini, Y. (2021). Metacognition as a core skill for wise decision-making in higher education: investigating gender differences. *Journal of Applied Research in Higher Education*. 10.1108/JARHE-11-2020-0400

Adetola, O. J., Aghazadeh, S., & Abdullahi, M. (2021). Perceived Environmental Concern, Knowledge, and Intention to Visit Green Hotels: Do Perceived Consumption Values Matter? *Pakistan Journal of Commerce and Social Science*, 15(2).

Adhiatma, A., Muna, N., & Fachrunnisa, O. (2019). Business and Leisure "Bleisure" in Organization: Antecedents and Outcomes. *JDM: Jurnal Dinamika Manajemen/ Jurnal Dinamika Manajemen Jurusan Manajemen Fakultas Ekonomi Universitas Negeri Semarang, 10*(2), 216–228. 10.15294/jdm.v10i2.19783

Agenda. (n.d.). World Economic Forum. https://weforum.org/agenda/

Agnihotri, A. (2024, January 4). The Era of Bleisure Travel: Remote and Hybrid Work Trends Inspire a Fusion of Business and Leisure on Work Trips. *Hindustan Times*. https://www.hindustantimes.com/lifestyle/travel/the-era-of-bleisure-travel-remote-and-hybrid-work-trends-inspire-a-fusion-of-business-and-leisure-on-work-trips-101704342757445.html

Aguilera, A. (2008). Business travel and mobile workers. *Journal of Transportation Research Part A: Policy andPractice, 42*(8), 1109-1116.

Aguilera, A. (2008). Business Travel and Mobile Workers. *Transportation Research Part A, Policy and Practice*, 42(8), 1109–1116. 10.1016/j.tra.2008.03.005

Ahmad, S. (2024, May 13). *What is the Importance of Bleisure Travel?*https://satgurutravel.com/importance-of-bleisure-travel/

Alfakihuddin, M. L. B. (2023). Dampak dari Pemasaran Hijau dan Iklan Hijau pada Niat Beli Produk Kecantikan pada Generasi Z. *SEIKO: Journal of Management \& Business, 6*(2).

Alghizzawi, M., Habes, M., Al Assuli, A., & Ezmigna, A. A. R. (2024). Digital Marketing and Sustainable Businesses: As Mobile Apps in Tourism. In Hamdan, A., & Aldhaen, E. S. (Eds.), *Artificial Intelligence and Transforming Digital Marketing* (pp. 3–13). Springer Nature Switzerland. 10.1007/978-3-031-35828-9_1

Allen, T., Johnson, R., Kiburz, K., & Shockley, K. (2012). Work—family conflict and flexible work arrangements: Deconstructing flexibility. *Personnel Psychology*, 66(2), 345–376. 10.1111/peps.12012

Allied Market Research. (2023). Global Bleisure Tourism Market Outlook 2032. https://www.alliedmarketresearch.com/bleisure-tourism-market

Alp, B., & Ayyıldız, A. Y. (2020). A new opportunity in tourism market: Bleisure. *Journal of Tourism & Gastronomy Studies*, 8(1), 336–354. 10.21325/jotags.2020.551

Anable, J., & Gatersleben, B. (2005). All work and no play? the role of instrumental and affective factors in work and leisure journeys by different travel modes. *Transportation Research Part A, Policy and Practice*, 39(2–3), 163–181. 10.1016/j.tra.2004.09.008

Anderson, R. I., Lewis, D., & Parker, M. E. (1999). Another Look at the Efficiency of Corporate Travel Management Departments. *Journal of Travel Research*, 37(3), 267–272. 10.1177/004728759903700308

Andresen, M., Biemann, T., & Pattie, M. W. (2015). What makes them move abroad? Reviewing and exploring differences between self-initiated and assigned expatriation. *International Journal of Human Resource Management*, 26(7), 932–947. 10.1080/09585192.2012.669780

Aquino, R. S., & Porter, B. A. (2022). Contemporary Issues in Tourism Management in the Philippines. *Perspectives on Asian Tourism*, (Part F190), 3–19. 10.1007/978-981-19-4497-0_1

Argan, M. (2013). *Rekreasyon yönetimi*. Anadolu Üniversitesi Web-ofset Tesisleri.

Arnfalk & Kogg. (2003). Service Transformation - Managing a Shift from Business Travel to Virtual Meetings. *Journal of Cleaner Production,* 11(8 SPEC.), 859–72. .10.1016/S0959-6526(02)00158-0

Aroles, J., Granter, E., & de Vaujany, F. X. (2019). 'Becoming Mainstream': The Professionalisation and Corporatisation of Digital Nomadism. *New Technology, Work and Employment*, 35(1), 114–129. 10.1111/ntwe.12158

Arora, N., Malik, G., & Chawla, D. (2019). Factors Affecting Consumer Adoption of Mobile Apps in NCR: A Qualitative Study. *Global Business Review*, 21(1), 176–196. 10.1177/0972150919876748

Asero, V., Gozzo, S., & Tomaselli, V. (2015). Building Tourism Networks through Tourist Mobility. *Journal of Travel Research*, 55(6), 751–763. 10.1177/0047287515569777

Astina, I. K., Sumarmi, S., & Kurniawati, E. (2021). Tourism in coastal areas: its implication to improve economic and culture acculturation (case study in goa China Beach, Malang). *Geo Journal of Tourism and Geosites*, 37(3), 740–746. 10.30892/gtg.37302-704

Axtell, C., Hislop, D., & Whittaker, S. (2008). Mobile Technologies in Mobile Spaces: Findings from the Context of Train Travel. *International Journal of Human-Computer Studies*, 66(12), 902–915. 10.1016/j.ijhcs.2008.07.001

Baker, M. J., & Cameron, E. (2008). Critical success factors in destination marketing. *Tourism and Hospitality Research*, 8(2), 79–97. 10.1057/thr.2008.9

Bąk, M., & Borkowski, P. (2015). Applicability of ICT solutions in passenger transport - case studies from different European backgrounds. *Transport*, 30(3), 372–381. 10.3846/16484142.2015.1079552

Balasubramanian, K., Kunasekaran, P., Konar, R., & Sakkthivel, A. M. (2022). *Insights for a Changing World* (Vol. II). Integrating augmented reality (AR) and virtual reality (VR) as marketing communications channels in the hospitality and tourism service sector. *In Marketing Communications and Brand Development in Emerging Markets*. Springer International Publishing.

Baltezarević, R., Baltezarević, B., & Baltezarević, V. (2022). The role of travel influencers in sustainable tourism development. *International Review (Steubenville, Ohio)*, (3-4), 125–129. 10.5937/intrev2204131B

Bandyopadhyay, R., Morais, D. B., & Chick, G. (2008). Religion and identity in India's heritage tourism. *Annals of Tourism Research*, 35(3), 790–808. 10.1016/j.annals.2008.06.004

Banerji, D., Rashideh, W., Arora, B., & Pratihari, A. R. (2021). Application potential of Blockchain technologies in the travel and tourism industry. In *Blockchain Applications in IoT Ecosystem* (pp. 289–299). Springer International Publishing. 10.1007/978-3-030-65691-1_19

BANI: What is it, and how can it help us? (n.d.). Impact International. https://www.impactinternational.com/blog/2023/10/bani-what-it-and-how-can-it-help-u

Barret, D. (2020). Estimating, monitoring and minimising the travel footprint associated with the development of the Athena X-ray Integral Field Unit: An on-line travel footprint calculator released to the science community. *Experimental Astronomy*, 49, 183–216. 10.1007/s10686-020-09659-832836797

Barros, C. P. (2006). Earnings, schooling and social capital of cooperative managers. *Annals of Public and Cooperative Economics*, 77(1), 1–20. 10.1111/j.1370-4788.2006.00295.x

Barten, M. (2024). 7 Tips for Hotels to Attract More Bleisure Travelers. Retrieved from https://www.revfine.com/bleisure/

Baruch, Y., Yochanan, A., & Tung, R. (2016). Career Mobility in a Global Era: Advances in Managing Expatriation and Repatriation. *The Academy of Management Annals*, 10(1), 841–889. 10.5465/19416520.2016.1162013

Bassyiouny, M., & Wilkesmann, M. (2023). Going on Workation – Is Tourism Research Ready to Take off? Exploring an Emerging Phenomenon of Hybrid Tourism. *Tourism Management Perspectives*, 46, 101096. Advance online publication. 10.1016/j.tmp.2023.101096

Batala, B., & Slevitch, L. (2024). Keeping two balls in the air: The bleisure travel experience. *Annals of Tourism Research Empirical Insights*, 5(1), 100115. 10.1016/j.annale.2023.100115

Beaverstock, Derudder, Faulconbridge, & Witlox. (2016). *International Business Travel in the Global Economy.*

Beaverstock, J. V., Derudder, B., Faulconbridge, J. R., & Witlox, F. (2009). International Business Travel: Some Explorations. *Geografiska Annaler. Series B, Human Geography*, 91(3), 193–202. 10.1111/j.1468-0467.2009.00314.x

Becker, G. S. (1962). Investment in Human Capital: A Theoretical analysis. *Journal of Political Economy*, 70(5, Part 2), 9–49. 10.1086/258724

Bekele, M. K., Pierdicca, R., Frontoni, E., Malinverni, E. S., & Gain, J. (2018). A survey of augmented, virtual, and mixed reality for cultural heritage. *Journal on Computing and Cultural Heritage*, 11(2), 1–36. 10.1145/3145534

Bell, R. A., & Morey, R. C. (1995). Increasing the Efficiency of Corporate Travel Management through Macro Benchmarking. *Journal of Travel Research*, 33(3), 11–20. 10.1177/004728759503300303

Benckendorff, P. J., Xiang, Z., & Sheldon, P. J. (2019). *Tourism information technology*. CABI. 10.1079/9781786393432.0000

Benzies, K. M., Premji, S., Hayden, K. A., & Serrett, K. (2006). State-of-the-Evidence Reviews: Advantages and Challenges of Including Grey Literature. *Worldviews on Evidence-Based Nursing*, 3(2), 55–61. 10.1111/j.1741-6787.2006.00051.x17040510

Bergström, G. (2010). Consequences of Overnight Work Travel for Personal Social Relations: Problems, Promises, and Further Repercussions. *Mobilities*, 5(3), 369–386. 10.1080/17450101.2010.494841

Berkery, E., Morley, M. J., Tiernan, S., Purtill, H., & Parry, E. (2017). On the Uptake of Flexible Working Arrangements and the Association with Human Resource and Organizational Performance Outcomes. *European Management Review*, 14(2), 165–183. 10.1111/emre.12103

Bezovski, Z. (2016). The future of the mobile payment as electronic payment system. *European Journal of Business and Management*, 8(8), 127–132.

Bhuiyan, K. H., Jahan, I., Zayed, N. M., Islam, K. M. A., Suyaiya, S., Tkachenko, O., & Nitsenko, V. (2022). Smart tourism ecosystem: A new dimension toward sustainable value co-creation. *Sustainability (Basel)*, 14(22), 15043. 10.3390/su142215043

Bi, N., Yin, C. Y., & Chen, Y. (2020). A bittersweet experience! The effect of mixed emotions on business tourists' revisit intentions. *Journal of Travel & Tourism Marketing*, 37(6), 695–710. 10.1080/10548408.2020.1795047

Bjerkan, K., & Øvstedal, L. (2018). Functional requirements for inclusive transport. *Transportation*, 47(3), 1177–1198. 10.1007/s11116-018-9939-7

Blackshaw, T. (2017). Decentring Leisure: Rethinking Leisure Theory (Book Review). *Annals of Leisure Research*, 20(2), 240–242. 10.1080/11745398.2016.1254798

Bleisure Travel: The Challenges & Rewards. (2023b, August 3). https://www.linkedin.com/pulse/bleisure-travel-challenges-rewards

Boerman, S. C., Willemsen, L. M., & Van Der Aa, E. P. (2017). This post is sponsored. *Journal of Interactive Marketing*, 38, 82–92. 10.1016/j.intmar.2016.12.002

Bogdan, S. (2018). Millennials: A new trend for the tourism industry. *Annals of Spiru Haret University.Economic Series 18*, (3), 109–122. 10.26458/1838

Bowie, D., & Buttle, F. (2004). *Hospitality marketing*. Routledge.

Bozzi, N. (2020). #digitalnomads, #solotravellers, #remoteworkers: A Cultural Critique of the Traveling Entrepreneur on Instagram. *Social Media + Society*, 6(2). Advance online publication. 10.1177/2056305120926644

Brewer, A. (1998). Work design, flexible work arrangements and travel behaviour: Policy implications. *Transport Policy*, 5(2), 93–101. 10.1016/S0967-070X(98)00003-1

BridgeStreet. (2014). Bleisure report. London. Retrieved from February 7, 2022, from Bridge Street, Global Hospitality http://skift.com/wp-content/uploads/20 14/10/BGH-Bleisure-Report-2014.pdf

Brightbill, C. K. (1960). *The challenge of leisure*. Prentice-Hall.

Briliana, V., & Prasetio, A. B. (2018). Some antecedents and effects of using mobile apps in tourism marketing. Proceedings of the 7th International Conference on Entrepreneurship and Business. 10.1080/08989575.2017.1337993

Brower, J., LaBarge, M., White, L., & Mitchell, M. (2020). Examining responsiveness to an incentive-based mobile health app: Longitudinal observational study. *Journal of Medical Internet Research*, 22(8), e16797. 10.2196/1679732773371

Buhalis, D., Leung, D., & Rob, L. R. L. (2011). eTourism: critical information and communication technologies for tourism destinations. *In CABI eBooks* (pp. 205–224). https://doi.org/10.1079/9781845937621.0205

Buhalis, D. (2000). Marketing the competitive destination of the future. *Tourism Management*, 21(1), 97–116. 10.1016/S0261-5177(99)00095-3

Buhalis, D., Harwood, T., Bogicevic, V., Viglia, G., Beldona, S., & Hofacker, C. (2019). Technological disruptions in services: Lessons from tourism and hospitality. *Journal of Service Management*, 30(4), 484–506. 10.1108/JOSM-12-2018-0398

Cacioppo, J. T., Gardner, W. L., & Berntson, G. G. (1999). The affect system has parallel and integrative processing components: Form follows function. *Journal of Personality and Social Psychology*, 76(5), 839–855. 10.1037/0022-3514.76.5.839

Caffyn, A. (2012). Advocating and implementing slow tourism. *Tourism Recreation Research*, 37(1), 77–80. 10.1080/02508281.2012.11081690

Caicedo-Barreth, A., Pavón, E. S., & Santos, L. L. (2020). Competitiveness of Guayaquil towards bleisure tourism. *European Journal of Tourism. Hospitality and Recreation*, 10(2), 118–133. 10.2478/ejthr-2020-0010

Camilleri, M. A. (2018). *The Tourism Industry: An Overview.*

Campos, A., Fanjul, M., & Moital, M. (2016). Segmenting the business traveler based on emotions, satisfaction, and behavioral intention. *Psychology & Marketing, 33*(2), 82–93. 10.1002/mar.20856

Capistrano, R. C., & Notorio, P. A. (2020). A content analysis of the future of tourism through the presidential state of the nation address in the Philippines (1987-2019). *Journal of Tourism Futures*, 7(1), 131–146. 10.1108/JTF-05-2020-0075

Carlson Wagonlit Travel. (2016). *Combing business and leisure trips: A quantitative look at the bleisure phenomenon.*

Carlson Wagonlit Travel. (2016). Combing business and leisure trips: A quantitative look at the bleisure phenomenon. In CWT Solution Group White Paper. available at https:// www.mycwt.com/content/dam/cwt/pdf/insights/20160712-solutions-group -whitepaper-bleisure.pdfretrived on 28th April 2024

Carvache, F. M., Perez, O. A., Carvache, F. O., Víquez, P. A. G., & Carvache, F. W. (2020a). The perceived value in ecotourism related to satisfaction and loyalty: A study from Costa Rica. *Geographica Pannonica*, 24(3), 229–243. 10.5937/gp24-25082

Carvache-Franco, M., Carvache-Franco, W., Carvache-Franco, O., Hernández-Lara, A. B., & Buele, C. V. (2020b). Segmentation, motivation, and sociodemographic aspects of tourist demand in a coastal marine destination: A case study in Manta (Ecuador). *Current Issues in Tourism*, 23(10), 1234–1247. 10.1080/13683500.2019.1600476

Carvache-Franco, M., Solis-Radilla, M. M., Carvache-Franco, W., & Carvache-Franco, O. (2023). Push and pull motivations as demand predictors of coastal and marine destinations: A study in Acapulco, Mexico. *Tourism Planning & Development*, 20(6), 1000–1018. 10.1080/21568316.2021.1945673

Çetinsöz, B. C., & Hazarhun, E. (2020). Turizm endüstrisinde yeni bir trend: Bleisure seyahatler ve motivasyon unsurları. *Journal of Recreation and Tourism Research*, 7(4), 500–527.

Çetinsöz, B. C., & Hazarhun, E. (2020). Turizm Endüstrisinde Yeni Bir Trend: Bleisure Seyahatler Ve Motivasyon Unsurları. *Journal Of Recreation and Tourism Research*, 7(4), 500–527. 10.31771/jrtr.2020.75

Chan, E. Y. (2024). Digital Consumer Behavior. In *Consumer Behavior in Practice: Strategic Insights for the Modern Marketer* (pp. 127–144). Springer Nature Switzerland. 10.1007/978-3-031-50947-6_7

Chang, L., & Chung, K. (2018). Leisure tourism connection behaviors by life stage and gender. *International Journal of Culture, Tourism and Hospitality Research*, 12(3), 292–309. 10.1108/IJCTHR-03-2018-0036

Cha, S. H., Ma, J. H., Seo, J., Kim, J. I., & Han, S. (2023). Empirical comparison of spatial experience between photo-based IVE and real space. *Architectural Science Review*, 66(1), 1–16. 10.1080/00038628.2022.2134089

Cheeyong, K., Kim, J. C., Jung, S. H., & Kim, E. K. (2017). Marine leisure sports based on realistic VR system for Bleisure Busan. *International Journal of Grid and Distributed Computing*, 10(10), 69–78. 10.14257/ijgdc.2017.10.10.06

Chen, C., Petrick, J. F., & Shahvali, M. (2014). Tourism experiences as a stress reliever. *Journal of Travel Research*, 55(2), 150–160. 10.1177/0047287514546223

Cheng, S. C., & Kao, Y. H. (2022). The impact of the COVID-19 pandemic on job satisfaction: A mediated moderation model using job stress and organizational resilience in the hotel industry of Taiwan. *Heliyon*, 8(3), e09134. 10.1016/j.heliyon.2022.e0913435342829

Chen, H. (2017). A pilot study of business travelers' stress-coping strategies. *Tourism and Hospitality Research*, 19(2), 252–258. 10.1177/1467358417740747

Chen, Y. C., Li, R. H., & Chen, S. H. (2013). Relationships among adolescents' leisure motivation, leisure involvement, and leisure satisfaction: A structural equation model. *Social Indicators Research*, 110(3), 1187–1199. 10.1007/s11205-011-9979-2

Chen, Y., Mak, B., & McKercher, B. (2011). What Drives People to Travel: Integrating the Tourist Motivation Paradigms. *Journal of China Tourism Research*, 7(2), 120–136. 10.1080/19388160.2011.576927

Chevron, J., & Primeau, M. (1996). The telecommuting innovation opportunity. *Journal of Consumer Marketing*, 13(4), 40–48. 10.1108/07363769610124537

Chevtaeva, E. (2021). Coworking and Coliving: The Attraction for Digital Nomad Tourists. In *Information and Communication Technologies in Tourism 2021* (pp. 202–209). Springer International Publishing. 10.1007/978-3-030-65785-7_17

Chiang, H. S., & Huang, T. C. (2015). User-adapted travel planning system for personalized schedule recommendation. *Information Fusion*, 21, 3–17. 10.1016/j.inffus.2013.05.011

Chircu, Kauffman, & Keskey. (2001). Maximizing TheValue of Internet-Based Corporate Travel Reservation Systems. *Communications of the ACM,* 44(11).

Choi, G., Kim, J., Sawitri, M. Y., & Lee, S. K. (2020). Ecotourism {Market} {Segmentation} in {Bali}, {Indonesia}: Opportunities for {Implementing} {REDD}+. *Land (Basel)*, 9(6), 186. 10.3390/land9060186

Choo, J., Desa, N., & Asaari, M. (2016). Flexible working arrangement toward organizational commitment and work-family conflict. *Studies in Asian Social Science*, 3(1). Advance online publication. 10.5430/sass.v3n1p21

Choudhury, R., & Mohanty, P. (2018). Strategic Use of Social Media in Tourism Marketing: A Comparative Analysis of Official Tourism Boards. *Atna Journal of Tourism Studies, 13*(2), 41-56. https://doi.org/https://doi.org/10.12727/ajts.20.4

Chung, J. Y., Choi, Y. K., Yoo, B. K., & Kim, S. H. (2020). Bleisure Tourism Experience Chain: Implications for Destination Marketing. *Asia Pacific Journal of Tourism Research*, 25(3), 300–310. 10.1080/10941665.2019.1708760

Coffey, J. K., Shahvali, M., Kerstetter, D. L., & Aron, A. (2024). Couples vacations and romantic passion and intimacy. *Annals of Tourism Research Empirical Insights*, 5(1), 100121. 10.1016/j.annale.2024.100121

Cohen, S. A., & Gossling, ¨. S. (2015). A darker side of hypermobility. *Environment and Planning A. Environment & Planning A*, 47(8), 166–1679. 10.1177/0308518X15597124

Connolly, F., & Gärling, T. (2023). The relationships between income, life satisfaction and emotional well-being in european countries differing in wealth. *International Journal of Psychology*, 58(6), 594–604. 10.1002/ijop.1293537572010

Cook, D. (2023). What is a digital nomad? Definition and taxonomy in the era of mainstream remote work. *World Leisure Journal*, 65(2), 256–275. 10.1080/16078055.2023.2190608

Cordes, K. A., & Ibrahim, H. M. (2003). *Applications in recreation and leisure: for today and the future* (3rd ed.). McGraw-Hill.

Correia, A., Kozak, M., & Ferradeira, J. (2013). From tourist motivations to tourist satisfaction. *International Journal of Culture, Tourism and Hospitality Research*, 7(4), 411–424. 10.1108/IJCTHR-05-2012-0022

Coşkun, G. (2021). Cultural diffusion theory and tourism implications. *International Journal of Geography and Geography Education (IGGE)* (Vol. 43). https://orcid.org/0000-0002-5200-6370

Crompton, J. (1979). Motivations for a Leisure Vacation. *Annals of Tourism Research*, 6(4), 408–424. 10.1016/0160-7383(79)90004-5

Crompton, J. L., & McKay, S. L. (2002). Motives of visitors attending festival events. *Annals of Tourism Research*. Advance online publication. 10.1016/S0160-7383(97)80010-2

Çulfacı, G., Onursoy, F. M., & Akın, M. H. (2024). Business Travel and Bleisure Tourism A Study on The Travel Motivations of Academics. *GSI Journals Serie A: Advancements in Tourism Recreation and Sports Sciences*, 7(2), 406–423. 10.53353/atrss.1403738

Cunningham, J., Mangematin, V., O'Kane, C., & O'Reilly, P. (2016). At the frontiers of scientific advancement: The factors that influence scientists to become or choose to become publically funded principal investigators. *The Journal of Technology Transfer*, 41(4), 778–797. 10.1007/s10961-015-9400-4

Dahlin, K., Taylor, M., & Fichman, M. (2004). Today's Edisons or Weekend Hobbyists: Technical Merit and Success of Inventions by Independent Inventors. *Research Policy*, 33(8), 1167–1183. 10.1016/j.respol.2004.06.003

Danna, K., & Griffin, R. W. (1999). Health and well-being in the workplace: A review and synthesis of the literature. *Journal of Management*, 25(3), 357–384. 10.1177/014920639902500305

Das, M. P. (2023). Technology and Guest experience: Innovations reshaping hotel management. *International Journal for Multidimensional Research Perspectives*, 1(3), 76–95.

Davidson, R. (2003). Adding Pleasure to Business. *Journal of Convention & Exhibition Management*, 5(1), 29–39. 10.1300/J143v05n01_03

Delgado-Ballester, E., Navarro, A., & Sicilia, M. (2012). Revitalising brands through communication messages: The role of brand familiarity. *European Journal of Marketing*, 46(1/2), 31–51. 10.1108/03090561211189220

Denstadli, J. M. (2004). Impacts of Videoconferencing on Business Travel: The Norwegian Experience. *Journal of Air Transport Management*, 10(6), 371–376. 10.1016/j.jairtraman.2004.06.003

Desideria, G., & Bandung, Y. (2020). User efficiency model in usability engineering for user interface design refinement of mobile application. *J. ICT Res. Appl*, 14(1), 16–33. 10.5614/itbj.ict.res.appl.2020.14.1.2

Deterding, S., & Dixon, D. (2011). From Game Design Elements to Gamefulness: Defining "Gamification." Proceedings. The 15th International Academic MindTrek Conference, 9-15. 10.1145/2181037.2181040

Díaz-Parra, O., Fuentes-Penna, A., Marroquín-Gutiérrez, F., Rodríguez-Lara, B. M., Salgado Ramírez, J. C., Trejo-Macotela, F. R., & Aguilar-Ortiz, J. (2023). Smart Tourism: Technologies to Improve Tourism. In Ruiz-Vanoye, J. A. (Ed.), *Management, Technology, and Economic Growth in Smart and Sustainable Cities* (pp. 83–96). IGI Global., 10.4018/979-8-3693-0373-3.ch005

Dickmann, M. (2012). Why do they come to London? Exploring the Motivations of Expatriates to Work in the British Capital. *Journal of Management Development*, 8(31), 783–800. 10.1108/02621711211253240

DiClemente, C. C., Prochaska, J. O., Fairhurst, S. K., Velicer, W. F., Velasquez, M. M., & Rossi, J. S. (1991). The process of smoking cessation: An analysis of precontemplation, contemplation, and preparation stages of change. *Journal of Consulting and Clinical Psychology*, 59(2), 295–304. 10.1037/0022-006X.59.2.2952030191

Dieffenbacher, F. S. (2023, September 3). *BANI World: What is it and Why We Need it?* Digital Leadership. https://digitalleadership.com/blog/bani-world/#:~:text=The%20BANI%20effect%20refers%20to

Dimitriou, C. K., & AbouElgheit, E. (2019). Understanding generation Z's travel social decision-making. *Tourism and Hospitality Management*, 25(2), 311–334. 10.20867/thm.25.2.4

Djafarova, E., & Rushworth, C. (2017). Exploring the credibility of online celebrities' Instagram profiles in influencing the purchase decisions of young female users. *Computers in Human Behavior*, 68, 1–7. 10.1016/j.chb.2016.11.009

Djurica, M., & Djurica, N. (2010). *Tourism destination marketing management, faculty of tourism and hospitality management in opatija. Biennial International Congress, Tourism & Hospitality Industry, University of* Rijeka, Faculty of Tourism & Hospitality Management, 890-901.

Doherty, N., Richardson, J., & Thorn, K. (2013). Self-initiated expatriation. *Career Development International*, 18(1), 6–11. 10.1108/13620431311305917

Dragomir, L., Girniceanu, A., & Mazilu, M. (2021). Trends in worldwide tourism in 2020. *Quaestus*, 18, 28–41.

Economist. (2019). The 2019 Bleisure barometer: Asia's best cities for work and recreation. London: The Economist Intelligence Unit.

Economist. (2019). The 2019 Bleisure barometer: Asia's best cities for work and recreation. London: The Economist Intelligence Unit. https://www.insidethegames.biz/media/file/135299/ECO056-JP-ANA-Bleisure-Business-and-Leisure-5-ver20190212.pdf

Egencia & Expedia. (2013). Expedia and Egencia unveil the future of travel report. PR Newswire Association LLC. Retrieved from https://search-proquestcom.zorac .aub.aau.dk/ docview/1496067552?accountid=8144

Elbaz, A., Salem, I., Elsetouhi, A., & Abdelhamied, H. (2020). The moderating role of leisure participation in work—Leisure conflict for the reduction of burnout in hotels and travel agencies. *International Journal of Tourism Research*, 22(3), 375–389. 10.1002/jtr.2342

Elias, S. (2024). Economic impact of tourism in developing countries. *Indian Scientific Journal of Research in Engineering and Management*, 08(04), 1–5. 10.55041/ IJSREM30010

Elshaer, I., & Saad, S. (2021). Entrepreneurial resilience and business continuity in the tourism and hospitality industry: The role of adaptive performance and institutional orientation. *Tourism Review*, 77(5), 1365–1384. 10.1108/TR-04-2021-0171

El-Sofany, H. F., & Abou El-Seoud, S. (2023). The Effectiveness of Tourism in KSA Using Mobile App During COVID-19 Pandemic. *Artificial Intelligence and Online Engineering*.

Erkan, I., & Evans, C. (2016). The influence of eWOM in social media on consumers' purchase intentions: An extended approach to information adoption. *Computers in Human Behavior*, 61, 47–55. 10.1016/j.chb.2016.03.003

Expedia. (2018). Unpacking bleisure traveler trends. Retrieved from https://bit.ly/ bleisure-trends

Expedia. (2018). Unpacking bleisure traveler trends. Retrieved from https://bit.ly/ bleisure-trends https://go2.advertising.expedia.com/rs/185-EIA-216/images/Bleisure %20Select%20Meeting.pdf

Expedia. (2018). Unpacking bleisuretraveler trends. Retrieved from https://bit.ly/ bleisure-trends

Ezeuduji, I. O. (2024). Bleisure travel reimagined: Implications for research. *International Conference on Tourism Research, 7*(1), 2-9.

Ezeuduji, I. O. (2024). Bleisure Travel Reimagined: Implications for Research. *Proceedings of the 7th International Conference on Tourism Research, 7*(1), 2-9. 10.34190/ictr.7.1.2194

Farida, U. (2020). The effect of flexible working arrangements on work engagement of online motorcycle taxi drivers. *Psychological Research and Intervention*, 3(2), 92–99. 10.21831/pri.v3i2.42196

Fay, D., & Frese, M. (2001). The concept of personal initiative (personal initiative): An overview of validity studies. *Human Performance*, 14(1), 97–124. 10.1207/S15327043HUP1401_06

Floričić, T., & Pavia, N. (2021). Linkage of leisure with remote work and digital nomadism in tourist accommodation facilities. 6th International Scientific Conference ToSEE-Tourism in Southern and Eastern Europe 2021: ToSEE–Smart, Experience, Excellence & ToFEEL–Feelings, Excitement, Education, Leisure (ToSEE 2021). 10.1504/IJTMKT.2023.127322

Fong, C. T. (2006). The Effects of Emotional Ambivalence on Creativity. *Academy of Management Journal*, 49(5), 1016–1030. 10.5465/amj.2006.22798182

Fong, N. M., Fang, Z., & Luo, X. (2015). Geo-conquesting: Competitive locational targeting of mobile promotions. *JMR, Journal of Marketing Research*, 52(5), 726–735. 10.1509/jmr.14.0229

Frochot, I., Montémont, V., & Violier, P. (2024). *Post-Covid hypermobile tourist practices facing environmental challenges*. Mondes Du Tourisme., 10.4000/tourisme.6689

Fuzi, A. (2015). Co-working spaces for promoting entrepreneurship in sparse regions: The case of South Wales. *Regional Studies, Regional Science*, 2(1), 462–469. 10.1080/21681376.2015.1072053

Gabelaia, I., & McElroy, J. W. (2023, October). The Impact of User-Generated Marketing on Creating Greater Audience Connections and Brand Loyalty. In *International Conference on Reliability and Statistics in Transportation and Communication* (pp. 389-403). Cham: Springer Nature Switzerland.

Gale, T. (2009). Urban beaches, virtual worlds and 'the end of tourism'. *Mobilities*, 4(1), 119–138. 10.1080/17450100802657996

García, M. (2016). Turismo de reunionesen la ciudad de Mar de Plata: Situación actual desde la percepción del Mar del Plata Convention & Visitors Bureau. Universidad Nacional de Mar del Plata.

Geng, Y., Zhang, X., Juan, G., Yan, Y., & Chen, L. (2024). Bibliometric analysis of sustainable tourism using CiteSpace. *Technological Forecasting & Social Change. Technological Forecasting and Social Change*, 202, 123310. 10.1016/j.techfore.2024.123310

Gerdenitsch, C., Kubicek, B., & Korunka, C. (2015). Control in flexible working arrangements. *Journal of Personnel Psychology*, 14(2), 61–69. 10.1027/1866-5888/a000121

Giri, P. (2023). *Social Media and Emerging Public Sphere: A Study of Northeast India* (Doctoral dissertation).

Global Business Travel Association. (2023). Global Business Travel Industry Forecast Is for Accelerated Rebound, Spending to Reach $1.8 Trillion by 2027. Retrieved from https://www.hospitalitynet.org/news/4117734.html

Global, H. I. S. (2020). İş seyahatleri ve küresel seyahat riskleri raporu. Retrieved from https://www.hisglobal.com.tr/uploads/HIS_travel_is_seyahati_ve_kuresel_seyahat_riskleri_raporu_mayis2020.pdf

Goecke, R. (2020). The Evolution of Online Booking Systems. In Xiang, Z., Fuchs, M., Gretzel, U., & Höpken, W. (Eds.), *Handbook of e-Tourism*. Springer. 10.1007/978-3-030-05324-6_27-1

Gordon, A. (2023). The Role of Public Transportation Systems in Promoting Sustainable Mobility in Green Cities. *Advances in Urban Resilience and Sustainable City Design*, 15(6), 1–18.

Gössling, S., & Lane, B. (2015). Rural tourism and the development of Internet-based accommodation booking platforms: A study in the advantages, dangers and implications of innovation. *Journal of Sustainable Tourism*, 23(8-9), 1386–1403. 10.1080/09669582.2014.909448

Grant, A. M., Berg, J. M., & Cable, D. M. (2014). Job Titles as Identity Badges: How Self-Reflective Titles Can Reduce Emotional Exhaustion. *Academy of Management Journal*, 57(4), 1201–1225. 10.5465/amj.2012.0338

Greenhaus, J. H., & Beutell, N. J. (1985). Sources of conflict between work and family roles. *Academy of Management Review*, 10(1), 76–88. 10.2307/258214

Green, P. (2020). Disruptions of self, place and mobility: Digital nomads in Chiang Mai, Thailand. *Mobilities*, 15(3), 431–445. 10.1080/17450101.2020.1723253

Griffin, J., Youm, Y., & Vivari, B. (2019). Stakeholder engagement strategies after an exogenous shock: how philip morris and r. j. reynolds adapted differently to the 1998 master settlement agreement. *Business & Society, 60*(4), 1009–1036. 10.1177/0007650319870818

Groen, B., Triest, S., Coers, M., & Wtenweerde, N. (2018). Managing flexible work arrangements: Teleworking and output controls. *European Management Journal*, 36(6), 727–735. 10.1016/j.emj.2018.01.007

Gross, M., & Huang, S. (2013). The domestic development experience of a hotel firm with chinese characteristics. *Cornell Hospitality Quarterly*, 54(2), 211–224. 10.1177/1938965512466286

Gunasekar, S., Patri, R., & Narayanan, B. (2017). International Tourist arrival in India. *Foreign Trade Review*, 53(1), 12–28. 10.1177/0015732516681882

Gunn, R. W., Carberry, D. P., Frigo, R., & Behrens, S. (1993). Shared services: major companies are re-engineering their accounting functions. *Management Accounting (USA), 75*(5), 22-35. https://link.gale.com/apps/doc/A14836435/AONE?u=anon~54b151d2&sid=googleScholar&xid=979f5a55

Gunthorpe, W., & Lyons, K. (2004). A Predictive Model of Chronic Time Pressure in the Australian Population: Implications for Leisure Research. *Leisure Sciences*, 26(2), 201–213. 10.1080/01490400490432127

Guo, C., Porshitz, E., & Alves, J. (2013). Exploring career agency during self-initiated repatriation: A study of Chinese sea turtles. *Career Development International*, 18(1), 34–55. 10.1108/13620431311305

Gustafson, P. (2012). Managing business travel: Developments and dilemmas in corporate travel management. Tourism Management, 33(2), 276–284. https://doi.org/.tourman.2011.03.00610.1016/j

Gustafson, P. (2012). Travel time and working time: What business travellers do when they travel, and why. *Time & Society, 21*(2), 203–222. 10.1177/0961463X12444057

Gustafson, P. (2012). Managing Business Travel: Developments and Dilemmas in Corporate Travel Management. *Tourism Management*, 33(2), 276–284. 10.1016/j.tourman.2011.03.006

Gustafson, P. (2013). Business Travel from the Traveller's Perspective: Stress, Stimulation and Normalization. *Mobilities*, 9(1), 63–83. 10.1080/17450101.2013.784539

Güzel, Ö., Sahin, I., & Ryan, C. (2020). Push-motivation-based emotional arousal: A research study in a coastal destination. *Journal of Destination Marketing & Management*, 16, 1–11. 10.1016/j.jdmm.2020.100428

Hacıoğlu, N. (2003). *A. Gökdeniz ve Y. Dinç*. Boş Zaman Ve Rekreasyon Yönetimi-Örnek Animasyon Uygulamaları, Detay Yayıncılık.

Ha, H., & Perks, H. (2005). Effects of consumer perceptions of brand experience on the web: Brand familiarity, satisfaction and brand trust. *Journal of Consumer Behaviour*, 4(6), 438–452. 10.1002/cb.29

Hargittai, E., Piper, A. M., & Morris, M. R. (2019). From internet access to internet skills: Digital inequality among older adults. *Universal Access in the Information Society*, 18(4), 881–890. 10.1007/s10209-018-0617-5

Haris, R., & Leiper, N. (n.d.). *Sustainable Tourism: An Australian Perspective*. Butterworth-Heinemann.

Hazar, A. (2003). *Rekreasyon ve animasyon (2. baskı)*. Detay Yayıncılık.

Helme, E. (2023). The role of authentic communication on perceived information credibility in influencer marketing.

Hensellek, S., & Puchala, N. (2021). *The Emergence of the Digital Nomad: A Review and Analysis of the Opportunities and Risks of Digital Nomadism*. 10.1007/978-3-030-62167-4_11

Herbert, D. T. (1988). Work and leisure: Exploring a relationship. *Area*, 20(3), 241–252.

Hidayah, A., Singh, J., & Hussain, I. (2021). Impact of flexible working arrangements in the public sector in Indonesia. *International Journal of Human Resource Studies*, 11(2), 38. 10.5296/ijhrs.v11i2.18458

Hornung, S., Rousseau, D., & Glaser, J. (2008). Creating flexible work arrangements through idiosyncratic deals. *The Journal of Applied Psychology*, 93(3), 655–664. 10.1037/0021-9010.93.3.65518457493

Howe-Walsh, L., & Schyns, B. (2010). Self-initiated expatriation: Implications for HRM. *International Journal of Human Resource Management*, 21(2), 260–273. 10.1080/09585190903509571

Hsu, T. K., Tsai, Y. F., & Wu, H. H. (2009). The preference analysis for tourist choice of destination: A case study of Taiwan. *Tourism Management*, 30(2), 288–297. 10.1016/j.tourman.2008.07.011

Huang, X., Chen, M., Wang, Y., Yi, J., Song, Z., & Ryan, C. (2022). Visitors' spatial-temporal behaviour and their learning experience: A comparative study. *Tourism Management Perspectives*, 42, 100951. 10.1016/j.tmp.2022.100951

Hudson, S., Huang, L., Roth, M. S., & Madden, T. J. (2016). The influence of social media interactions on consumer–brand relationships: A three-country study of brand perceptions and marketing behaviors. *International Journal of Research in Marketing*, 33(1), 27–41. 10.1016/j.ijresmar.2015.06.004

Huettermann, M., Thimm, T., Hannich, F., & Bild, C. (2019). Requirements for future digital visitor flow management. *Journal of Tourism Futures*, 5(3), 241–258. 10.1108/JTF-03-2019-0023

Hur, W.-M., Ahn, K., & Kim, M. (2011). Building brand loyalty through managing brand community commitment. *Management Decision*, 49(7), 1194–1213. 10.1108/00251741111151217

Hussain, S., Singh, A. M., Mohanty, P., & Gavinolla, M. R. (2023). Next generation employability and career sustainability in the hospitality industry 5.0. *Worldwide Hospitality and Tourism Themes*, 15(3), 308–321. 10.1108/WHATT-01-2023-0011

Hussein, S., & Ahmed, E. (2022). Mobile Application for Tourism: The Case of Egypt. *International Journal of Customer Relationship Marketing and Management*, 13(1), 1–29. 10.4018/IJCRMM.290415

Igor, K., Alexander, K., Mikhail, G., Catherine, A., & Pandey, B. (2021). Mobile Application Based Intelligent Role of Information Technologies in Tourism Sector. *International Journal of Aquatic Science*, 12(2), 2706–2731.

Ingrassia, M., Bellia, C., Giurdanella, C., Columba, P., & Chironi, S. (2022). Digital influencers, food and tourism—A new model of open innovation for businesses in the Ho. Re. Ca. sector. *Journal of Open Innovation*, 8(1), 50. 10.3390/joitmc8010050

Jalilvand, M. R., & Samiei, N. (2012). The impact of electronic word of mouth on a tourism destination choice. *Internet Research*, 22(5), 591–612. 10.1108/10662241211271563

Jammu & Kashmir seeing a tourism boom, here's why. (2024, March 22). *CNBC TV18. Com.* Retrieved May 11, 2024, from https://www.cnbctv18.com/videos/economy/jammu-and-kashmir-seeing-a-tourism-boom-here-why-19349801.htm

Jammu & Kashmir to see major boost in business, tourism investment. (2022, November 26). The Economic Times. Retrieved May 12, 2024, from https://travel.economictimes.indiatimes.com/news/destination/states/jammu-kashmir-to-see-major-boost-in-business-tourism-investment/95780265

Javits, O. (2019). *Social media influencers in destination marketing. A case study of Visit Tampere, Finland* (Master's thesis).

Jensen, C. R., & Guthrie, S. (2006). *Outdoor recreation in america* (6th ed.). Human Kinetics. 10.5040/9781492597438

Jeppesen, L. B., & Lakhani, K. R. (2010). Marginality and Problem-Solving Effectiveness in Broadcast Search. *Organization Science*, 21(5), 1–18. 10.1287/orsc.1090.0491

Jiang, Y., Gu, Z., & Law, R. (2020). Understanding bleisure travelers: A systematic literature review. *Journal of Travel Research*, 59(8), 1344–1361.

Jimenez Ruiz, A. E., Bhartiya, S., & Bhatt, V. (Eds.). (2024). *Promoting Sustainable Gastronomy Tourism and Community Development*. IGI Global. 10.4018/979-8-3693-1814-0

Jin, S. A., & Phua, J. (2014). Following celebrities' tweets about brands: The impact of Twitter-Based electronic Word-of-Mouth on consumers' source credibility perception, buying intention, and social identification with celebrities. *Journal of Advertising*, 43(2), 181–195. 10.1080/00913367.2013.827606

Jones, A. (2013). Conceptualising Business Mobilities: Towards an Analytical Framework. *Research in Transportation Business & Management*, 9, 58–66. 10.1016/j.rtbm.2013.08.003

Joo, D., & Woosnam, K. M. (2020). Measuring tourists' emotional solidarity with one another: A modification of the emotional solidarity scale. *Journal of Travel Research*, 59(7), 1186–1203. 10.1177/0047287519878503

Kabassi, K. (2010). Personalizing recommendations for tourists. *Telematics and Informatics*, 27(1), 51–66. 10.1016/j.tele.2009.05.003

Kachniewska, M. (2016). Bleisure: business and leisure equilibrium in contemporary hotel chains. Routledge Handbook of Hotel Chain Management, 542–554. https://doi.org/10.4324/9781315752532.ch45

Kaplan, A. M., & Haenlein, M. (2010). Users of the world, unite! The challenges and opportunities of Social Media. *Business Horizons*, 53(1), 59–68. 10.1016/j.bushor.2009.09.003

Karl, K., Peluchette, J., Hall-Indiana, L., & Harland, L. (2005). Attitudes toward Workplace Fun: A Three Sector Comparison. *Journal of Leadership & Organizational Studies*, 12(2), 1–17. 10.1177/107179190501200201

Karusala, N., Vishwanath, A., Vashistha, A., Kumar, S., & Kumar, N. (2018, April). " Only if you use English you will get to more things" Using Smartphones to Navigate Multilingualism. In *Proceedings of the 2018 CHI Conference on Human Factors in Computing Systems* (pp. 1-14).

Khairawati, S. (2019). Effect of customer loyalty program on customer satisfaction and its impact on customer loyalty. *International Journal of Research in Business and Social Science, 9*(1), 15–23. 10.20525/ijrbs.v9i1.603

Khan, I., Melro, A., Amaro, A. C., & Oliveira, L. (2020). Systematic review on gamification and cultural heritage dissemination. *Journal of Digital Media & Interaction*, 3(8), 19–41.

Khoo-Lattimore, C., & Yang, E. C. L. (2018). Asian Youth tourism: contemporary trends, cases and issues. In *Perspectives on Asian tourism* (pp. 1–13). 10.1007/978-981-10-8539-0_1

Kim, D. Y., Lehto, X. Y., & Morrison, A. M. (2007). Gender differences in online travel information search: Implications for marketing communications on the internet. *Tourism Management*, 28(2), 423–433. 10.1016/j.tourman.2006.04.001

Kim, H., Joun, H. J., Choe, Y., & Schroeder, A. (2019). How can a destination better manage its offering to visitors? Observing visitor experiences via online reviews. *Sustainability (Basel)*, 11(17), 4660. 10.3390/su11174660

Kim, J. H., Ritchie, J. R. B., & McCormick, B. (2010). Development of a Scale to Measure Memorable Tourism Experiences. *Journal of Travel Research*, 51(1), 12–25. 10.1177/0047287510385467

Kim, K., Oh, I. K., & Jogaratnam, G. (2007). College student travel: A revised model of push motives. *Journal of Vacation Marketing*, 13(1), 73–85. 10.1177/1356766706071201

Kim, S.-E., Kim, H., Jung, S., & Uysal, M. (2023). The Determinants of Continuance Intention toward Activity-Based Events Using a Virtual Experience Platform (VEP). *Leisure Sciences*, 1–26. 10.1080/01490400.2023.2172116

Kim, S.-H., Holland, S., & Han, H.-S. (2012). A Structural Model for Examining how Destination Image, Perceived Value, and Service Quality Affect Destination Loyalty: A Case Study of Orlando. *International Journal of Tourism Research*, 15(4), 313–328. 10.1002/jtr.1877

King, B., Lejealle, C., & Chapuis, J. M. (2023). Educational travellers and destination appeal: Deconstructing intrinsic motivations. *Journal of Vacation Marketing*, 29(1), 38–53. 10.1177/13567667221078241

Kiráľová, A., & Pavlíčeka, A. (2015). Development of social media strategies in tourism destination. *Procedia: Social and Behavioral Sciences*, 175, 358–366. 10.1016/j.sbspro.2015.01.1211

Kizildag, M., Doğru, T., Zhang, T., Mody, M., Altin, M., Ozturk, A., & Ozdemir, O. (2019). Blockchain: A paradigm shift in business practices. *International Journal of Contemporary Hospitality Management*, 32(3), 953–975. 10.1108/IJCHM-12-2018-0958

Kleiber, D. A., Walker, G., & Mannell, R. C. (2011). a Social Psychology of Leisure (2nd ed.). State College: Venture Publishing, Inc. https://lccn.loc.gov/2011929715

Kluin, J. Y., & Lehto, X. Y. (2012). Measuring family reunion travel motivations. *Annals of Tourism Research*, 39(2), 820–841. 10.1016/j.annals.2011.09.008

Kolb, A. Y., & Kolb, D. A. (2005). Learning styles and learning spaces: Enhancing experiential learning in higher education. *Academy of Management Learning & Education*, 4(2), 193–212. 10.5465/amle.2005.17268566

Kong, H. M., Witmaier, A., & Ko, E. (2021). Sustainability and social media communication: How consumers respond to marketing efforts of luxury and non-luxury fashion brands. *Journal of Business Research*, 131, 640–651. Advance online publication. 10.1016/j.jbusres.2020.08.021

Kong, X., Eisele, W., Zhang, Y., & Cline, D. (2018). Evaluating the impact of real-time mobility and travel time reliability information on truck drivers' routing decisions. *Transportation Research Record: Journal of the Transportation Research Board*, 2672(9), 164–172. 10.1177/0361198118797508

Kossek, E., & Kelliher, C. (2022). Making flexibility more i-deal: advancing work-life equality collectively. *Group & Organization Management, 48*(1), 317–349. 10.1177/10596011221098823

Kraaijenbrink, J. (2022, June 23). What BANI Really Means (And How It Corrects Your World View). *Forbes*. https://www.forbes.com/sites/jeroenkraaijenbrink/2022/06/22/what-bani-really-means-and-how-it-corrects-your-world-view/?sh=3a0d6cbe11bb

Kumar, N., & Sharma, S. (2019). Are they really happy? Insights into the Medical Tourists' Satisfaction in Delhi Hospitals. *African Journal of Hospitality, Tourism and Leisure*, 8(4). www.ajhtl.com

Kurkland, N. B., & Bailey, D. E. (1999). The advantages and challenges of working here, there anywhere, and anytime. *Organizational Dynamics*, 28(2), 53–68. 10.1016/S0090-2616(00)80016-9

Kwan, M., & Tong, L. (2023). Exemplifying Exceptional Hospitality: Creating Unforgettable Home Away From Home Experiences For a Diverse Range of Discerning Guests- A Case Study of Intercontinental Zhuhai Hotel. *Gulf Journal of Advance Business Research*, 1(1), 44–59.

Laczkovich, I. (2018). Social Media Influencers in the Travel Industry: an analysis.

Lazer, D. M. J., Baum, M. A., Benkler, Y., Berinsky, A. J., Greenhill, K. M., Menczer, F., Metzger, M. J., Nyhan, B., Pennycook, G., Rothschild, D., Schudson, M., Sloman, S. A., Sunstein, C. R., Thorson, E. A., Watts, D. J., & Zittrain, J. L. (2018). The science of fake news. *Science*, 359(6380), 1094–1096. 10.1126/science.aao299829590025

Lee, A., Toombs, A. L., & Erickson, I. (2019). Infrastructure vs. Community: Co-spaces Confront Digital Nomads' Paradoxical Needs. *Extended Abstracts of the 2019 CHI Conference on Human Factors in Computing Systems*. 10.1145/3290607.3313064

Lee, J., & Hammer, J. (2011). Gamification in Education: What, How, Why Bother? Gamification in Education: What, How, Why Bother? *Academic Exchange Quarterly*, 15(2), 1–5.

Lee, T., & Crompton, J. (1992). Measuring novelty in tourism seeking. *Annals of Tourism Research*, 19(4), 732–751. 10.1016/0160-7383(92)90064-V

Lee, T.-H., & Jan, F.-H. (2022). Development and Validation of the Smart Tourism Experience Scale. *Sustainability (Basel)*, 14(24), 16421. 10.3390/su142416421

Lehto, X. Y., Kirillova, K., Wang, D., & Fu, X. (2024). Convergence of boundaries in tourism, hospitality, events, and leisure: Defining the core and knowledge structure. *Journal of Hospitality & Tourism Research (Washington, D.C.)*, 48(3), 407–419. 10.1177/10963480221108667

Leiper, N., Witsel, M., & Hobson, J. P. (2008). Leisure travel and business travel. *Asian Journal of Tourism and Hospitality Research*, 2(1), 1.

Leong, A., Yeh, S. S., Hsiao, Y. C., & Huan, T. C. (2015). Nostalgia as travel motivation and its impact on tourists' loyalty. *Journal of Business Research*, 68(1), 81–86. 10.1016/j.jbusres.2014.05.003

Le, T. H., Arcodia, C., Novais, M. A., & Kralj, A. (2019). What we know and do not know about authenticity in dining experiences: A systematic literature review. *Tourism Management*, 74, 258–275. 10.1016/j.tourman.2019.02.012

Lichy, J., & McLeay, F. (2018). Bleisure: Motivations and Typologies. *Journal of Travel & Tourism Marketing*, 35(4), 517–530. 10.1080/10548408.2017.1364206

Lim, X.-J., Cheah, J.-H., Morrison, A. M., Ng, S. I., & Wang, S. (2022). Travel app shopping on smartphones: Understanding the success factors influencing in-app travel purchase intentions. *Tourism Review*, 77(4), 1166–1185. 10.1108/TR-11-2021-0497

Lipsa, S., & Dash, R. K. (2024). A seven-year analysis of the tourism sector of India with a prediction model—A case study of smart tourism. *Smart Tourism*, 5(1), 2526. 10.54517/st.v5i1.2526

Li, S., Robinson, P., & Oriade, A. (2017). Destination Marketing: The Use of Technology since the Millennium. *Journal of Destination Marketing & Management*, 6(2), 95–102. 10.1016/j.jdmm.2017.04.008

Litchfield, R. C., & Woldoff, R. A. (2023). Digital nomads: curiosity or trend? *Handbook of Virtual Work*, 186–196. 10.4337/9781802200508.00018

Litvin, S. W., Goldsmith, R. E., & Pan, B. (2018). A retrospective view of electronic word-of-mouth in hospitality and tourism management. *International Journal of Contemporary Hospitality Management*, 30(1), 313–325. 10.1108/IJCHM-08-2016-0461

Liu, H., Huang, Y., Gao, M., & Stebbins, R. (2021). From serious leisure to devotee work: An exploratory study of yoga. *Leisure Studies*, 41(3), 405–419. 10.1080/02614367.2021.1980087

Liu, H., Wu, L., & Li, X. (2019). Social media envy: How experience sharing on social networking sites drives millennials' aspirational tourism consumption. *Journal of Travel Research*, 58(3), 355–369. 10.1177/0047287518761615

Lo, A., & Lee, C. (2011). Motivations and perceived value of volunteer tourists from Hong Kong. *Tourism Management*, 32(2), 326–334. 10.1016/j.tourman.2010.03.002

López-González, J. L. (2023). Job Touristification: Bases for the Critique of a Social Acceleration Phenomenon Manifested in Bleisure and Workation | La Turistificación Del Trabajo: Bases Para La Crítica de Un Fenómeno de La Aceleración Social Manifestado En El Bleisure y El Workation. *Cuadernos de Relaciones Laborales*, 41(2), 335–348. 10.5209/crla.87872

Lou, C., & Yuan, S. (2019). Influencer marketing: How message value and credibility affect consumer trust of branded content on social media. *Journal of Interactive Advertising*, 19(1), 58–73. 10.1080/15252019.2018.1533501

Lubbe, B. (2019). The economic impact of tourism. *Tourism Management*, 40(2), 211–221. 10.1016/j.tourman.2013.06.003

Lubbe, B. (2020). Business Travel: A Perspective Paper. *Tourism Review*, 75(1), 113–116. 10.1108/TR-05-2019-0178

Lu, L., & Hu, C. (2005). Personality, leisure experiences and happiness. *Journal of Happiness Studies*, 6(3), 325–342. 10.1007/s10902-005-8628-3

Luxford, A. M. Y., & Dickinson, J. E. (2015). The role of mobile applications in the consumer experience at music festivals. *Event Management*, 19(1), 33–46. 10.3727/152599515X14229071392909

Madeira, S., Branco, F., Gonçalves, R., Au-Yong-Oliveira, M., Moreira, F., & Martins, J. (2021). Accessibility of mobile applications for tourism—Is equal access a reality? *Universal Access in the Information Society*, 20(3), 555–571. 10.1007/s10209-020-00770-3

Mak, A. H. (2017). Online destination image: Comparing national tourism organisation's and tourists' perspectives. *Tourism Management*, 60, 280–297. 10.1016/j.tourman.2016.12.012

Mangold, W. G., & Faulds, D. J. (2009). Social media: The new hybrid element of the promotion mix. *Business Horizons*, 52(4), 357–365. 10.1016/j.bushor.2009.03.002

Mareš, J. (1998). *Styly učení žáků a studentů.* Portál. https://is.muni.cz/el/sci/podzim2015/XS150/um/02_XS150_Styly_uceni.pdf

Martín, E. (2011). *El turismo de negocios: unaactividaden auge. Espacios y destinosturísticosentiempos de globalización y crisis. XII Coloquio de Geografía del Turismo, Ocio y Recreación de la Asociación de GeógrafosEspañoles*. AGE.

Maslow, A. H. (1943). A Theory of Human Motivation. In *Originally Published in Psychological Review* (Vol. 50). www.excelcentre.net

Mason, K. J. (2017). *The Propensity of Business Travellers to Use Low Cost Airlines.*

Matsushita, K. (2023). How the Japanese workcation embraces digital nomadic work style employees. *World Leisure Journal*, 65(2), 218–235. 10.1080/16078055.2022.2156594

Mccabe, S., & Stokoe, E. H. (2004). Place And Identıty In Tourısts' accounts. *Annals of Tourism Research*, 31(3), 601–622. 10.1016/j.annals.2004.01.005

McNaught, C., & Lam, P. (2014). Using Wordle as a Supplementary Research Tool. *The Qualitative Report*, 15(3). Advance online publication. 10.46743/2160-3715/2010.1167

Medaille, A. (2010). The Power of Play: Fostering Creativity and Innovation in Libraries. *Journal of Library Innovation*, 1(October), 8–23.

Medlik, S. (2003). *Dictionary of travel, tourism, and hospitality.* Butterworth-Heinemann.

Mehra, P. (2023). Unexpected surprise: Emotion analysis and aspect based sentiment analysis (ABSA) of user generated comments to study behavioral intentions of tourists. *Tourism Management Perspectives*, 45, 101063. 10.1016/j.tmp.2022.101063

Meng, F., Tepanon, Y., & Uysal, M. (2008). Measuring tourist satisfaction by attribute and motivation: The case of a nature-based resort. *Journal of Vacation Marketing*, 14(1), 41–56. 10.1177/1356766707084218

Mercan & Sandikci. (2024). *Bleisure Tourism: Business and Leisure Together.*

Mercan, R., & Sandıkcı, M. (2024). Bleisure Tourism: Business and Leisure Together. In *Future Tourism Trends Volume 1 (Building the Future of Tourism).* Emerald Publishing Limited. 10.1108/978-1-83753-244-520241001

Mercan, R., & Sandıkcı, M. (2024). Bleisure Tourism: Business and Leisure Together. In *Future Tourism Trends Volume 1: Tourism in the Changing World* (pp. 3-15). Emerald Publishing Limited.

Mercan, R., & Sandıkcı, M. (2024). Bleisure tourism: Business and leisure together. In *Future tourism trends volume 1: Tourism in the changing world.* Emerald Publishing Limited.

Merkel, J. (2022). *Coworking Spaces as destinations and new stakeholders in hospitality ecosystems.* https://www.researchgate.net/publication/361794319

Meyer, D. H., Brightbill, K. C., & Sessoms, D. H. (1969). *Community recreation a guide to ıts organization* (4th ed.). Prentice Hall.

Miao, L., Yang, F. X., Im, J., & Zhang, Q. (2024). Flexwork and Flextravel. *Annals of Tourism Research*, 106, 103763. Advance online publication. 10.1016/j.annals.2024.103763

Mihalic, T. (2016). Sustainable-responsible tourism discourse–Towards 'responsustable'tourism. *Journal of Cleaner Production*, 111, 461–470. 10.1016/j.jclepro.2014.12.062

Milosh, P. (2023). *Evolving Preferences.* Understanding Contemporary Luxury Hotel Guests. [Bachelor's thesis, Jyväskylä: Jamk University of Applied Sciences]

Mody, M. A., Jung, S., Dogru, T., & Suess, C. (2022). How do consumers select between hotels and Airbnb? A hierarchy of importance in accommodation choice. *International Journal of Contemporary Hospitality Management*, 35(4), 1191–1218. 10.1108/IJCHM-12-2021-1551

Mohanty, P., Shreya, V., & Choudhury, R. R. (2021). Information and Communications Technology for Overtourism Management: An Exploration. In *Overtourism, Technology Solutions and Decimated Destinations* (pp. 81-98).

Mohanty, P., Dhoundiyal, H., & Choudhury, R. (2022). Events tourism in the eye of the COVID-19 storm: Impacts and implications. In *Event Tourism in Asian Countries* (pp. 97–114). Apple Academic Press. 10.1201/9781003161134-6

Moschis, G. P. (2022). *Marketing Travel & Leisure Services*. Vol. Part F379.

Moutinho, L. (2000). *Strategic management in tourism*. Cabi. 10.1079/9780851992822.0000

Mueller Correa & Marina. (2022). *Social Media Storytelling: A New Zealand Study of the Use of Narratives to Engage with the Public* (Doctoral dissertation, Auckland University of Technology).

Mull, R. F., Bayless, K. G., Ross, C. M., & Jamieson, L. M. (1997). *Recreational sport management* (3rd ed.). Human Kinetics.

Muntean, C. I. (2011). Raising Engagement in ELearning through Gamification. Proceedings. The 6th International Conference on Virtual Learning ICVL 2011, (1), 323-329.

Murchie, F. (2014). "Bleisure" - mixing business with leisure. Retrieved from https://www. relocatemagazine.com/articles/4344bleisure-mixing-business-with-leisure

Nath, R., & Murthy, N. R. V. (2004). A Study of the Relationship Between Internet Diffusion and Culture. *Journal of International Technology and Information Management*, 13(1). Advance online publication. 10.58729/1941-6679.1247

NCR. (2019). National car rental. State of business travel survey fact sheet. Retrieved from www.nationalcar.com/en/blog/2019-state-of-business-travel-survey-fact-sheet.html

Netto, A. P. (2009). What is tourism? Definitions, theoretical phases and principles. *Philosophical issues in tourism, 37*, 43-62.

Nunes, L. (2019). *Sustaining a digital online influence through personal branding: a case study of travel bloggers*. University of Johannesburg.

OEDC. (2020). OEDC Economic outlook, June 2020. Retrieved from https://www.oecd.org/economic-outlook/june-2020/

Ohlan, R. (2017). The relationship between tourism, financial development and economic growth in India. *Future Business Journal*, 3(1), 9–22. 10.1016/j.fbj.2017.01.003

Okumus, B., & Bilgihan, A. (2014). Proposing a model to test smartphone users' intention to use smart applications when ordering food in restaurants. *Journal of Hospitality and Tourism Technology*, 5(1), 31–49. 10.1108/JHTT-01-2013-0003

Olszewski-Strzyżowski, D. J. (2022). Promotional activities of selected National Tourism Organizations (NTOs) in the light of sustainable tourism (including sustainable transport). *Sustainability (Basel)*, 14(5), 2561. 10.3390/su14052561

Orel, M. (2019). Coworking environments and digital nomadism: Balancing work and leisure whilst on the move. *World Leisure Journal*, 61(3), 215–227. 10.1080/16078055.2019.1639275

Osakwe, S. (2023). Travelling Arrangements and Requirements in Corporate Organisations. *Innovative Journal of Arts and Social Sciences, 5*(5), 31-43.

Othman, M. K., Aman, S., Anuar, N. N., & Ahmad, I. (2021). Improving children's cultural heritage experience using game-based learning at a living museum. *Journal on Computing and Cultural Heritage*, 14(3), 1–24. 10.1145/3453073

Ozdemir & Celebi. (2023). *Bleisure Trends: Combining Business and Leisure Travel.*

Ozdemir, G., & Celebi, D. (2023). Bleisure trends: Combining business and leisure travel. *Routledge Handbook of Trends and Issues in Global Tourism Supply and Demand*, 411–420. https://doi.org/10.4324/9781003260790-41/BLEISURE-TRENDS-GOKCE-OZDEMIR-DUYGU-CELEBI

Özgürel, G. (2022). A Research on Determining the Destination Quality Perceptions and Intentions to Revisit of Bleisure Tourists: İstanbul Case. www.academia.edu. https://www.academia.edu/91300746/A_Research_on_Determining_the_Destination_Quality_Perceptions_and_Intentions_to_Revisit_of_Bleisure_Tourists_%C4%B0stanbul_Case

Özoğul Balyali, T. (2024). Female digital nomads' destination experiencescape perspective. *Worldwide Hospitality and Tourism Themes*, 16(3), 282–293. Advance online publication. 10.1108/WHATT-03-2024-0051

Pan, T. J. (2012). Motivations of volunteer overseas and what we learned – The experience of Taiwanese Students. *Tourism Management*, 33(6), 1493–1501. 10.1016/j.tourman.2012.02.003

Paraskevaidis, P., & Andriotis, K. (2017). Altruism in tourism: Social exchange theory vs altruistic surplus phenomenon in host volunteering. *Annals of Tourism Research*, 62, 26–37. 10.1016/j.annals.2016.11.002

Park, S., Lehto, X., & Kang, J. (2024). Balancing Work and Leisure: Unraveling Constraints on Work-Leisure Integration in Bleisure Travel. *International Journal of Hospitality & Tourism Administration*, 1–27. Advance online publication. 10.1080/15256480.2024.2344226

Parry, R. W. A., Saxena, S., Ahmad, S. I., & Basheer, I. (2023). Investigating Consumer Purchase Intentions and Social Media Advertising Attributes Among Generation-Z: An Empirical Study in the Region of Jammu and Kashmir. Top of Form. *The Journal of Research Administration*, 5(2), 8965–8979.

Passmore, A., & French, D. (2001). Development and administration of a measure to assess adolescents' participation in leisure activities. *Adolescence*, 36(141), 67–75.11407636

Patsy, E., Alfakihuddin, M. L. B., Butar Butar, N. A., & Nethania, P. (2023). Corporate action on plastic pollution (the body shop case study). *Jurnal Ekonomi*, 12(2), 1350–1355.

Pearce, A. (2015). Internationalisation strategy implemented through Faculty Exchange: Strategic Entrepreneurship in a "new" United Kingdom University. *International Journal of Business Innovation & Research.*, 10(1), 43–64. 10.1504/IJBIR.2016.073243

Pearce, P. L., & Lee, U. I. (2005). Developing the Travel Career Approach to Tourist Motivation. *Journal of Travel Research*, 43(3), 226–237. 10.1177/0047287504272020

Pencarelli, T. (2020). The digital revolution in the travel and tourism industry. *Information Technology & Tourism*, 22(3), 455–476. 10.1007/s40558-019-00160-3

Pereira, V., Gupta, J. J., & Hussain, S. (2019). Impact of travel motivation on tourist's attitude toward destination: Evidence of Mediating Effect of destination image. *Journal of Hospitality & Tourism Research (Washington, D.C.)*, 46(5), 946–971. 10.1177/1096348019887528

Perles-Ribes, J. F., Ramón-Rodríguez, A. B., Moreno-Izquierdo, L., & Such-Devesa, M. J. (2019). Online reputation and destination competitiveness: The case of Spain. *Tourism Analysis*, 24(2), 161–176. 10.3727/108354219X15525055915518

Petrenko, A., Ekinil, G., & Provotorina, V. (2023). Organization of Bleisure-Tourists Service as a Factor of Sustainable Development of the Tourism Sector of the Rostov Region. *E3S Web of Conferences*, 381. 10.1051/e3sconf/202338101084

Pham, H. C., Duong, C. D., & Nguyen, G. T. (2024). What drives tourists' continuance intention to use ChatGPT for travel services? A stimulus-organism-response perspective. *Journal of Retailing and Consumer Services*, 78, 103758. 10.1016/j.jretconser.2024.103758

Phosikham, T. (2010). Heritage sites as tourist attractions: A case study of Luang Prabang, Lao People's Democratic Republic [Master's Thesis, Lincoln University]. Lincoln University Archive. http://hdl.handle.net/10182/2584

Pike, S. (2012). *Destination marketing*. Routledge. 10.4324/9780080568935

Pillai, R., & Sivathanu, B. (2020). Adoption of AI-based chatbots for hospitality and tourism. *International Journal of Contemporary Hospitality Management*, 32(10), 3199–3226. 10.1108/IJCHM-04-2020-0259

Pine, B. J., & Gilmore, J. H. (1998). Welcome to the experience economy. *Harvard Business Review Press*, 76(4), 97–105.10181589

Pine, J., & Gilmore, J. H. (2011). *The Experience Economy: Past, Present and Future*. Handbook on the Experience Economy., 10.4337/9781781004227.00007

Pinho, M., & Marques, J. (2021). Business tourism in Porto: An empirical investigation of its potentialities and development challenges. *International Journal of Tourism Cities*, 7(1), 1–12. 10.1108/IJTC-05-2019-0071

Pinho, M., & Marques, J. (2021). The Bleisure Tourism Trend and the Potential for This Business-Leisure Symbiosis in Porto. *Journal of Convention & Event Tourism*, 22(4), 346–362. 10.1080/15470148.2021.1905575

Pisoňová, M. (2015). Creation and Results of a Research Project with a Focus on School Management for Teachers. *Acta Technologica Dubnicae*, 5(2), 14–30. 10.1515/atd-2015-0062

Pizam, A., Neumann, Y., & Reichel, A. (1979). Tourist satisfaction: Uses and misuse. *Annals of Tourism Research*, 6(2), 195–197. 10.1016/0160-7383(79)90146-4

Pizam, A., Uriely, N., & Reichel, A. (2000). The intensity of tourist–host social relationship and its effects on satisfaction and change of attitudes: The case of working tourists in Israel. *Tourism Management*, 21(4), 395–406. 10.1016/S0261-5177(99)00085-0

Platon, O. E. (2023). Using Instagram Marketing: Creating the Perception of a Tourism Destination Experience and Influencing the Travel Decision-Making Process. *Challenges of the Knowledge Society*, 669-676.

Plog, S. (2001b). Why destination areas rise and fall in popularity: An update of a Cornell Quarterly classic. *The Cornell Hotel and Restaurant Administration Quarterly*, 42(3), 13–24. 10.1016/S0010-8804(01)81020-X

Porter, M. (1985). *The Competitive Advantage: Creating and Sustaining Superior Performance*. Hbs.edu. https://www.hbs.edu/faculty/Pages/item.aspx?num=193

Prochaska, J. O., Norcross, J. C., & DiClemente, C. C. (2013). Applying the Stages of Change. In *Oxford University Press eBooks* (pp. 177–181). 10.1093/med:-psych/9780199845491.003.0034

Puerta López, M. E., Pindado Martínez, J., & González Alvarado, T. E. (2023). The resilience of corporate tourism: Bleisure, digitalization, and sustainability. *Mercados y Negocios*, 2023(48), 53–74. 10.32870/myn.vi48.7679

Puerta, M., Pindado, J., & González, T. (2023). *The Resilience of Corporate Tourism : Bleisure*. Digitalization.

Qazi, S., & Baig, S. (2024). Promoting Tourism via Instagram: A Study of Instagram Users and the Role of Tourism Companies in Pakistan. Journalism. *Politics & Society*, 2(01), 1–20.

Quiaoit, M., & Furuya, H. (2022). Analysis of travel reviews on the philippine tourism experience by word2vec model. *Doboku Gakkai Ronbunshu, 77*(5), I_253-I_268. 10.2208/jscejipm.77.5_I_253

Rachmat, Z., Rukmana, A. Y., Nurendah, Y., Ashari, D. R. W., Donoriyanto, D. S., Bait, J. F., & Kasmita, M. (2023). *Strategi Bisnis Digital dan Implementasinya*. Get Press Indonesia.

Rainoldi, M., Ladkin, A., & Buhalis, D. (2024). Blending work and leisure: A future digital worker hybrid lifestyle perspective. *Annals of Leisure Research*, 27(2), 215–235. 10.1080/11745398.2022.2070513

Rakshit, S., Islam, N., Mondal, S., & Paul, T. (2021). Mobile apps for SME business sustainability during COVID-19 and onwards. *Journal of Business Research*, 135, 28–39. 10.1016/j.jbusres.2021.06.00534751197

Ralston, R., Downward, P., & Limsdon, L. (2004). The expectation of volunteers prior to the XVII Commonwealth Games, 2002: A qualitative study. *Event Management*, 9(1/2), 13–26. 10.3727/1525995042781084

Ramanjulu, D. (2024). Detours and delays: Navigating the pandemic's impact on India's transport sector and tourism. *EPRA International Journal of Economic and Business Review*, 22–27. 10.36713/epra16460

Ramaswami, A., Carter, M., & Dreher, G. (2016). Expatriation and career success: A human capital perspective. *Human Relations*, 69(10), 1–29. 10.1177/0018726716630390

Ramos, C. M., Costa, T., Severino, F. S., & Calisto, M. L. (2024). *Social Media Strategies for Tourism Interactivity*. IGI Global. 10.4018/979-8-3693-0960-5

Rasoolimanesh, S. M., Chee, S. Y., & Ragavan, N. A. (2024). From Mindset to Practice: How employees' attitudes impact tourism businesses' sustainability practices. *International Journal of Hospitality & Tourism Administration*, 1–31. 10.1080/15256480.2024.2344224

Rastogi, R. M. H., & Patil, A. (2015). Segmentation analysis of domestic tourists — A case study. *KSCE Journal of Civil Engineering*, 19(5), 1509–1522. 10.1007/s12205-015-0673-9

Rees, C. S., Breen, L. J., Cusack, L., & Hegney, D. (2015). Understanding individual resilience in the workplace: The international collaboration of workforce resilience model. *Frontiers in Psychology*, 6. Advance online publication. 10.3389/fpsyg.2015.0007325698999

Reichenberger, I. (2017). Digital nomads – a quest for holistic freedom in work and leisure. *Annals of Leisure Research*, 21(3), 364–380. 10.1080/11745398.2017.1358098

Respatyanti, Y. R. (2019). *Enhancing the Information Availability of Indonesia's Tourism Destinations Through A Travel App*. Victoria University of Wellington. https://openaccess.wgtn.ac.nz/ndownloader/files/31689896

Reynolds, S., Schultz, F., & Hekman, D. (2006). Stakeholder theory and managerial decision-making: Constraints and implications of balancing stakeholder interests. *Journal of Business Ethics*, 64(3), 285–301. 10.1007/s10551-005-5493-2

Richards, G., & Munsters, W. (Eds.). (2010). *Cultural tourism research methods*. Cabi. 10.1079/9781845935184.0000

Richardson, J. (2006). Self directed expatriation: Family matters. *Personnel Review*, 35(4), 469–486. 10.1108/00483480610670616

Rijal, S., Badollahi, M. Z., & Haryanto, B. (2021). *Tourism turbulance*. Advances in Economics, Business and Management Research/Advances in Economics, Business and Management Research. 10.2991/aebmr.k.211223.009

Ringer, G. (2016). *Social media travel in Caribbean island destinations*. L'Harmattan.

Roblin & Matthew, (2017). Blogs for The Digital Agency etravelseo. com–Online Travel Marketing.

Roby, H. (2014). Understanding the Development of Business Travel Policies: Reducing Business Travel, Motivations and Barriers. *Transportation Research Part A, Policy and Practice*, 69, 20–35. 10.1016/j.tra.2014.08.022

Rose, T., & Williams, D. (2015). Nurse leadership: The importance of balancing work with leisure. *Nurse Leader*, 13(3), 60–62. 10.1016/j.mnl.2014.08.004

Ross, G. F., & Iso-Ahola, S. E. (1991). Sightseeing tourists' motivation and satisfaction. *Annals of Tourism Research*, 18(2), 226–237. 10.1016/0160-7383(91)90006-W

Rukmana, G. M., Amin, K., Rahmah, A. H., Sabtohadi, J., Bisnis, F. E., Politik, D., Muhammadiyah, U., Timur, K., Brida, P., & Kartanegara, K. K. (2023). Existence of co-working space to support local industries in Samarinda. *Jurnal Scientia, 12*. https://infor.seaninstitute.org/index.php

Saldana, J. (2021). *The Coding Manual for Qualitative Researchers*. SAGE Publications Ltd - Torrossa. https://www.torrossa.com/en/resources/an/5018667

Sardest, Z. F., & Ivanauskas, V. O. (2019). Bleisure Tourism'Impact of Employees' Motivations and Quality of life. *Unpublished Master Thesis). Aalborg University, Denmark.*

Schänzel, H. A., Smith, K. A., & Weaver, A. (2005). Family holidays: A research review and application to New Zealand. *Annals of Leisure Research*, 8(2-3), 105–123. 10.1080/11745398.2005.10600965

Seabra, C., Vicente, M., Silva, C., & Abrantes, J. L. (2014). Motivation and involvement ın ınternational tourism. *International Journal of Multıdisciplinarity in Business and Science*, 2(2), 1–15.

Setiani, S. S., Setiawati, E., Suryono, C., Yen, Y. F., Dewi, R. P., Khalim, A., & Irawan, J. A. (2024). Optimization Integrated Marketing Communication Model as Strategic Approach to Boost Cirebon Business Leisure. *International Journal Of Accounting, Management, And. Economic Research Journal*, 2(1), 33–44.

Shaheer, I., Lee, C., & Carr, N. (2021). Factors motivating working holiday travel: The case of Latin American visitors to New Zealand. *Tourism and Hospitality Research*, 21(3), 330–343. 10.1177/14673584211003630

Shao, C., Ciampaglia, G. L., Varol, O., Yang, K., Flammini, A., & Menczer, F. (2018). The spread of low-credibility content by social bots. *Nature Communications*, 9(1), 4787. Advance online publication. 10.1038/s41467-018-06930-730459415

Sharkey, J. (2001). Leisure activities are increasingly being fitted in to help make life on the road less difficult. The New York Times, New York, NY, C6.

Sharma, S. K. (2013). Destination marketing: An integrated marketing communication approach. *Journal of Management and Marketing Research*, 12, 1–11.

Sherry, L. (2015). A method for quantifying travel productivity for corporate travel managers. *Journal of Air Transport Management*, 42, 118–124. 10.1016/j.jairtraman.2014.09.012

Shrivastava, J., Srivastava, K. A., Kumar, M., & Yadava, R. L. (2021, April 29-30). 2021). Android Application Development Based Tourist Guiding Mobile Application Using Java & XML Coding. 2021 IEEE International Conference on Nanoelectronics, Nanophotonics, Nanomaterials, Nanobioscience & Nanotechnology (5NANO). 10.1108/JHTI-02-2022-0087

Sigala, M., & Gretzel, U. (Eds.). (2017). *Advances in social media for travel, tourism and hospitality: New perspectives, practice and cases*). 10.4324/9781315565736

Singh, M., Verma, V., Gopal, R., & Aggarwal, P. (2022). Hospitality Education: Past, Present, and Future. Present and Future (June 6, 2022).

Slevitch, L., Chandrasekera, T., Mejia-Puig, L., Korneva, K., & Akosa, J. S. (2022). Virtual Reality images' impact on cognition and affect in hotel promotions: Application of self-reported and psycho-physiological measures. *Journal of Hospitality and Tourism Management*, 53, 176–187. 10.1016/j.jhtm.2022.10.005

Sohaili, N., Aminudin, N., & Amir, A. (2022). Exploring Items for Measuring Behavioural Intention among Bleisure in Malaysia: An Exploratory Factor Analysis. *Article in International Journal of Academic Research in Business and Social Sciences*. 10.6007/IJARBSS/v12-i11/15164

Sohaili, N. L. M., Aminudin, N., & Amir, A. F. (2022). Bleisure Motivation Towards Leisure Attraction: A Systematic Literature Review. *International Journal of Academic Research in Business & Social Sciences*, 12(11), 910–922. 10.6007/IJARBSS/v12-i11/15626

Sohaili, N. L. M., Aminudin, N., & Amir, A. F. (2022). Bleisure motivation towards leisure attraction: A systematic literature review. *Social Sciences*, 12(11), 910–922.

Sohaili, N. L. M., Aminudin, N., & Amir, A. F. (2022). Bleisure Motivation Towards Leisure Attraction: A Systematic Literature Review. *Social Sciences*, 12(11), 910–922.

Soliman, M., & Al Balushi, M. K. (2023). Unveiling destination evangelism through generative AI tools. *ROBONOMICS: The Journal of the Automated Economy*, 4(54), 1.

Solis-Radilla, M. M., Carvache-Franco, M., Carvache-Franco, O., & Carvache-Franco, W. (2021). Motivations as predictive variables of satisfaction and loyalty in coastal and marine destinations: A study in Acapulco, Mexico. *International Journal of Tourism Cities*, 7(3), 767–782. 10.1108/IJTC-12-2020-0283

Sommet Education. (2022, January 5). Evolution of workspace and rising popularity of "bleisure" post-covid. Hospitality Inspired. https://hospitalityinspired.sommet-education.com/index.php/news-insights/trends-hospitality/evolution-workspace-and-rising-popularity-bleisure-post-covid

Spanaki, M., Παπαθεοδώρου, A., & Παππάς, N. (2021). Tourism in the post covid-19 era: Evidence from hotels in the north east of England. *Worldwide Hospitality and Tourism Themes*, 13(3), 357–368. 10.1108/WHATT-01-2021-0013

Spreitzer, G. M., Cameron, L., & Garrett, L. (2017). Alternative Work Arrangements: Two Images of the New World of Work. *Annual Review of Organizational Psychology and Organizational Behavior*, 4(1), 473–499. 10.1146/annurev-orgpsych-032516-113332

Srivastava, U. K. (2024). A study of global trade war and its impact on Indian economy. *International Journal for Multidisciplinary Research*, 6(2), 14813. Advance online publication. 10.36948/ijfmr.2024.v06i02.14813

Staines, G. L. (1980). Spillover versus compensation: A review of the literature on the relationship between work and nonwork. *Human Relations*, 33(2), 111–129. http://hdl.handle.net/2027.42/67317. 10.1177/001872678003300203

Stanford University Press. (2019). *A Theory of Cognitive Dissonance | Leon Festinger*. Sup.org. https://www.sup.org/books/title/?id=3850

Starĉević, S., & Konjikušić, S. (2018). Why millenials as digital travelers transformed marketing strategy in tourism industry. *International Thematic Monograph Tourism in Function of Development of the Republic of Serbia - Tourism in the Era of Digital Transformation*, University of Kragujevac,221-24. https://ssrn.com/abstract=3280320

Stoecklin, M. P., Singh, K., Koved, L., Hu, X., Chari, S. N., Rao, J. R., . . . Schales, D. L. (2016). Passive security intelligence to analyze the security risks of mobile/BYOD activities. *IBM Journal of Research and Development, 60*(4), 9:1-9:13. 10.1147/JRD.2016.2569858

Stone, M.J., & Petrick, J.F. (2013). The Educational Benefits of Travel Experiences: A Literature Review, *Journal of Travel Research: A Quarterly Publication of the Travel and Tourism Research Association*, 52(6), 731-744. 10.1177/0047287513500588

Streimikiene, D., Svagzdiene, B., Jasinskas, E., & Simanavicius, A. (2021). Sustainable tourism development and competitiveness: The systematic literature review. *Sustainable Development (Bradford)*, 29(1), 259–271. 10.1002/sd.2133

Sunaryo, S., Sawitri, H., Suyono, J., Wahyudi, L., & Sarwoto, S. (2022). Flexible work arrangement and work-related outcomes during the COVID-19 pandemic: Evidence from local governments in Indonesia. *Problems and Perspectives in Management*, 20(3), 411–424. 10.21511/ppm.20(3).2022.33

Sun, P., Cárdenas, D. A., & Harrill, R. (2015). Chinese Customers' Evaluation of Travel Website Quality: A Decision-Tree Analysis. *Journal of Hospitality Marketing & Management*, 25(4), 476–497. 10.1080/19368623.2015.1037977

Surge in solo travel; J&K, Manali preferred travel destinations: Report. (2023, July 2). *Business Standard.* https://www.business-standard.com/india-news/surge-in-solo-travel-j-k-manali-preferred-travel-destinations-report-123070200268_1.html

Susilo, D., & Santos, , M. C. (2023). Digital Marketing Communication for Promoting Philippines Tourism. *International Journal of Research and Review*, 10(6), 209–220. 10.52403/ijrr.20230625

Swaminathan, R. (2022). How Can Resilience Create and Build Market Value? *Journal of Creating Value*, 8(2), 204–218. 10.1177/23949643221125287

Tan, W. (2020). Destination selection: Influence of tourists' personality on perceived travel constraints. *Journal of Vacation Marketing*, 26(4), 442–456. 10.1177/1356766720942556

Tejedor, B., & Aguirre, A. (1998). Proyecto Logos: investigación relativa a la capacidad de aprender de las empresas españolas. Boletín de estudios económicos, 53, 231.

Tene, O. (2011). Privacy: The new generations. *International data privacy law, 1*(1), 15-27.

Teodoro, R., Ozturk, P., Naaman, M., Mason, W., Lindqvist, J., Tech, C., & York, N. (2014). The Motivations and Experiences of the On-Demand Mobile Workforce. Performing Crowd Work, 236-247. 10.1145/2531602.2531680

Tham, A., Mair, J., & Croy, G. (2020). Social media influence on tourists' destination choice: Importance of context. *Tourism Recreation Research*, 45(2), 161–175. 10.1080/02508281.2019.1700655

The Future Laboratories. (2008). The trend tracker. https://www. thefuturelaboratory.com/trend-tracker

The Future Laboratories. (2008). The trend tracker. https://www.thefuturelaboratory.com/trend-tracker

The Independent. (2009, Dec. 11). Top 10 travel trends in 2010 - look out for "granny chic," "ecoluxe," "bleisure" trips.

The Sunday Times. (2010). Bleisure travel: the best of both worlds.

Thomas, J. (2023, November 23). *77+ Bleisure Travel Statistics [Updated 2022]*. Stratos Jet Charters, Inc. https://www.stratosjets.com/blog/bleisure-travel-statistics/

Thorn, K. (2009). The relative importance of motives for self-initiated mobility. *Career Development International*, 14(5), 441–464. 10.1108/13620430910989843

Thynk. (n.d.). Bleisure the new holy grail for revenue generation in hospitality? Thynk. https://thynk.cloud/blog/bleisure-for-revenue-generation

Tomazos, K. (2022). Social media influencers and tourism sustainability: the good, the irritating, and the desperate. In *Handbook of innovation for sustainable tourism* (pp. 250–273). Edward Elgar Publishing.

Torkildsen, G. (2005). Leisure and recreation management *(fifth edition)*. London And Newyork: Taylor and Francis Group. 10.4324/9780203401651

Torkildsen, G. (1999). *Leisure and recreation management*. Spon Press.

Tretyakevich, N. (2015). Corporate mobility: Impacts on life domains and implications, (Ph.D), Faculty of Economics Universita della Svizzera İtaliana.

Tsaur, S. H., & Tsai, C. H. (2023). Bleisure Travel Experience: Scale Development and Validation. *Journal of Travel & Tourism Marketing*, 40(1), 21–37. 10.1080/10548408.2023.2199773

TUİK. (2024). Türkiye istatistik kurumu. Retrieved from. https://data.tuik.gov.tr/Bulten/Index?p=Turizm-Istatistikleri-IV.-Ceyrek:-Ekim---Aralik,-2023-53661#:~:text=Geli%C5%9F%20ama%C3%A7lar%C4% B1na%20g%C3%B6re%20ziyaret%C3%A7iler%2C%20IV.&text=Y%C4%B1ll%C4%B1k%20olarak%20de%C4%9Ferlendirildi%C4%9Finde%20ziyaret%C3%A7ilerin%20geli%C5%9F,ve%20arkada%C5%9F%20ziyareti%22%20amac%C4%B1yla%20geldi, Accessed: 07.05.2024.

TURSAB. (2024). Türkiye sehayat acantaları birliği. Retrieved from. https://www.tursab.org.tr/assets/pdf/tursab-akademi/e-egitim/konu-ozetleri/unite-08.pdf

Tussyadiah, I. P., & Zach, F. J. (2012). The role of geo-based technology in place experiences. *Annals of Tourism Research*, 39(2), 780–800. 10.1016/j.annals.2011.10.003

Umarov, S., Durmanov, A., Kilicheva, F., Murodov, S., & Sattorov, O. (2019). Greenhouse vegetable market development is based on the supply chain strategy of the Republic of Uzbekistan. *International Journal of Supply Chain Management*, 8(5), 864–874.

Ünal, A., & Özgürel, G. (2021). A research on determining the destination quality perceptions and intentions to revisit of bleisure tourists: İstanbul case. *Tourism and Recreation*, 3(1), 1–10.

Unger, O., & Uriely, N. (2022). The bleisure memories of business travelers. *Annals of Tourism Research*, 97, 103497. 10.1016/j.annals.2022.103497

Unger, O., & Uriely, N. (2023). Reflections on Hypermobility: A Study of Business Travelers during the COVID-19 Pandemic. *Tourism and Hospitality Research*. Advance online publication. 10.1177/14673584231184160

Unger, O., Uriely, N., & Fuchs, G. (2016). The business travel experience. *Annals of Tourism Research*, 61, 142–156. 10.1016/j.annals.2016.10.003

Unpacking Bleisure Traveler Trends. (n.d.). https://info.advertising.expedia.com/bleisure-travel-trends

UNWTO. (2017). *Overview of the meetings industry in Asia*. UNWTO.

UNWTO. (2020). El turismo internacional sigue adelantado a la economía global. Ginebra: UNWTO.

UNWTO. (2022). El turismo internacional consolida su fuerte recuperación en medio de crecientes desafíos. Ginebra: UNWTO.

Uysal, M., & Jurowski, C. (1994). Testing the push and pull factors. *Annals of Tourism Research*, 21(4), 844–846. 10.1016/0160-7383(94)90091-4

Vaismoradi, M., Turunen, H., & Bondas, T. (2013). Content analysis and thematic analysis: Implications for conducting a qualitative descriptive study. *Nursing & Health Sciences*, 15(3), 398–405. 10.1111/nhs.1204823480423

Valsaraj, B. P., More, B., Biju, S., Payini, V., & Pallath, V. (2021). Faculty experiences on emergency remote teaching during COVID-19: A multicentre qualitative analysis. *Interactive Technology and Smart Education*, 18(3), 319–344. 10.1108/ITSE-09-2020-0198

Van der Merwe, P., Slabbert, E., & Saayman, M. (2011). Travel motivations of tourists to selected marine destinations. *International Journal of Tourism Research*, 13(5), 457–467. 10.1002/jtr.820

Van Harreveld, F., Rutjens, B. T., Schneider, I. K., Nohlen, H. U., & Keskinis, K. (2014). In doubt and disorderly: Ambivalence promotes compensatory perceptions of order. *Journal of Experimental Psychology. General*, 143(4), 1666–1676. 10.1037/a003609924588217

Vargas-Sánchez, A., Fotiadis, A., Manuel Alcaraz, J., Castellanos-Verdugo, M., Manuel Hernández-Mogollón, J., Pierre Levy-Mangin, J., Manuel Berbel-Pineda, J., José Martínez-López, F., Riquel-Ligero, F., Miguel Rodríguez-Antón, J., Francesc Valls-Giménez, J., Abbate, T., Aguas, P., Jere Jakulin, T., Morvillo, A., Nigro, C., Allee, J., Chung-chi Wu, S., Jafari, J., & Sheldon, P. (2020). A critical review of literature in the rising tide of social media towards promoting tourism. *Enlightening Tourism: A Pathmaking Journal, 10*(2), 270–305. 10.33776/et.v10i2.4887

Vayghan, S., Baloglu, D., & Baloglu, S. (2023). The impact of utilitarian, social and hedonic values on hotel booking mobile app engagement and loyalty: A comparison of generational cohorts. *Journal of Hospitality and Tourism Insights*, 6(5), 1990–2011. 10.1108/JHTI-06-2022-0229

Viacava, G., Bresciani, S., & Caputo, A. (2021). COVID-19 and the bleisure travellers: An investigation on the aftermaths and future implications.

Voll, K., Gauger, F., & Pfnür, A. (2023). Work from anywhere: traditional workation, coworkation and workation retreats: a conceptual review. *World Leisure Journal*, 65(2), 150–174. 10.1080/16078055.2022.2134199

von Zumbusch, J. S. H., & Lalicic, L. (2020). The role of co-living spaces in digital nomads' well-being. *Information Technology & Tourism*, 22(3), 439–453. 10.1007/s40558-020-00182-2

Walia, S., Kour, P., Choudhary, P., & Jasrotia, A. (2023). COVID-19 and the bleisure travellers: An investigation on the aftermaths and future implications. *Tourism Recreation Research*, 48(5), 657–667. 10.1080/02508281.2021.1946653

Wang, X. (2020). Personalized recommendation framework design for online tourism: Know you better than yourself. *Industrial Management & Data Systems*, 120(11), 2067–2079. 10.1108/IMDS-05-2020-0278

Wearing, S. (2001). *Volunteer tourism: Experiences that make a difference*. Cabi. 10.1079/9780851995335.0000

Wee, H., Kamarulzaman, N., & Anas, M. (2022). MICE industry survival: A systematic literature review. *International Journal of Academic Research in Business & Social Sciences*, 12(11). Advance online publication. 10.6007/IJARBSS/v12-i11/15622

Weng, Y. (2024). Explore how to refine social media marketing strategies and shape consumer travel preferences: An in-depth study on Airbnb. *Advances in Economics. Management and Political Sciences*, 74(1), 68–74. 10.54254/2754-1169/74/20241499

Whang, H., Yong, S., & Ko, E. (2016). Pop culture, destination images, and visit intentions: Theory and research on travel motivations of Chinese and Russian tourists. *Journal of Business Research*, 69(2), 631–641. 10.1016/j.jbusres.2015.06.020

Wharton, A., Chivers, S., & Blair-Loy, M. (2008). Use of formal and informal work–family policies on the digital assembly line. *Work and Occupations*, 35(3), 327–350. 10.1177/0730888408316393

What is Bleisure? Benefits & Challenges | Uber for Business. (n.d.). Uber. https://www.uber.com/us/en/business/articles/what-is-bleisure-travel/

White, M. (2012). Digital workplaces: Vision and reality. *Business Information Review*, 29(4), 205–214. 10.1177/0266382112470412

World Economic Forum. (2015). The travel & tourism competitiveness report 2015. Geneva: WEF. https://www3.weforum.org/docs/gcr/2015-2016/Global_Competitiveness_Report_2015-2016.pdf

Xiang, Z., & Gretzel, U. (2010). Role of social media in online travel information search. *Tourism Management*, 31(2), 179–188. 10.1016/j.tourman.2009.02.016

Yadav, S. (2023, June 4). Bleisure is back and transforming the travel and hospitality sector. ET HospitalityWorld. https://hospitality.economictimes.indiatimes.com/news/speaking-heads/bleisure-is-back-and-transforming-the-travel-and-hospitality-sector/100738316

Yang, Z., Yin, M., Xu, J., & Lin, W. (2019). Spatial evolution model of tourist destinations based on complex adaptive system theory: A Southern Anhui, China case study. *Journal of Geographical Sciences*, 29(8), 1411–1434. 10.1007/s11442-019-1669-z

Ye, X., Li, S., Das, S., & Du, J. (2023). Enhancing routes selection with real-time weather data integration in spatial decision support systems. *Spatial Information Research,* 1-9.

Yoo, H., McIntosh, A., & Cockburn-Wootten, C. (2016). Time for me and time for us: Conference travel as alternative family leisure. *Annals of Leisure Research*, 19(4), 444–460. 10.1080/11745398.2016.1147361

Yoo, K., & Gretzel, U. (2011b). Influence of personality on travel-related consumer-generated media creation. *Computers in Human Behavior*, 27(2), 609–621. 10.1016/j.chb.2010.05.002

Yoon, Y., & Uysal, M. (2005). An examination of the effects of motivation and satisfaction on destination loyalty: A structural model. *Tourism Management*, 26(1), 45–56. 10.1016/j.tourman.2003.08.016

Yousaf, A., Amin, I., & Santos, J. C. (2018). Tourists' Motivations to Travel: A Theoretical Perspective on the Existing Literature. *Tourism and Hospitality Management*, 24(1), 197–211. 10.20867/thm.24.1.8

Yuan, S., & Lou, C. (2020). How Social Media Influencers Foster Relationships with Followers: The Roles of Source Credibility and Fairness in Parasocial Relationship and Product Interest. *Journal of Interactive Advertising*, 20(2), 133–147. 10.1080/15252019.2020.1769514

Zak, K. (2016). Maximizing the value of conferences to communities: 'Bleisure Travel' and 'Bizcations' emerge with social media boosts.

Zeng, B., & Gerritsen, R. (2014). What do we know about social media in tourism? A review. *Tourism Management Perspectives*, 10, 27–36. 10.1016/j.tmp.2014.01.001

Zheng, K., Kumar, J., Kunasekaran, P., & Valeri, M. (2022). Role of smart technology use behaviour in enhancing tourist revisit intention: the theory of planned behaviour perspective. *European Journal of Innovation Management*, (ahead-of-print).

Zimmerman, K. (2017, June 6). How Millennials Are Being Creative With Their Travel. *Forbes*. https://www.forbes.com/sites/kaytiezimmerman/2017/06/06/how-millennials-are-being-creative-with-their-travel/?sh=5a0e28ce18a8

Zubair, S., Zubair, M., & Anwar, M. (2022). The study of advancement in the tourism and hospitality industry post Covid-19 pandemic.

About the Contributors

Swati Sharma earned her Ph.D. from Kurukshetra University, India and has qualified UGC NET twice. She is currently Associate Professor at Amity Institute of Travel & Tourism, Amity University, Noida. With 18 years of experience in travel & tourism academia and industry, she has made significant contributions to the area of tourism. Dr. Sharma has a strong interest in MICE Tourism and Destination Image and has published extensively on related topics. She has been invited to speak at numerous conferences and seminars on tourism and related fields. She keeps a track of the changing dimensions of business travel. Dr. Sharma's previous works include one edited book on "Tourist Behaviour" published by Apple Academic Press, USA; one book on "Research Methodology" and one on "Ethical Aspects of Business in Tourism". She brings a unique perspective to the current book, drawing on her extensive knowledge and experience in tourism and hospitality academia.

Narendra Kumar earned his Ph. D. from JS University, Shikohabad, India and currently working as Assistant Professor at Amity Institute of Travel & Tourism, Amity University, Noida. With 23 years of experience in travel & tourism, he has made significant contributions to the area of tourism education. Dr. Kumar has a strong interest in Business travel, tourist behaviour and visitor experiences and has published extensively on related topics. In addition to his academic pursuits, Dr. Kumar is actively involved in helping young graduates of tourism and hospitality domain to help them in establishing their start-ups. He has been invited to speak at numerous conferences and seminars on tourism and related fields and his current research focuses on student mentoring. Dr. Kumar's previous works include one edited book on "Tourist Behaviour" published by Apple Academic Press, USA; one book on "Digital Marketing" and one on "Ethical Aspects of Business in Tourism".

Vasco Ribeiro dos Santos holds a Ph. D. in Business Sciences with specialization in Marketing from Fernando Pessoa University, Portugal. He also earned a PhD in Tourism from Seville University, Spain. Vasco also holds a Post-Doc in Innovation Management applied to Sustainable Luxury Tourism from Aveiro University, Portugal. Currently he is the coordinator of the Master Degree in Business Management at the Higher Institute of Management and Administration of Santarém (ISLA Santarém) along with coordinator of the Degree in Commercial Management at the Higher Institute of Management and Administration of Santarém. Vasco has been author of scientific papers and book chapters. His research areas include luxury tourism, sustainable tourism, ethical marketing, wine marketing, wine tourism, and employer branding.

Karen Miranda-Fernandez holds a doctoral degree in Business Management specialized in Hospitality Management earned at Philippine Women's University, Manila. She is the Vice President for Southeast Asia of the Asia Pacific Institute for Events Management (APIEM) and President of APIEM Events Management Services. She has been appointed as visiting professor in UCSI University, Management and Science University, Universiti Teknologi MARA (UiTM), and Olympia College in Malaysia; Universitas Maarif Hasyim Latif, Universitas Prasetiya Mulya, Sahid Tourism Institute of Surakarta, and Bandung Institute of Tourism in Indonesia; National Institute of Development Administration (NIDA), Maha Sarakham University, Naresuan University, North Bangkok University, and Burapha University in Thailand; and Chung Hua University and Ming Chuan University in Taiwan. She was a postdoctoral scholar at School of Events, Tourism and Hospitality in Leeds Beckett University, United Kingdom. She holds master's degree in Business Administration major in Hotel and Restaurant Management earned at Philippine Women's University, Manila. Her research interests include events management, sustainable tourism, and hospitality management.

* * *

Muhammad Lukman Baihaqi Alfakihuddin is a faculty member at Sampoerna University. He has over 15 years of experience in education and a proven track record of successfully improving academic results. Lukman is a graduate of the Florida Institute of Technology and is actively involved in researching topics such as marketing, the green economy, carbon credits, and sustainable strategies. Lukman has written and disseminated journals ranging from strategies for MOOC learning to digital business. Additionally, he has authored several book chapters on Management Strategic, Business Ethics, and Digital Marketing Strategies. Before joining Sampoerna University, he served as an associate researcher at Cornell University. Furthermore, he has undertaken various community service projects spanning across Indonesia, from Aceh to South Sulawesi.

Sreeparna Bhattacharyya, an accomplished academician, an Assistant Professor (Management) at Bharatiya Vidya Bhavan Institute of Management Science, Kolkata, and a PhD Scholar in Management (Human Resource Management) at Silver Oak University, Ahmedabad, India focusing on 'Sustainable HRM'. She holds a Master's in Arts Degree in Psychology (I/O) from IGNOU and a Master's in Business Administration Degree with a focus on Human Resource Management (Major) and Marketing (Minor) from Heritage Business School, Kolkata (MAKAUT, formerly known as WBUT) with 1st Class. She is also pursuing her Post Graduate Diploma in Applied Statistics (Specialization in Operations & Decisions Science) from IGNOU. With a prolific research output, Sreeparna has authored publications spanning national and international repute journals and book chapters on Behavioural Science. She actively engages in academic discourse and has presented at national and international conferences, where she bagged "The Best Paper Award" in the General Management track at the 'South Asia Pacific International Conference on Changing Business Practices in the Current Environment-2024' organized by N L Dalmia Institute of Management, Mumbai. Beyond academia, she serves as a resource person in various workshops, conferences, and professional courses. Her commitment is underscored by her role as the Sub-Editorial Committee Member of the 'Kolkata Kindle', a journal of the National Human Resource Development Network (NHRDN), Kolkata Chapter. She is a Life-Member of NHRDN, Kolkata Chapter along with reviewers of reputed Scopus-Indexed journals and book chapters. She has also played a key role as an Editorial Member of the 26th NHRDN National Conference – 'Beyond Tomorrow: New Age People Processes' organized by the NHRDN Kolkata Chapter.

Sarani Bhaumik is a well-recognized tourism academician, having fifteen years of professional experience including working in the tourism industry, teaching, training and research. She is pursuing her Ph.D. in Management from Aliah University, Kolkata. She also obtained few professional courses like a Post-Graduate Diploma in Teaching and Research In Management, a Post-Graduate Diploma in Instructional Design, a Post-Graduate Diploma in Instructional Design, a graduate Diploma in Educational Administration and Supervision, Post-Graduate Diploma in Event Management and Promotions, Post-Graduate Diploma in Public Relations, Post Graduate Diploma in Entrepreneurship, Post Graduate Diploma in International Business and Operations, Post Graduate Diploma in Human Resource Management, Post Graduate Diploma in Marketing Management, Diploma in Training & Development, Diploma in IATA/UFTAA Foundation and EBT Course, Enter the world of Amadeus (ETWA-AMA), Enter the world of Automated Ticketing (ETWAT-AMA) from various recognised institutions. She has published many papers in international and national journals and also contributed many book chapters. She is a lifetime member of the Indian Society for Training & Development (ISTD), All India Management Association (AIMA), Local Management Association: Calcutta Management Association, National Human Resource Development Network (NHRDN), Responsible Tourism Society of India (RTSOI), Indian Society for Technical Education (ISTE) & Associate member of Public Relation Society of India (PRSI). Her current research interests are Intangible Cultural Heritage (ICH) based Tourism, Responsible Tourism and Community Development.

Sarbari Bhowmick is pursuing MBA in Tourism Management from The University of Burdwan. She has completed her Bachelor's in Business Administration (BBA) in Travel & Tourism from School of Management Sciences, Maulana Abul Kalam Azad University of Technology, West Bengal, India with 1st class. Sarbari, a novice but dedicated researcher in this field. In the very short span of time she has published a few papers in refereed journals as well as indexed Book chapters. She has a keen interest in the field of travel and tourism with a special interest to ICH.

Rashmiranjan Choudhury, an enthusiast of nature, traveller by passion and researcher by profession, holds the academic position of Assistant Professor at Jain University, Bangalore. Prior to that, he was associated with Chandigarh University and guest faculty at North-Eastern Hill University. Dr. Choudhury holds doctoral degree in Tourism and Hotel Management from North-Eastern Hill University and a JRF awardee from the University Grant Commission, Govt. of India. In research contribution he has interests Community-based Tourism, Technology in tourism, Sustainability, and Smart tourism etc. He has presented several research papers in various conferences, published several articles in referred research journals, and contributed three book chapters under reputed publishers including Routledge, Apple Academic press, IGI publishers.

Nagarjuna G. is an Assistant Professor in the Department of Tourism Management, School of Business and Management, Bannerghatta Campus, Christ (Deemed to be University). Before starting his academic career, he worked in Holiday Bliss as an executive in tour operations. Later, he joined Christ University as a Research Assistant for the Major Research Project on "An Evaluation of Eco and Sustainable Tourism Practices of Selected Resorts in Karnataka". He holds a doctoral degree in the sustainable tourism practices of Karnataka. He started his full-Time academic career by joining the Department of Tourism Studies in Indian Academy Degree College, later served as an assistant professor at Mount Carmel College, Bangalore. He has presented research and conceptual papers in seminars and conferences at national and international level. He has published articles in acclaimed journals and also participated in research workshops.

Sandeep Guleria has been in the field of Tourism since, 2005. For all these years, he has been into academics, research and promotion of Tourism in different parts of our nation. Born in 1983, he completed his initial education and graduation in Dharamshala, Himachal Pradesh, India. He did his Master of Tourism Administration and later Doctorate in Tourism with specialization in Tourist Behavior from HP University Shimla. He served as Asst. Professor, HOD and Officiating Principal in one of the colleges affiliated to Punjab Technical University, in Chandigarh for more than 10 years. Presently he is heading over the Department of Tourism in University Institute of Tourism and Hospitality Management at Chandigarh University, Mohali, Punjab. He has published many research papers, articles and chapters in national, international journals and books. He has been instrumental for promoting tourism education to under privileged students of tribal areas of Himachal Pradesh, Sikkim, Arunachal Pradesh and Assam.

Shilpi Gupta is a Research Scholar - AITT, Amity University, Noida, UP, India Assistant Professor - UITHM, Chandigarh University, Punjab, India.

Tuğçe Merve İnak Özberk completed her doctoral studies in the Department of Business Administration - Marketing Program at Muğla Sıtkı Koçman University, with a thesis titled "Factors Influencing Marina Customers' Marina Preferences." She obtained her master's degree in Logistics Management with a thesis on "Port Competition Focused on Intermodal Transportation." During her master's program, she also completed a project at Hochschule Bremen University in Germany under the ERASMUS program, gaining a different perspective and valuable experience. Currently, she works as a Lecturer Doctor in the Marina and Yacht Management Program at Muğla Sıtkı Koçman University Datça Kazım Yılmaz Vocational School. She also serves as the Head of the Marina and Yacht Management Program and as the Assistant Director of the Vocational School. Dr. İnak Özberk teaches courses in marketing as well as in maritime logistics, marine tourism, and marina management, making significant contributions through her academic work. Her previous works include an article titled "Examining Factors Affecting Marina Customers' Preferences According to Demographic Characteristics" and a book on "Marina Management Service Quality, Customer Satisfaction, and Customer Loyalty." Her research areas include consumer marketing, digital marketing, service marketing, and marina management.

Md. Tariqul Islam is a Ph.D. student in Hospitality and Tourism at Taylor's University, Malaysia. He holds a Master of Science (by research) in Tourism from Universiti Putra Malaysia, Malaysia. He graduated with distinction in Airlines, Tourism, and Hospitality from Lovely Professional University, India. Tariqul has published several research articles in ABDC- listed and Scopus-indexed journals and presented the findings of his research at various national and international conferences. His area of research includes consumer behaviour and technology adoption.

Monisha Juneja is working as an Assistant Lecturer at State Institute of Hotel Management, Indore, Madhya Pradesh (India). Completed Ph.D. from Amity University, Noida (India) in Travel and Tourism. Previous industry experience includes working in 5-star hotel brands like The Park Hotels and The Oberoi's. With over nine years of academic experience teaching at the school level and in institutes affiliated to NCHMCT, Noida (India). Her primary research area includes Cultural Heritage, World Heritage Sites (WHS), Tourist experience and perception. Has published work in Scopus-indexed journals and presented papers at national and international conferences.

Levent Karadağ works as Assoc. Prof. at Mugla Sıtkı Kocman University-Datça Kazım Yılmaz Vocational School. He holds a bachelor's degree in tourism management. He did his master's degree in Tourism Management program on "Consumer decision-making process in tourism: A research on family groups who visit Turkey". He completed his PhD on "The importance of touristic product diversification in the development of sustainable tourism strategies: A sample of Muğla" in the Department of Business Administration Program.

Rupam Konar is the Programme Director for the Doctor of Philosophy (Hospitality & Tourism) and Master of Science (Tourism) programmes. Dr. Konar is also a Senior Lecturer in the School of Hospitality, Tourism & Events at Taylor's University, Malaysia. He also serves as a managing editor for the SCOPUS-indexed Asia Pacific Journal of Innovation in Hospitality and Tourism and as an Associate Director at the Centre for Research and Innovation in Tourism (CRiT). Dr. Rupam is a Certified Microsoft Innovative Educator. His specialization area includes service innovation, service delivery, and service design within the hospitality industry. Within his research interest, he has published in many international refereed journals, and books and has successfully complemented many national and privately funded research projects. With his gained years of experience in the hospitality sector and academia, he is now really intrigued by the possibilities and innovative changes he can contribute to these industries.

Jeetesh Kumar is Head of Research at the Faculty of Social Sciences & Leisure Management, Taylor's University, Malaysia. Dr Jeetesh earned his doctorate in Hospitality and Tourism from Taylor's University Malaysia and a professional Master's in Hospitality and tourism from the University of Toulouse, France. He is also a tourism academician at the School of Hospitality, Tourism and Events, Associate Director for Information Management & Documentation at the Centre for Research and Innovation in Tourism (CRiT), and Hub Leader - "Responsible Tourism for Inclusive Economic Growth" hub under Sustainable Tourism Impact Lab at Taylor's University, Malaysia. His research areas include Economic Impacts, Economic Modelling, MICE, and Behavioural Studies.

Johnpaul M. is currently an Assistant Professor in the Department of Management Studies at the Central University of Kerala. Dr. John earned a Bachelor's Degree in Economics from the prominent Loyola College in Chennai, as well as a Master's Degree in Business Administration and MA Economics from Osmania University in Hyderabad. He earned his Ph.D. and cleared the AP SET and UGC NET in Management. From 2009 until June 2022, he was an Assistant Professor at Mahatma Gandhi University's Department of Management Studies in Nalgonda. He additionally served as a Hostel Warden, Coordinator for the Academic Audit Cell, NSS Programme Officer, and in a variety of other academic and administrative posts at MGU. To his credit, he has over 13 years of teaching experience. He has published 15 research papers in national and international journals. He has delivered 17 papers at national and international conferences. He has participated in various Faculty Development Programs. He has written one edited book, "Responsible Marketing for Sustainable Business". His teaching topics include marketing, marketing research, strategic management, international business strategy, and managerial economics.

Subhadip Majumder is Professor and Corporate Chef at Silver Mountain School of Hotel Management in Kathmandu, Nepal. He is also Academic Head for Queen Margaret University's "Bachelor of Arts in International Culinary Arts" curriculum. He holds an Honorary Doctorate (PhD) in Hotel Management with a Food Production Specialisation from Washington University in Seattle, USA. His efforts are further recognised by 9 patents and 2 design patents. He wrote 12 books and 3 chapters. He has 12 academic research papers and there are upcoming. He lectures and researches on food production, hospitality trends, food journalism, food and architecture, and food nutrition. He was Head of School for Lovely Professional University's School of Hotel Management and Tourism before this. HACCP Auditor, Government of India-recognized hotel andragogy trainer, and AHLEI-certified hotel educator. He is a lifelong member of WACS, IFCA, CAFR, ISHE, CAWB, and WCCF.

Mridula Mishra is experienced professional and a dedicated researcher in field of tourism and heritage. She is working as an Assistant Professor in Amity School of Travel and Tourism, Noida, UP, part of Amity University, India, India. She is a consultant, scholar, distinguished academician and a thoughtful academic leader in true sense who is known for his passion to bring practical orientation to academics in Tourism and Hospitality across different levels of education specifically focusing tourism and Heritage as a base. She has been associated with Vasanta College, Rajghat, Varanasi, BHU Varanasi and Indian Institute of Tourism and Travel, Noida.

Priyakrushna Mohanty is an Assistant Professor at the Department of Business Administration, Christ University, Bengaluru, India. He was a former U.G.C. Senior Research Fellow at the Department of Tourism Studies, Pondicherry University, India, where he received his Ph.D. in Tourism Studies. PK is also an awardee of the prestigious Travel Corporation (India) Gold Medal for his outstanding performance in his Master's Degree in Tourism Studies from Pondicherry University, India. He also holds a Master's Degree in Finance along with three PG Diploma Degrees in Rural Development, Research Methodology, and Teaching Skills. He has published over forty papers in international and national journals and edited books. He has presented more than thirty papers at both international and national conferences to his name. Several national and international institutes have invited him as a guest speaker. He is the co-editor for five book projects with prestigious publishers like Routledge, Emerald, Springer Nature, and CABI. PK is passionate about academic areas of Research Methodology, Tourism Sustainability, Sustainable Livelihood, Events Tourism, and e-Tourism, along with Gender issues in Tourism Development.

Nitish Ojha is a distinguished scholar, Researcher, and mentor having rich Industrial experience as well as varied experience in Teaching and Research. He has academic experience of over 15 years with renowned universities like American University of Europe, University of Stirling UK, and others where he worked in the capacity of Faculty and Researcher, also worked as a Core Member of Research and Development in many Indian Universities i.e., Chandigarh University, LPU, Amity University. He has worked as a software engineer in Nokia Siemens Network, India. He served in several research projects in different profiles of researchers funded by DST/MCIT/MOHFW Govt. of India having National and International importance at IIT Delhi and in AIIMS. Areas of interest include Cyber Security, AI, Risk Management, Privacy and Cyber Law.

John Ericson A. Policarpio is a University Professor on both Undergraduate and Graduate programs in Business, Tourism, and Hospitality, an Academic Researcher, a Book Author, a PACUCOA Accreditor, a Sales & Marketing Trainer, Business Consultant, Travel Agency Owner, and a Hotelier. He recently finished his Doctor of Business Administration (DBA) degree at Olivarez College where he received the Highest Academic Distinction Award and the Best Corporate Development Research for his dissertation on Luxury Tourism in Asia. He obtained his master's degree in business administration – Top Executive Program at the Pamantasan ng Lungsod ng Maynila (PLM). He finished his Bachelor of Science in Tourism Major in Airline Operations degree at PATTS College of Aeronautics where he topped his class as the batch Cum Laude and Academic Excellence Awardee. He is an Internationally Certified Event Educator, Event Manager, and Event Planner by the Asia Pacific Institute for Events Management (APIEM) in Leeds, United Kingdom. He is also a Certified Tourism Professional (CTP) recipient by the Institute of Tourism and Hospitality Professionals in London, United Kingdom. He is also a Distinguished Program Specialist for the Certification in Hospitality and Tourism Technology Service Professionals. He is also a Distinguished Program Reviewer for Travel & Tourism Supervision microbadge. Dr. Policarpio is also a Certified Amadeus GDS Trainer. He is a Member of the Southeast Asia Research Academy (SEARA) Batch 10. A Hotelier by profession, Dr. Policarpio held numerous positions in the Accommodation Sector, particularly in the Sales & Marketing Department. He started as a Reservations Associate all the way to become the Head of Sales & Marketing Department for Five years. Currently, Dr. Policarpio is connected with a number of colleges and universities as Professor in the tourism, hospitality, and business administration programs. Among these schools are Olivarez College, University of Perpetual Help System DALTA, St. Scholastica's College Manila, and Trinity University of Asia.

Indu Ranga, Assistant Professor at Christ University's Department of Tourism Management, holds a doctoral degree from Maharshi Dayanand University, with gold medals for her Master's and Bachelor's in Tourism Management. With over ten faculty development programs attended, she excels in research software like Smart PLS-SEM, SPSS, NVivo, and VOSviewer, conducting insightful research. She has presented more than seventeen papers at international and national conferences. She has published research articles, book chapters in Scopus, ABDC, Web of Science-indexed and U.G.C. journals, and edited books focusing on Online Travel Communities, Social Media in Tourism, and Responsible Tourism.

Chetna Sharma is an Independent Journalist from Jammu & Kashmir, India. She has worked as a TV News Anchor and a field reporter in both National and Regional TV News Channels under the parent body, JK MEDIA PVT. LTD. At present, she is a Doctoral Research Scholar (Pursuing PhD in Mass Communication) from Sharda University, Greater Noida, Uttar Pradesh. Her research specialisation includes Cultural Communication, Development Communication and Theories of Mass Communication.

Devika Sood holds PhD degree from Amity University, Master's degree in Travel and Tourism, in addition to her Bachelor's degree in Science from St. Bede's College. With 18 years of extensive corporate working experience, her career has been marked by achievements in lead generation, business development, and operations within the inbound tourism segment, specializing in the MICE (Meetings, Incentives, Conferences, and Exhibitions) segment.

Angelina Priscilla Tan is a double degree student, currently pursuing her studies at both the University of Arizona in the USA and Sampoerna University. Her academic focus lies in Management, where she demonstrates a profound dedication to her studies. Beyond her academic pursuits, Angelina has authored several impactful books on topics ranging from Green Economy to Business and Travel, showcasing her diverse interests and intellectual prowess.

Index

A

B

C

D

I

V

W

Z

www.ingramcontent.com/pod-product-compliance
Lightning Source LLC
LaVergne TN
LVHW081349300926
849161LV00008B/2105
* 9 7 9 8 3 6 9 3 4 3 5 4 8 *